T0397678

Rules to Infinity

Rules to Infinity

The Normative Role of Mathematics in Scientific Explanation

MARK POVICH

OXFORD UNIVERSITY PRESS

OXFORD
UNIVERSITY PRESS

Oxford University Press is a department of the University of Oxford. It furthers the University's objective of excellence in research, scholarship, and education by publishing worldwide. Oxford is a registered trade mark of Oxford University Press in the UK and certain other countries.

Published in the United States of America by Oxford University Press
198 Madison Avenue, New York, NY 10016, United States of America.

Library of Congress Cataloging-in-Publication Data
Names: Povich, Mark, author.
Title: Rules to infinity : the normative role of mathematics in
scientific explanation / [Mark Povich]
Description: New York, NY, United States of America :
Oxford University Press, [2024] | Includes bibliographical
references and index.
Identifiers: LCCN 2024030420 (print) | LCCN 2024030421 (ebook) |
ISBN 9780197679005 (hardback) | ISBN 9780197679036 (others) |
ISBN 9780197679029 (others) | ISBN 9780197679012 (epub)
Subjects: LCSH: Religion and science. | Science—Philosophy. |
Mathematics—Philosophy.
Classification: LCC BL240.3 .P685 2024 (print) | LCC BL240.3 (ebook) |
DDC 121/.4—dc23/eng/20240905
LC record available at https://lccn.loc.gov/2024030420
LC ebook record available at https://lccn.loc.gov/2024030421

DOI: 10.1093/oso/9780197679005.001.0001

Printed by Marquis Book Printing, Canada

To my parents, without whom I would be nothing,

and

to Carl, without whom I would be something unimaginably different

Contents

Preface

I have always considered platonism—by which I mean the traditional version I first learned about as an undergraduate, which consists of metaphysical, epistemological, and semantic theses to the effect 1) that there exist *abstract objects* or *abstracta*, such as numbers, propositions, and properties, not located in space or time, nor causally contacting anything in space or time, 2) that we come to know of their existence and features via some occult intuitive sense, and 3) that these abstract objects are described by and make true our true claims and beliefs about them—a philosophical embarrassment. And the idea, popular in post-Quinean philosophy, that not only are platonism and scientific naturalism compatible, but that the latter entails the former, has always seemed to me a sick joke. (Even if the appeal to intuition was replaced by a confirmational holism according to which our knowledge of the existence of abstract objects and their properties consists merely in the assumedly naturalistically explainable knowledge of the scientific theories that appeal to them.) The Quinean idea derives from the well-known "indispensability argument" for platonism: briefly, that the indispensability of numbers (for example) to science commits us to their existence, where "indispensability" usually means that our scientific theories are improved, according to some criteria, by quantification over them (Quine 1976; Putnam 1979). In this book, I am more concerned with the indispensability argument's so-called enhanced descendent: briefly, that the indispensability of, for example, numbers to certain scientific *explanations* commits us to their existence; numbers sometimes play an indispensable, ontologically committing, *explanatory* role in science. This argument is intended to be an enhancement over the original indispensability argument due to its emphasis on the *explanatory* role of numbers (Baker 2009). This enhanced indispensability argument (EIA) is simply a version of the original indispensability argument according to which explanatory power is the feature of our scientific theories that is improved by quantification over numbers. As with the original indispensability argument, the anti-platonist or nominalist could resist the EIA by denying the indispensability claim: the appeal to mathematical objects is explanatorily dispensable (see, e.g., Field 1980).

One could also resist the explanatory claim: the appeal to mathematical objects, while indispensable, is not explanatory (see, e.g., Saatsi 2011). I will do neither here. I will accept that mathematical objects play an indispensable explanatory role in science, and I will give an account of how such indispensably or *distinctively* mathematical explanations (DMEs) work (Lange 2013b), but I will deny that this indispensability ontologically commits us to the existence of numbers in any substantive sense. The EIA rests on a *descriptivist* and *anti-normativist* assumption about the nature of pure mathematical discourse, i.e., that the function of this discourse is to describe substantive bits of extra-linguistic reality. However, by being *normativists*, according to whom mathematical truths express conceptual rules, we can accept an indispensable explanatory role for mathematics, while insisting that we are only committed to numbers in the deflationary Carnapian sense in which "There are numbers" is an analytic truth, which comes with the straightforward epistemology of conceptual analysis, and which should not be objectionable to any anti-platonist or even nominalist. If you'll permit a pun: just as vegetarians should not object to synthetic meat, nominalists should not object to analytic abstracta. Of course, nominalists may object to the very idea of analyticity, but that is not the point. Vegetarians should not object to synthetic meat, even if they think synthetic meat is impossible.[1]

Many of the ideas defended in this book go back to philosophers like Carnap and Wittgenstein, but I hope to freshen them up by placing them in modern philosophical garb along with some flashy accessories, such as an argument for their compatibility with truth-conditional semantics and a compatible account of mathematical applications and modeling. I will also give a novel, counterfactual account of how DMEs work.

The neo-Carnapian view I will defend has been germinating for a long time. The first big step in its direction was taken when I inculcated an idea of one of my mentors, John Heil. From John I learned a critique of a still dominant and largely implicit conception of the relation between language and reality, a critique versions of which are increasingly popular (Heil 2003; see also Armstrong 2004; Dyke 2007; Linnebo 2018; Rayo 2013; Cameron 2010; Thomasson 2007b). It was also John (Heil 2003, 185–186) who first introduced me to the modal normativism—though he didn't call it that—that forms the backbone of my philosophy of mathematics and my argument

[1] Don't take the pun too seriously. Perhaps there are reasons for a vegetarian to object to synthetic meat.

for the invalidity of the EIA. I fear he would be mortified by the normativist label and the deflationary metaontological destination to which he inadvertently led me. Forgive me, John; I still think truthmaking is a coherent, useful idea, though less useful than some have tried to make out—and I actually do *not* think John is in the latter camp!

Eventually I came across the work of Amie Thomasson, who quickly seemed to me to be the most convincing and most Carnapian neo-Carnapian. It wouldn't be a stretch to say that one aim of the present book is to defend the applicability of her work on metaphysical modality to mathematical modality. The label "normativism" itself comes from her. I have benefited immensely from her work and our personal correspondence.

My counterfactual account of DME has also had a long gestation period. I first gained sympathy for counterfactual accounts of scientific explanation while being involved in debates regarding mechanistic explanation in cognitive science (e.g., Povich 2015). My thinking about scientific explanation generally is heavily influenced by my mentor and dissertation advisor, Carl F. Craver. It was from Carl that I first learned as an undergraduate that scientific explanation was a topic of philosophical investigation. I co-authored with Carl a critique of Lange's account of DME that forms part of Chapter 2, which was my first foray into the DME debate (Craver and Povich 2017). It was at this time that I started thinking about how to create a counterfactual account of DME. Carl's influence extends far beyond this, though. It is fair to say that I would not be a philosopher at all without him.

I would also like to thank many people and audiences who have given me feedback and support over the years: Andre Ariew, Paul Audi, Sam Baron, Dan Burnston, Earl Conee, Carl F. Craver, Mike Dacey, Dylan Doherty, Chris Dorst, William Fitzpatrick, Juliet Floyd, Stuart Glennan, Leonard Green, Steven Gross, Philipp Haueis, John Heil, Eric Hochstein, Philippe Huneman, Kareem Khalifa, Jens Kipper, Arc Kocurek, Daniel Kostić, Marc Lange, Eddy Lazzarin, Øystein Linnebo, Ron Mallon, Joe McCaffrey, Christiane Merritt, Gualtiero Piccinini, Christopher Pincock, Anya Plutynski, Agustín Rayo, Collin Rice, Sarah Robins, Felipe Romero, Kate Schmidt (née Shrumm), Rick Shang, Zeynep Soysal, Julia Staffel, Catherine Stinson, Caroline Stone, Brian Talbot, Amie Thomasson, Dan Weiskopf, Kit Wellman, David Wright, Tom Wysocki, and audience members at the 2014, 2016, 2018, and 2020–2021 Philosophy of Science Association conferences, the 2014 St. Louis Area Philosophy of Science Association (SLAPSA) conference, the 2023 Scientific Understanding and Representation (SURe) conference, and the 2023 International Society for the History of Philosophy and Social Studies of Biology (ISHPSSB) conference. I apologize if I have forgotten anyone. I thank Francis Milford for over a decade of friendship and her permission to use her wonderful artwork for the cover. I thank Lisa Wright at the Digitization Lab at the University of Rochester Libraries for digitization of the artwork. I thank the Humanities Center at the University of Rochester for awarding me one of the inaugural Faculty Open Access Publishing Grants to make this book open access. I thank Peter Ohlin and Chelsea Hogue at Oxford University Press for this astonishing opportunity, their endless patience, and their assistance in making everything go smoothly. Finally, I thank three anonymous reviewers at OUP, one of whom gave invaluable, detailed comments on the manuscript. This book is much better than it otherwise would have been thanks to them.

Some material of Chapter 2 is reprinted from Mark Povich and Carl F. Craver, "The Directionality of Distinctively Mathematical Explanations," *Studies in History and Philosophy of Science Part A* 62 (2017): 31–38, with permission from Elsevier. Some material of Chapter 2 is reprinted by permission from Springer Nature:, Mark Povich, "Modality and Constitution in Distinctively Mathematical Explanations," *European Journal for Philosophy of Science* 10, no. 3 (2020): 1–10. Some material of Chapter 2 comes from Mark Povich, (2023b), "A Scheme Foiled: A Critique of Baron's Account of Extra-mathematical Explanation," *Mind.* Most of Chapter 3 is used with permission of University of Chicago Press, from Mark Povich, "Minimal Models and the Generalized Ontic Conception of Scientific Explanation," *British Journal for the Philosophy of Science* 69, no. 1 (2018): 117–137, permission conveyed through Copyright Clearance Center, Inc. Most of Chapter 4 is used with permission of University of Chicago Press, from Mark Povich, "The Narrow Ontic Counterfactual Account of Distinctively Mathematical Explanation," *British Journal for the Philosophy of Science* 72, no. 2 (2021b): 511–543, permission conveyed through Copyright Clearance Center, Inc. Material in Chapter 5 was published in Mark Povich, "A Conventionalist Account of Distinctively Mathematical Explanation," *Philosophical Problems in Science (Zagadnienia Filozoficzne W Nauce)* 74 (2023): 171–223. The material in Chapter 8 on Linnebo and on the omega rule is currently being worked up into papers (Povich n.d.-a, n.d.-b).

The book proceeds as follows: Chapter 1 is a big-picture introduction in which I expand on the metaontological and other themes very briefly touched on in this preface, and I situate my position.

Chapter 2 characterizes our central topic, distinctively mathematical explanation, describes many prominent examples, and presents three desiderata that any philosophical account of DME should satisfy: it should accommodate and explicate the modal import of some DMEs (Baron 2016); it should distinguish uses of mathematics in scientific explanation that are distinctively mathematical from those that are not (Baron 2016); and it should accommodate the directionality of DMEs (Craver and Povich 2017). I then illustrate how two recent accounts (Baron 2019; Lange 2013b) fail to meet some or all of the desiderata.

Chapter 3 concerns renormalization group (RG) explanations, which are explanations that use a distinctive mathematical procedure called the RG method. I argue that the distinctiveness of this mathematical procedure does not imply that RG explanations are DMEs, contra Reutlinger (2014). Instead, RG explanations are standard causal, mechanistic, or otherwise ontic explanations. This position is defended against criticisms by Batterman and Rice (2014).

Chapter 4 presents and defends my own account of DME, which I call the Narrow Ontic Counterfactual Account (NOCA). I argue that NOCA satisfies the three desiderata presented in Chapter 2. In this chapter, I make free use of and appeal to platonistic language and entities, e.g., abstract mathematical objects and the instantiation relation between abstract mathematical objects and concrete objects to ground the relevant countermathematicals (i.e., counterfactuals with mathematically impossible antecedents) of which NOCA makes use. By placing DMEs within a counterfactual account of scientific explanation, NOCA provides a unification of the causal and the non-causal, the ontic and the modal, by identifying a common core that all scientific explanations share and in virtue of which they are explanatory: their ability to provide counterfactual information and answer what-if-things-had-been-different questions (w-questions) (Woodward 2003).

Chapter 5 argues that NOCA's use of platonistic language need not be taken to imply platonism in any traditional, substantive sense. The inference from the correctness of NOCA to platonism—which is an instance of the enhanced indispensability argument—goes through only if one assumes that the mathematical truths employed in DMEs, and in an account of DMEs, serve the function of substantively describing mathematical reality. Instead, I argue for the normativist thesis that mathematical truths express actual conceptual rules—rules governing the use of our mathematical concepts. I also give a normativist account of instantiation and countermathematicals.

I further argue that normativistically deflating NOCA does not reduce its explanatory power, nor its claim to be an *ontic* account of DME. More generally, normativism blocks any enhanced indispensability inference from the existence of DMEs—no matter the account of them—to platonism. I illustrate this by showing how normativism similarly deflates other ontic accounts of DME, such as Pincock's (2015) abstract dependence account and Baron's (2024) Pythagorean account. To be clear, NOCA and normativism are independent—it is possible for one to be right and the other wrong. Most of the material in this chapter is adapted from work that is currently under review (Povich n.a.).

Chapter 6 defends an inferentialist account of mathematical conceptual content. I argue for a broad normative inferentialist account of applied mathematical concepts, according to which their content is determined by the inferential rules governing them, including their empirical application conditions, which are structural. This latter aspect of the view should be very clearly distinguished from the view that usually goes by "structuralism" in philosophy of mathematics, according to which pure mathematics describes structures. I don't think pure mathematics describes anything. In fact, I think the appeal of structuralism often rests precisely on an invalid inference from "mathematical concepts have structural content" to "pure mathematics describes structures." I also defend the compatibility of normativism, deflationism, and inferentialism with truth-conditional semantics. I argue that this compatibility is possible, in part, because normativism is a thesis about the *function* of mathematical discourse, truth-conditional semantics is, obviously, a *semantic* thesis, and these are consistent with a variety of *metasemantic* theses. I hope that my argument will be useful for defenders of other positions who have gotten flak for supposedly being inconsistent with truth-conditional semantics (e.g., moral expressivists, epistemic expressivists, projectivists about laws of nature).

Chapter 7 defends an inferentialist account of the content of scientific models, including mathematical models, that I call the fully inferentialist theory (FIT). According to FIT, the content of a model (mathematical or otherwise) is determined by the inferences that are to be made with it, and the inferences that are to be made with it are determined by the form of the model and the denotational conventions surrounding it. I argue that the role of denotation can be interpreted normatively as expressing the validity of rules of surrogative inference. My thinking on scientific models has benefited greatly from correspondence with Dan Burnston. The material in this chapter is adapted from our joint work that is currently under review (Povich and Burnston n.a.). Dan should not be saddled with any of the other views presented in this book.

Chapter 8 compares my mathematical normativism with prominent related positions in philosophy of mathematics: conventionalism, fictionalism, and neo-Fregeanism. Although I am most sympathetic to Warren's (2020) conventionalism, and I don't really see it as a rival, I note some important points of disagreement regarding the nature of conventionalist explanation, the (non)conventionality of metamathematics, and how we follow the ω-rule. Field (2022) has recently raised some objections to conventionalism and has suggested that it is equivalent to fictionalism. I respond to these objections. Then I discuss Plebani's (2018) take on a recent debate between Contessa (2016) and Thomasson (2013, 2014, 2017b) regarding fictionalism and deflationism, and I offer a Carnapian way forward. Part of that debate is mirrored in a debate between Linnebo (2018) and Rayo (2013), and I offer a Carnapian way forward there too.

Chapter 9 concludes the book. After summarizing the main theses and arguments, I discuss areas of future work. These include but are certainly not limited to the strengths of different kinds of necessity, including natural necessity, and DME-adjacent explanations.

1

Introduction

Scientific Explanation, Mathematics, and Metaontology

1.1. Introduction: Scientific Explanation

One central aim of science is to provide explanations of natural phenomena. Explanation is a scientific achievement distinct from description, prediction, and confirmation. What is the nature of the achievement of explanation? What role(s) does mathematics play in achieving this aim? How does mathematics contribute to the explanatory power of science? In this book, I defend answers to these questions. Specifically, I defend an ontic conception of scientific explanation, a normativist account of mathematics, and I combine these into a normativist-cum-ontic account of the distinctive role of mathematics in scientific explanation. In this section, I briefly expand on these views, which recur throughout the book.

The central idea of mathematical normativism, common though perhaps inchoate among many members of the Vienna Circle, is that mathematics contributes to the explanatory power of science by *expressing* conceptual or semantic norms or rules, primarily rules for transforming empirical descriptions.[1] Mathematics should not be thought of as *describing*, in any substantive sense, anything, let alone an abstract realm of eternal mathematical objects, as traditional platonists have thought. A pure mathematical claim such as "3 is prime" should be thought of as expressing a semantic rule according to which it is *correct* to apply "is prime" when it is *correct* to apply "3."[2] We then use this rule to transform empirical descriptions such "there are three particles" into "there are a prime number of particles."

[1] This is idea goes back at least to Wittgenstein ([1956] 1978, 2013).

[2] Where I judge irrelevant, I ignore the distinctions between terms and concepts, and between sentences and propositions. This shouldn't, I hope, affect any of the points I make here. This leads me sometimes to play fast and loose with the use of quotation marks. My hope is that this won't get me into trouble. Note also that when I speak of a sentence being analytic, I don't just mean a string of marks or sounds, but a *meaningful* string, what Ludwig (n.d.) and Thomasson (2020a) call a *statement*. How could a meaningless string be *true*, let alone true in virtue of *its meaning*?

Rules to Infinity. Mark Povich, Oxford University Press.
DOI: 10.1093/oso/9780197679005.003.0001

In the following chapters, I update this normativist view of mathematics with contemporary philosophical tools like semantic deflationism, the idea, roughly, that the truth concept is governed solely by the "equivalence schema": "*p*" is true if and only if *p*.[3] Truth is thus not a substantive property. This is not to deny that there are substantive ways the world must be for some propositions to be true. But the substantiveness of the truth of "*p*" comes down to the substantiveness of the fact that *p*. For example, the truth of "snow is white" requires that the world be a certain way—such that snow is white; whereas the non-substantiveness of the truth of, say, "2 is prime" comes down to the non-substantiveness of the fact that 2 is prime. As I explain below, this truth and its associated fact are non-substantive because they are analytic. I argue that this combination of normativism and deflationism is compatible with the mainstream semantic theory, truth-conditional semantics. This allows the normativist to accept that there are mathematical truths and that they can play explanatory roles in science, while resisting the platonistic idea that there exist abstract mathematical objects that explain such truths or explain the truth of such truths.

I combine this philosophy of mathematics with a particular account of the distinction between scientific explanations that are in some sense distinctively mathematical—that explain natural phenomena in some uniquely mathematical way—and those that are only standardly mathematical. In *standardly* mathematical explanations in science, the mathematics plays a merely representational role; i.e., it merely represents the explanatorily relevant features, such as the quantities and magnitudes associated with explanatorily relevant causes. In *distinctively* mathematical explanations (DMEs), the mathematics is supposed to do something more than this; it bestows upon the explanandum (i.e., the thing to be explained) a kind of necessity that mere effects of causes do not possess (Lange 2013b, 2016). In Chapter 2, I present desiderata for any account of DME and criticize competing accounts for their failure to meet them. In Chapter 8, I critique other prominent views in the philosophy of mathematics such as fictionalism, conventionalism, and neo-Fregeanism.

I call my account of DME—which will be presented in Chapter 4—the Narrow Ontic Counterfactual Account (NOCA). NOCA is an ontic account of explanation, meaning that it takes the explanandum, explanans (i.e., the

[3] Or: the proposition that *p* is true if and only *p*. There are many ways of cashing out semantic deflationism (see, e.g., Horwich 1998b), and for my purposes I don't need to commit to any of them.

thing doing the explaining), and explanatory relations between them to be objective, "worldly" objects, properties, and relations. One might reasonably suspect that an ontic of DME would be committed to platonism. If mathematical facts are among the explanans in DMEs, and these facts are objective, (other-?)worldly facts, then platonism seems to follow inescapably. (Or perhaps there follows an empiricism according to which mathematical facts are concrete, empirical facts, but I won't be going that route either. More on empiricism in Chapter 6.) I will argue that platonism does not follow.

NOCA is an ontic conception of explanation. I hold an ontic conception of scientific explanation generally. That is, I think *all* scientific explanations appeal to objective relations between objective phenomena. In every case, the objective explanatory relation that holds between objective explanans and objective explanandum is a kind of counterfactual dependence relation. The explanandum counterfactually depends on the explanans—if the explanans hadn't occurred, then the explanandum wouldn't have occurred—and this counterfactual dependence holds in virtue of some objective relation between them, such as causation or constitution (or perhaps others). By "objective," I mean mind-independent, in the sense that whether the explanans, explanandum, and explanatory relation between them exists is not up to us explainers. I don't think the definition of "ontic" should rule out the possibility of ontic explanation in the cognitive and social sciences, including sociology and linguistics; brains, beliefs, social (including linguistic) conventions, etc. are perfectly objective in the sense that matters for ontic explanation, and only on exceedingly controversial and exceedingly rare philosophical views can such things not enter into causal or other natural relations. Brains, conventions, etc. are in principle scientifically manipulable and apt to figure in causal explanations, as explanantia and as explananda.

Thus, all scientific explanations follow a single pattern: they all exhibit (represent) relations of counterfactual dependence that hold in virtue of some ontic relation that holds between explanandum and explanans and in virtue of which they count as explanations.[4] I call this the *generalized ontic*

[4] Specifically, what matters is the representation of *patterns* of counterfactual dependence that hold in virtue of some ontic relation. It is not simply that *x* explains *y* if and only if *y* counterfactually depends on *x* in virtue of some ontic relation that holds between them. Preemption cases and others from the causation literature are relevant here. The breaking of the bottle does not counterfactually depend on Suzy's throwing her rock if Billy threw his right after (or if he threw his at the same time or if he would've thrown his if Suzy hadn't thrown hers). But this needn't undermine the claim that Suzy's throw explains the breaking of the bottle in these scenarios. For, as Woodward (2003, 86) points out, when it comes to causal explanation, "once we have been given information about the complete patterns of counterfactual dependence in [these kinds of] cases as well as a description of

conception. NOCA thus portrays DME as a component in an intuitive typology of kinds of explanation that are individuated by the ontic relation in virtue of which the relation of counterfactual dependence holds between explanans and explanandum. When the relation of counterfactual dependence holds in virtue of a causal relation between explanans and explanandum, we have a causal explanation. When the relation of counterfactual dependence holds in virtue of a constitutive mechanistic relation between explanans and explanandum, we have a constitutive mechanistic explanation (see Craver 2007; Craver, Glennan, and Povich 2021). When the relation of counterfactual dependence holds between a mathematical explanans and a natural explanandum in virtue of some other relation—perhaps instantiation—we have a DME, but more on this in Chapter 4. NOCA thus unifies causal and non-causal, ontic and modal. We will also see in Chapter 5 that, for the normativist, DME is a very special kind of quasi-causal or quasi-mechanistic explanation.

So, that's the ontic conception, or my version of it. Why hold it? I believe it is the best account of what is distinctive about the scientific achievement of explanation. It satisfies two widely held desiderata for any adequate account of scientific explanation: 1) it demarcates explanation from other scientific achievements, like description, prediction, and confirmation, and 2) it provides norms for evaluating explanations (Craver 2014; Craver and Kaplan 2020). Proponents of the ontic conception "believe one cannot satisfy these desiderata without taking a stance on the kinds of worldly (that is, ontic) relations that a putative explanation must reveal to count as explanatory" (Craver and Kaplan 2020, 294). (Note that it is no part of my understanding of the ontic conception that an explanation *is* something ontic, like a cause or a mechanism, and *not* a representation, text, model, etc.) There are questions surrounding what the norms of explanation are and whether an ontic conception of explanation supplies the right ones. For example, many have thought that an ontic conception implies that the more detailed an explanation, the better (e.g., Batterman and Rice 2014; Chirimuuta 2014). I think Craver and Kaplan (2020) have adequately dispelled this myth.

This is not to deny there is room for "pragmatic context" or "interests" in the evaluation of explanations. It is uncontroversial—and I think consistent with an ontic account—that whether and to what extent a putative

the actual course of events, it appears that nothing has been left out that is relevant to understanding why matters transpired as they did." The existence of preemption cases and others does not preclude a counterfactual account of causal (or other) explanation.

explanation reveals relevant worldly facts depends on who is consuming it (Povich 2021a). Some might argue that this gives up the game (e.g., Wright and van Eck 2018). If they want to call the generalized ontic conception "the generalized epistemic conception," that's fine. What matters is the view itself. Although many of the arguments in this book refer to "the generalized ontic conception," the substance of those arguments doesn't hinge at all on whether interests are included in the evaluation of explanations or what the view is called. For example, in Chapter 3, I argue against certain accounts of renormalization group (RG) explanation and in favor of an account in line with the generalized ontic conception. My arguments concern how RG explanations work. Similarly, in Chapter 4, I argue against certain accounts of DME and in favor of an account in line with the generalized ontic conception (i.e., NOCA). In Chapter 5, I argue that NOCA remains consistent with the generalized ontic conception even after its platonistic language is normativistically deflated. All these arguments concern how DMEs work. Nothing at all of substance in this book changes if we include interests in the evaluation of explanations and call my view "the generalized epistemic conception." Wright and van Eck (2018), critics of the ontic conception, cite approvingly Bokulich's (2016) distinction between "conceptions" of explanation, which concern what explanations *are*, and "accounts" of explanation, which concern how they work. If you want to call the generalized ontic conception "the generalized ontic *account*," fine by me. I don't mind what you call it; I mind that it is a monistic, counterfactual view of scientific explanation that unifies causal explanations, RG explanations, and DMEs, and that it still covers DMEs once they are normativistically deflated. More on the generalized ontic conception in Chapter 3. For now, let us move on to metaontology.

1.2. Metaontology

I believe the package of views going by various names such as "pragmatism," "functional pluralism," and "deflationary (or minimalist) metaontology" (e.g., Brandom 1994; Price 2011; Thomasson 2014, 2020a) provides the most plausible, illuminating, and naturalistic picture of, well, everything. (Obviously these views are not the same and their proponents have disagreements.) In particular, of human beings and our practices. Functional pluralism is the thesis that not all declarative sentences have the function of describing or representing the world, in any substantive sense (Price 2011).[5] Usually, this functional pluralist thesis is combined with the claim that thinking otherwise has led much philosophy astray and is the cause of many philosophical problems and confusions. Deflationary or minimalist metaontology is basically the thesis that, at least for some things, existence is cheap (see, e.g., Linnebo 2018; Thomasson 2014; Warren 2020). Often, and historically, the cheapness of the existence of some class of entities (e.g., mathematical entities like numbers, sets) is cashed out in terms of some kind of dependence on language or conceptual scheme. In other words, the existence of such-and-such entities is cheap because they are a product of our language or conceptual scheme. Of course, we must be very careful with that kind of talk, because we usually *don't* want to say that such entities did not exist before human minds or language, or wouldn't have existed if human minds or language hadn't. I take "pragmatism" to be roughly the combination of functional pluralism and deflationary metaontology, and I take it to be roughly equivalent to what goes by the name "neo-Carnapianism" these days. Neo-Carnapianism is the metaontology with which I am most sympathetic,[6] so I will expand on it below.

Admission: unfortunately, I cannot give a thorough defense of the metaontological views I hold, and which will pop up frequently throughout the book. Certainly, I will respond to many objections along the way, but other controversial theses are more or less assumed. The most significant, and central for my purposes, is the thesis that there are analytic or conceptual[7] truths. The analytic/synthetic (A/S) distinction has been seeing something of a comeback. This thesis plays a crucial role in my Carnapian style of pragmatism. (Some pragmatists, such as Amie Thomasson, embrace it; others, such as Michael Williams, eschew it.)[8] Analytic truths have traditionally been said to be those owing their truth to the meanings of their constituent terms alone. This is usually called the *metaphysical* sense of analyticity.[9]

[5] Sometimes one who believes that a class of terms doesn't describe is called an "anti-representationalist" about that class.

[6] I have also been influenced by Azzouni (2004), Balaguer (2021), Eklund (2013), Hirsch (2011), Putnam (1981, 1987), Sellars (see, e.g., his essays collected in Scharp and Brandom 2007), and Wittgenstein ([1956] 1978, 1976), among others.

[7] I use "analytic truth" and "conceptual truth" interchangeably.

[8] Putnam (1981, 1987) and Hirsch (2011) are sometimes described as neo-Carnapians, although they don't rely on the A/S distinction. Perhaps a *neo*-Carnapian is one who says many similar things that Carnap says about (meta)ontology, but who rejects the A/S distinction, and one who says many similar things that Carnap says about ontology *and* accepts the A/S distinction is just a Carnapian.

[9] See Boghossian (1996) for the classic distinction between epistemic and metaphysical analyticity, including a critique of the latter and a defense of the former.

For example, the sentence "bachelors are unmarried" is true *because* the terms therein have certain meanings and *not* because of the way the (extra-linguistic) world is. This has intuitive appeal. After all, make any change in the extra-linguistic world you want and you will not change the truth-value of the sentence, but you can change its truth-value by changing the meanings of its constituent terms.[10] This seems to imply that the true of an analytic statement makes no demands on the world. Synthetic truths have traditionally been said to be those owing their truth both to the meanings of their constituent terms *and* to the way the world is. The sentence "bachelors are unhappy" is true—if it is true—because the terms therein have certain meanings *and* because of the way the (extra-linguistic) world is. If that claim is false, it is synthetically, not analytically, false—false because the concepts therein have certain meanings and because of the way the (extra-linguistic) world is. The thesis that there are analytic truths in this traditional metaphysical sense has had respectable defenses recently (e.g., Rabinowicz 2010; Russell 2008; Warren 2015b), and I will return to it below and in Chapter 8. According to the epistemic sense of analyticity, analytic truths are those knowable by grasp of their meanings alone. Thomasson has given the epistemic understanding of analyticity a normative twist, according to which, "mastery of the relevant linguistic/conceptual rules *entitles* one to accept the conceptual truth (without the need for any further investigation), and . . . rejecting it would be a *mistake*" (2014, 238–239, my emphasis; see also Thomasson 2007b for further defense of analytic truth). On this view, the claim that bachelors are unmarried is analytic because mere mastery of the terms involved entitles one to accept its truth.[11] Those who accept epistemic analyticity and deny metaphysical analyticity need to explain either 1) how there can be epistemically analytic truths that make demands on the world, which sounds a lot like the synthetic a priori,[12] or 2) how epistemically analytic truths make no

[10] Obviously, this is also true of some non-analytic truths, such as "water is H_2O" and other a posteriori necessities, but normativists break such truths into an analytic and a synthetic component. See the refences in note 15 of this chapter. I discuss a posteriori necessity a bit more in Chapter 9.

[11] As defenders of analyticity since Grice and Strawson (1956) have noted, acceptance of analyticity is compatible with Quine's claim that all statements are in principle revisable in the light of experience. A revision of an analytic statement results in a change of meaning, and we may alter the meanings of our terms because experience suggests that it would be useful to do so.

[12] Boghossian (1996) writes that the positivists appealed to metaphysical analyticity for the purpose of taming necessity. This is true, but I think they—ever so concerned to avoid the synthetic a priori—also appealed to metaphysical analyticity to avoid a priori truths that make demands on the world (at least those that aren't as harmless as indexical truths like "I exist" [Evans 1979]). I think the same consideration partly explains why they inferred conventionalism or non-descriptivism (Boghossian calls it "non-factualism") from the practice of implicit definition, an inference Boghossian finds inexplicable. It is explicable if one is concerned about a priori truths that make

demands on the world, without appeal to metaphysical analyticity. Though I will not provide much by way of direct argument for the thesis that there are analytic truths in either sense (though see Chapter 8), you should see the book itself as an argument: look at all you can do if you accept analytic truth! Obviously, those unconvinced by the book will make the same exclamation sarcastically.

However, Boghossian (1996) famously argued against metaphysical analyticity, which he says is required to make sense of the "linguistic theory of necessity"—the thesis that necessity is explained by linguistic conventions. The thought is that metaphysical, not epistemic, analyticity is required to make sense of the claim that analytic truths make no demands on the world. However, normativism does not say that linguistic conventions are truthmakers of necessities. Normativism's non-descriptivism entails that

demands on the world, for conventionalism and non-descriptivism are ways of cashing out the idea that implicit definitions (which are analytic) make no demands on the world. Boghossian gives the contingent a priori as an example of a class of stipulative, a priori truths that *do* make demands on the world. (He doesn't put it that way; he says they express something factual.) One of Kripke's famous examples of a contingent a priori truth is "stick S is one meter long," where the length of S is used to define (i.e., to fix rigidly the reference of) the meter. But, first, this is widely recognized to be controversial (Noonan 2014, 174; see also Chapter 16 of Soames 2003). Even Kripke (1980, 63) said that it "seems plausible" that "in some sense" one who learns an a priori contingency does not learn some contingent information about the world, some new contingent fact one didn't know before, which sounds to me like skepticism about the idea that a priori contingencies of this kind make demands on the world. I think this "seems plausible" because it is correct. The ease with which trivial examples of the contingent a priori can be multiplied ought to make us suspicious of its metaphysical importance. All the phenomenon requires is rigidly fixing the reference of a designator with a description of an accidental property of the designated object, and these distinctions—the rigid/non-rigid and the accidental/essential—which are wholly explanatory of the contingent a priori, at least Kripke's variety, can be understood wholly semantically or conventionalistically (Sidelle 1989, 1992, 1995). Let "Macky" rigidly designate the sock on my left foot at time t_0. "Macky is on Mark's left foot at t_0" seems as contingent a priori as "stick S is one meter long." I've learned nothing new, but only reformulated something I already knew, that the sock on my left foot at t_0 is on my left foot at t_0. There are different ways, some of which require a distinction between sentences and propositions that for ease of exposition I have so far avoided, of explaining why Kripke's examples are either a priori or contingent but not both, or, if both, as harmless to conventionalism as "I exist," and I needn't commit myself to any of them here (see, e.g., Baker and Hacker 2005; Donaldson and Wang 2022; Evans 1979; Hughes 2004; Noonan 2014; Soames 2003; Thomasson 2020a; Warren 2022a). If there are contingent a priori truths, they, like necessary a posteriori truths, complicate but do not undermine the idea that necessity and a priority are explained by convention—just sometimes in different ways, such that these come apart (see, e.g., Sidelle 1989 on the necessary a posteriori and Warren 2022a on the contingent a priori). Depending on what exactly we mean by "analytic" and "place demands on the world," we may even want to say that some of these truths are analytic *and* place demands on the world, but in a way that doesn't threaten either conventionalism or the claim that the truths of logic and mathematics are analytic and place no demands on the world. (Warren 2022a might be an example of this.) Second, Boghossian's appeal to the contingent a priori doesn't help explain how it could be that the *necessary* a priori truths of mathematics and logic with which the positivists were primarily concerned could make demands on the world.

analyticities require no truthmakers and make no demands on the world.[13] Furthermore, the dependence of necessity on convention that normativism accepts is not the usual counterfactual kind. Einheuser (2006, 2011), whose work features prominently in Chapter 5, has convincingly argued that conventionalists—among whom normativists would be included—need only the idea that adopting an alternative conceptual scheme would result in different necessities, as judged from *within* the alternative scheme. This notion of dependence is all that is required by normativism (and by the linguistic theory of necessity). I argue for this in greater detail in Chapter 8.[14]

Speaking of conventionalism—the thesis that mathematical and logical truths are in some sense conventional, based on convention, explained by convention, etc.—while writing this manuscript, I read Jared Warren's (2020) wonderful book *Shadows of Syntax: Revitalizing Logical and Mathematical Conventionalism.* I think his book successfully rebuts most of the influential objections to analyticity and conventionalism, including Boghossian's. The philosophy of mathematics I present here is certainly of a piece with his. In fact, while I have disagreements with some of Warren's specific claims, which I will address in Chapter 8, I take Warren's conventionalism and mathematical normativism to be roughly equivalent, differing mainly in emphasis. Throughout this book, I will help myself to both normativistic and conventionalistic turns of phrase. Let me briefly explain both views and why I will treat them as equivalent. A more elaborate presentation of normativism comes in Chapter 5.

[13] Nyseth (2021) argues that normativists should not say that analyticities have no truthmakers, but should instead say that in analyticities the application conditions of the concepts involved are "fulfilled no matter what the world is actually like" (280). (Thomasson [2007b, 70] in fact makes the latter point. Cf. Sidelle [2009, 229] and Warren [2020, 178–179]. Also see Rayo [2013] for similar thoughts on "trivial truth conditions.") Note that this is not an epistemic point what we *know* or *can know* applies to what, but a point about our application conditions and how they can conspire to produce a truth that places no demands on the world. Other defenders of analyticity make this point too. This seems to me like a way of *explaining why* analyticities have no truthmakers. If Nyseth is right, it is not normativism's thesis that the function of mathematics is not to describe but to express conceptual rules that *explains why* analyticities make no demands on the world, but the fact that they have application conditions that are fulfilled no matter what. Note that Nyseth (277n18) says that the conventionalisms of Sidelle and Einheuser, to whom I make extensive appeal, are compatible with his argument. In the course of Nyseth's argument, he claims that, according to normativism, analyticities are true *because* they express rules (275). But that is dangerously close to saying analyticities describe or are made true by rules, which normativists deny. Nyseth's claim is accurate only if "because" is read counterconceptually. I discuss this idea in greater detail in Chapters 5 and 8, where I also offer more arguments for the claim that analyticities place no demands on the world. See Asay (2020) for a truthmaker theoretic argument that analyticities require no truthmakers.

[14] See also note 9 of Chapter 5.

Thomasson's (2020a, 2021) modal normativism is somewhat similar to expressivism about metaphysical modality, the thesis that claims about what is metaphysically necessary or (im)possible do not *describe* anything, but *express* something. (We needn't worry here about what exactly *metaphysical* modality is.) Expressivists can disagree about *what* is expressed by terms of whatever class about which they are expressivists, though usually it is a mental state of some motivational, non-belief kind. In Thomasson's case, though, what is expressed is conceptual/semantic rules[15] or consequences thereof, i.e., conventional rules for how to use words and concepts. Note that a metaphysically modal claim is not *about* those rules. For example, according to Thomasson, a metaphysical necessity such as that a statue cannot survive being squashed is an expression of rules of use for our statue concept—the statue concept is not to be applied after squashing.[16] Although Thomasson's normativism concerns specifically *metaphysical* modality, it is easily generalizable to mathematics, which I will do in this book. According to mathematical normativism, mathematical claims do not describe, in any substantive sense, anything, but instead are *expressions* of conceptual rules or consequences thereof.

Thomasson's normativism is only somewhat similar to traditional expressivism, because she accepts the existence of modal truths, facts, and descriptions as long as all of these things are understood in suitably deflationary senses (Thomasson 2020a; see also Baker and Hacker 2009). Since it's necessary that bachelors are unmarried, we can trivially derive that "it's necessary that bachelors are unmarried" is true, using the equivalence schema. Thus, there are modal truths. Deflationists often accept similar equivalence schemata, such as: it is a fact that p if and only if p. Since it's necessary that bachelors are unmarried, we can trivially derive that it is a fact that it's necessary that bachelors are unmarried. Thus, there are modal facts. The mathematical normativist is similarly capable of recognizing mathematical truths and mathematical facts. Thus, the problem of "creeping minimalism" in metaethics (Dreier 2004) arises here as well. In metaethics,

[15] Rules which may include empirical variables to account for a posteriori necessities (Sidelle 1989; Thomasson 2020a; Warren 2022b), but these, as well as *de re* necessities, are irrelevant to the present work. However, see Chapter 9 for brief discussion of posteriori necessities.

[16] It may be more complicated than this. Perhaps there are circumstances where the statue concept might still apply after squashing, but normally we wouldn't say that the squashed clay is the *same* statue. But this—talk of persistence conditions, identity conditions, and so on—is all still expressing conceptual rules, rules about when concepts are to be applied and, in the case of persistence and identity conditions, reapplied.

this is the problem of how to distinguish moral expressivism from moral realism once the expressivist adopts semantic minimalism or deflationism and is thereby able to say everything the realist says. There are several proposals for solving this problem in metaethics. Adjusting Simpson's (2020) solution in metaethics to the topic of mathematics, we could say that mathematical normativism differs from platonism in not having to appeal to mathematical facts to explain (the content of) mathematical language and thought (see also Brandom's 2008 explanation of modal language). For example, the normativist wouldn't (and can't) say that the mathematical facts make the mathematical truths true or explain why they are true. The mathematical truths and facts have been so deflated that no explanatory relation can hold between them. I think this is right, but to address the problem in modality and mathematics, I think the easiest solution is to appeal to analyticity, something usually not open to metaethicists, since most these days don't believe that moral truths are analytic.[17] In other words, both platonist and normativist say that numbers exist (for example), but the former takes this to be a synthetic claim and the latter takes it to be analytic. Avoiding the problem of creeping minimalism—i.e., making the required distinctions between "substantive" and "non-substantive" reference, existence, etc.—might be harder, I think, for those deflationists (such as Michael Williams) who eschew analyticity.[18]

This is all quite similar to Warren's (2020) conventionalism, according to which all mathematical truths in a language are fully explained by (the validity of) the basic inference rules of that language. For Warren, for the basic inference rules to fully explain a mathematical truth is for the mathematical truth to be derivable solely from the basic inference rules. (I don't think Warren is clear enough about the sense of "explanation" here, a point on which I expand in Chapter 8.)

Notably, according to Warren's (2020) conventionalism, it is not the case that mathematical truths *describe* conventions. You could say that arithmetical truths describe numbers because their terms refer to numbers, but such reference—and, therefore, existence—is a trivial byproduct of our arithmetical language. For example, let us assume our arithmetical language

[17] For a detailed exploration of the similarities and differences between philosophical problems of morality and mathematics, see Clarke-Doane (2020).

[18] This "substantive"/"non-substantive" distinction is the same one Linnebo (2018) is after with his distinction between thick and thin objects. He notes that the analytic/synthetic distinction, if workable, does the trick, but he prefers to make the distinction using "sufficiency", which I discuss in Chapter 8.

is formally modeled by first-order Peano arithmetic, one of whose basic inference rules allows the derivation of "N0" (i.e., "zero is a number") from no premises. From this, we can easily derive "there is a number" via the introduction rule for the existential quantifier. Thus, the existence of numbers is analytic, because it is a consequence of our basic inference rules; it is a trivial byproduct of our arithmetical language. Thomasson and Warren are both deflationary "trivial realists" in mathematical ontology.

There are some obvious differences between Warren's and Thomasson's views, but I will treat them as equivalent when the differences are irrelevant. One important difference is Warren's emphasis on syntactic inference rules and Thomasson's emphasis on semantic application conditions. Now, Thomasson accepts that rules governing application conditions might not be the only kinds of rule that are expressed by modal claims (Thomasson 2023, 21n20), and Warren accepts that application conditions can be meaning-determining (Warren 2022a, 46). (They also both accept the semantic and epistemic legitimacy of implicit definition as a meaning-determining practice.) Since in this book I am mostly concerned with the use of mathematics in scientific explanations, I will mostly be concerned with mathematical concepts that have application conditions. I think it is best to treat mathematical claims that involve concepts that *don't* have application conditions as expressing syntactic rules of inference governing the use of those concepts, more along the lines of Warren's conventionalism. I don't think there is any inconsistency here in the "different" treatments of mathematical claims that involve empirically applicable concepts and those that don't. Warren takes the basic syntactic inferences rules in any language to be automatically valid, i.e., (logically) necessarily truth preserving. It is not as if I am appealing to two radically different philosophies of mathematics, and, for the purposes of this book, I don't think there is a philosophically significant difference between saying that "bachelors are unmarried" expresses a rule according to which "bachelor"[19] may only be applied when "unmarried" applies and saying that it expresses a rule according to which one may only infer that someone is a bachelor when he is unmarried. Some inference rules contain terms that possess application conditions. In such cases, such rules governing inference can also be viewed as rules governing application. Since in this book I am mainly concerned with the use of mathematics in scientific explanations, I will speak of rules governing application rather than

[19] Throughout the book, I will ignore the copula when writing predicates.

inference. When I want to remain neutral on whether a rule is semantic or not, I will simply talk of linguistic or conceptual rules.

Another apparently significant difference is the fact that Thomasson is an expressivist and Warren is not—he's an inferentialist, according to whom the meanings of mathematical terms are determined by their inference rules. (More on inferentialism in Chapter 6.) However, Thomasson is not an expressivist in the traditional sense, which is one reason she prefers the term "normativism". Normativism is not a semantic or metasemantic thesis, like traditional expressivism, which has an "ideational" (meta)semantics according to which the *meaning* of the relevant class of terms is determined by the mental states they express; normativism is a *functional* thesis, a thesis about the function of a class of terms.[20] In fact, like Warren, Thomasson (2020a, 79) is an inferentialist, and the normativist's functional thesis is entirely open to Warren. Thomasson even supports the same kind of bilateralist inferentialism about logic that Warren (2020, 126) supports. This is why I take conventionalism and normativism to be roughly equivalent, differing mainly in emphasis. What for Warren is fully explained by (the validity of) basic inference rules, is for Thomasson an expression of conceptual rules or their consequences. This is not to say there are no important differences between Warren and Thomasson. Another important difference is that Thomasson's inferentialism is normative and Warren's isn't.[21] But this difference will not be relevant until Chapter 6, where I side with Thomasson (though my normative inferentialism is naturalistic, so maybe it isn't far from Warren's after all).

I said above I would come back to Carnap. Normativism and neo-Carnapianism are distinct theses. Normativism is a thesis about the function of a class of terms, and I think it is best to view neo-Carnapianism as a metaphilosophical thesis: it is (or entails) a view about the nature of philosophy, and metaphysics in particular. According to it, philosophical questions are resolvable via some combination of conceptual analysis, empirical investigation, and normative, pragmatic considerations. There is no *special* or distinctive metaphysical method. Philosophical questions that seem

[20] One could interpret normativism as an empirical hypothesis about the function of a class of terms, as Thomasson (2022) seems to. However, I think one could also interpret normativism as a normative claim that the function of a class of terms ought to be such-and-such. See Chapter 6 for discussion.

[21] It also seems that they disagree about how to accommodate the contingent a priori (Thomasson 2020a; Warren 2022a) and about the (un)importance of quantifier variance (Thomasson 2014; Warren 2020).

unresolvable are conceptually confused and require either conceptual repair or rejection.

Carnap's metaphilosophy is closely associated with the distinction between internal and external (I/E) questions. Carnap held that existence questions (e.g., "Are there numbers?"), conceived as internal to a framework, can be straightforwardly answered via conceptual analysis and empirical investigation. To answer the question "Does Bigfoot exist?," conceived as an internal question, you need to determine what that means, i.e., what it would take for Bigfoot to exist, and then undertake empirical investigation to determine whether those conditions are actually met. Existence questions that are conceived as external to a framework are either pragmatic questions or senseless pseudo-questions. Note that the same question can be conceived internally or externally. What exactly it means to ask a question internal or external to a framework depends on what frameworks are, and there is debate about what exactly a framework is (Eklund 2013, 2016). I won't discuss all the options, but I think everything I argue in this book is compatible with the idea that a framework is a fragment of language. On this understanding of a framework, to ask an internal question is simply to ask a question in a particular language (fragment), and to ask an external question is either to ask what language to use or to say something nonsensical like "Answer this question but ignore its actual meaning: are there numbers?" (Eklund 2013, 232).[22] As Eklund notes, so far this seems pretty trivial and doesn't seem immediately to have any deflationary metaontological implications. "There are numbers" may be true in some languages and false in others, but it doesn't mean the same thing in those languages. I think that's right—*so far* there are no deflationary metaontological implications.

This is why the A/S distinction is important. The way I see it, the entirety of Carnap's deflationary metaontology rests on two claims: the A/S distinction holds in natural languages like ours (Carnap 1955), and there is no such thing as the one true language. It is these two claims that allow Carnap to say that all questions are either answerable by conceptual analysis, empirical investigation, or normative pragmatic considerations, or they are senseless. Eklund (2013, 245) is understandably curious why, if this is right, Carnap (1950) focused on the I/E distinction, rather than the A/S distinction, in his

[22] Compare explicit denials of analytic truths, like "Bachelors are married." These can only be interpreted as being about language (e.g., as being suggestions to change language) or as based on confusion (Burgess, Cappelen, and Plunkett 2020; Thomasson 2017a). I return to this below.

anti-metaphysical arguments.[23] It's a great question. I'm not sure; perhaps he assumed that readers knew that, according to him, frameworks come with an A/S distinction and that it determines how questions within a framework are answered. The fact that Carnap (1950) states that some questions can be answered by conceptual analysis alone shows that he was assuming the A/S distinction. Regardless of what Carnap's view was, I will present mine. I will make explicit the relation I see between ontological questions, external questions, and analyticity.

On the relation between the A/S and I/E distinctions, Eklund argues the following (2013, 237, original emphasis):

> Carnap is actually drawing a *tripartite* distinction: between questions internal to a framework, questions about which framework we should choose to employ, and the pseudo-questions—the supposed theoretical external questions. What Quinean criticism of the analytic/synthetic distinction threatens is the distinction between *the first two* categories: change in theory and change in language cannot be separated in the way Carnap assumes. But even if this distinction collapses, Carnap's critique of ontology still stands. For the *third* category, that of the supposed pseudo-questions, can remain untouched.

Of course, the very *idea* of pseudo-questions doesn't require the A/S distinction—one could make sense of the idea in other ways—but I think an intuitive understanding of what pseudo-questions are and why they can only sensibly be interpreted as questions about which language to use arises quite naturally from the A/S distinction. In other words, there is an important and motivated connection between the account of ontological questions, external questions, and analyticity. Eklund would argue otherwise—he would argue that a questioner asks a pseudo-question (i.e., a putatively *theoretical*, rather than practical, external question) when the questioner knows what's true in the language, and the questioner is not asking a practical question about which language to use. Here there is no mention of analyticity. True, but when the questioner knows what's true in the language and still asks an

[23] Basically the same thing happens in Section V of Carnap's ([1937] 2001) *Logical Syntax of Language*. He makes a distinction between what he calls "object-questions," which concern extralinguistic objects, and "logical questions," which concern linguistic objects, that is similar to the I/E distinction; he argues that metaphysical questions are pseudo-object-questions that are actually logical questions; and the A/S distinction, although central throughout *Logical Syntax*, doesn't figure in his discussion.

existence question, the question rests on the questioning of an analytic truth; i.e., they would consider their question answered if they accepted an analytic truth.[24] And it is the fact that their question rests on the questioning of an analytic truth that helps motivate the idea that they must be asking a question about which language to use, since analytic truths express linguistic rules. If they aren't asking such a question, they are asking a pseudo-question. That is the connection between external questions and analyticity. Let me illustrate how when the questioner has been told what's true in the language and still asks an existence question, the question always rests on the questioning of an analytic truth. (To be clear, I mean here that an external question always rests on the questioning of something that is an analytic truth in the framework of the thing whose existence is being questioned.) A philosopher asks us "Are there numbers?" First, we see if they intend this as an internal question. Internal questions concern what's true in our language and are answerable via empirical and conceptual means. Considered as an internal question, it can be answered by purely conceptual means. We may explain to them why "there are numbers" is true in our language via the derivation of that claim from the Peano axioms (again, assuming our arithmetical language is modeled by these axioms). They persist in their questioning, which clearly rests on the questioning of an analytic truth, namely, the analytic truth that there are numbers. Obviously, if they accepted the analytic truth that there are numbers, they would consider their question answered. Since the question rests on the questioning of an analytic truth—an expression of a rule for the use of language—they can only sensibly be asking a pragmatic question about the use of language. The alternative is that they are asking a senseless pseudo-question, a question whose terms are *not* governed by their standard rules of use (Thomasson 2015, 39).

You may think this can't be an adequate account of everything Carnap regarded as a pseudo-question. For example, he regarded "Are there tables?," construed as an external question not about language, as a pseudo-question, yet this question doesn't rest on the questioning of an analytic truth. This is wrong. Construed as an external question, the question *does* rest on the questioning of an analytic truth; therefore, if it is not about language use, it is a pseudo-question. Let me illustrate. A philosopher asks us, "Are there tables?" First, we see if this is meant as an internal question. We explain to them

[24] Thus, I hold the position mentioned by Eklund (2013, 245) that "all properly ontological disputes turn on analytic claims."

why "there are tables" is true in our language. It doesn't really matter whether they *agree* that "there are tables" is true in our language. If they continue to question whether there are tables, their question will rest on the questioning of an analytic truth. Suppose they agree that it is true in our language but continue to question. Then their question rests on the questioning of the analytic truth (A): if "there are tables" is true in our language, then there are tables. If they accepted (A), they would consider their question answered, since they accept the antecedent.

If they didn't agree that "there are tables" is true in our language, they could accept (A). Their continued questioning would thus not rest on the questioning of *that* analytic truth. But it would still rest on the questioning of *some* analytic truth. Such a philosopher might say, "I accept (A). I just deny its antecedent—I don't think that 'there are tables' *is* true in our language. I think that what it takes for it to be true in our language is for there to be a certain kind of composite object, but I don't believe in composite objects. I only believe in simples." They thus accept (A), but they still do not accept an analytic truth: that if there are simples arranged table-wise, then there are tables. If they accepted this analytic truth, their question would be answered, since they accept its antecedent. The same goes for other ontologists. The nihilist might say, "I accept (A). I just deny its antecedent—I don't think that it *is* true in our language. I think that what it takes for it to be true is for there to be a certain kind of composite object, but I don't believe in *anything*." But they still deny an analytic truth: that if it is tabling,[25] then there are tables. If they accepted this analytic truth, their question would be answered. Each of these antecedents is simply a *different way of describing* what it would take for "there are tables" to be true (cf. Heil 2003, 177; Rayo 2013, 31; Thomasson 2014, 106–107). For a Carnapian, ontologies are languages. I think this goes for all ontologists who would deny that "there are tables" is true in our language. In fact, I think it's what distinguishes the skeptical ontologist from the delusional person. For the skeptical ontologist, as opposed to the delusional person, there is some *p* such that *p* analytically entails that tables exist, and they believe that *p*.[26] (*X* analytically entails *Y* if and only if "if *X*, then *Y*" is an analytic truth.) Since they believe some such *p* and deny that tables exist,

[25] This is the feature-placing language of ontological nihilists (Hawthorne and Cortens 1995).

[26] Thus, for the delusional person, for all *p*, if *p* analytically entails that tables exist, then they don't believe that *p*.

there is some analytic truth of the form "if *p*, then tables exist" that they deny. Their questioning thus rests on the questioning of some analytic truth.[27]

Thus, external questions, at least external existence questions like the one we've been considering, rest on the questioning of an analytic truth. As I said, I don't think it's impossible to explicate the I/E distinction in a way that doesn't appeal to analyticity. However, I think appealing to analyticity can give a better account of *why* one who says, "I know 'there are tables' is true in our language, but are there tables?" (and similar things) can only sensibly be asking which language to use. It is because that question rests on the questioning of a truth that is analytic in the framework of the object whose existence is being questioned, a truth which is simply an expression of linguistic rules for the use of terms for that object. A truth, furthermore, that serves as an introduction rule for the relevant term—the analytic conditionals the questioner questions are precisely the kinds used to introduce new terms into a language. An external existence question thus questions the introduction of new terms. Note that the denial of such analytic conditionals needn't betray any conceptual incompetence; it can betray a refusal to adopt a linguistic framework (see Chapter 8 for elaboration of the points in this paragraph).

The A/S distinction thus supplies a direct connection between asking an external existence question and asking about a linguistic framework. Accounts of the I/E distinction that don't appeal to analyticity (e.g., Bird 2003; Eklund 2013) seem not to explain this. Or, if they do, they rely on something like inference to the best explanation (IBE): why can one who says, "I know 'there are tables' is true in our language, but are there tables?" only sensibly be asking which language to use? Because there is no better explanation of what they could be asking. Now, I don't think there's anything wrong with IBE—in fact, I'm going to use it right now—but I think appealing to analyticity gives a better explanation of why someone who asks an external question is either asking a question about language use or asking a pseudo-question. And I've got a feeling that the analyticity-denier's intuition that there is no better explanation rests on a tacit appeal to analyticity. The intuition that there is no better explanation likely arises from the judgment that the external questioner must not mean what we mean by the relevant terms.

[27] The same line of reasoning in this paragraph also applies to the philosopher who questions the existence of numbers. They might disagree that "there are numbers" is true in our language. But there is certainly some *p* such that *p* analytically entails that numbers exist, and they believe that *p*, since *for all p*, *p* analytically entails that numbers exist, because "numbers exist" is analytic. Thus, there is certainly some analytic conditional of the form "if *p*, then numbers exist" that they deny.

According to Eklund (2013, 236), "One can believe that one and the same string of symbols can have different meanings in different languages while thinking that there can be no analytic truths." I'm not so sure, at least in a natural language context. What considerations justify one's belief that the same word is being used with a different meaning? A likely, though perhaps not the only, source for a judgment of difference in meaning is the prior judgment that someone has denied an analyticity. You judge that I mean something different by a word than you do because I deny something you take to be analytic. You might object that you can justifiably believe that our meanings differ simply by observing our wildly different uses, without appeal to analyticity. But your judgment that differences in our uses amount to differences in *meaning* requires the judgment that such differences are in *meaning-constitutive* or *meaning-determinative uses.* Your judgments that our differences in use are meaning-constitutive are judgments about my considered uses of a word "*w*" in conditions *c*, where you take it to be analytic that "*w*" does not apply in *c*; i.e., you take "if . . . *c* . . . , then . . . ~*w*" to be analytic. Such uses reveal that I deny an analyticity, and thereby justify your belief that I mean something different, rather than merely believe something different, than you do. For example, if I consistently apply "bachelor" ("*w*") to married men (*c*), you will conclude that we mean different things, rather than that I merely have a strange belief, *because* you believe that "if someone is a married man, then he is not a bachelor" ("if . . . *c* . . . , then . . . ~*w*") is analytic. If you didn't think that was analytic, you would conclude that I have a strange belief, not that we mean different things. Deniers of the A/S distinction deny that there is a distinction between a change in meaning and a change in belief. For, to change what I mean is to change my mind about an analytic sentence, and to change what I believe is to change my mind about a synthetic sentence. But this applies interpersonally too: for us to differ in what we mean is for us to disagree about an analytic sentence, and for us to differ in what we believe is for us to disagree about a synthetic sentence. A judgment that the external questioner must not mean what we mean—a judgment that there is a difference in meaning, not mere belief—thus seems to rely on a judgment that we disagree about an analyticity, revealing a tacit acceptance of the A/S distinction. Note that this account of the I/E distinction does not require the postulation of different concepts of existence (see Hirsch's 2011 work on quantifier variance).

I conclude, acknowledging that my argument is far from conclusive, that appealing to analyticity gives us the best account of the distinction between internal and external questions and of why external questions are either questions about which language to use or pseudo-questions.

Now, you may be wondering how this all squares with an ontic account of DME. How can a Carnapian normativist hold an *ontic* account of DME? Regarding the compatibility of normativism and an ontic account of DME, I argue in Chapter 5 that NOCA does not cease to be an ontic account after being deflated by normativism. The short explanation is: normativism reconceives the metaphysical nature of the explanans and explananda of DMEs, and this allows the normativist to see ontic accounts of DME, including NOCA, as roundabout ontic accounts of what people think and say. After all, for the mathematical normativist, mathematical truths express conceptual/semantic rules—what people think and say is all there is to explain, and it can be explained ontically.

Regarding the compatibility of deflationary metaontology and the generalized ontic conception, I will say this. In this book, I am only concerned to deflate mathematics; I will only briefly discuss deflationary metaontology in other areas. However, there is much debate over whether one can say some of the deflationary things I want to say in one area without its generalizing to a global deflationism and ultimately global anti-realism (see, e.g., Price et al. 2013). And the brand of deflationary metaontology with which I am most sympathetic is Carnap's (1950), which is certainly global in character. One might therefore reasonably worry whether the generalized ontic conception requires a kind of metaphysical realism with which Carnapian metaontology is incompatible. I don't think they are incompatible. First, unlike the other metaontological deflationists just cited who worry about global anti-realism, I accept the A/S distinction. For me, deflating mathematics means making it analytic. You cannot similarly deflate tables and chairs. The existence of tables and chairs is not analytic, and if you tried to make it so by stipulating the analyticity of "tables exist," you would simply change the meaning of the word.[28] "But isn't the existence of tables relative to a linguistic framework for Carnap?" Not in any problematic sense. A framework in which "tables exist" is false is one in which "tables" (or "exists") means something different. A framework is just a language (fragment). For Carnap, there is a world out there, and we can talk about it in many different ways. Ontologies are languages, so while one philosopher may say that tables exist and another may

[28] As Warren (2020, 232–233) points out, this defuses a standard objection to us defenders of analytic existence claims: why can't we make the existence of God analytic? By all means, make "God exists" analytic. Unfortunately, you won't have established what you think you have.

say that only particles arranged table-wise exist, they are merely talking about the same thing in different languages (Dyke 2007; Heil 2003; Hirsch 2011; Putnam 1981, 1987; Rayo 2013; Thomasson 2014).

The generalized ontic conception does not require *ontological* realism—the idea that there is one correct ontology, one correct language in which to describe the world. Take a straightforward causal explanation: the bottle broke because Suzy threw a rock at it. The ontology of rocks and bottles simply doesn't matter. It matters not a bit to the generalized ontic conception whether what Suzy threw was a substance, a bunch of simples arranged rock-wise, a part of the universe that was rock-ing, or whatever.[29] So, when the generalized ontic conception says that the explanans—here, the rock—must be objective in order to explain, it does not mean that rocks as such (rather than simples arranged rock-wise) must figure in the one true ontology, nor that the explanans must be described in a certain language. It just means that the rock must be mind-independent; whether it is, is in part an *empirical* matter—I take it that, for example, whether consciousness collapses the wave function has some *empirical* bearing on it.[30]

The generalized ontic conception requires what we might call "empirical objectivity" or "empirical realism" as opposed to "ontological objectivity" or "ontological realism."[31] There are many ontologically different but empirically equivalent ways of describing the real, mind-independent explanandum, explanans, and explanatory relation. In fact, ontologists often *insist* that different ontological theories are empirically indistinguishable (e.g., Merricks 2011; van Inwagen 1995). I take this to be obvious—e.g., no possible experience could distinguish between the truth of the claim that there are substantial rocks and the truth of the claim that there are only particles arranged rock-wise. If they were empirically distinguishable, ontologists would be doing empirical investigation.

Hofweber (2016) agrees that different ontological hypotheses are *phenomenologically* indistinguishable, but he thinks they are still *empirically* distinguishable. His argument is that our perceptual beliefs are about objects, not

[29] This idea does not imply that the bottle's breaking is wildly causally overdetermined, since these descriptions of the cause are just different ways of describing the same thing. See Thomasson (2007b) on the confusion of overdetermination and causal exclusion arguments against ordinary objects.

[30] Sidelle (2016, 71–72) doubts whether "there is mind-independent matter" has a metaphysically unloaded, framework-internal sense. I think it does for the reason just given.

[31] "The concept of reality occurring in these internal questions is an empirical, scientific, non-metaphysical concept. To recognize something as a real thing or event means to succeed in incorporating it into the system of things at a particular space-time position so that it fits together with the other things as real, according to the rules of the framework" (Carnap 1950, 22).

simples arranged object-wise (for example), and these beliefs are defeasibly justified. We may have justified beliefs about simples arranged object-wise, but these are not *perceptual* beliefs; these are beliefs downstream from our justified perceptual beliefs about objects. He writes, "The belief that there are simples arranged chair-wise is not a perceptual belief at all, and it can't be in our perceptual system" (192). I'm not sure what he means by "it can't be in our perceptual system." He can't mean that we can't have perceptual beliefs with that content because we can't perceive individual simples, for perceiving simples arranged chair-wise needn't require that ability. Maybe he just means we can't have perceptual beliefs with that content because beliefs with that content are always downstream of perceptual beliefs about objects. If that's just a claim about us, as our psychologies actually are, then it's plausible.[32] However, I see nothing incoherent in the idea of a linguistic community that learns the language of simples arranged object-wise first, and only later comes to talk about objects. It seems plausible that the members of such a community would form perceptual beliefs about simples arranged object-wise and that their beliefs about objects would be downstream. That our own conceptual development didn't happen this way and that, perhaps for contingent social, historical, and neurological reasons no community would conceptually develop this way, doesn't undercut the point. (See Thomasson 2019b on the development of language for ordinary objects.) I want to emphasize that I am arguing against the idea that ontological claims are empirically distinguishable; I am not arguing against the justification of our perceptual beliefs in ordinary objects.[33]

Now on to the book's central foil: the enhanced indispensability argument for platonism.

1.3. The Enhanced Indispensability Argument

Some of the most influential arguments for platonism have been and continue to be indispensability arguments. The thought is that we ought to be platonists because mathematics is indispensable to us, in some way that needs to be cashed out. According to the Quine-Putnam version of this argument,

[32] Though not unassailable. Brandom (2015, Chapter 2) discusses a Sellarsian account of perception that, I think, would allow one to perceive simples arranged object-wise.

[33] Hofweber (2016) has a second argument for empirical distinguishability that appeals to scientific confirmation, but, as he acknowledges, this argument relies on the first.

we ought to be platonists because our best scientific theories indispensably quantify over mathematical objects, where this means that every theory that doesn't quantify over mathematical objects is worse, by some standard (e.g., simplicity, fruitfulness, predictive power, etc.) (see, e.g., Quine 1976; Putnam 1979). Baker (2009, 613) christened the following version of this argument the "enhanced indispensability argument" (EIA), which focuses on *explanatory power*, i.e., on DMEs:

(1) We ought rationally to believe in the existence of any entity that plays an indispensable explanatory role in our best scientific theories.
(2) Mathematical objects play an indispensable explanatory role in science [i.e., there are DMEs].
(3) Hence, we ought rationally to believe in the existence of mathematical objects.

Many critics of the EIA have denied the second premise, the existence of DMEs (e.g., Melia 2000; Daly and Langford 2009; Saatsi 2011). They insist that in all putative DMEs, the mathematics is playing a merely representational role. As far as I know, no one has denied the first premise. It expresses a widespread scientific realist attitude in contemporary philosophy of science. And no one, as far as I know, has argued that the EIA is invalid. But that's what I think, and that's what I will argue.

At least, I think it's invalid when properly formulated. For, the premises appear to be category mistakes. How could an *entity* play a role in a *theory*? Entities play roles—e.g., causal or functional roles—in the world, but not in theories. Instead, I think the argument is better rendered as something like (EIA'):

(1') We ought rationally to believe in the existence of any entity referred to by a concept that plays an indispensable explanatory role in our best scientific theories.
(2') Mathematical concepts play an indispensable explanatory role in science [i.e., there are DMEs].
(3') Hence, we ought rationally to believe in the existence of mathematical objects.

But this isn't valid. For, we need:

(2.5') Mathematical concepts refer to mathematical objects.

And here's why I think the EIA' is invalid: I argue that (2.5') is false, at least if reference is here understood as a substantial relation, as surely it must be for any proponent of the EIA'. If the reference of mathematical concepts can be got for cheap, then the existence of mathematical objects can be got for cheap, and there's no point in using the EIA' to secure their existence. The proponent of the EIA is after something more. After all, no proponent of the EIA' would be satisfied with the merely *analytic* truth of "mathematical concepts (successfully) refer to mathematical objects" or "there are mathematical objects," which normativists and conventionalists accept. For the EIA' proponent, reference is not cheap—it is by playing an indispensable explanatory role in our best scientific theories that we are entitled to believe that a concept succeeds in referring. Let us say that *X*s exist analytically (synthetically) when "*X*s exist" or "there are *X*s" is an analytic (synthetic) truth.[34] With the analyticity of existence comes the analyticity of successful reference and vice versa: "*X*s exist" is an analytic (synthetic) truth if and only if "'*X*' refers successfully" is an analytic (synthetic) truth (holding fixed the actual meaning of "*X*"—it is given the actual meaning of "5" that "'5' refers successfully" is analytic). The proponent of the EIA is after the *synthetic* existence of mathematical objects and *synthetic* successful reference of mathematical concepts. A central aim of this book is to show how normativism can deflate even ontic accounts of DME, rendering the EIA' invalid when understood platonistically, i.e., when reference and existence are understood synthetically.

Note that (2.5') is not meant to imply *successful* reference. If it did, (2.5') alone would take us to platonism. The distinction between reference and successful reference is common. Obviously, we could do away with the distinction, treating reference as essentially successful, and restate the argument with (2.5') as "Mathematical concepts refer to mathematical objects, if they refer," or "Mathematical concepts purport to refer to mathematical objects," mutatis mutandis. I will stick with the distinction between reference and successful reference.

Given that the proponent of the EIA is after synthetic reference and synthetic existence, an even more explicit formulation is as follows (EIA*):

(1*) We ought rationally to believe in the synthetic existence of any entity synthetically referred to by a concept that plays an indispensable explanatory role in our best scientific theories.

[34] It is best to read this claim schematically, rather than as a universal quantification. If you worry that I'm quantifying into a quotational context, see Chapter 8's discussion of Linnebo for a more careful account of analytic existence claims.

(2*) Mathematical concepts play an indispensable explanatory role in science [i.e., there are DMEs].
(3*) Mathematical concepts synthetically refer to mathematical objects.
(4*) Hence, we ought rationally to believe in the synthetic existence of mathematical objects.

To believe in the synthetic existence of *X*s, I don't think it's necessary to believe that *X*s exist *and* to believe that "*X*s exist" is synthetic. You don't need the concept of the synthetic to believe in the synthetic existence of *X*s. To believe in the synthetic existence of *X*s is just to believe that *X*s exist, where the proposition that *X*s exist is a synthetic proposition. This doesn't require possession of the concept of the synthetic. The synthetic proposition that *X*s exist is different from the analytic proposition that *X*s exist because "*X*s exist" means different things depending on whether it is analytic or synthetic. In Chapter 6, I defend an inferentialist account of meaning according to which meaning is determined by inferential rules. Since "*X*s exist" has different inferential rules governing it depending on whether it is analytic or synthetic—e.g., if it's analytic, but not if it's synthetic, you are allowed to infer it anywhere in a proof—it means different things depending on whether it is analytic or synthetic.

Premise (3*) is simply the denial of normativism. To (purport to) refer synthetically is to refer successfully synthetically, if reference is successful at all. So, if mathematical concepts refer synthetically to mathematical objects, that implies that if they succeed, their successful reference is synthetic. In other words, according to (3*), if "'5' refers successfully to 5" is true, it is synthetically true. So, (3*) implies that sentences like "'5' refers successfully to 5" (and, so, "5 exists") are synthetic; but these are analytic according to the normativist. (3*) says that mathematics describes in the substantive sense denied by normativism. Thus, the EIA* is invalid without begging the question against the normativist. She can accept the existence of DMEs while denying platonism, because she denies (3*).

She could also deny (1*), of course, but she needn't. I am taking (1*) to be equivalent to "If a concept plays an indispensable explanatory role in our best scientific theories, we ought to believe in the synthetic existence of any entity it synthetically refers to."[35] Call this (1a*). The normativist can accept (1a*). Call a concept that plays an indispensable explanatory role in our best

[35] And I take (1a*) to be equivalent to "If a concept plays an indispensable explanatory role in our best scientific theories, then, if it synthetically refers to an entity, we ought to believe in the synthetic existence of that entity (i.e., we ought to believe that the concept's synthetic reference is successful)." The normativist can accept this because she thinks mathematical concepts don't meet the second, embedded antecedent.

scientific theories an "i-concept." The normativist can agree with (1a*) that we ought to believe in the synthetic existence of any entity an i-concept synthetically refers to, because she thinks mathematical i-concepts don't synthetically refer to anything, so there's nothing to believe synthetically exists. Thus, the normativist can accept the scientific realist sentiment of (1) by accepting (1a*). One could instead take (1') to mean "If a concept plays an indispensable explanatory role in our best scientific theories, we ought to believe it synthetically refers successfully." Call this (1b*). The normativist would deny (1b*). She thinks mathematical concepts are i-concepts, but that they don't synthetically refer successfully. If (1b*) were used as the first premise, then the EIA* would seem to me valid without premise (3*), but still not valid without an anti-normativist premise, this time premise (1b*).

Let me stress that I think that many mathematical concepts are descriptive and in fact successfully describe, but only in applied contexts. I will give an account of their descriptive content in Chapter 6. But the applied uses of mathematical concepts are not the *distinctive* uses that figure in DMEs—the applied uses are merely representational uses. In DMEs, mathematical concepts appear in truths both of pure and applied mathematics, but it is the appearance of truths of pure mathematics that supposedly gives DMEs their ability to support platonism in the EIA.[36] In other words, the indispensable explanatory role appealed to in the EIA is not the representational role. Recall that those who deny the existence of DMEs do so by claiming that all uses of mathematics within them are representational. So, premise (3*) doesn't mean that mathematical concepts can be empirically applied, something no normativist need deny; it means that *pure* mathematics describes mathematical objects.

1.4. Summary

The idea that pure mathematics is not descriptive in any substantive sense is not new. As I mentioned, many of the positivists, especially Wittgenstein in different ways in different periods, held something like it. Their views have come under heavy fire over the decades, though, and I believe that normativism provides the most plausible way of resurrecting their view from the ashes. I will discuss normativism in detail in Chapter 5. First, I must elaborate on our central topic: distinctively mathematical explanation (DME).

[36] I will leave the asterisk off when it doesn't matter which version of the EIA I'm referring to.

2

Distinctively Mathematical Explanation

2.1. Introduction

In this chapter[1] I characterize distinctively mathematical explanation (DME), describe many prominent examples, and present three desiderata that any philosophical account of DME should satisfy: it should accommodate and explicate the modal import of some DMEs (Baron 2016); it should distinguish uses of mathematics in scientific explanation that are distinctively mathematical from those that are not (Baron 2016); and it should accommodate the directionality of DMEs (Craver and Povich 2017). I then show how two recent accounts of DME fail to satisfy some or all of the desiderata: Lange (2013b, 2016) and briefly Baron (2019). Baron's (2020) newer, counterfactual account will be critiqued in Chapter 4, where I present my own counterfactual account. Baron's (2024) newest Pythagorean account will be addressed in Chapter 5, because the points I make require normativist concepts I elaborate in that chapter.

Section 2.2 introduces the phenomenon of DME, presents examples, and explains the desiderata for any account of DME. Sections 2.2.1–2.2.9 critique Lange's (2013b) account of DME. Section 2.3 critiques Baron's (2019) account.

2.2. Distinctively Mathematical Explanations

DMEs work primarily by showing a natural explanandum (i.e., the thing to be explained) to follow in part from a mathematical fact. Many[2] DMEs thus

[1] Much of the material from the first few sections of this chapter is adapted with some revisions from Craver and Povich (2017). I will accordingly use plural first-person pronouns and possessives when drawing from that collaborative work and singular when the ideas are wholly mine.

[2] I will be noncommittal for now whether they all work this way. In Chapter 4, I will argue that they do.

Rules to Infinity. Mark Povich, Oxford University Press. © Oxford University Press 2024.
DOI: 10.1093/oso/9780197679005.003.0002

show that the explanandum had to happen, in a sense stronger than any ordinary causal law can supply. As a paradigmatic example, consider Trefoil Knot (Lange 2013b). The explanandum is the fact that Terry failed to untie his knot. The explanantia (i.e., the things that explain) are the empirical fact that his knot is a trefoil knot and the mathematical (knot theoretic) fact that the trefoil knot is distinct from the unknot (i.e., mathematically cannot be untied). The unknot is a single closed loop (think torus or donut), while the trefoil knot has three crossing loops. That the trefoil knot is distinct from the unknot, and so, mathematically, cannot be untied, means that there are no 'admissible' moves of twisting, lifting, or crossing strands without cutting them (the so-called Reidemeister moves) that can transform the trefoil knot into the unknot. Thus, the explanantia ensure mathematically that Terry will fail to untie his knot; his success is mathematically impossible. Some (e.g., Kuorikoski 2021) deny the existence of DMEs. It will become apparent in Chapter 4 why I think they exist and what I think demarcates them from standardly mathematical explanations. More examples are given below.

Trefoil Knot illustrates three desiderata for an account of DME: modality, distinctness, and directionality.

> *The Modal Desideratum*: an account of DME should accommodate and explicate the modal import of some DMEs. (Baron 2016)

Terry's failure is modally robust—he could not succeed. An account of DME should capture and explicate this modal robustness. (Note that this desideratum allows that some DMEs are not modally robust; see note 2).

> *The Distinctiveness Desideratum*:[3] an account of DME should distinguish uses of mathematics in explanation that are distinctively mathematical from those that are not. (Baron 2016)

Bromberger's (1966) flagpole[4] is an example of an explanation that uses mathematics but is not a DME. This is widely agreed upon, and I will use this as my paradigm of *standardly* mathematical explanation throughout the book. The explanandum is the fact that the length of a flagpole's shadow is *l*.

[3] Baron (2016) calls this the genuineness constraint.

[4] The example actually comes from Salmon (1989), who gives it the name "Bromberger's flagpole." Bromberger (1966) himself uses slightly different examples to make the same point.

The explanantia are the empirical facts that the angle of elevation of the sun is θ, the height of the flagpole is h, and light propagates in straight lines, and the mathematical fact that $\tan \theta = h/l$. Precise explanations of why this example is an example of only *standardly* mathematical explanation may depend on one's account of DME, but the central idea is that in this example the mathematics is playing a merely representational role, where this means that the mathematics is merely representing what is in fact doing the real explanatory work (i.e., the physical causes). There are two ways an account of DME might fail to meet the distinctiveness desideratum: it might count as distinctively mathematical an explanation that is not, and it might count as not distinctively mathematical an explanation that is.

> *The Directionality Desideratum*: an account of DME should accommodate the directionality of DME. (Craver and Povich 2017; Povich and Craver 2018)

Bromberger's flagpole explanation is reversible: one can derive the flagpole's height from the length of the flagpole's shadow and other relevant facts. For Bromberger (and Salmon 1984), the example demonstrates an *asymmetry* in *natural* explanations that the covering-law model could not accommodate. This model held that to explain is to derive a description of the explanandum from descriptions of laws of nature and initial conditions. The covering-law model is thereby shown to be an inadequate account of the norms of scientific explanation. Accommodating the directionality of scientific explanations is thus a desideratum generally. Craver and Povich (2017) argue that, analogously, the explanation of Trefoil Knot can be "reversed"[5] to form an argument that fits Lange's (2013b) account of DME but is not explanatory. In fact, there's an algorithm for such a reversal: Simply take the explanandum and the empirical premise, swap them, and negate them, akin to turning a modus ponens into a modus tollens. Thus, change the explanandum to "Terry's knot is not trefoil." Change the empirical premise to "Terry untied his knot." The mathematical premise is the same: the trefoil knot is distinct from the unknot. This reversal should not count as an explanation; Terry's untying his knot doesn't explain why his knot is non-trefoil.

[5] Craver-Povich reversals in this sense are not strict reversals—simple swaps of explanandum and explanans—like the well-known reversal of Bromberger's flagpole. Henceforth, I will drop the scare quotes.

These desiderata should not be controversial. They help to show why DMEs are distinctive and explanatory. They are arguably constitutive of DME. An account of DME that does not meet *further* desiderata—such as, e.g., that the account should comport well with intra-mathematical explanation—would not be ideal, but an account that violates the modality, distinctiveness, or directionality desiderata is arguably not an account of DME at all.

Before moving on to Lange's account of DME, let me present more prominent examples. DMEs have no canonical form, but examples are readily reconstructed as arguments in which a description of an explanandum phenomenon follows from an empirical premise (EP) describing the relevant natural facts,[6] and a mathematical premise (MP) describing one or more more-than-merely-naturally-necessary facts. The following examples are readily found in the literature:

> **Strawberries:** Why did Mary fail to divide her strawberries among her three kids?[7] Because she has 23 strawberries (EP), and 23 is not divisible by 3 (MP).[8]
>
> **Bridges**: Why did Marta fail to walk a path through Königsberg in 1735, crossing each of its bridges exactly once (i.e., an Eulerian walk)? Because, that year, Königsberg's bridges formed a connected network with four nodes (landmasses); three nodes had three edges (bridges); one had five (EP), and only networks that contain either zero or two nodes with an odd number of edges permit an Eulerian walk (MP).

[6] Lange might object to the inclusion of the empirical premise in this formulation. Instead, he might treat the empirical premise as a presupposition of the why question: "Why did Mary fail to divide her 23 strawberries evenly among her three kids?" Answer: "Because 23 is indivisible by 3." In what follows, all of our examples can be so translated without affecting the principled incompleteness in the cases, but this reformulation comes at considerable cost to the clarity with which the incompleteness can be displayed (see Section 2.2.4).

[7] Or "Why didn't she on some particular occasion?" or "Why didn't anyone ever?" or, modally, "Why *couldn't* anyone ever?" I will discuss the distinction between modal and non-modal explananda later. Lange intends all these explananda to be explained by the same explanans. A similar multiplicity of explananda can be generated for the examples below.

[8] This example is reconstructed as a sketch of a deductive argument. We would have to tighten the bolts to make the argument valid (e.g., no cutting of strawberries is allowed), but the general idea is clear enough. The empirical premise works by describing the natural features of a system. They specify, for example, the relevant magnitudes (Mary starts with 23 strawberries), and the causal or otherwise relevant dependencies among them. Some DMEs might be inductive. For example, one might explain why fair dice will most likely not roll a string of 10 consecutive double-6s on mathematical grounds, using logical probability and some mathematics. See also the Chopsticks example below.

Chopsticks: Why is it likely that more tossed chopsticks will be oriented horizontally rather than vertically? Because they were tossed randomly (EP), and there are more ways for a chopstick to be horizontal than to be vertical (MP). (If we focus on the sphere produced by rotating the chopstick through three dimensions, a chopstick can be horizontal anywhere near the equator; it is vertical only near the poles.)

Cicadas: Why do cicadas have prime life-cycle periods? Because it is evolutionarily advantageous to have a life cycle that minimizes intersection with those of your periodic predators (EP), and prime periods minimize intersection (MP). (We assume cicadas evolve what is evolutionarily advantageous.)

Honeycombs: Why do honeybees produce hexagonal honeycomb cells? Because honeybees divide their combs (which are planar regions with dividing walls of negligible thickness) into regions of equal area (EP), and a hexagonal grid uses the least total perimeter in dividing a planar region into regions of equal area (MP).[9]

Pendulum: Why does Patty's pendulum have at least four equilibrium configurations? Because Patty's pendulum is a double pendulum (EP), and any double pendulum's configuration space is a torus with at least four stationary points (MP).

2.2.1. Lange on Distinctively Mathematical Explanation

In "What Makes a Scientific Explanation Distinctively Mathematical?" (2013b), Lange uses the above examples to argue that certain natural phenomena are best explained by appeal to mathematical, rather than natural,

[9] I've described Cicadas and Honeycombs the way they are usually described in the literature (e.g., Baker 2005). The cicada explanandum is also sometimes described as being that cicadas have 13- and 17-year life cycles (e.g., Baron, Colyvan, and Ripley 2017). Baron et al. also describe Honeycombs as follows: Why do honeybees produce hexagonal honeycombs? Because they are under evolutionary pressure to produce the largest honeycomb cells using the least wax (EP), and hexagons are the most efficient method of tessellating a surface into regions of equal area with least total perimeter (MP). These differences between examples are unimportant, for the basic logic is the same: a description of the explanandum phenomenon follows from an empirical premise and a mathematical premise. Lange, however, "narrows" these two explananda: for him, the explananda are that cicadas with prime life-cycle periods tend to suffer less from predation by predators with periodic life cycles than do cicadas with composite periods, and that honeybees use at least the amount of wax they would use to divide their combs into hexagons of equal area. Lange thinks the explananda as usually described have causal (etiological and constitutive) explanations. The narrower explanations, Lange argues, have DMEs. My account of DME—the Narrow Ontic Counterfactual Account (NOCA)—agrees with this narrowing idea. NOCA will be presented in Chapter 4.

facts. In other words, he argues by way of example that there are DMEs, whose core explanatory facts are modally stronger than facts about, e.g., statistical relevance, causation, or natural law, and he gives an account of how such DMEs work. A DME might describe causes, Lange allows, but its explanatory force derives ultimately from appeal to facts that are "more necessary" than causal laws. Lange advances this thesis to argue for the importance of a purely modal view of explanation (a view that emphasizes necessities, possibilities, and impossibilities, showing that an event had to happen or could not have happened) in contrast to an ontic view (a view that associates explanation with describing the relevant natural facts, e.g., about how the event was caused or how its underlying mechanisms work).

Lange operates with a narrower understanding of the ontic conception. He describes it as the view that all explanations are causal. He cites Salmon, who claimed, "To give scientific explanations is to show how events and statistical regularities fit into the causal structure of the world" (Salmon 1977, 162)[10] and "to understand why certain things happen, we need to see how they are produced by these mechanisms [processes, interactions, laws]" (Salmon 1984, 132). He also cites Lewis (1986, 217) ("Here is my main thesis: to explain an event is to provide some information about its causal history") and Sober (1984, 96) ("The explanation of an event describes the 'causal structure' in which it is embedded").[11] In contrast to Lange, we adopt a more inclusive understanding of the ontic (see Chapters 1 and 3) that embraces any natural regularity (Salmon 1989; Craver 2014; Povich 2018), e.g., statistical relevance (Salmon 1977), natural laws (Hempel 1965), or contingent compositional relations might also figure fundamentally in explanation. Lange's arguments should, however, work equally well against this broader understanding of the ontic conception, given that he uses the examples to show that some explanations of natural facts depend fundamentally on relations of necessity that are stronger than mere natural necessity.

We think Lange's account of DME is flawed. Specifically, it fails to account for the directionality implicit in his examples of DME.[12] This failure

[10] See the passages quoted in Chapter 3 for evidence that Salmon did not think the ontic conception was strictly causal.

[11] One can believe that mechanistic explanation is important without believing that all explanations are causal or mechanical. We show why $C = 2\pi r$ without describing mechanisms. We explain why Obama can sign treaties without describing causes. Explanations in epistemology, logic, and metaphysics often work without describing causes. The question here is not whether one should be a pluralist about explanation but about whether Lange's account of DME is complete and whether his contrast with the ontic conception is substantiated by his examples.

[12] See Craver (2016) for a discussion of directionality problems in network explanation.

threatens Lange's argument because it shows that his examples do not, in fact, derive their explanatory force from mathematical relations alone (independent of ontic considerations). The inadequacy is in each case easily remediable by appeal to ontic facts that account for why the explanation is acceptable in one direction and unacceptable in the other. That is, Lange's exemplars of DME appear to require for their adequacy appeal to natural, ontic facts about, e.g., causation, constitution, and natural regularity. In Chapters 4 and 5, I give my own ontic account of DME that preserves the requisite directionality.

2.2.2. Lange's Modal Account

Lange's goal is to show "how distinctively mathematical explanations work" by revealing the "source of their explanatory power" (2013b, 486). He accepts as a basic constraint on his account that it should "fit scientific practice," that is, that it should judge as "explanatory only hypotheses that would (if true) constitute genuine scientific explanations" (486). In short, the account should not contradict too many scientific commonsense judgments about whether an explanation is good or bad. Lange's goal and his guiding constraint are conceptually related: to identify the source of an explanation's power requires identifying the key features that sort acceptable explanations from unacceptable explanations of that type. In causal explanations, for example, much of the explanatory power comes from knowledge of the causal relations among components in a mechanism. Bad causal explanations of this kind fail when they misrepresent the relevant causal structure (in ways that matter). In DMEs, on Lange's view, the explanatory force comes from mathematical relations that are 'more necessary' than mere causal or correlational regularities.

Given this setup, Lange's account of the explanatory force of DMEs can be undermined by examples that fit Lange's account but that would be rejected as bad explanations as a matter of scientific common sense. The account would fail to identify fully the explanatory force in such explanations and so would fail to account for the norms governing such explanations.

The question is whether the mathematical premises are supplying the bulk of the "force" of the explanation. Central to Lange's broader purposes is the claim that DMEs gain their explanatory force from non-causal, and more broadly, non-ontic sources: i.e., stronger-than-naturally-necessary relations.

Explanatory priority flows downward from the more necessary to the less necessary:

> In my view, the order of causal priority is not responsible for the order of explanatory priority in distinctively mathematical explanations in science. Rather, the facts doing the explaining are eligible to explain by virtue of being modally more necessary even than ordinary causal laws (as both mathematical facts and Newton's second law are) or being understood in the why question's context as constitutive of the physical task or arrangement at issue. (2013b, 506)

For Lange, DMEs gain their explanatory force from the fact that they rely fundamentally on mathematical relations that are more necessary than are relations of causation and natural law. The norms by which good DMEs are sorted from bad DMEs would, according to this account, turn on the relevant mathematics and facts about how that mathematics is being applied. In the following section we argue that Lange's analysis is inadequate.

2.2.3. The Inadequacy of Lange's Account

Lange's account currently leaves unspecified a crucial feature for sorting good from bad DMEs. It thereby fails to meet the directionality desideratum. One can generate explanations that fit Lange's form that appear to violate our commonsense norms about the acceptable and unacceptable directions of scientific explanation. If one is committed to the existence of DMEs, then one must find a way to reconcile the directionlessness of many applications of mathematics with the directionality of scientific explanations. My own account—the Narrow Ontic Counterfactual Account (NOCA), presented in Chapter 4—can do this. The kinds of relation described in algebra, geometry, and calculus are directionless; with addition or division, a variable on one side of the equation can be moved to the other side. They have no intrinsic left-right directions; rather, these must be imposed from the outside. This is why Lange's examples of putative distinctively mathematical explanation face a directionality challenge. Each of Lange's examples can be reversed to yield an argument that appeals to the same mathematical premise and that has the same form as Lange's examples but that would not be counted as an acceptable explanation (absent considerable revision in scientific common sense). Consider, for example:

Reversed Strawberries. Why doesn't Mary have 23 strawberries? Because she divided her strawberries equally among her three kids (EP) and 23 is indivisible by 3 (MP).

From a commonsense perspective, at least, Mary's even-numbered pile of strawberries explains but is not explained by her dividing the pile equally among the children.[13] (And surely the number of children Mary had is not explained by her distribution of strawberries today, though a mathematical argument of that sort could be constructed as well.) Note further that the implicit directionality in this explanation is plausibly accounted for by ontic assumptions about the kinds of relations that properly carry explanatory force: i.e., that Mary's pile is the cause (the source) of the portions each kid gets. In contrast, the portions do not cause the number of strawberries or the number of children. The trefoil knot example faces a similar reversal:

Reversed Trefoil Knot: Why doesn't Terry have a trefoil knot? Because Terry untied the knot (EP) and the trefoil knot is distinct from (i.e., not isotopic to) the unknot (MP).

But it would seem more in line with scientific common sense to explain why Terry has a particular kind of knot by describing how he tied it and not by describing his ability or inability to untie it.

Reversed Bridges: Why did either zero or two of Königsberg's landmasses have an odd number of bridges in 1756? Because Marta walked through town, hitting each bridge exactly once (EP) and only networks containing zero or two nodes with an odd degree permit such an Eulerian path (MP).

[13] Catherine Stinson (personal communication) emphasizes that this claim must be bracketed to nonintentional contexts. Mary might decide, for example, to bake a certain number of cookies knowing they will have to be evenly divided among her kids, or she might decide to have three kids because she decides that three is the maximum number of children she can support on her income. These are intentional, causal explanations.

As in the other examples, Königsberg's layout is arguably better explained by the decisions of the Burgermeister than by Marta's walk, yet facts about Königsberg's layout follow reliably from descriptions of either.

> **Reversed Chopsticks:** Why were the chopsticks tossed non-randomly? Because it was likely that more of the tossed chopsticks were oriented vertically than horizontally (EP) and there are more ways for a chopstick to be horizontal than to be vertical (MP).

In this reversal, the unexpected number of vertically oriented chopsticks provides evidence that some biasing force must be acting upon them (much as deviations from the Hardy-Weinberg equilibrium detect selective forces). As in Lange's forward-directed version of the example, the argument here is inductive. But while we are apt to count Lange's original example as explanatory, it seems more fitting with scientific common sense to describe Reversed Chopsticks as describing an evidential, not explanatory, relation.

> **Reversed Cicadas:** Why isn't it evolutionarily advantageous to have a life cycle that minimizes intersection with those of your periodic predators? Because cicadas don't have prime life-cycle periods (EP), and prime periods minimize intersection (MP). (We assume cicadas evolve what is evolutionarily advantageous.)

Here again it seems that we would conflate evidence and explanation if we were to count this reversal as an explanation. Suppose we find a population of cicadas that doesn't have a prime life-cycle period. We know that prime periods minimize intersection, so this gives us reason to conclude that minimizing intersection must not be evolutionarily advantageous in this population. However, an *explanation* of why minimizing intersection is not evolutionarily advantageous would presumably need to cite things such as its unexpectedly deleterious effects in this hypothetical population.

> **Reversed Honeycombs:** Why don't honeybees divide their combs (which are planar regions with dividing walls of negligible thickness) into regions of equal area? Because they don't produce hexagonal honeycomb cells (EP), and a hexagonal grid uses the least total perimeter in dividing a planar region into regions of equal area (MP).

Like Reversed Cicadas, here biological considerations seem required for an *explanation* of why honeybees don't divide their combs into regions of equal area. The premises have merely given us a reason to believe that. The mathematical premise is directionless, but the explanatory force runs in a preferred direction. And finally:

> **Reversed Pendulum:** Why isn't Patty's pendulum a double pendulum? Because Patty's pendulum doesn't have at least four equilibrium configurations (EP), and any double pendulum's configuration space is a torus with at least four stationary points (MP).[14]

But surely Patty's engineering explains the kind of pendulum she has or does not have better than does the fact that the pendulum has more or fewer than four equilibrium points (again, outside intentional contexts).

Each of Lange's examples can be used to generate a putative DME, with the same mathematical premise and the same form, that few scientists would accept as a genuine explanation. Given that Lange is not aiming to revise radically our scientific commonsense ideas about the nature of scientific explanation, it would appear that Lange's account of DME is inadequate.

To amplify this point, note that each example of reversal seems to confuse justification and explanation (see Hempel's [1965] distinction between reason-seeking and explanation-seeking why-questions). An argument justifies believing thesis P (at least partially) when it provides evidence that P. The pristine form of the covering-law model, i.e., one conjoined to the strongest form of the explanation-prediction symmetry thesis, can be seen as attempting to erase this boundary. The goal was to cast explanation as fundamentally an epistemic achievement: explanation is reduced to rational expectation. The problem, of course, is that one can have reason to believe P without explaining P. An Archaeopteryx fossil gives one reason to believe

[14] There are many other putative examples of DME. I haven't yet seen one that can't be reversed. To give one more that is often cited (Baker 2005; Colyvan 2001; Lange 2016; Daly and Langford 2009): Why is it that at any given time there exist two antipodal (i.e., exactly opposite) points on the Earth that have the same temperature? Because temperature is a continuous function (EP), and, by the intermediate value theorem, given a continuous function on a surface there must be a point where the difference in values between antipodal points is zero (MP). The reversal is: Why isn't temperature continuous? (Suppose we lived in a world where it wasn't continuous.) Because at any given time there do not exist two antipodal points on the Earth that have the same temperature (EP), and, by the intermediate value theorem, given a continuous function on a surface there must be a point where the difference in values between antipodal points is zero (MP). The Borsuk-Ulam theorem can be used to give a similar explanation of why it is that at any given time there exist two antipodal points on the Earth that have the same temperature as well as pressure.

that Archaeopteryx once existed, but it does not explain Archaeopteryx's existence. The same point has been made time and again: with barometers and storms, spots and measles, yellow fingers and lung cancer, and roosters and sunrises. Indicators are not always explainers. It was in recognition of this problem that defenders of the covering-law model quickly backed away from strong forms of the explanation-prediction symmetry thesis and sought other means to account for the directionality of scientific explanations. It was in the face of these challenges that Salmon raised his flag in favor of the ontic conception.

Yet precisely the same problem appears to arise for Lange's examples: we learn something about Terry's knot when we learn he's untied it; we learn something about Königsberg's bridges from Marta's stroll; we learn something about our chopsticks when we observe their contra-normal behavior; we learn something about evolutionary advantage when we observe the life cycles of cicadas; we learn something about honeycombs from their structure; and we learn something about a pendulum from how many equilibrium configurations it has. But learning something about the system is not in all cases tantamount to explaining that feature of the system.

Lange argues that the order of explanatory priority in his examples follows the degree of modal necessity, with more necessary things explaining less necessary things. Yet this restriction on DMEs cannot block the above examples. After all, the same mathematical laws are involved in the forward and reversed cases. We have simply changed the empirical facts. The problem appears to be that the mathematics in these examples is sufficiently flexible that it doesn't seem to have the resources internal to it to account for the directionality enforced in scientific common sense. Some extra ingredient is required to sort genuine DMEs from pretenders and, specifically, to sort explanation from justification. In other words, these putative cases of distinctively modal, mathematical explanations of natural phenomena appear to retain an ineliminable ontic component, perhaps working implicitly in the background, but required to account for the preferred direction to the explanation. In the cases as described, causation seems a plausible candidate for supplying directionality: Mary's pile explains the kids' allotment, and not vice versa, because the allotment is produced from the pile. The trefoil knot explains the failure to untie it, and not vice versa, perhaps because structures constrain functions and not vice versa. Similarly, the structure of Königsberg's bridges explains which walks are possible around town, but the walks do not explain the structure of the town. Perhaps the movement of the sticks does not explain the forces acting on the sticks because the pattern in the sticks is not causally relevant to the forces acting upon them. Perhaps what is evolutionarily advantageous explains the presence of a trait, and not vice versa, because what is evolutionarily advantageous is causally relevant to the existence and persistence of selectable traits. Perhaps the structure of honeycombs explains the amount of wax used, but not vice versa, because the structure of a honeycomb determines the amount of wax needed to build it. And perhaps the shape of Patty's pendulum is explained by her desires in choosing it and not by the fact that it does or does not have four stable equilibrium points precisely because Patty's desires are causally relevant and (in most non-intentional contexts) the four equilibrium points are not. In other words, in each case, it would appear that various ontic assumptions about what can explain what are called upon to sort out the appropriate direction of the explanation and to weed out inappropriate applications of the same argumentative forms appealing to the same mathematical laws.[15] However, appealing to some ontic relation like causation to account for directionality seems to result in the denial of the existence of DMEs—all of the examples are standard causal explanations.

The dialectical situation might be expressed as a tension between three propositions: first, that there are DMEs; second, that DMEs are directionless; and third, that explanations of natural phenomena are not directionless. Denying the first is obviously not an option for any defender of DME. Denying the third requires significant, I think devastating, revisions to scientific common sense. I will deny the second. I argue in Chapters 4 and 5 that narrowing the explananda of DMEs allows me to demarcate them from standardly mathematical explanations while retaining directionality—the explananda of DMEs cannot explain their explanantia. One might also deny that mathematics is directionless. Perhaps some areas of mathematics enforce a direction that corresponds to the explanatory norms in a given domain (Philippe Huneman, personal communication). This appears not to be the case in Lange's examples, but it does not follow that there are no such cases.

[15] Aggregative explanations apply to constitutive relations but exhibit a preferred direction. The mass of the pile of sand is explained by summing the masses of the individual grains. But one can infer the mass of an individual grain from the mass of the whole and the mass of the other grains. This aggregative explanation appears to have the same simple mathematical structure as Strawberries. In this case, it is a constitutive (not causal) relation that apparently accounts for the preferred direction. Perhaps parts explain wholes and not vice versa: an ontic commitment.

Even if one is tempted to give up on the first proposition and to deny that there truly are DMEs, Lange's discussion highlights an important feature of causal and mechanistic explanation that has thus far received very little attention: namely, that all mechanisms are constrained to work within the space of logical and mathematical possibility. If how something works is explained by revealing constraints on its operation (as Craver and Darden [2013], for example, appear to suggest), then one cannot neglect these modal constraints in a complete understanding of mechanistic explanation.

2.2.4. Presuppositions and Constitutive Contexts

Although we have modeled our reconstructions on Lange's discussion, in which he explicitly states that contingent, empirical facts are part of the explanantia (2013b, 506), he may object to the form of the examples. He considers and rejects the following pseudo-explanation:

> Why are all planetary orbits elliptical (approximately)? Because each planetary orbit is (approximately) the locus of points for which the sum of the distances from two fixed points is a constant [EP], and that locus is (as a matter of mathematical fact) an ellipse [MP]. (2013b, 508)

Like the previous examples, this one has an empirical premise and a mathematical premise. This is not a DME, according to Lange, because "the first fact to which it appeals [i.e., EP] is neither modally more necessary than ordinary causal laws nor understood in the why question's context to be constitutive of being a planetary orbit (the physical arrangement in question)" (508). However, if we presuppose that the planetary orbits in question are just those that are loci of points for which the sum of the distances from two fixed points is a constant, then that fact is understood in the why-question's context to be constitutive of being a planetary orbit. The why-question then becomes: Why are all planetary orbits that are loci of points for which the sum of the distances from two fixed points is a constant, elliptical? It is constitutive of the planetary orbits in question that they are loci of points for which the sum of the distances from two fixed points is a constant. The DME is that those loci are necessarily ellipses. Should Lange object to our reversed examples on similar grounds, their empirical premises can also be presupposed and shifted into their associated why-questions. For example, in Reversed Trefoil Knot, instead of asking, "Why doesn't Terry have a trefoil knot?" and stating as an empirical premise that Terry untied the knot, we could instead ask, "Why isn't the knot Terry untied a trefoil knot?" Now the former empirical premise is part of the constitutive context of the why-question. We presuppose that Terry untied his knot, rather than stating it as an empirical premise. This seems to fit Lange's criteria for DME.

Lange could respond to this move by distinguishing between what is *understood* to be constitutive of the physical task or arrangement at issue and what is *actually* constitutive of the physical task or arrangement at issue.[16] Lange could then argue that, for example, it is actually constitutive of the physical task or arrangement at issue that Terry's knot is a trefoil knot. However, Lange could continue, in the version of Reversed Trefoil Knot where we presuppose that Terry untied his knot, that fact is not actually constitutive of the physical task or arrangement at issue. We are unsure how this distinction between what is "understood" to be and what is "actually" constitutive could be drawn. When we request an explanation for the fact that Terry failed to untie his knot, we grant that context determines that it is actually (and not merely understood to be) constitutive of that fact that his knot is a trefoil knot. However, when we request an explanation for the fact that the knot Terry untied isn't a trefoil knot, it seems to us constitutive of that very fact that Terry untied his knot. It wouldn't be the same explanandum had Terry not untied his knot. We do not see how one can claim that Terry's untying the knot is merely understood to be constitutive of this explanandum, while claiming that the knot's being a trefoil knot is actually constitutive of the former explanandum.

We don't think there's anything objectionable about so restricting the range of our explananda/why-question (e.g., to just those planetary orbits that are loci of points for which the sum of the distances from two fixed points is a constant). Notice that such a restriction is required of Lange's examples as well. For example, it is not constitutive of all knots that they contain trefoil knots; it is constitutive only of the knot under consideration, which actually contains a trefoil knot. Nor is it constitutive of all pendula that they are double pendula; nor of all arrangements of strawberries and children that there are 23 of the former and 3 of the latter; nor of all bridges that they have a non-Eulerian structure. This response to our challenge, in other

[16] Note that Lange (2013b) always speaks of what is "understood" to be constitutive in the context of the why-question (e.g., 491, 497, 506, 507, 508).

words, requires an account of how context determines what is constitutive of the physical task or arrangement in question,[17] especially if it relies on a distinction between what is actually and what is merely understood to be constitutive in a given context.

2.2.5. Modal and Ontic Aspects of Mechanistic Explanations

Return again to the flagpole and the shadow. As discussed above, Bromberger and Salmon used this example to demonstrate the directionality of scientific explanations. They enlist this point to argue for an ineliminable causal (or more broadly, ontic) component in our normative analysis of scientific explanation. We have used the same strategy to argue for an ineliminable ontic component in Lange's examples of DME. But the example can be yoked for another duty.

One might, in fact, describe the flagpole example as a distinctively mathematical (or at least trigonometric) explanation of a natural phenomenon, one that calls out for a distinctively modal interpretation. *Presupposing* that the angle of elevation of the sun is θ and that the height of the flagpole is h (and the flagpole and ground are straight and form a right angle, and that the system is Euclidean, etc.), why is the length of the flagpole's shadow l? Once the contingent causal facts are presupposed in our empirical premise, the only relevant fact left to do the explaining seems to be the trigonometric fact that $\tan \theta = h/l$. Moreover, once these natural facts are presupposed, the length of the flagpole's shadow seems to follow by trigonometric necessity. So, if we package all the natural facts into an empirical premise and highlight the relation $\tan \theta = h/l$, which is crucial for the argument to work, then we might see this as a case in which the bulk of the explanatory force is carried by a trigonometric function. The example thus seems to provide a recipe for turning at least some mechanistic explanations into distinctively mathematical explanations: simply package all of the empirical conditions, such as the rectilinear propagation of light, or the Euclidean nature of spacetime, into the empirical premise or the context of the request for explanation, and leave a mathematical remainder or a tautology to serve as the premise with stronger-than-natural necessity.[18]

[17] This worry is raised by Pincock (2015, 875).

[18] This could presumably be done with any kind of necessity. For example, take an explanation one of whose premises is a *conceptual* necessity. Fix or presuppose all the premises other than the

The importance of geometry to mechanistic explanation is readily apparent in artifacts, such as the coupling between an engine and the drive crankshaft of a car. Machamer, Darden, and Craver (2000) describe the organization of such mechanisms as geometrico-mechanical in nature. Vertical motion produced by explosions in the piston chambers drives the pistons out. The center of each piston is connected via a rod to the crankshaft at some distance (r) from the center of the crankshaft so that when the piston is driven out, the crankshaft is rotated in a circle. This mechanism very efficiently transfers the vertical force of the pistons into a circular motion that drives the car forward. These engine parts are organized geometrically in circles and triangles. The angle of the connecting rod, for example, determines the position of the piston, though the explanation would appear to work the other way around. Yet these mathematical facts surely are relevant to why the car accelerates as it does and not faster or slower.[19]

But as Lange's examples aptly illustrate, mathematics appears to play an essential role in mechanistic explanations in at least many areas of science.

conceptual necessity. You then have a distinctively *conceptual* explanation. Lange appears to recognize this possibility (2013b, 504).

[19] Baron, Colyvan, and Ripley (2017; see also Chirimuuta 2018) propose assimilating this mathematical dependence to a "counterfactualist" account of explanation (i.e., an account according to which explanatory power consists in the ability to answer what-if-things-had-been-different questions, or w-questions) and they show how to assess the relevant counterpossible counterfactuals within a structural equation modeling framework. I return to their work in Chapters 4 and 5. We find this assimilation plausible but as yet inadequate, because Baron et al. (and Chirimuuta) do not address the question of which true counterfactuals are explanatorily relevant and which are not. For example, there are contexts in which it is true that had the flagpole's shadow been length l then the flagpole's height would have been h. There are also contexts in which it is true that had Mary divided her strawberries evenly among her children, then 23 would have been divisible by 3. Thus, there is a similar problem of directionality with respect to counterfactuals: in one direction, a counterfactual can seem explanatory; in the other direction, it does not seem explanatory. We think that the distinction between explanatorily relevant and irrelevant counterfactuals must be made by appeal to ontic considerations (Salmon 1984; Povich 2018), and this is precisely what I will do in Chapters 4 and 5.

Note that if counterfactualists such as myself are right, this will go some way to dissolving the distinction between ontic and modal conceptions of explanation, which is a central task of this book. According to counterfactualists, causal, mechanistic, distinctively mathematical, and all other kinds of explanation derive their explanatory power from their ability to answer w-questions about their explananda. No one, as far as we know, takes the distinction between causal and mechanistic explanation to be significant enough to warrant relegating each to a different conception of explanation. The distinction between them is real and there is disagreement about how to make it, but, even noting the real differences between causal and constitutive relevance, no one takes the distinction to mark two wholly different conceptions of what it means to explain. If the counterfactualists are right, the distinction between distinctively mathematical explanations and causal/mechanistic explanations seems as insignificant for the theory of explanation as the distinction between causal and mechanistic explanation. There is no philosophically significant reason to lump a few kinds of explanation together and say that they explain in accordance with an "ontic conception" and the others in accordance with a "modal conception." For the counterfactualist, all are simply species of a genus, and all explain by providing answers to w-questions. This is what my generalized ontic conception, of which NOCA is a component, seeks to accomplish.

After all, the space of possible mechanisms is constrained by the space of mathematical (and logical) possibility. If one considers the mechanisms of sound transduction in the inner ear, one finds an arrangement most similar to the engine and the crankshaft, except in this case the mechanism converts vibrations in the air into vibrations in fluid. Still, parts are arranged geometrically. Likewise, when we look into the intricate mechanisms of gating ion channels, we seem to find structures that are understood geometrically, in terms of sheets and helices, which structures allow or prohibit certain activities (Kandel et al. 2013). Structural information has been essential to understanding the mechanisms of protein synthesis and inheritance and to understanding features of macro evolution (Craver and Darden 2013). Perhaps not all of these explanations are distinctively mathematical, but the mathematics does ineliminable work in revealing how the mechanism operates, how it can operate, and how it cannot.

This blend of the mathematical and the mechanical (or more broadly, the ontic) is, in fact, precisely what one would expect based on the history of the mechanical philosophy. Aristotle's (1936) (or pseudo-Aristotle's) mechanics works fundamentally by reducing practical problems to facts about circles. Hero of Alexandria and Archimedes, though celebrated for the practical utility of their simple machines, viewed those machines equally as geometrical puzzles to be solved. Descartes' conception of the mechanistic structure of the world was directly connected with his planar representation of geometrical space, in which extended things interact through contact. Galileo demonstrated his results with thought experiments, such as the Tower of Pisa, that rely on basic mathematical truths (i.e., an object cannot both accelerate and decelerate at the same time). Newton wrote the *Principia*, like the great physicists before him, in the language of geometry. Dijksterhuis (1986) closes his masterly *Mechanization of the Scientific World Picture* with the cautionary note that "serious misconceptions would be created if mechanization and mathematization were presented as antitheses" (500). It is a misconception because the mathematization of nature and the search for basic mechanistic explanatory principles have been treated historically as distinct aspects of the same explanatory enterprise. The very idea of mechanism, and the idea of the world as a causal nexus, has always been expressed in tandem with, rather than in opposition to, the idea that the book of nature is written in the language of mathematics and the belief that a primary aim of science is to leave nothing in words.

2.2.6. Modality and Constitution in Distinctively Mathematical Explanations

Lange (2018) has replied that his account can avoid our (Craver and Povich 2017) critique that his account flouts the directionality desideratum. Specifically, Lange argues that in legitimate DMEs, but not in their reversals, the empirical fact appealed to in the explanation is understood to be constitutive of the physical task or arrangement at issue in the explanandum.

I argue that Lange's reply is unsatisfactory because it leaves the crucial notion of being "*understood* to be constitutive of the physical task or arrangement" obscure in ways that fail to block reversals except by an apparent ad hoc stipulation or by abandoning the reliance on understanding and instead accepting a strong realism about essence. In Section 2.2.7, I briefly review the directionality objection and Lange's (2018) reply. In Section 2.2.8, I argue that the notion of "constitution" to which Lange appeals cannot exclude our reversals, on pain of abandoning a purely modal conception of DME. In Section 2.2.9, I present some non-explanatory reversals whose empirical facts are plausibly "understood to be constitutive of the physical task or arrangement," thus meeting Lange's criteria for DME.

2.2.7. Directionality and Lange's Reply

Our (Craver and Povich 2017) argument is premised on the fact that each of Lange's DMEs can be reversed to yield an argument of the same form that appeals to the same mathematical facts but is not an acceptable explanation. For example, recall that in Reversed Bridges, the explanandum is the fact that Königsberg's bridges in 1735 did not form a network with a certain topology, viz., with four nodes, three of which had three edges and one of which had five (see Craver 2016). The explanantia are the empirical fact that Marta completed an Eulerian walk through the bridges and the mathematical fact that only networks that contain either zero or two nodes with an odd number of edges permit Eulerian walks. Similarly, in Reversed Trefoil Knot, the explanandum is the fact that Terry does not have a trefoil knot. The explanantia are the empirical fact that Terry untied his knot and the mathematical fact that the trefoil knot is distinct from the unknot. We argued that these reversals fit Lange's criteria for DME: the mathematical facts are modally more necessary than causal laws and we stipulate that the empirical facts are understood to be constitutive of the physical task or arrangement at issue (so that, for example, it becomes constitutive of Terry's knot that he untied it).

In reply, Lange (2018, 87) argues:

> By making the fact that Terry untied the shoelace a presupposition of the why question, we have not made Terry's having untied the shoelace understood as part of what constitutes the physical task or arrangement at issue. Terry's untying the knot does not help to make the knot trefoil (or non-trefoil). As an analogy, suppose I ask you to bring me some salt. If I add that salt is my favorite spice, this does not change what it takes to bring me some salt. What is understood as constituting salt does not change when I add that it is my favorite spice.

It is plausible that presupposing the fact that Terry untied his knot makes that fact part of what constitutes *the explanandum*—it helps make the explanandum, the fact to be explained, the fact that it is. It would not be the same explanandum-fact had Terry not untied his knot.[20] What is less clear, though, is whether presupposing this fact makes Terry's having untied his knot part of *what constitutes the physical task or arrangement at issue.* Lange thinks not, as the quotation makes clear. Let us call the former idea "explanandum-constitution" and the latter "task-constitution." Lange seems to be arguing that DMEs require task-constitution—only presuppositions that partly constitute the physical task or arrangement at issue, not the explanandum-fact, result in a DME. In other words, task-constitution enforces the required directionality (or accounts for the directionality intuition) of DMEs—the "forward cases" rely on task-constitution, while their reversals do not.

Note that, for Lange, whether the empirical facts are understood to be constitutive of the physical task or arrangement at issue must be a relatively objective or non-psychological matter. Lange's use of the word "understood" makes it seem like this is at least partly a psychological matter. If it were not partly non-psychological, then what is understood to be constitutive of the physical task or arrangement at issue would be up to those requesting an explanation. There would be nothing to exclude our reversals; we could

[20] Prima facie, the fact that Terry does not have a trefoil knot is different from the fact that Terry does not have a trefoil knot in the knot he untied.

simply stipulate that in some context the person requesting an explanation understands the empirical facts in their reversals to be constitutive of the physical task or arrangement at issue. Indeed, we understood them this way ourselves. I return to this point below.

2.2.8. Explanandum-Constitution

Recall that Lange seemed originally to intend DMEs to conform to a modal conception of explanation that denies any ontic requirements on explanation (Lange 2013b, 509–510). Indeed, part of Lange's motivation, at least in (2013b),[21] was arguably to elevate the "modal" conception of explanation from its neglected status in contemporary philosophy relative to the epistemic and ontic conceptions (Salmon 1989).

Our objections were designed to show that a complete account of DMEs cannot dispense with ontic constraints. In this section, I explain why explanandum-constitution must also result in a DME, if DME is understood in the purely modal sense in which Lange (2013b, 509–510) seemed originally to intend it.

According to Lange (2013b, 2016), DMEs are distinctive because they reveal their explananda to be mathematically necessary or impossible. The explanantia of a DME make its explanandum *mathematically inevitable* (Lange 2013b, 487) or *mathematically necessary* (488) or make the non-obtaining of its explanandum *mathematically impossible* (496).[22] This is the source of the distinctive explanatory power of DMEs, according to Lange. The fact that Terry has a trefoil knot, together with the mathematical fact that the trefoil is distinct from the unknot, *makes mathematically inevitable* or *makes mathematically necessary* that he will fail to untie it or *makes mathematically impossible* that he will untie it. Furthermore, Terry's failure to untie his knot, even together with the relevant mathematical fact, does not necessitate that his knot is a trefoil knot, so the exact reversal is not a DME.

[21] Lange's (2016, especially Chapter 3) later account of "explanations by constraint" (of which DMEs are one variety) goes far beyond any traditional modal conception, but I do not have the space here to give his full account the attention it deserves. Here I am only concerned with the extent to which ontic, non-modal elements must be considered in an account of the explanatory power of DMEs. See Section 2.2.9 below for an argument that there are still reversals even if Lange is right that explanandum-constitution does not result in a DME.

[22] There are similar statements in the book (Lange 2016, 30, 37, 38). I find these claims hard to square with Lange's other claim that the explananda of DMEs need not be necessary (131).

This might make it seem as if Lange's account does not face directionality problems.

However, all of the purely modal relations that hold between the explanantia and the explanandum of a DME hold in our reversals as well. On purely modal readings, "*x* makes *y* necessary" means "necessarily, if *x*, then *y*": every possible world in which *x* obtains is a world in which *y* obtains. Likewise, "*x* makes *y* impossible" means "necessarily, if *x*, then ~*y*": every possible world in which *x* obtains is a world in which *y* does not obtain.[23] So, the fact that Terry untied his knot, together with the mathematical fact that the trefoil knot is distinct from the unknot, *makes mathematically inevitable* or *makes mathematically necessary* that he did not have a trefoil knot in it or *makes mathematically impossible* that he had a trefoil knot in it. This is because every possible world in which Terry has a trefoil knot is a world where he fails to untie it, and every possible world in which Terry untied the knot is a world where it was not a trefoil knot. Therefore, if Terry's untying his knot does *not* help to make necessary that his knot was not a trefoil knot, or to make impossible that it was a trefoil knot, as Lange claims, then Lange must not be working with purely modal readings of "to make necessary" and "to make impossible." Notice, too, that it is precisely the presupposition that Terry untied his knot that is what helps to make necessary that it was not a trefoil knot or to make impossible that it was; had we presupposed instead something irrelevant, like that the trefoil knot is his favorite knot (on analogy with Lange's response quoted above), that presupposition would not have helped to make necessary that it was not a trefoil knot or to make impossible that it was, since it is not true that every possible world in which the trefoil knot is Terry's favorite knot is a world where his knot is not a trefoil knot. Therefore, explanandum-constitution also results in a DME, when DMEs are understood in the purely modal sense Lange seemed originally to defend. Lange's (2018) reply does not address this central point.

For many purposes, however, purely modal notions of necessitation and "making impossible" are inadequate (e.g., Schaffer 2010). On the purely modal reading of the former, for example, every contingent fact (and every necessary fact too) necessitates every necessary fact (e.g., the fact that my couch is red necessitates the fact that 2 + 2 = 4) and, for the latter, every contingent fact (and every necessary fact too) makes impossible every impossible fact (e.g., the fact that my couch is red makes impossible the fact that

[23] *X* makes *y* impossible if and only if *x* makes ~*y* necessary.

$2 + 2 = 5$). A possible substitute for the purely modal notion of necessitation is grounding (e.g., the fact that my couch is red does not ground the fact that $2 + 2 = 4$). Perhaps the explanans-facts of a DME, but not its reversal, ground (at least partially) their explanandum. However, if Lange appeals to a notion that is not purely modal, such as grounding, then he will be conceding our main point that some ontologically substantial relation is required to account for the directionality of DMEs.

Lange (2018, 87) might be right that he does not need a general account of what is and what is not constitutive of the physical task or arrangement at issue, and the distinction between task-constitution and explanandum-constitution might effectively sort cases into those that intuitively are DMEs and those that are not, but without an account of *why* only task-constitution results in a DME, the distinction remains ad hoc. Let us follow Lange, though, in taking only task-constitution to result in a DME. Even then, reversals can still be constructed.

2.2.9. Task-Constitution

It turns out that our reversals do not rely on task-constitution only because their explananda are characterized in a certain way. Each of their reversals can easily be rewritten as examples that rely on task-constitution. Before seeing how, note that two of our reversals that Lange does not discuss arguably rely on task-constitution: Reversed Pendulum and Reversed Chopsticks. In Reversed Pendulum, the explanandum is the fact that Patty's pendulum is not a double pendulum and the explanantia are the empirical fact that Patty's pendulum does not have at least four equilibrium configurations and the mathematical fact that the double pendulum's configuration space is a torus with at least four stationary points.[24] In this reversal, presupposing the empirical fact plausibly makes it understood to be constitutive of the arrangement (i.e., the pendulum) in question.

In Reversed Chopsticks, the explanandum is the fact that the chopsticks were tossed non-randomly and the explanantia are the empirical fact that it was likely that more of the tossed chopsticks were oriented vertically than horizontally and the mathematical fact that there are more ways for a

[24] If this seems like a definitional explanation rather than an explanation of a natural fact, consider making the explanandum the fact that Patty's pendulum does not have a flexible joint in it. The same explanation applies. Thanks to Mark Alford for this suggestion.

chopstick to be horizontal than to be vertical. In this reversal, presupposing the empirical fact plausibly makes it understood to be constitutive of the arrangement (i.e., this collection of tossed chopsticks) in question. So, even if the distinction between explanandum-constitution and task-constitution is part of Lange's explanation for why Reversed Bridges and Reversed Trefoil Knot are not DMEs, this cannot be the reason why the Reversed Chopsticks and Reversed Pendulum are not DMEs.

To return to the main point: the reason that some of our reversals rely on explanandum-constitution and others rely on task-constitution has to do with the nature of their empirical explanantia. Many of the explananda in Lange's examples are event- or action-oriented: they describe the (necessary) non-occurrence of an event or action. In our reversals, negations of Lange's explananda become the empirical explanantia. Then, when we presuppose those empirical explanantia, we presuppose that someone succeeds in some action (e.g., untying a knot or crossing some bridges). The result of this presupposition is not task-constitution: it is not plausible that any of the relevant actions partly constitute a task or arrangement at issue. However, the explananda in Chopsticks and Pendulum do not consist of the (necessary) non-occurrence of an event or action; they consist of some object's, or collection's, having some property. Thus, when we reverse those examples and presuppose their empirical explanantia, the result is task-constitution.

Therefore, we can make reversals that rely on task-constitution out of all our examples by revising the explananda slightly. Thus, consider a revision to Reversed Trefoil Knot. The explanandum is still the fact that Terry does not have a trefoil knot. The explanantia are the now-revised empirical fact that Terry's knot is isotopic to the unknot and the mathematical fact that the trefoil knot is distinct from the unknot. This reversal plausibly fits the criteria for DME: its mathematical fact is modally more necessary than ordinary causal law and presupposing the empirical fact makes it understood to be constitutive of the arrangement (i.e., the knot) in question.

Next, consider revising the explanandum in Bridges to the fact that Königsberg's bridges did not permit an Eulerian walk. In the reversal of this revision, the explanandum is the fact that Königsberg's bridges did not form a connected network with four nodes (landmasses), three of which had three edges (bridges) and one of which had five. The explanantia are the empirical fact that Königsberg's bridges formed a connected network that permitted an Eulerian walk and the mathematical fact that only networks that contain either zero or two nodes with an odd number of edges permit an Eulerian walk. Presupposing the empirical fact plausibly makes it understood to be constitutive of the arrangement (i.e., the bridges) in question.

Lange could respond that a knot's pattern of overs and unders is constitutive of it and that a network's pattern of nodes and edges is constitutive of it. In contrast, the isotopy of a knot to the unknot follows logically from its pattern of overs and unders, but it is not constitutive of the knot (Lange, personal communication),[25] and whether a network permits an Eulerian walk follows logically from its pattern of nodes and edges, but it is not constitutive of it. This might[26] be true when the knot is considered as a topological individual or when the network is considered as a "graphical individual." However, Lange acknowledges that there are contexts where a knot is not considered as a topological individual (2018, 87) (and presumably he would say there are contexts where a network is not considered as a graphical individual). For example, when considered as a historical individual, a knot's pattern of overs and unders is not constitutive of it (87). There seems nothing to prevent us, then, from stipulating contexts in which a knot's isotopy to the unknot is constitutive of it and a network's permitting an Eulerian walk is constitutive of it. As what kinds of individual would the knot and the network be considered in such a context? I know of no name for these kinds of individuals, since contexts are simply stipulated for them—call them an "isotopic individual," the kind of individual such that when a knot is considered as one, its isotopy to the unknot is constitutive of it, and an "Eulerian individual," the kind of individual such that when a network is considered as one, its permitting an Eulerian walk is constitutive of it. Practicing knot and graph theorists may not find conceiving of their subject matter this way useful, but that does not show that such a conception is impossible, nor does Lange's account currently prevent such a conception from occurring in an explanatory context.

It would appear, therefore, that Lange's response thus far is only palliative. Even if Lange can mount a non–ad hoc argument that only task-constitution results in a DME, he will need to appeal to something else to exclude

[25] This is what Lange (2018) has in mind when he says, "Terry's untying the knot does not help to make the knot trefoil (or non-trefoil)" (87). Obviously, it was possible from the beginning to argue that in our (Craver and Povich 2017) original reversals there was task-constitution as well; that we stipulated a context in which the knot is considered as an individual such that Terry's untying the knot helps to make it the kind of individual it is. However, this context (and this kind of individual) seems far more artificial than the one stipulated above, thus making the case far less plausible.

[26] This is arguably false on the standard modal account of essential properties. See two paragraphs below.

these revised reversals, as well as the Reversed Pendulum and Reversals Chopsticks, which arguably already satisfy his criterion, whatever it should turn out to be.

One route for Lange to exclude these reversals is to exclude the kinds of individual to which they appeal (such as the "isotopic individual" and the "Eulerian individual"), because they are not *real* kinds of individual. There are at least two problems with this strategy. First, it presupposes a strong realism about individuals and their essential properties (what Sidelle [1992] calls a "privileged ontology" with objective identity conditions) and an account of essential properties that does not follow the standard modal account. For, on that account, a knot's isotopy to the unknot is essential to it, considered as a topological individual, since there is no possible world where it exists as the topological individual that it is and is not isotopic to the unknot (similarly for the network). Second, this move takes much of the psychological element out of what is *understood* to be constitutive of the task or arrangement at issue, which plays a large role in Lange's account. This understanding determines what kind of individual a task or arrangement is considered and, thus, whether the explanation proffered is distinctively mathematical at all. At the very least, this move places heavy constraints on what can legitimately be so understood.

Finally, even if Lange can address my previous points, it seems we can simply modify the examples again. In the knot case, let us replace the empirical explanans with the fact that Terry has a Thistlethwaite knot. A Thistlethwaite knot is isotopic to the unknot. The explanandum is still the fact that Terry does not have a trefoil knot. Thus, the explanantia are the empirical fact that Terry has a Thistlethwaite knot and the mathematical fact that the trefoil knot is distinct from the unknot. This case seems to fit Lange's account of DME: it appeals to a mathematical fact, and the empirical fact is more clearly constitutive of the physical arrangement or task at issue, since a Thistlethwaite knot is a standard topological individual defined by its pattern of overs and unders. In the Bridges, let us replace the empirical explanans with the fact Königsberg's bridges formed a $K_{2,2}$ network, a complete bipartite graph that permits an Eulerian walk.[27] The explanandum is still the fact that Königsberg's bridges did not form a connected network with four nodes (landmasses), three of which had three edges (bridges) and one of

[27] $K_{2,2}$ consists of two sets of two nodes, where each node of the first set is connected to each node of the second.

which had five. Thus, the explanantia are the empirical fact that Königsberg's bridges formed a $K_{2,2}$ network and the mathematical fact that only networks that contain either zero or two nodes with an odd number of edges permit an Eulerian walk. This case also seems to fit Lange's account of DME: it appeals to a mathematical fact, and the empirical fact is more clearly constitutive of the physical arrangement or task at issue, since a $K_{2,2}$ network is a standard graphical individual defined by its pattern of nodes and edges. These cases fit Lange's account, and they do not appeal to any contrived, stipulated individuals to which Lange might object.[28]

To summarize: for an argument to be a DME, according to Lange (2013b, 2016), each of its premises must be either modally more necessary than ordinary causal laws (as the mathematical premises are) or understood to be constitutive of the physical task or arrangement at issue (as the empirical facts are). The mathematical premises of all our reversals meet the former condition. The debate is thus over (i) whether the empirical facts in their reversals meet the second condition or whether they are only understood to be constitutive of their *explananda* and (ii) whether arguments whose empirical facts are only understood to be constitutive of their *explananda* are DMEs.

I argued that explanations whose empirical facts are understood to be constitutive of their explananda, but not the task or arrangement at issue, must be DMEs, on pain of abandoning their purely modal character. But I also presented some new (and old) reversals and argued that their empirical facts can be understood to be constitutive of the physical tasks or arrangements at issue. I have shown that a slight revision of the explanandum-statement in each case yields an example that sidesteps Lange's response. While Lange's examples explain why I know or should believe that *p*, they do not explain why *p*. My hope is that my arguments go some way toward tilting the scales away from a modal conception of DME and toward something like an ontic conception or counterfactual account of DME.[29]

[28] Perhaps you think that these arguments require additional premises—that the Thistlethwaite knot is isotopic to the unknot and that $K_{2,2}$ permits an Eulerian walk, respectively. Even if that's true, there is nothing in Lange's account that implies DMEs can only have one mathematical premise. In fact, some of his other examples seem to have more than one mathematical premise, such as Pendulum.

[29] Lange (2021) has recently argued for a neo-Aristotelian metaphysics of mathematics. We needn't discuss it here because it is simply intended to supply a metaphysics for his account of DME—the account itself has not changed.

2.3. Baron's Deductive-Mathematical Account

Before moving to the next chapter, I want briefly to critique another modal, law-based account of DME due to Baron (2019). Baron (2020) also has a counterfactual account, which I critique in Chapter 4 before presenting my own, and a newer Pythagorean (2024) account, which I critique in Chapter 5.

Baron (2019) has argued that his deductive-mathematical (DM) account of DME can satisfy the modal and distinctiveness desiderata. He does not consider the directionality desideratum. My aim here is to express briefly some skepticism about whether it satisfies the distinctiveness and directionality desiderata. I do not pretend to show that the DM account *cannot* satisfy these desiderata, for reasons I make clear below.

Baron's (2019) DM account of DMEs is as follows:

1. [DMEs] are sound arguments.
2. The conclusion of a [DME] is a proposition stating the physical phenomenon to be explained.
3. Among the premises of a [DME] there must be at least one mathematical claim.
4. If the mathematical claim were removed from the premises of an explanatory argument, then the argument would become invalid.
5. The proposition stating the physical phenomenon is 'essentially deducible' from the argument's premises.
6. Such arguments obey relevance logic.[30]

Claims 1–4 are self-explanatory. Claims 5 and 6 require some elaboration. "Essential deducibility" in claim 5 is defined as follows:

> A non-mathematical claim P is essentially deducible from a premise set S that includes at least one mathematical sentence M just when for an appropriate choice of expressive resources there is a sound derivation of P from S and either for the same choice of expressive resources there is no sound derivation of P from a premise set S* that includes only physical

[30] Claims 1–4 constitute Baron's (2019) "basic DM theory"; 5 and 6 are additions meant to handle certain problems with 1–4; claim 5 was added to satisfy the distinctiveness desideratum and claim 6 was added to handle the irrelevance problems that face deductive-nomological accounts. I have replaced occurrences of "extra-mathematical explanation" with "DME" throughout.

> sentence[s] or all sound derivations of P from premise sets $S_1 \ldots S_n$ each of which includes only physical sentences are worse than the mathematical derivation or for all appropriate choices of expressive resources the best derivations use M. (2019, 693)

The basic idea is that an argument is a DME just when it is sound, one of its premises states a mathematical fact, and the argument is better than any sound argument for the explanandum that does not invoke a mathematical premise. "Better," for Baron (2019), is meant to track normative explanatory criteria like unity (or strength) and simplicity (more on these presently). When ranking arguments overall, one must balance simplicity and unity. The essential deducibility constraint is intended to make the DM account satisfy the distinctiveness desideratum. For claims 1–4 count all explanations that use mathematics as DMEs, and claim 5 is intended to fix this.

However, it is arguable whether claim 5 does the fix, because it is not clear that it can exclude the flagpole case. Arguably, the flagpole argument *is* better (i.e., stronger and simpler) than any sound arguments for the same explanandum that do not invoke any mathematical premises. By "simplicity," Baron means the number of premises in an argument. Baron relativizes strength or unificatory power to a choice of expressive resources and basic predicates. This is because strength is a measure of the deductive consequences of a premise set, and what can be deduced from a premise set depends on expressive resources and basic predicates. The basic predicates are those in the mathematical and scientific vocabulary in which the argument is couched. So, for example, the basic predicates in a biological explanation that invokes number theory are biological and number-theoretic predicates. An argument, then, is stronger or more unifying than another, both of which employ the same basic predicates, when more conclusions can be deduced from its premises. If Baron's account is to exclude the flagpole argument, there must be an argument for that conclusion that does not invoke any mathematical premises and is just as strong and simple as the argument that does. Baron has not shown what that argument is and, so, has not excluded the flagpole case. The examples I give below suggest that there are no such arguments to be found.

Claim 6 requires that DMEs obey relevance logic. This is meant to handle irrelevance problems that have long been known to afflict deductive-nomological accounts of explanation. Adding "2 + 2 = 4" to the premises of any sound argument results in a second sound argument. The second argument counts as an explanation if the first one does, even if the fact that 2 + 2 = 4 is irrelevant to the conclusion. Relevance logic requires the premises of an argument to be relevant to their conclusion (and the antecedents of conditionals relevant to their consequents). For Baron, premises are relevant to their conclusion just when all the information contained within the conclusion is contained within the premises and each premise contains some part of the information in the conclusion.

It seems to me that Baron's DM account does not satisfy the distinctiveness or directionality desiderata.[31] Trefoil Knot and Reversed Trefoil Knot can both be expressed as sound arguments (Craver and Povich 2017) that adhere to the DM model. In argument form, Trefoil Knot can be expressed as:

1. Terry has a trefoil knot. (empirical premise)
2. The trefoil knot is distinct from the unknot. (mathematical premise)
C. Terry failed to untie his knot.

And Reversed Trefoil Knot can be expressed as:

1. Terry untied his knot. (empirical premise)
2. The trefoil knot is distinct from the unknot. (mathematical premise)
C. Terry does not (or did not) have a trefoil knot.

This reversal is a sound argument. It contains a mathematical premise without which it would not be valid. It contains no irrelevant premises. Thus, the reversal satisfies conditions 1–4 and 6. What about 5? Is there a better (i.e., stronger and simpler) (or not worse) argument for the fact that Terry does not (or did not) have a trefoil knot that does not invoke a mathematical premise? There may be a straightforward causal explanation of that fact that doesn't invoke any mathematical premises, but is that argument simpler and stronger (or at least not less simple and strong)? It is hard to see how it could be. For, 1) it is overwhelmingly likely that any causal explanation of this explanandum will have more than two premises—it will presumably need to cite things such as the production of the knot Terry does have, how he acquired it, perhaps his intentions, etc.[32]—so, will be less simple, and 2) the causal

[31] I'm not convinced it satisfies the modality desideratum either, because there is nothing modally robust about his explananda themselves.

[32] Also, Baron hasn't told us how to individuate premises. Presumably a conjunction shouldn't count as one premise. How should we count premises?

explanation will presumably use different predicates than the reversal, which seems to make comparisons of strength impossible, since Baron relativizes strength to a set of expressive resources and basic predicates. Baron needs to specify what exactly the argument for the reversed explanandum is that strikes a better (or not worse) balance of simplicity and strength, without mathematical premises, than the reversed argument given above, or else his DM account will incorrectly count Reversed Trefoil Knot as a DME.

Perhaps the simpler and stronger non-mathematical argument for Reversed Trefoil Knot's explanandum goes something like this:

1. For any person *x*, if *x* untied their knot, then *x* does not have a trefoil knot.
2. Terry untied his knot.
C. Terry does not have a trefoil knot.

There are no mathematical premises, and the argument is just as short, therefore, simple. It doesn't seem as strong, though. The first premise can be used to derive conclusions about any actual person who has untied a knot. But it seems that the previous, mathematical premise can be used to derive many more conclusions, conclusions about all possible attempts to untie trefoil knots.[33] Furthermore, if Baron *does* mount an argument that this argument is just as strong, then it seems his account will incorrectly exclude Trefoil Knot. For, consider the following argument:

1. For any person *x*, if *x* has a trefoil knot, then *x* will fail to untie it.
2. Terry has a trefoil knot.
C. Terry failed to untie his knot.

There are no mathematical premises, and the argument is just as short. If Baron wants to claim that the previous argument is stronger than Reversed Trefoil Knot, then this one should be stronger than Trefoil Knot. Thus, the same reasoning used to exclude the Reversed Trefoil Knot would exclude Trefoil Knot as well.

The non-mathematical alternative to Reversed Trefoil Knot was not as strong because its main premise could not be used to derive as many conclusions. What if we modally "pumped up" the main premise of the

[33] I thank an anonymous reviewer for this important point.

non-mathematical argument, so that more conclusions could be derived from it? Consider:

1. For any possible knot x, if x can be untied, then x is not a trefoil knot.
2. Terry untied his knot.
C. Terry does not have a trefoil knot.

This first premise seems just as strong as that of Reversed Trefoil Knot. There are two things to note, though. First, what is the nature of the possibility appealed to in the premise? If the premise is to be just as strong as the mathematical premise, then the possibility must be a mathematical possibility. But that seems to imply that this is not a non-mathematical premise. If not, Baron should say why. Second, as before, if Baron *does* mount an argument that this premise is just as strong and that it is non-mathematical, then it seems his account will incorrectly exclude Trefoil Knot. Simply replace the mathematical premise of Trefoil Knot with this one, and we have an argument that is just as strong, with no mathematical premises, thus excluding Trefoil Knot.

Thus, it is doubtful whether Baron's DM account can meet the distinctiveness and directionality desiderata.

2.4. Summary

In this chapter, I introduced DME and presented many well-known examples of it. I also critiqued two prominent accounts of DME. Before presenting my own account in Chapter 4, I address a kind of explanation that uses a distinctive mathematical method—renormalization group (RG) explanation. I argue that while the mathematical method is distinctive, the explanations the method offers are not DMEs (contra Reutlinger 2014). They are instead standardly mathematical ontic explanations (contra Batterman and Rice 2014).

3

Renormalization Group Explanation

3.1. Introduction

While acknowledging the widespread use of causal explanation in science, a number of prominent philosophers of science have begun exploring its limits (see Batterman 2002a, 2002b; Huneman 2010; Rice 2012, 2015; Woodward 2013). Recently, some have claimed that renormalization group (RG) explanation is inconsistent with causal or otherwise ontic accounts of scientific explanation. Reutlinger (2014) argues that it is a kind of distinctively mathematical explanation (DME). Batterman and Rice (2014; henceforth "B&R") argue that it provides a "minimal model explanation," which, while not exactly a DME, is not a standard ontic explanation either. These philosophers have brought important and successful modeling techniques to bear on the philosophy of scientific explanation. Nevertheless, there are significant limitations to their project. It is my aim here to spell out these limitations and provide an alternative proposal. I argue that, while not necessarily causal, extant RG explanations are ontic explanations and are not DMEs.

B&R focus on minimal models, which are "used to explain patterns of macroscopic behavior across systems that are heterogeneous at smaller scales" (349). This widespread class of models, they argue, has explanatory power that cannot be captured by what they call "common features" approaches to explanation. According to common features approaches, 1) explanations accurately represent all and only[1] the features relevant to their explananda (i.e., the things being explained), and 2) the explanatoriness of a representation consists in its representing relevant features (351).[2] Common features

[1] Depending on the explanatory representation used, some irrelevant features must be represented. For example, if our explanatory representation is pictorial, it must be colored some way, even if color is not relevant to the explanandum phenomenon. Ideally the modeler will flag any potential confusions. See Weisberg (2013, §3.3) for a related discussion of the role of modelers' intentions in determining what he calls "representational fidelity criteria", standards for evaluating a model's representational accuracy.

[2] (1) is not just a restatement of (2). One could hold that accurate representation is necessary but not sufficient for explanation. This appears to be close to B&R's view (351, 356).

Rules to Infinity. Mark Povich, Oxford University Press. © Oxford University Press 2024.
DOI: 10.1093/oso/9780197679005.003.0003

approaches include not only mechanistic approaches (Craver 2006; Glennan 2002; Kaplan 2011) and causal and difference-making approaches (Salmon 1984, 1989; Strevens 2008; Woodward 2003), but also Pincock's (2012) structuralist or mapping account, which explicates the explanatory role of mathematics in terms of its ability to mirror certain ontic structures. Any philosophical theory of explanation according to which accurate representation is responsible for explanatory power is a common features approach, whether or not the features represented are causes (B&R, 351).

B&R argue that common features approaches fail to capture the explanatoriness of minimal models because, even when a minimal model is minimally accurate, it is not its accuracy that accounts for its explanatoriness. Rather, minimal models are explanatory in virtue of "there being a story about why large classes of features are irrelevant to the explanandum phenomenon" (356).

In this chapter, I argue for negative and positive theses. My negative theses are 1) that RG explanations are not DMEs and 2) that B&R's account of the explanatoriness of minimal models fails. Regarding 1), I argue that the RG method simply reveals the causes or other ontic features responsible for the explanandum. RG explanations are thus causal or otherwise ontic explanations, and RG is merely a distinctive method for producing causal or otherwise ontic explanations. Regarding 2), I argue as follows. B&R require that three questions be answered in order to provide the above-mentioned story about why large classes of features are irrelevant. I will henceforth refer to these as the "Three Questions":

Q1. Why are these common features necessary for the phenomenon to occur?
Q2. Why are the remaining heterogeneous details (those left out of or misrepresented by the model) irrelevant for the occurrence of the phenomenon?
Q3. Why do very different [fluids and populations] have features . . . in common?[3] (361)

My critique consists of two parts. First, the method they propose to answer the Three Questions is unable to answer them, at least by itself.

[3] I have slightly altered the wording of Q3 to capture both models, thereby avoiding unnecessary repetition.

Second, answers to the Three Questions are unnecessary to account for the explanatoriness of minimal models. I argue for this second claim in two ways. First, I analogize their strategy to one in a more commonplace case of multiple realizability. In the case I present, it is evident that answering analogues of the Three Questions is unnecessary to explain multiple realizability. Second, I argue that if answers to the Three Questions were necessary, a regress would loom. B&R need to explain why, if the Three Questions are necessary, we should stop asking where they say we should. Of course, according to B&R, the Three Questions are not further questions, in addition to the question of what makes minimal models explanatory; the Three Questions just are those that need to be answered in order to account for the explanatoriness of minimal models. My analogy is intended to show that that is not the case.

My positive thesis is that a common features approach can account for the explanatoriness of minimal models.[4][5] B&R are (probably)[6] right that mechanistic and difference-making accounts cannot do the job, but an account much like the one proposed by Bokulich (2011), Rice himself (2013), and Saatsi and Pexton (2013) can. They follow Woodward (2003) in requiring that an explanation represent counterfactual dependence relations between the explanandum phenomenon and the features on which it depends, but they drop the requirement that these counterfactual dependence relations be construed causally. The reason for this is that the counterfactual dependence relations represented by some models, such as B&R's minimal models, cannot very plausibly be given a causal interpretation.

On this view, explanatory power consists in the ability to answer what-if-things-had-been-different questions (w-questions). I argue that this requires commitment to an ontic conception of scientific explanation (Salmon 1984) and that philosophers of science have been mistaken in equating the ontic conception with the causal-mechanical account of explanation. As we will see, Salmon seems not to have equated them.

[4] Lange (2015) also made this point, although he does not develop the positive proposal I do. He also made an objection to B&R similar to one of mine about regress. These and any other commonalities were arrived at independently.

[5] I also think that the common features that are shared between minimal models and real-world systems are what justifies scientists' applications of the former to the latter, though I do not have space to argue for this here.

[6] It is somewhat plausible that at least some of the common features in B&R's minimal models can be given a causal interpretation. On the account proposed here, though, this is not what makes these features explanatory. I briefly expand on this at the end of Section 3.4.

My proposal is consistent with many things B&R have themselves written in the past.[7] It seems that their desire to avoid anything like a common features approach has driven them too far, apparently past things they have said before. In the present atmosphere in philosophy of science, it is a significant enough achievement to have brought to philosophical focus important modeling methods in physics and biology that emphasize the systematic neglect of causal detail. B&R have rightly stressed the importance of this neglect, but this importance need not drastically change our account of scientific explanation.

The rest of the chapter is organized as follows. In Section 3.2, I present the minimal models whose explanatoriness B&R argue cannot be accounted for by a common features approach. These are the Lattice Gas Automaton (LGA) model of fluid dynamics and Fisher's model of 1:1 sex ratios. In Section 3.3, I present and critique B&R's account of the explanatoriness of these minimal models, as well as Reutlinger's claim that RG explanations are DMEs. Reutlinger's claim is incorrect because it too tightly ties the kind of explanation an explanation is to the method of constructing it. For B&R, any account of minimal models must answer the Three Questions, and answers are provided by the RG and universality classes.[8] I argue that the Three Questions cannot in fact be answered by RG alone. I then argue that regardless of whether RG answers the Three Questions, they do not need to be answered in order to give an account of the explanatoriness of LGA and Fisher's model. I give two arguments for this. First, I show that answers to analogues of the Three Questions are unnecessary in an analogous case of multiple realizability. Batterman (2000) has argued that RG explains multiple realizability generally, so I take it that my analogy is apt and generalizable to B&R's models. Second, I argue that if answering the Three Questions were necessary for an account of the explanatoriness of B&R's minimal models, a regress would loom.

In Section 3.4, I provide my own common features account of the explanatoriness of B&R's minimal models: the generalized ontic conception mentioned in Chapter 1. I argue that minimal models are explanatory because they accurately represent the relevant objective dependence relations,

[7] For examples, see note 24, Batterman's remarks below on pain, and Rice (2013): "*in some cases counterfactual information can be explanatory without tracking any relationships of causal dependence*" (20, original emphasis).

[8] Of course, in biological contexts some mathematical method(s) other than RG must be employed, though B&R are silent on what these methods might be.

that is, the objective features of the world on which the explanandum phenomenon counterfactually depends. I argue, for reasons different than Wright (2012), that it is a mistake to equate the ontic conception of scientific explanation with the causal-mechanical account of explanation (Craver [2014] gestures at this idea in his defense of the ontic conception). A viable general theory of scientific explanation can be constructed by combining insights from Salmon (1984, 1989) and Woodward (2003), while realizing that there are noncausal kinds of ontic dependence.

Nevertheless, I do briefly consider the idea that some of the objective dependence relations in B&R's minimal models can be given a causal interpretation. I do this simply because I do not think a causal interpretation is as obviously wrong as B&R imply. A causal interpretation is more plausible for some common features than others, though I do not commit myself here to a causal interpretation of any of them.

On my account, RG plays a central role in discovering explanatorily relevant features and demonstrating that they are relevant (Section 3.3 shows how). This makes RG not a kind of explanation distinct from common features or ontic explanation, but an essential method scientists use to construct such explanations.

3.2. B&R's Minimal Models

B&R present two minimal models whose explanatoriness they argue cannot be captured by a common features approach. These are the Lattice Gas Automaton (LGA) model of fluid dynamics and Fisher's optimality model of 1:1 sex ratios.

LGA accurately predicts macroscopic fluid behavior that is described by the Navier-Stokes equations ("Navier-Stokes behavior," for short). The model consists of a hexagonal lattice on which each particle has a lattice position and one of six directions of motion (momentum vectors). Each particle moves one step in its direction of motion, and if some "collide," so that their total momentum adds to zero, then those particles' directions of motion rotate 60° (see Figure 3.1). With thousands of particles and steps, and some smoothing out of the data, an overall pattern of motion emerges that is incredibly similar to real fluid motion (Goldenfeld and Kadanoff 1999, 87).

The second model presented by B&R is Fisher's model of the 1:1 sex ratio. The biological question that Fisher's (1930, 141–143) model was designed to

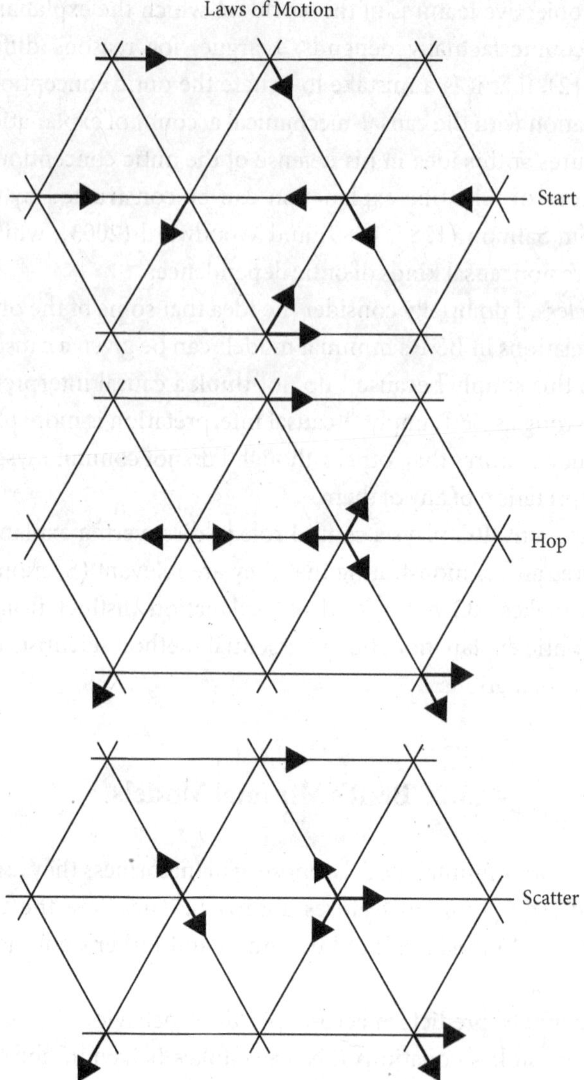

Figure 3.1 The Lattice Gas Automaton. From Goldenfeld and Kadanoff (1999, p.88, Figure 1). Reprinted with permission from AAAS.

answer is why population sex ratios are often 1:1. Hamilton (1967) provides a succinct summary of Fisher's argument. If males are less common than females in a population, then a newborn male has better mating prospects than a newborn female. In this situation, parents genetically disposed to have male offspring will tend to have more than the average number of grandchildren. This will cause the genes for the tendency to have male offspring to spread. As male births become more common and a 1:1 sex ratio nears, the advantage of the tendency to produce males disappears. Since the same reasoning holds if females are the more common sex, 1:1 is the equilibrium sex ratio (Hamilton 1967, 477).

If, then, male and female offspring cost the same amount of resources on average, a 1:1 sex ratio will result. More generally, any sex ratio can be calculated as $C_M/(C_M + C_F)$, where C_M is the average resource cost of one male offspring and C_F is the average resource cost of one female offspring (B&R, 367).

3.3. B&R's Account of the Explanatoriness of Minimal Models

B&R's account of the explanatoriness of their minimal models makes use of the concepts of the RG and universality classes. Here I explain these concepts and how they fit into B&R's account.

RG is a method of coarse-graining, reducing degrees of freedom or the number of details. B&R (362) discuss one such procedure: Kadanoff's block spin transformation. Consider a lattice of particles, each with an up or down spin. Group the spins into blocks of, for example, four spins and average over each block. One averaging procedure is called 'majority rule', in which a block of four spins is replaced by the most common spin in the block. If there is no most common spin, choose one randomly (see McComb 2004). This reduces the number of spins in the lattice by a factor of four. The length between spins, or the lattice constant, is greater after averaging, so it is then rescaled to the old lattice constant (see Figure 3.2). Near a critical point, the length across which spins are correlated, or the correlation length, increases and eventually diverges to infinity. When this is the case, averaging over correlated blocks of spins and then rescaling the lattice preserves the macroscopic behavior of the lattice with fewer degrees of freedom (microscropic details) (Huang 1987, 441–442). The irrelevant details are thereby eliminated.

With the concept of RG in hand, we can define a universality class. After repeated application of RG, certain systems will reach the same fixed point, a state at which RG no longer has an effect. The class of all systems that will reach the same fixed point after repeated application of RG is a universality class.

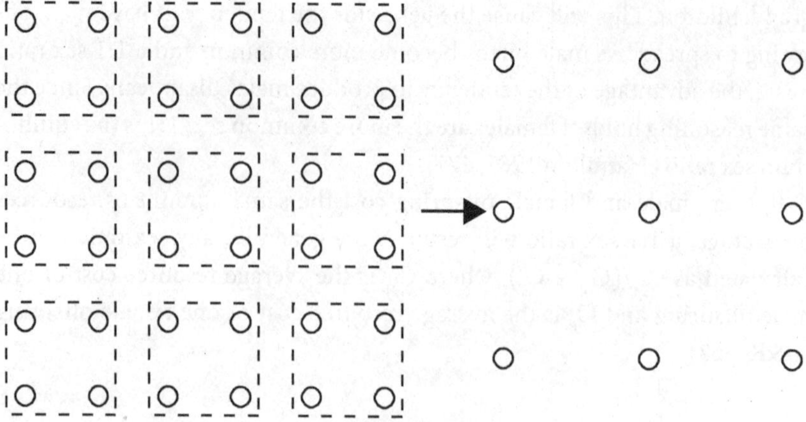

Figure 3.2 Blocking lattice spins. From McComb (2003, p.40, Figure 1.8). Reprinted with permission from David McComb.

Using RG, it can be discovered that all systems exhibiting Navier-Stokes behavior, including LGA, form a universality class that shares the following three features:

1. Locality: A fluid contains many particles in motion, each of which is influenced only by other particles in its immediate neighborhood.
2. Conservation: The number of particles and the total momentum of the fluid is conserved over time.
3. Symmetry: A fluid is isotropic and rotationally invariant. (B&R 360; from Goldenfeld and Kadanoff 1999, 87)

Similarly, an RG-type story would show that all populations exhibiting a 1:1 sex ratio, including Fisher's model, form a universality class and share the feature of linear substitution cost; that is, the average resource cost of male offspring is equal to the average resource cost of female offspring.

According to B&R, although RG demonstrates that diverse systems share features with their minimal models, it is not this fact that accounts for the explanatoriness of their minimal models. An account of why minimal models are explanatory must, according to them, answer the Three Questions presented above. B&R argue that RG answers Q2, for both LGA and Fisher's model, because the RG transformation eliminates details that are irrelevant. They write, "By performing this [RG] operation repeatedly, one can answer question Q2 because the transformation in effect eliminates details or degrees of freedom that are irrelevant" (362). However, RG alone does not answer this. Q2 asks why the heterogeneous details are irrelevant and RG only shows us that the details are irrelevant. The answer appears to be that "the details are irrelevant because, as RG shows, the same macro-behavior results no matter the details." But this is uninformative.[9]

RG is also supposed to answer Q3 by demonstrating that all the fluids within LGA's universality class share the common features of locality, conservation, and symmetry, and that all populations in Fisher's model's universality class share linear substitution cost (363, 372). B&R write:

> A derivative, or *by-product*, of this [RG] analysis is the identification of the shared features of the class of systems. In this case, the by-product is a realization that all the systems within the universality class share the common features locality, conservation, and symmetry. Thus, we get an explanation of why these are the common features as a by-product of the mathematical delimitation of the universality class. (363, their emphasis)

The byproduct is merely the identification of the shared features, not why they are shared. Again, RG merely shows that these features are shared across diverse systems, not why they are shared. Perhaps B&R's suggestion is that the fact that RG demonstrates that the details are irrelevant explains why the common features are shared. But this boils down to "These features are shared across diverse systems because no other features are shared." This is also uninformative. RG alone does not explain why locality, symmetry, and conservation are present in, for example, water and LGA, but not anisotropic liquid crystals. Answering that question requires investigation of specific fluids. One reason why liquid crystals are not in the same universality class as LGA and water is that their often rod-shaped particles result in directional preference and lack of symmetry (Priestley et al. 1975). Liquid crystals therefore cannot be accurately modeled using the unmodified Navier-Stokes equations. The addition of a stress tensor or coupling with a Q-tensor system is required to take into account the anisotropy of liquid crystals (Badia et al. 2011; Paicu and Zarnescu 2012). Similarly for Fisher's

[9] An anonymous referee suggests the possibility that in this case there is no clear distinction between showing why and showing that the details are irrelevant. I agree that in the LGA case the distinction seems blurry. However, there are clear cases. For example, the entire cerebellum appears to be irrelevant to consciousness, even though it contains more neurons than the cerebral cortex. Knowing this does not tell one why the cerebellum is irrelevant—according to one popular theory, it has to do with the cerebellum's lack of informational integration (Tononi and Koch 2015).

model: RG alone does not explain why the average resource cost of male and female offspring is equal in, for example, sheep, mule deer, and so on, but not in, for example, bees.

Finally, the answer to Q1 follows from the answers to Q2 and Q3. Obviously, if B&R are mistaken about their answers to Q2 and Q3, then they are also mistaken about Q1.

Perhaps I have interpreted B&R too narrowly, and they do not mean that RG alone can answer their Three Questions. If I am right about RG, B&R are wrong merely about how to go about answering the Three Questions, not that answers are required. Next, then, I present two arguments that such a story is not required, that answering their Three Questions is unnecessary for an account of the explanatoriness of LGA and Fisher's model.

The first argument rests on an analogy with a commonplace case of multiple realizability. Batterman (2000; 2002b, §5.5) has plausibly argued that universality just is multiple realizability:

> That microstructurally different systems fall in the same universality or equivalence class, is the physicists' way of saying that the upper level universal behavior is multiply realized. And so, the explanation of the universality of the behavior is an explanation of the behavior's multiple realizability. (2000, 129)

The diverse systems in a universality class multiply realize some universal behavior. Therefore, Batterman argues, RG or similar methods can explain cases of multiple realizability. The following analogy, then, is apt, and the lessons derived therefrom should generalize to B&R's account of LGA and Fisher's model. If the lessons do not generalize, B&R need to explain why.

Diverse fluids exhibit similar behavior (e.g., critical behavior) under certain conditions (e.g., near critical points). Similarly, diverse objects, such as apples, tomatoes, and bowling balls, exhibit similar behavior (e.g., rolling) under certain conditions (e.g., on an incline plane).[10] Rolling under these conditions is universal, or multiply realizable, in apples, tomatoes, and bowling balls; apples, tomatoes, and bowling balls are in the same universality class with respect to rolling. We would like to know why this is; why apples, tomatoes, and bowling balls all roll on an incline plane. These diverse objects behave similarly in certain conditions in virtue of possessing

[10] And in a suitable gravitational environment and so on.

a similar property, (approximate) sphericity. It is their (approximate) sphericity that disposes them all to roll when placed on an incline plane. That fact could be discovered by some RG-like method. That they all share the relevant property of sphericity and that all of their other properties, such as size[11] and color, are irrelevant to rolling on an incline plane is what explains this similar behavior and allows us to answer w-questions about it. A minimal model of spherical objects would be in the same universality class as apples, tomatoes, and bowling balls, and would explain their similar behavior in certain conditions in virtue of accurately representing the relevant property, (approximate) sphericity. Why should our account of the explanatoriness of B&R's minimal models differ from this one?

The further question—Why are the remaining heterogeneous details, such as the size, material, and color of these objects, irrelevant for the disposition to roll?—which is analogous to B&R's Q2, is unnecessary for an account of the explanatoriness of our minimal model of spherical objects. Why, for example, the color of an object does not matter to its rolling on an incline plane is a question that can only be answered by a physical investigation into the dispositions bestowed by color. An investigation in color physics would reveal why the disposition to roll on an incline plane is not one of the dispositions bestowed by color. Such an investigation would be unnecessary for knowing or showing that color is irrelevant to the disposition to roll and, therefore, unnecessary for an account of the explanatoriness of our minimal model of rolling.

The question analogous to B&R's Q3 is "Why do very different objects, such as apples, tomatoes, and bowling balls, all have sphericity in common?" Intuitively, an answer to this question is beside the point to answering the question of why these objects behave similarly in certain conditions, why they all roll when placed on an incline plane. Furthermore, this question seems to have no good answer. Yet the absence of an answer does not suggest that there is no explanation of these diverse objects' disposition to roll on an incline plane. Similarly, there may be no good answer to the question of why some diverse fluids share locality, conservation, and symmetry, or why some diverse populations share linear substitution cost. The story about why large classes of features are irrelevant that is required by B&R may not be available. This analogy should motivate the claim that such a story is unnecessary

[11] Obviously, there are limits in the example as described. For example, if the size of the bowling ball (or apple or tomato) were too large, it would crush the incline plane, unless the plane is sufficiently strong. Assume all these deviant cases are excluded.

to answer the question of what makes LGA and Fisher's model explanatory. B&R need to say why answers to the Three Questions are necessary in the cases of LGA and Fisher's model, but not in my rolling case or similar cases of multiple realizability.

The above analogy is entirely consistent with Batterman's own remarks on the multiple realizability of pain:

> Suppose that physics tells us that the physical parameters α and γ are the (only) relevant physical parameters for the pain universality class. That is, that N_h, N_r, and N_m have these features in common when certain generalizations or regularities about pain are the manifest behaviors of interest observed in each of humans, reptiles, and martians. Equivalently, physics has told us that all the other micro-details that legitimately let us think of N_h, N_r, and N_m as heterogeneous are irrelevant. We then have our explanation of pain's realizability by wildly diverse realizers. (2000, 133; see also 2002b, §5.5)

This appears to be a common features explanation of exactly the type given above for the multiple realizability of rolling on an incline plane. N_h, N_r, and N_m are the realizers of pain in humans, reptiles, and Martians, respectively. They are all in the pain universality class. An RG-type procedure might discover that α and γ are the only relevant common features shared by these realizers. This would be enough to explain the multiple realizability of pain in humans, reptiles, and Martians. Further questions such as why humans, reptiles, Martians, sentient robots, and everything else in the pain universality class have the pain-conferring features α and γ in common may have no good answer. Answers to the Three Questions are therefore unnecessary for an explanation of the multiple realizability of pain.

There is another reason why answering the Three Questions is unnecessary. Were answers necessary for an account of the explanatoriness of LGA and Fisher's model, a regress would loom. B&R write, "Simply to cite locality, conservation, and symmetry as being explanatorily relevant actually raises the question of why those features are the common features among fluids" (361). Similarly:

> Common features accounts would likely cite the fact that the different fluids have locality, conservation, and symmetry in common as

> explanatorily relevant and maybe even as explanatorily sufficient. However, as we emphasized in section 3.3, this is a mistake. The fact that the different fluids all possess these common features is also something that requires explanation. (374)

Common features are insufficient to explain macroscopic fluid behavior because, B&R argue, they do not answer the further question of why these features are common. With respect to 1:1 sex ratios, B&R write:

> Were we simply to cite the fact that all these populations have the common feature of linear substitution cost, we would fail to explain this universal behavior. The reason for this is that we can equally well ask why the populations of different species distinguished by different mating strategies, and so on, all exhibit a linear substitution cost and why they display the 1:1 sex ratio. (374)

This appears to be an injunction against explanations that appeal to things that also require explanation.[12] But if it is a mistake to explain something by appeal to something else that requires explanation, then nearly all explanations are mistaken. B&R need to explain why the chain of explanation should stop where they say it should.

Before moving on to my own account of minimal models, I want to critique Reutlinger's (2014) claim that RG explanations are DMEs. Interestingly, Reutlinger claims this even though he also claims that RG explanations do not exploit mathematical necessity, in contrast to Lange's (2013b) characterization of them. Rather, for Reutlinger, the mathematical operations involved in RG account for RG's explanatory power, and this makes them distinctively mathematical. He writes:

> The mathematical explanatory power is derived from . . . the [RG] transformations and flow of Hamiltonians [to a fixed point]. Both the transformations and the 'flow' are mathematical operations, which, ultimately, serve the purpose to reveal something that two fluids have in common despite the fact that their "real physical" Hamiltonians (or "initial physical manifolds") are strikingly different. (2014, 1166, 1168)

[12] This point is also made by Lange (2015, 303–304).

I agree that the mathematical operations of RG reveal common features, but I do not agree that those operations are the sole contributors of explanatory power. If that were true, we would seem to have a case where representing the things on which an explanandum depends does not contribute explanatory power, but the methods used to reveal, discover, or demonstrate the relevance of those things do. This seems false in my multiple realizability of rolling example, in which case it cannot be true of explanations of multiple realizability in general. That is, it seems false that representing their shared (approximate) sphericity does not contribute explanatory power to the explanation of the multiple realizability of rolling by apples, tomatoes, and bowling balls, but that the method(s) used to reveal, discover, or demonstrate that (approximate) sphericity is the only relevant, common property does contribute. Similarly for the multiple realizability of pain, briefly discussed above. Rather, representing the only relevant common features on which our explanandum depends is what contributes explanatory power, by allowing us to answer w-questions about it. The methods, mathematical or not, that we use to discover that (approximate) sphericity is the only relevant property do not contribute any explanatory power in themselves; they are simply tools used in the construction of the "common features" explanation. This is how I see the role of RG. Note that if Reutlinger's distinctively mathematical account is to be extended to other minimal models, some analogues of the mathematical operations of RG must be specified, since those are the operations that he argues contribute explanatory power. In biological contexts, for example, it is unclear what such operations could be.

To conclude this section, I have found two problems with B&R's account of the explanatoriness of their minimal models. First, it does not appear that RG alone can answer the Three Questions. Perhaps they did not mean to imply as much. The second problem is that answering the Three Questions is unnecessary. I gave two arguments for this. First, it is plausible that answers to analogous questions in similar cases of multiple realizability are unnecessary (and potentially unavailable, without thereby threatening explanation), and, second, were answers to the Three Questions necessary, a regress would loom. I then argued that Reutlinger is incorrect that RG explanations are DMEs, because the RG method is merely a mathematical method used to construct a common features explanation. I now expand my own common features account.[13]

[13] Perhaps it will be said that I have missed the distinctive feature of Fisher's model: that it is an equilibrium explanation. According to Sober (1983), "Where causal explanation shows how the

3.4. Generalizing the Ontic Conception

The account I propose is similar to the accounts proposed by Bokulich (2011), Reutlinger (2016, 2017), Rice himself (2013), Saatsi and Pexton (2013), though I give my account an ontic spin.[14] These authors follow Woodward (2003) in requiring that an explanation answer w-questions. According to Woodward, an explanation "must enable us to see what sort of difference it would have made for the explanandum if the factors cited in the explanans [i.e., the thing that explains] had been different in various possible ways" (2003, 11). This requires the accurate representation of the objective relations of dependence between the explanandum phenomenon and the features on which it depends.

Woodward is explicit that it is in virtue of conveying counterfactual information that causal claims are explanatory (2003, 210–220). Since noncausal dependence relations can also convey counterfactual information, they can, therefore, also be explanatory.[15] For example, Saatsi and Pexton (2013) present an explanation of Kleiber's law, an allometric scaling law that relates an organism's body mass to a biological observable (West et al. 1999). The precise details of the explanation are irrelevant for our purposes. What matters here is that there is a feature, the scaling exponent, that counterfactually depends on the dimensionality of the organism. It is plausible that this counterfactual dependence relation contributes explanatory power, yet it is implausible that the dimensionality of organisms is a causal variable that can, in practice or in theory, be intervened upon (Saatsi and Pexton 2013, 620).

Salmon (1984, 1989) distinguished between epistemic, modal, and ontic conceptions of explanation. These are conceptions of what a scientific

event to be explained was in fact produced, equilibrium explanation shows how the event would have occurred regardless of which of a variety of causal scenarios actually transpired" (202). Equilibrium explanations show how many of the causal details are irrelevant to the explanandum. This presents no challenges I have not already discussed here at length. The common features account given here is much like Rice's (2012) own account of equilibrium explanation. B&R seem to be thinking of optimality explanation as a kind of equilibrium explanation and of equilibrium explanation as a kind of RG explanation.

[14] See also Ruben's (1990) "realist" account of explanation that emphasizes determinative and dependency relations and Thalos' (2002) discussion of causal dependence as only one form of explanatory dependence.

[15] Woodward (2003, §5.9) himself suggests dropping the causal requirement in certain cases where an interventionist interpretation is implausible. See also Strevens (2008, 177–180).

explanation aims to show of the explanandum phenomenon: that it is expected to occur, that it had to occur, and that it fits "into a discernible pattern," respectively (1984, 121). For Salmon, the "discernible pattern" into which the explanandum phenomenon is fit is structured by causal processes, causal interactions, and causal laws (1984, 132). "[W]e explain," wrote Salmon, "by providing information about these patterns that reveals how the explanandum-events fit in" (1989, 121). Explanation is not about nomic expectability or nomic necessity, but about fitting the explanandum into "discernible patterns," "relationships that exist in the world" (1984, 121). This need not be construed solely causally—it is a mistake to equate the ontic conception with the causal-mechanical account of explanation. Salmon actually did not think causation was essential to the ontic conception:

> It could fairly be said, I believe, that mechanistic explanations tell us how the world works. These explanations are local in the sense that they show us how particular occurrences come about; they explain particular phenomena in terms of collections of particular causal processes and interactions—or, perhaps, in terms of noncausal mechanisms, if there are such things. (1989, 184)[16]

For Salmon, what was essential to the ontic conception was that "the explanation of events consists of fitting them into the patterns that exist in the objective world" (1989, 121). We can and should hold on to the ontic conception while accepting many of the criticisms and limitations of causal explanation, including those provided by B&R. There are noncausal dependence relations in which an explanandum phenomenon can stand to other worldly items. Explanation remains, then, a matter of fitting the explanandum phenomenon into "discernible patterns" and "relationships that exist in the world," all while acknowledging that these worldly patterns and relationships can be noncausal.

[16] See also, for example, "[T]he ontic conception focuses upon the fitting of events into natural regularities. Those regularities are *sometimes*, if not always, causal" (Salmon 1989, 120, my emphasis), and "[E]xplanations reveal the mechanisms, causal *or other*, that produce the facts we are trying to explain" (121, my emphasis). Salmon says that Railton's (1978, 1981) account is an ontic conception even though "[h]is view is more lenient than mine with regard to noncausal explanation" (1989, 121). Salmon also clearly thought that laws, construed as *ontic regularities*, can be explanatory (see, e.g., 1984, 17–18, 121; 1989, 120). See especially (1989, 120, 129) for explicit claims that a focus on the laws themselves, rather than law-*statements*, leads to the ontic conception.

The ontic-epistemic debate has shifted twice since Salmon (Illari 2013). Salmon framed the debate in terms of what explanations do. After Salmon, the debate was framed metaphysically, as a debate about what explanations are. The ontic conception was associated with the claim that scientific explanations *are* things in the world (almost always causes and causal dependence relations); the epistemic conception was associated with the claim that scientific explanations *are* epistemic states or representations. Craver's (2014) most recent formulation of the ontic conception backs away from the metaphysical claim that explanations are ontic structures in the world and focuses on demarcatory and normative constraints on explanation.[17] Craver (2014) writes that according to the ontic conception, "in order to satisfy these two objectives [of explanatory demarcation and explanatory normativity], one must look beyond representational structures to the ontic structures in the world" (28). That is, attention to ontic structures, rather than epistemic or representational form, is required in order to demarcate explanation from other scientific achievements, like prediction, and to distinguish good from bad explanations, how-possibly from how-actually explanations, and explanatorily relevant from irrelevant features (2014, 51).[18]

The generalized ontic conception, then, is an ontic conception because it embraces Craver's claim that achieving the objectives of explanatory demarcation and normativity requires attention to the ontic. It is generalized because it says that attention to more of the ontic than just the causal-mechanical is required to achieve those objectives—attention is required to all ontic structures on which an explanandum might depend and all ontic relations that might ground this dependence. My account of DME, which I present in Chapters 4 and 5, falls under this generalized ontic conception.

The ontic conception, unhindered by a strictly causal-mechanical interpretation, retains the ability to demarcate explanation from description and prediction. Explanations provide information about relations of ontic dependence, causal and noncausal, which can be used to answer w-questions about the explanandum phenomenon. Understanding is possessing this information and, therefore, knowing answers to w-questions.[19] Norms of

[17] According to Illari (2013, 241), Craver holds that this has always been the debate.

[18] Under this framing of the debate, Wright (2012) overemphasizes the role that lexical ambiguity plays in the case for the ontic conception. The argument, which I do not have space here to defend, for Craver's claims about explanatory demarcation and normativity does not require any lexical ambiguity of the term "explanation".

[19] More needs to be said about understanding than I am able to say here. See, for example, Strevens (2013) for the kind of view to which I am sympathetic.

explanation immediately fall out of this account: the more information one has about the *relevant* dependencies, the more w-questions can be answered, the better the explanation of that phenomenon, all else equal (see Craver and Kaplan 2020 for more on norms of explanation and Povich 2021a for a discussion of explanatory information).

Let me clarify the relation between the aspect of my account that emphasizes dependence relations and the counterfactual aspect that emphasizes the ability to answer w-questions. These aspects are tightly intertwined, but relations of dependence are not "analyzed" in terms of counterfactuals or "reduced" to counterfactuals. Analysis and reduction apply to terms, concepts, or theories, not the things to which they refer. Rather, relations of counterfactual dependence hold in virtue of, or are grounded in, relations of ontic dependence. Like supervenience, counterfactual dependence is a modal concept (Heil 2003, 37). Different relations of ontic dependence could ground supervenience, including, among others, identity, constitution, and causal sufficiency (67). Supposing that what grounds counterfactual dependence relations also makes (descriptions of) them true, we can put this in terms of truthmakers: relations of ontic dependence provide truthmakers for counterfactuals.[20]

It is only with information about dependence that one can answer w-questions. This is why the ontic aspect of my account is inseparable from the counterfactual aspect. This is why one cannot say that explanation is a matter of answering w-questions, but not a matter of accurately representing ontic dependencies. Bokulich (2011), Rice (2013), and Saatsi and Pexton (2013) emphasize the importance for explanation of the ability to answer w-questions and are silent about ontic relations, but these issues cannot be separated. Consider the counterfactual "If population P had lacked linear substitution cost, it would not have a 1:1 sex ratio." What grounds this counterfactual is the (perhaps causal) dependence between the population's linear substitution cost and its 1:1 sex ratio. Those who think of explanation in terms of the ability to answer w-questions should therefore embrace the ontic account presented here.

The ontic aspect of my account also allows one to distinguish explanatorily relevant from irrelevant counterfactuals. The length of a flagpole's

[20] Though I think this way of putting it is illuminating, it is controversial both in light of possible-world semantics for counterfactuals and in light of disagreement about the relation between grounding and truthmaking. For a survey of possible relations between grounding and truthmaking, see Griffith (2014).

shadow can be derived from the height of the pole and the angle of elevation of the sun (Bromberger 1966). This derivation is symmetric. That is, one can also derive the height of the flagpole from the length of a flagpole's shadow and the angle of elevation of the sun. It seems, then, that if the shadow had been longer and the sun in the same position, then the flagpole would have been higher. Yet it does not seem true that this explains the height of the flagpole. Here it is plausible that the explanatory asymmetry is provided by causal asymmetry: the derivation of the length of the pole's shadow counts as explanatory because that derivation, but not the reverse derivation, tracks causes (Hausman 1998; Woodward 2003). This lesson can be generalized to cases of noncausal dependence: in general, when there are explanatory asymmetries, these are due to asymmetries in ontic dependence.

Symmetry provides a nice example of something on which fluid behavior noncausally depends. As I mentioned above, there are fluids, like anisotropic liquid crystals, that have a preferential alignment due to their banana- and rod-shaped molecules and therefore cannot be accurately modeled using the unmodified Navier-Stokes equations. The dependence of the macro-behavior of liquid crystals on the shape of their particles is plausibly not a causal dependence or mechanistic dependence. A feature or disposition of the whole liquid, its macro-behavior, depends on the features of its mereological parts, so construing this dependence causally is inappropriate (assuming, plausibly, that parts and wholes cannot stand in causal relations to each other; see Craver and Bechtel 2007). Yet, it is also plausible that the particles are not a mechanism that produces, underlies, or maintains the fluid's macro-behavior. Mechanisms are organized in a way mere aggregates are not (Craver 2001), and, while I recognize that there is something of a continuum here, fluid particles do not appear to have the requisite organization to constitute a mechanism. Here, then, is an instance of ontic dependence that is neither causal nor mechanistic but is asymmetric and can be used to answer w-questions about fluid behavior.[21]

B&R remark only in passing that it "stretches the imagination" to think of locality, symmetry, conservation as causally relevant (360).[22] I agree, but I do think it is plausible that linear substitution cost can be given a causal

[21] I suspect that many explanations of dispositions in terms of their micro-bases will have this noncausal, non-mechanistic structure.

[22] Lange (2015, 300) points out that this is plausible if it means that locality, symmetry, and conservation are not causes, but implausible if it means that they cannot figure in causal explanations. See also note 23 below.

interpretation, though I do not think a causal interpretation is required for that feature to be explanatory. Woodard (2003) has given the most influential account of causal relevance. Very briefly, according to Woodward, *x* is causally relevant to *y* if and only if a sufficiently surgical manipulation (or "intervention") of *x* would change *y*. Here, "sufficiently surgical" means that a manipulation of *x* that would change *y* would do so only via the pathway from *x* to *y*.

It is important to note that on Woodward's view, the manipulation need not be physically possible. All that is necessary is that relevant scientific theory be able to answer what would happen under the imagined intervention. For example, considering the counterfactual claim that changes in the position of the moon cause changes in the motion of the tides, Woodward writes:

> Newtonian theory and familiar rules about the composition of forces tell us how to subtract out any direct influence from such a process so that we can calculate just what the effect of, say, doubling of the moon's orbit (and no other changes) would be on the tides, even though it also may be true that there is no way of actually realizing this effect alone. In other words, Newtonian theory itself delivers a determinate answer to questions about what would happen to the tides under an intervention that doubles the moon's orbit, and this is enough for counterfactual claims about what would happen under such interventions to be legitimate and to allow us to assess their truth. (2003, 131)

If physical theories and biological theories can tell us what would happen under hypothetical interventions, then causal relevance can be established.

A causal interpretation of linear substitution cost is plausible on a manipulationist account. Recall that linear substitution cost is equality between the average resource costs of male and female offspring. Here is a hypothetical intervention on average resource cost: inject all and only the males of a population with a fluid that has the effect of raising their metabolism and increasing their average resource cost. Do this over many generations in a population that initially had a 1:1 sex ratio and you will eventually see a deviation from a 1:1 sex ratio.

One might object that this hypothetical intervention does not show that linear substitution cost is causally relevant to 1:1 sex ratios, only that metabolism is causally relevant, since this is what was manipulated. This objection is conceptually confused. In the case at hand, manipulating metabolism just is manipulating average resource cost. It does not matter if manipulating metabolism were but one way among many of manipulating average resource cost. There are usually many different ways to manipulate a variable. Although, according to the generalized ontic conception, linear substitution cost need not be causally relevant to be explanatorily relevant, it plausibly is causally relevant on the manipulationist account.

It is much less plausible that conservation and locality are causally relevant to the macro-behavior of fluids. Conservation is a paradigm law of nature. It is hard to imagine any hypothetical interventions that would alter this regularity. One can imagine "local miracles," local speedings up, slowings down, and poppings into and out of existence of a fluid's particles, and this would certainly change the macro-behavior of the fluid. Physical theory might even be able tell us what would happen in such a contranomic or counterlegal scenario, but it is highly implausible to construe laws as causally relevant in the interventionist sense because laws are not events or objects and particles are mereological parts of the fluid.[23]

According to the generalized ontic conception, then, LGA explains Navier-Stokes behavior and Fisher's model explains 1:1 sex ratios in virtue of accurately representing all and only the relevant features: symmetry, locality, and conservation for fluid behavior, and linear substitution cost for 1:1 sex ratios. Knowing that these features alone are the relevant ones allows one to answer w-questions about fluid behavior and 1:1 sex ratios. The essential role RG plays is in discovering and demonstrating that these are the relevant features. RG and universality classes do not provide a kind of explanation distinct from common features explanations. Rather, RG and similar procedures are necessary methods used in the construction of common features explanations.[24]

[23] This is not to deny that conservation laws are causally relevant in the sense that they govern or constrain all *causal interactions*, in Salmon's (1984, 169–170) sense of that term. Nor am I denying that citing a law can provide information about a phenomenon's causal history (Skow 2014). I am only denying that conservation laws are causally relevant in the interventionist sense. See Lange (2007, 2011) for valuable discussions of the nature and explanatory status of conservation laws.

[24] Cf. Batterman (2000): "The RG type analysis illuminates those physical features that *are* relevant for the upper level universal behavior, *and at the same time demonstrates that all of the other details which distinguish the systems from one another are irrelevant*" (128, original emphasis). More compactly, "[RG] is a *method for extracting structures* that are, with respect to the behavior of interest, detail independent" (128, added emphasis). Also, B&R: "[T]here are a number of techniques for *demonstrating that* a large class of details of particular systems is irrelevant to their macroscale behavior" (371, added emphasis). These quotations are consistent with my account of the role of RG.

3.5. Summary

Batterman and Rice are at the forefront of a philosophical exploration of the limits of causal explanation. They have argued forcefully and plausibly that certain models in physics and biology are not explanatory in virtue of accurately representing causes (e.g., Batterman 2002a, 2002b; Rice 2012, 2013). Batterman and Rice (2014) use the minimal models to critique the explanatory requirement of accurate representation, regardless of whether the features accurately represented are causal.

According to B&R, the explanatoriness of LGA and Fisher's model is captured by a story about why heterogeneous details are irrelevant, a story that answers the Three Questions. I identified two problems with this account. First, RG alone cannot answer the Three Questions. Perhaps RG in conjunction with other methods can. Even so, the second problem is that answers to these questions are in fact unnecessary. I argued for this by showing 1) that answers to analogous questions in an analogous case of multiple realizability are unnecessary, and 2) that if answers to the Three Questions were necessary, a regress would loom.

B&R have rightly stressed the significance of RG explanation but have misplaced where that significance lies. These methods do not provide novel kinds of explanation. RG is a unique method that is necessary to extract the relevant features of the world that explain the phenomena in which physicists are often interested. The explanatoriness of the minimal models they present, LGA and Fisher's model, can be adequately captured by a common features approach, the generalized ontic conception. Though I argue in Chapters 4 and 5 that DMEs do fall under the generalized ontic conception, minimal models and other RG explanations are not DMEs, contra Reutlinger (2014). These minimal models explain by accurately representing the features on which their explananda causally or noncausally depend, and RG is simply a mathematical method for discovering these features. I now turn to my own account of DME, the Narrow Ontic Counterfactual Account (NOCA).

4

The Narrow Ontic Counterfactual Account

Now, if 6 turned out to be 9, I don't mind, I don't mind.

—Jimi Hendrix, 1967

4.1. Introduction

A simplistic and Whiggish history of the philosophy of scientific explanation, modeled after a terribly stripped-down reading of Salmon's (1989) *Four Decades*, might go as follows: In the beginning was Hempel, with whose covering law (CL) model of explanation[1] the main problems in the philosophy of explanation were thought, for the most part, to have been solved. There was peace in the land . . . for a while. Then came mumblings of discontent. For most of the problems that faced the CL model resulted, many thought, from its inability to account for the central role of causation in scientific explanation. Mumblings magnified into roars and the CL model was burst asunder. A new account of scientific explanation—the causal-mechanical account (Salmon 1989)—gained hegemony, and peace and consensus returned. In the past couple of decades, mumblings of discontent have started again to arise: equilibrium explanations (Sober 1983; Rice 2015), optimality explanations (Rice 2012, 2015), renormalization group (RG) explanations (Batterman and Rice 2014), topological explanations (Huneman 2010; Kostić 2020; Kostić and Khalifa 2021).[2] How can the causal hegemony in the philosophy of explanation account for all these?[3] The causal hegemony must give way to a new one, one that is either a more inclusive theory that

[1] Throughout, by "explanation" I mean "scientific explanation" and I will not attempt to distinguish this from other kinds of explanation (e.g., [purely] mathematical, moral, or metaphysical explanation).

[2] I discuss equilibrium, optimality, and RG explanations extensively in Chapter 3. I discuss topological explanations in Chapter 5.

[3] See Skow (2016) for a valiant effort to maintain the causal hegemony in the face of these alleged counterexamples, though he does add that not only causing, but grounding, can be explanatory. Claims that *all* explanation is causal are rare—this is one way in which the story is simplistic—though claims approaching that can be found in Salmon (1984) and Lewis (1986).

Rules to Infinity. Mark Povich, Oxford University Press. © Oxford University Press 2024.
DOI: 10.1093/oso/9780197679005.003.0004

covers both causal and non-causal explanation, or a principled explanatory pluralism according to which different kinds of explanation gain their explanatory force from ultimately different sources.

One of the strongest challenges to the causal-mechanical account of scientific explanation and to ontic accounts more generally is distinctively mathematical explanation (DME) (Baker 2005, 2012; Colyvan 1998; Lange 2013b; Leng 2005; Mancosu 2008; Steiner 1978). Unlike causal-mechanical explanations, DMEs do not seem to gain their explanatory power from accurately describing the causes of, or the mechanism that constitutes, the explanandum phenomenon (i.e., the phenomenon to be explained). Instead, DMEs work by showing the natural[4] explanandum to follow in part from a mathematical fact, a fact modally stronger than any fact about causes, mechanisms, and even natural laws.[5] In that sense, a DME shows that the explanandum *had to happen*, in a sense stronger than any ordinary causal law can supply.[6] I agree with Lange (2013b, 2016) about all this.

More needs to be said about DMEs before we can confidently assess the true strength of their challenge to the causal consensus and to explanatory monism generally. In this chapter, I begin to develop an account of DME that, while it challenges the causal consensus narrowly construed, paints causal-mechanical explanation and DME as species of a single ontic genus: both gain their explanatory power from ontically backed counterfactual dependence. Thus, my account of DME is still an ontic one, falling under the generalized ontic conception. In Section 4.2, I reiterate the three desiderata that any account of DMEs should satisfy: the modal, distinctiveness, and directionality desiderata. In short, it should account for the modal import

[4] I use "natural fact," "physical fact," and "empirical fact" synonymously, as distinguished from purely mathematical facts. For the purposes of this chapter, I take the distinction to be relatively self-evident, but I touch on it again later when I discuss mixed natural-mathematical facts.

[5] Lange (2013b, 504) also includes under the umbrella of explanations by constraint (of which DMEs are a species) explanations that show the explanandum to follow from any fact modally stronger than natural law, not just mathematical facts. Here, I limit myself to mathematical explanantia, but see note 21 and the discussion in Chapter 9.

[6] In his book, Lange (2016, 131) writes that the explananda of DMEs need not be necessary. I find this hard to square with Lange's repeated claims in that book and in (2013b) that DMEs work by showing their explananda to be necessary (e.g., 2013b, 485, 491; 2016: 30, 37, 38). His "type-(n)" and "type-(c)" explanations by constraint (of which DMEs are a species) are somewhat analogous to my "wide" and "narrowed" explanations. (Type-(m) DMEs explain modal facts. Modal explananda are addressed in Section 4.4.) I see two options here for my account: either 1) it is an account only of type-(c) and type-(m) DMEs, and I deny the existence of type-(n) DMEs; or 2) I add that a "wide" explanation is a DME if and only if it can be turned into a "narrowed" explanation that is a DME by shifting its empirical premise into the explanandum-statement. This would have the consequence that the original flagpole case is a DME, but this is arguably the case on Lange's account too (he seems to agree that it is in his 2018).

of some distinctively mathematical explanations, distinguish uses of mathematics in explanation that are distinctively mathematical from those that are not (Baron 2016), and account for their directionality (Craver and Povich 2017). In Section 4.3, I show how a recent counterfactual proposal (Baron 2020) is unlikely to satisfy at least one of the desiderata: the directionality desideratum. In Section 4.4, I show how my own counterfactual account, the Narrow Ontic Counterfactual Account (NOCA), can satisfy all three desiderata. According to counterfactualism about explanation, the explanatory relation—the relation that holds between explanantia (i.e., the things that explain) and explanandum—is a relation of counterfactual dependence. NOCA is a species of this kind of counterfactualism that makes use of a special narrowing procedure to satisfy the three desiderata. In Section 4.5, I consider a limitation of NOCA. For, although NOCA meets all the desiderata, it ultimately remains incomplete until the relation between mathematical facts and the natural facts that they explain, in virtue of which the latter counterfactually depend on the former, is demystified. In other words, this demystification challenge is the challenge of clarifying how natural facts can depend counterfactually only upon mathematical facts. I argue that the relation of instantiation helps to do the job, but demystification is not complete until I argue in Chapter 5 that normativism deflates this platonistic language. In Section 4.6, I consider some objections to NOCA.

4.2. Desiderata for an Account of Distinctively Mathematical Explanation

What should a philosophical account of DME do? Let us recall the three desiderata:

The Modal Desideratum: an account of DME should accommodate and explicate the modal import of some DMEs.

The Distinctiveness Desideratum: it should distinguish uses of mathematics in explanation that are distinctively mathematical from those that are not.

The Directionality Desideratum: it should accommodate the directionality of DME.[7]

[7] There may be good reasons to restrict this desideratum to non-modal explananda. I return to this issue below.

In DMEs, the explanandum is not shown merely to have occurred, but to have occurred with a certain modal force—the explanandum had to occur or be the case. This does not mean that the explananda of DMEs are themselves *modal facts*, though some can be (more on this at the end of Section 4.4). In other words, some DMEs show that the explanandum *had* to occur or be the case, with a modal strength proportional to the modal strength of the mathematical fact that explains it. This is the case even if the explanandum is not itself a modal fact (e.g., a fact about what can't or must happen). All the DMEs I consider here do possess a certain kind of necessity. Perhaps there are some DMEs whose explananda do not possess any kind of necessity. According to my account, there aren't. But if there are, then my account should be viewed as an account only of those DMEs that work by showing that the explanandum had to occur or be the case (but see note 6). My account is similarly restricted to explanations of natural facts in which the explanatory work is done entirely by mathematical facts and not by some combination of mathematical and natural facts. According to NOCA, the latter aren't DMEs.

My paradigm DME for this chapter will be Trefoil Knot. Recall that in this example, the explanandum is the fact that Terry failed[8] to untie his knot. The explanantia are the empirical fact that Terry has a trefoil knot and the mathematical fact that the trefoil knot is distinct from the unknot (a loop without knots), i.e., the trefoil knot cannot be untied. As Lange (2013b) notes, Terry's failure is modally robust. Terry did not fail because of any physical obstacle, limitation, or infelicity in the causal order. Terry *had* to fail, given that the knot was a trefoil knot. And this explains why he *did* fail. An account of DME needs to accommodate and explicate this modal import.

My paradigm standardly mathematical explanation (i.e., explanation that uses mathematics but isn't a DME) will be Bromberger's (1966) flagpole. Recall that in Bromberger's flagpole, the explanandum is the fact that the length of a flagpole's shadow is l. The explanantia are the empirical facts that the angle of elevation of the sun is θ and that the height of the flagpole is h[9] and the mathematical fact that $\tan \theta = h/l$. Here, it seems, the mathematics merely tracks the relevant causal structure, and the explanandum does not possess the modal strength of a DME's explanandum—the length of the flagpole's shadow did not *have* to be l. Another standardly mathematical

[8] The explanandum could be that Terry *had* to fail. For now, I stick to non-modal explananda. Modal explananda are considered at the end of Section 4.4.

[9] And the flagpole and ground are straight and form a right angle, the system is Euclidean, light travels in straight lines, etc.

explanation is Baron's (2016) train case. The explanandum is the fact that train T arrives at station S at 3:00 p.m. The explanantia are the empirical facts that T left from station S', 10 kilometers away, at 2:00 p.m., going 10 kph and the mathematical fact that 10/10 = 1. Again, the mathematics seems merely to track the relevant causal structure and the explanandum does not possess the modal strength of a DME's—the train did not *have* to arrive at 3:00 p.m.[10] I follow Baron (2016) in taking the intuitions behind these cases to be data that an account of DME must accommodate.

We should keep in mind the reversals presented in Chapter 2. Those who regard reversals as explanatory seem to be conflating evidence or justification with explanation, and any adequate account of DME should exclude these reversals. Before presenting my own counterfactual account of DME, in the next section I critique another recent counterfactual account (Baron 2020).

4.3. A Scheme Foiled: A Critique of Baron's Account of DME

Baron (2020) has recently presented what he calls the U-Counterfactual Theory ('U' for unifying or unification) of DME, or what he calls "extra-mathematical explanation". The U-Counterfactual Theory makes use of countermathematicals—counterfactuals with mathematically impossible antecedents, which I assume for the sake of argument are not trivially or vacuously true (Baron, Colyvan, and Ripley 2017). Baron's central explanatory concept, which demarcates explanatory from non-explanatory countermathematicals, is the "generalized counterfactual scheme". According to the U-Counterfactual Theory, roughly, a countermathematical is explanatory just when it is an instance of a generalized counterfactual scheme.

A generalized counterfactual scheme (similar to Kitcher's [1989] argument schemes) consists of 1) a counterfactual in which some or all of the non-logical expressions have been replaced with variables, 2) a set of filling instructions specifying the values the variables can take, and 3) a classification, which explains how an instance of the scheme is to be evaluated (Baron 2020).

[10] You might think this is false. *Given* the other facts, the train *did* have to arrive at 3:00 p.m. and the length of the flagpole's shadow *did* have to be *l*. I think there is something to this, but the reader should wait until I explain NOCA in Section 4.4.

On Baron's full account, a counterfactual CF, featuring a mathematically impossible antecedent, is explanatory just when:

(i) CF is an instance of a counterfactual scheme CS such that:
   (1) All of the instances of CS are true.
   (2) For at least two instances of CS, CF1 and CF2, CF1 and CF2 are nomically distinct.

(ii) There is no other counterfactual scheme CS* such that:
   (1) All of the instances of CS* are true.
   (2) For each instance of CS with consequents $c_1 \ldots, c_n$, there is a true instance of CS* with exactly that consequent.
   (3) For each instance of CS*, none of the antecedents of those instances involves a mathematical impossibility.
   (4) Each instance of CS is true, because the mathematical twiddles that realize each counterfactual's antecedent change the physical features in CS* that are responsible for unification in that scheme. (Baron 2020, 556)

CF1 and CF2 are nomically distinct when the physical laws relevant to the evaluation of those counterfactuals are different. The degree to which a counterfactual is explanatory is proportional to the number of nomically distinct instances of its associated generalized counterfactual scheme (Baron 2020, 549).

Baron (2020) uses Cicadas to show how the U-Counterfactual Theory works. As Baron presents the case,[11] the explanandum is the fact that two subspecies of cicada possess life cycles of 13 and 17 years, respectively. The explanation relies crucially on the number-theoretic fact that 13 and 17 are both co-prime with each of 2, 3, 4, 5, 6, 7, 8, and 9. To fit this example to the U-Counterfactual Theory, we need a generalized counterfactual scheme, such as:

(CS1) If $x_1 \ldots x_n$ had not been co-prime with $y_1, y_2, \ldots$, or y_m, the p_1, p_n would not have had x_n *U Cs*.

The filling instructions are:

[11] In Baker (2005, 230), the explanandum is slightly different: the fact that cicada life-cycle periods are prime.

(1) The p_n are periodical phenomena within any actual or physically possible system *S* that is under pressure to optimize some feature and where that feature is optimized just when for periodical phenomena $p^*_1 \ldots p^*_m$ that are in *S* and that are distinct from the p_n, the frequency of intersection between the p_n and the p^*_m is minimized.
(2) The x_i are numbers that are bijectively mapped to the p_n.
(3) The y_i are numbers that are bijectively mapped to the p^*_m.
(4) *U* is the unit of the p_n (e.g. years).
(5) The *Cs* are the type of period that characterizes the p_n (e.g. life cycles). (Baron 2020, 550)

Now consider this countermathematical:

> (CF1) If 13 and 17 had not been co-prime with 2, 3, 4, 5, 6, 7, 8, or 9, then North American cicadas would not have had 13- or 17-year life cycles. (Baron 2020, 542)

This countermathematical is an instance of the abovementioned generalized counterfactual scheme CS, reached by the abovementioned filling instructions. Furthermore, all of the instances of CS are true, and there is, according to Baron, plausibly no other counterfactual scheme that meets the criteria in (ii) above. I am skeptical of this last claim and will return to it in Section 4.3.2.

Furthermore, the U-Counterfactual Theory requires that there be at least two instances of CS that are nomically distinct. Baron's second instance uses an example of rotating gears. In this case, the explanandum is the fact a hypothetical company that aims to manufacture the longest lasting engine they can, manufactures an engine with large gears with either 13 or 17 teeth. The explanation relies on the number theoretic fact that 13 and 17 are both co-prime with each of 2, 3, 4, 5, 6, 7, 8, and 9. Supposing the company is constrained to manufacture small gears with between 2 and 9 teeth per gear and large gears with between 12 and 18 teeth per gear, large gears with either 13 or 17 teeth minimize wear on the small gears, maximizing the engine's longevity (Baron 2020, 546). This leads to the second instance of CS:

> (CF2) If 13 and 17 had not been co-prime with 2, 3, 4, 5, 6, 7, 8, or 9, the large gears in the company's engine would not have had 13 or 17 period rotations. (Baron 2020, 550)

CF1 and CF2 are nomically distinct, according to Baron (2020, 551), because the evaluation of CF1 involves the laws of evolution and natural selection, while the evaluation of CF2 involves the laws of mechanics. (One might deny that there are laws of evolution and natural selection and that these cases are nomically distinct. Here I assert only the conditional: if these two cases are nomically distinct, then so too are the two problem cases in Section 4.3.2 below.)

Since there are at least two nomically distinct instances of CS and all other conditions of the U-Counterfactual Theory are satisfied, CF1 and CF2 count as explanatory countermathematicals, and the cicada and gear cases count as DMEs. However, in the next three subsections, I argue that the U-Counterfactual Theory fails to meet the modal, distinctiveness, and directionality desiderata.

4.3.1. The Modal Desideratum

Though Baron (2020) does not consider whether the U-Counterfactual Theory meets the modal desideratum he presented in earlier work (Baron 2016), it seems to me that it does not. There is nothing necessary about Baron's explananda, the instances of "the p_1, p_n have x_n *U Cs*". Recall that perhaps not all explananda of DMEs are necessary. Perhaps these explananda—these *sets* of explananda, since these descriptions contain variables that can be filled in specific cases—are contingent. But even if the explanandum were necessary—and Baron thinks *some* explananda are—there is nothing in the U-Counterfactual Theory that explicates its necessity. Thus, even if Baron's account adequately handles DMEs with contingent explananda, it cannot handle those with necessary explananda, and thus is incomplete as an account of DME.[12]

[12] It will not do to say that being the consequent of a true countermathematical explicates the requisite necessity (when the explanandum is in fact necessary), since that would falsely imply that every true countermathematical has a necessary consequent. The countermathematicals throughout this chapter are plausibly true and have contingent consequents. Here is an unrelated, uncontroversial example: If Hobbes had squared the circle, sick children in the mountains of South America at the time would not have cared (Nolan 1997).

4.3.2. The Distinctiveness Desideratum

Baron's theory also fails to meet the distinctiveness desideratum, for two reasons: 1) it incorrectly counts his own paradigm example of DME as not a DME, and 2) it incorrectly counts Bromberger's flagpole example as a DME.

Recall that Baron asserts that there is no other counterfactual scheme that meets the criteria in (ii) above. I can now explain why I am skeptical of this. Consider a scheme that Baron says is not explanatory because its unifying power traces to the existence of an underlying physical twiddle: If *x*/*y* had not equaled *z*, then *c* would not have ended at *B**. Baron says this scheme has these two nomically distinct instances: 1) if 10/10 had not equaled 1, then train T's journey would not have ended at 3:00 p.m., and 2) if 50/1 had not equaled 50, then Suzy's refueling of her car would not have ended at 70 liters (2020, 555). The scheme is not explanatory because its unifying power is "due to an underlying physical correlate—an exchange rate [i.e., a rate of change; in the train case it is kilometers per hour and in the fuel case it is dollars per liter]—that we can get at by twiddling the mathematics" (558). Baron then claims, "There is no general physical twiddle that we can make to both the cicada system and the L-Engine system that would have the same upshot for both cases as the one produced by altering the co-primeness of 13 and 17" (558–559). But it strikes me that if rate of change can count as an underlying physical correlate we can get at by twiddling the mathematics in the train and fuel instances, then so can frequency of intersection in the cicada and gear instances. The relevant counterfactual scheme would be something like:[13]

[13] I think the following also works, but might be a bit more controversial:

(CS1**) If $x_1 \ldots x_n$ *U Cs* had not minimized the frequency of intersection with $y_1, y_2, \ldots,$ or y_m *U Cs*, the p_1, p_n would not have had x_n *U Cs*.

with instances

(CF1**) If 13- and 17-year life cycles had not minimized the frequency of intersection with 2-, 3-, 4-, 5-, 6-, 7-, 8-, or 9-year life cycles, then North American cicadas would not have had 13- or 17-year life cycles.

(CF2**) If 13 and 17 period rotations had not minimized the frequency of intersection with 2, 3, 4, 5, 6, 7, 8 or 9 period rotations, the large gears in the company's engine would not have had 13 or 17 period rotations.

I say these might be more controversial because one might think that the antecedents are mathematically impossible, but I do not think they are. They look superficially like mathematical impossibilities, but they are statements of *physical* impossibility that contain numerals. Compare: "If 2 sets of 2 *o* had not resulted in 4 *o*, then . . .", where "*o*" is an object variable. This antecedent is also a statement of physical impossibility that contains numerals and looks superficially like a mathematical impossibility. Perhaps in such a world a new object appears or disappears whenever 2 sets of 2 objects are gathered. In CF1** and CF2**, perhaps at certain times cicadas/gears appear or disappear

(CS1*) If the minimum frequency of intersection between the p_n and the p^*_m had been different, the p_1, p_n would not have had x_n *U Cs.*

where the filling instructions for the relevant variables are the same, yielding the following instances:

(CF1*) If the minimum frequency of intersection between North American cicadas and their predators had been different, then North American cicadas would not have had 13- or 17-year life cycles.

(CF2*) If the minimum frequency of intersection between large and small gears had been different, the large gears in the company's engine would not have had 13 or 17 period rotations.

Note that the minimum frequency of intersection must change if the mathematical twiddling in CS1 is to do its work. Baron makes much of this point for the train and fuel cases. If the minimum frequency of intersection between the p_n and the p^*_m does not change when the mathematical twiddling occurs, then the gear and cicada explananda remain the same, making the relevant instances of CS1 false. Changes in co-primeness have—and can only have—their intended effects on the explananda *because* these changes alter the minimum frequency of intersection. Thus, CF1* and CF2* are true, and CF1 and CF2 are true *because* CF1* and CF2* are true, as required by condition ii.4.[14] Thus, Baron's theory fails to meet the distinctiveness desideratum because it incorrectly counts his own paradigm example of a DME as not a DME.

Now I argue that Baron's theory incorrectly counts the case of Bromberger's flagpole as a DME. I present below a generalized counterfactual scheme and filling instructions by which a countermathematical can be deduced that, were it explanatory, would make Bromberger's flagpole a DME. Since it is agreed by all parties to the debate on DME that Bromberger's flagpole is not one, the countermathematical I will present is not explanatory, and the U-Counterfactual Theory fails to meet the distinctiveness desideratum.

or entire years/rotations appear or disappear. Such a world would be a strange world indeed, a physically impossible world certainly, but not mathematically impossible.

[14] In fact, I am suspicious of condition ii.4 in general, because I think *any* mathematical twiddling must have *some* physical correlate, not just for each instance of a scheme, but even a very general, 'scheme-level' correlate, if the twiddling is not to be explanatorily idle. But I neither argue for nor rely on this thesis here. See note 13 for further discussion.

Suppose that a flagpole casts a 15-foot shadow, that the angle of the sun's elevation is 40 degrees, and that the flagpole is 12.59 feet tall (approximately). Now consider this counterfactual scheme:

(CS2) If tan *z* had not equaled *x*/*y*, then the length of *P* would not have been *A U*.

And these filling instructions:

(1) θ is an acute angle in a Euclidean right triangular system *S*, *O* is the length of the side opposite θ in *S*, and *A* is the length of the side adjacent to θ in *S*.
(2) *x* is a non-negative real number mapped to *O*.
(3) *y* is a positive real number mapped to *A*.
(4) *z* is a non-negative real number mapped to θ.
(5) *P* is the adjacent side of an *S*.
(6) *U* is a unit of length (e.g., feet).[15]

The following countermathematical is an instance of the generalized counterfactual scheme, reached by following the filling instructions:

(CF3) If tan 40 had not equaled 12.59/15, then the length of the flagpole's shadow would not have been 15 feet.

Furthermore, the generalized counterfactual scheme CS2 is applicable across nomically distinct systems, since it applies to all right triangular systems, regardless of the physical laws governing those systems, and thus regardless of the physical laws relevant to the evaluation of CS2's instances. Here is another such instance. Suppose a painter is commissioned to paint the spandrel on the right side of a large archway at her local cathedral. She practices on a right triangular canvas which is 15 feet long, 12.59 feet tall, and has an internal angle of 40 degrees. The following countermathematical is an instance, using this example, of the same generalized counterfactual scheme CS2, reached by following the same filling instructions:

[15] For simplicity, I am going to ignore the angular units for θ.

(CF4) If tan 40 had not equaled 12.59/15, then the length of the canvas would not have been 15 feet.

The evaluation of CF3 involves the laws of optics governing the rectilinear motion of light, while the evaluation of CF4 involves the laws of mechanics. Furthermore, all of the instances of CS2 will be true, given that the filling instructions specify that only information pertaining to right triangles can be entered, and there is plausibly no other counterfactual scheme, CS2*, that meets the criteria in (ii) above. Thus, the U-Counterfactual Theory incorrectly counts CF3 and CF4 as explanatory and so counts Bromberger's flagpole and the canvas case as DMEs.

I just stated that there is plausibly no other counterfactual scheme, CS2*, that meets the criteria in (ii) above. However, consider the following:

(CS3) If the space *S* occupies had not been locally Euclidean, then the length of *P* would not have been *A U*.

with the same filling instructions for the relevant variables. I do not think this will work. It does not seem to be the case that every instance of CS3 is true. It may be true in the standard flagpole case where the length of the shadow is the explanandum, if we imagine keeping the position of the sun and height of the flagpole fixed and curving the space where the shadow is cast, much like curving the ground; then the length of the shadow will change. However, it does not generally seem to be the case that changing the curvature of space results in a change in the length of objects occupying it. A meter-long rod is still a meter long when slightly curved.

I do not think my response is conclusive, because there are some difficult conceptual issues surrounding the evaluation of this counterfactual. For example, I claimed that a meter-long rod is still a meter long when slightly curved. But this depends on what we mean by 'length'. I am relying on a non-Euclidean notion of length that, so to speak, 'follows the curve' of the rod. But if by 'length of the rod' we mean the distance of the *Euclidean* straight line connecting two ends of the rod, then a slightly curved rod is slightly shorter. When imagining the truth of the antecedent, what notion of length should we employ when evaluating the consequent: Euclidean or non-Euclidean? If Kripke (1980, 77) is right that in counterfactual reasoning we continue to use our actual conceptual conventions, it seems as though we should employ a Euclidean notion of length rather than a non-Euclidean one. On the other hand, Kocurek, Jerzak, and Rudolph (2020) have provided convincing counterexamples to Kripke's rule. Instead of trying to resolve these conceptual issues here, though, it is enough for me simply to say this: 1) If Baron keeps criterion ii.4, then the cicada case is not a DME, since the frequency of intersection is an underlying physical correlate of both the cicada and gear cases that we can get at by twiddling the mathematics. The cicada case is his *paradigm* DME, so this constitutes a failure to meet the distinctiveness desideratum. Furthermore, depending on the conceptual issues surrounding the evaluation of CS3 just mentioned, the flagpole case may count as a DME, which also constitutes a failure to meet the distinctiveness desideratum. 2) If Baron drops criterion ii.4, then the cicada case remains a DME, but the flagpole case now certainly counts as a DME, which constitutes a failure to meet the distinctiveness desideratum. Either way, Baron's theory fails to meet the distinctiveness desideratum.

Before showing how Baron's account fails to meet the directionality desideratum, let me very quickly point out that Reutlinger's (2016) counterfactual theory of explanation (CTE) also fails to meet the distinctiveness desideratum. Though, to be fair, he was not concerned to give an account *of DME*; he just wanted to show that his CTE could count examples like Bridges as explanations, not necessarily as distinctively mathematical ones. My point is that if one wanted to use CTE as an account of DME, one would fail. According to CTE, Bridges is explanatory because it meets the following conditions (740):

1. *The veridicality condition:* the premises and conclusion are all true.
2. *The implication condition:* the premises entail the conclusion.
3. *The dependency condition:* one of the premises supports at least one example of counterfactual dependence of the explanandum on the explanans.

The first two conditions are obviously met by Bridges, and it is true that if all landmasses were connected to an even number of bridges, or if exactly two were connected to an odd number of bridges, then Marta would not have failed to an Eulerian walk. However, this clearly does not distinguish DMEs from causal explanations. Bromberger's flagpole and any other causal explanation fit this model. There is not even a requirement that one of the premises state a mathematical fact (though that requirement wouldn't help). I return to Reutlinger below.

4.3.3. The Directionality Desideratum

With trivial changes to the flagpole countermathematical CF3, we can show that the U-Counterfactual Theory also incorrectly counts the *reversal* of Bromberger's flagpole as a DME. Take the height of the flagpole as the explanandum and simply change CF3 to:

(CF5) If tan 40 had not equaled 12.59/15, then the height of the flagpole would not have been 12.59 feet.

Could Baron adopt Lange's (2018) proposed solution to Craver-Povich reversals here? Recall that according to Lange, the fact described in the empirical premise in Craver-Povich reversals is not understood to be "constitutive of the physical task or arrangement at issue." In the "forward" case, it is understood to be constitutive of Terry's knot that it is trefoil. In contrast, in the reversal, it is not understood to be constitutive of Terry's knot that he untied it.

This response will not work for Baron. First, there is nothing in Baron's account remotely like this—there are no empirical premises/explanantia that could be understood as constitutive of the physical task or arrangement at issue. Second, even if Lange's proposal could somehow be grafted ad hoc onto Baron's account, I argued in Chapter 2 that Lange's proposal doesn't work. Third, this reversal is not of the Craver-Povich type, which is designed to target Lange's account and that Lange's response is supposed to avoid. This is a version of the standard flagpole reversal. Thus, Baron's U-Counterfactual Theory cannot satisfy the directionality desideratum.

4.4. The Narrow Ontic Counterfactual Account

I now present my own counterfactual account of DME: the Narrow Ontic Counterfactual Account (NOCA). It falls under the generalized ontic conception discussed in Chapter 3, according to which all explanations—causal and non-causal—count as explanations in virtue of the fact that they allow one to answer what-if-things-had-been-different questions (w-questions) about the explanandum phenomenon. In other words, all explanations exhibit relations of counterfactual dependence, regardless of whether that dependence has a causal basis (Povich 2018; Reutlinger 2016; Rice 2015;

Saatsi and Pexton 2013; Strevens 2008). *X* counterfactually depends on *y* if, and only if, were *y* the case, then *x* would be the case, and were ~*y* the case, then ~*x* would be the case (Lewis 1973, 563). If *x* and *y* are actually the case, then the first counterfactual is automatically true. It would be quite a victory for the counterfactualist if she can unify causal explanations and DMEs under a single, monistic account of explanation. How, then, does the counterfactualist account for DMEs? Can the counterfactualist satisfy all three desiderata? I will argue that she can.

Baron (2016) argues that the counterfactualist cannot satisfy the distinctiveness desideratum.[16] The counterfactualist, according to Baron, holds that an explanation is a DME when it shows a natural fact to depend counterfactually on a mathematical fact. However, this does not distinguish the train and flagpole cases from the trefoil knot case. In the train case, the explanandum depends counterfactually on the mathematical fact that 10/10 = 1. Were 10/10 = 2, then the train would have arrived at the station at 4:00 p.m. rather than 3:00 p.m. In the flagpole case, the explanandum depends counterfactually on the mathematical fact that $\tan \theta = h/l$. Were $\tan \theta = h/l^2$, then the length of the flagpole's shadow would have been the square root of *l* rather than *l*. So, naïve counterfactualism mistakenly counts the train and flagpole cases as distinctively mathematical, violating the distinctiveness desideratum.[17]

To get around this problem, I suggest that the counterfactualist follow Lange (2013b) in taking the explananda of DMEs to be of a special, narrow sort. This feature of Lange's account is often overlooked, but it is crucial. To spell this out, recall the following example from Lange (2013b, 508): "Why are all planetary orbits elliptical (approximately)? Because each planetary orbit is (approximately) the locus of points for which the sum of the distances from two fixed points is a constant, and that locus is (as a matter of mathematical fact) an ellipse." Lange argues that this is not a DME, and his reasons why are telling. According to Lange, this is not a DME because "the first fact to which it appeals is neither modally more necessary than ordinary causal laws nor understood in the why question's context to be constitutive of

[16] Reutlinger's (2016, 2017) counterfactualism explicitly denies the directionality desideratum for non-causal explanations.

[17] This depends on the non-triviality of counterfactuals with impossible antecedents, which is controversial (Lewis 1973). See Baron, Colyvan, and Ripley (2017) for a defense of non-triviality. I take non-triviality for granted throughout this chapter, and I offer a normativistic account of countermathematicals in Chapter 5.

being a planetary orbit (the physical arrangement in question)" (508).[18] Let us compare this to Trefoil Knot.

How exactly does Trefoil Knot, which is a DME, differ from the elliptical orbits case that Lange says is not a DME? Both use empirical and mathematical premises to derive (a description of) a natural fact. The difference, according to Lange, is that, in the latter, having a certain structure (i.e., [approximately] being the locus of points for which the sum of the distances from two fixed points is a constant) is *not* understood in the why-question's context to be constitutive of being a planetary orbit. In the former, having a certain structure (i.e., being a trefoil knot) *is* understood in the why-question's context to be constitutive of Terry's knot. In an important sense, the empirical facts in Trefoil Knot are metaphysically implicit in the explanandum, since they are partly constitutive of the physical task or arrangement at issue in the explanandum. To make this explicit, you could shift the empirical premise that Terry's knot is a trefoil knot into the explanandum-statement: the special, narrower explanandum is the fact that Terry failed to untie his trefoil knot.[19] This is the "narrow" to which is referred in the *Narrow* Ontic Counterfactual Account of DME.

Understanding this narrow construal of the explananda of DMEs allows us to see why Lange's strawberry example is a DME, too, even though it seems prima facie exactly like the train or flagpole case. Recall that the explanandum in Strawberries is the fact that Mary failed to divide evenly her strawberries among her children. The explanantia are the empirical facts that she has 23 strawberries and three children, and the mathematical fact that 23 is not divisible by 3. This would be like the train case, were it not for

[18] Later, Lange (2016, 419n35) treats narrowed explananda as conditional explananda: "if we have a scientific explanation in which the explanandum E follows from the explanans C by some mathematical proof, then (in an appropriate context) an answer to 'Why is it the case that if C, then E?' can be 'Because this conditional fact is mathematically necessary.'" I have no objection to thinking of narrowed explananda as conditional.

[19] As I mentioned in Chapter 2, Lange makes this narrowing move explicitly when he considers Cicadas and Honeycombs. He argues that, for Cicadas to be a DME, the explanandum must *not* be that cicada life-cycle periods are prime rather than composite numbers of years (2013b, 498–499), which is what the explanandum is usually taken to be (e.g., Baker 2005, 2009, 2012; Baron 2016; Lyon 2012). To make this a DME, "we narrow the explanandum to the fact that in connection with predators having periodic life-cycles, cicadas with prime periods tend to suffer less from predation than cicadas with composite periods do" (Lange 2013b, 499). This narrowed explanandum is the usual cicada explanandum, with that explanation's empirical explanans shifted into it. The reversed, narrowed explanandum would be the fact that some population of cicadas, which does not tend to suffer less from predation by predators with periodic life cycles than other populations (i.e., whose life-cycle period does not minimize intersection with predators' periods), does not have a prime life-cycle period.

the fact that Lange takes it as constitutive of the physical task at issue that Mary has 23 strawberries and three children. Therefore, in an important sense, the empirical premises do not function explanatorily like premises—they are not explanantia—and the explanandum could be stated more narrowly as the fact that Mary failed to divide her 23 strawberries evenly among her three children. This explanandum includes in it the empirical facts that were taken as premises before (i.e., that she has 23 strawberries and three children—obviously, the why-question's context also presupposes that Mary exists and attempts to make such a division).

NOCA thus provides a solution for the counterfactualist: an explanation is a DME just in case it shows a natural fact to depend counterfactually *only* on a mathematical fact.[20] This satisfies the distinctiveness desideratum by counting Trefoil Knot and the other cases, properly narrowed, as DMEs, and by not counting the train, flagpole, and elliptical orbit cases as DMEs. (According to NOCA, the original "wide" or "unnarrowed" versions of the Trefoil Knot and other cases are not DMEs, but this is consistent with what Lange [2013b] says on this issue. Of course, according to NOCA, properly narrowed versions of the train and flagpole cases *are* DMEs. But this is also consistent with Lange [2018].)[21]

This formulation of NOCA is but a promising first pass. We will see presently, when we consider just how the relevant counterfactuals are evaluated, that NOCA should say that an explanation is a DME just in case it shows a natural fact *(weakly) necessarily* to depend counterfactually *only* on a mathematical fact. We will also need to add a further necessitation condition to cover certain kinds of explanandum. This will all be explained in due course.

The same move of narrowing the explanandum also allows NOCA to satisfy the modal desideratum. Since the properly narrowed explanandum

[20] NOCA claims that in DME there is counterfactual dependence of a natural fact on a mathematical one. Thus, the truth of "asymmetric counterfactuals" like "had Patty's double pendulum not had at least four equilibrium configurations, then a double pendulum's configuration space would not be a torus with at least four stationary points" does not pose a problem. They are already not DMEs according to NOCA. Furthermore, in asymmetric counterfactuals, the explanandum-fact is not an instantiation of the explanans-fact (see Section 4.5).

[21] In note 5, I mentioned that Lange includes under the umbrella of explanations by constraint any explanation whose explanans is modally stronger than its explanandum and ordinary natural law, thereby constraining it. I expect that NOCA can accommodate these as well. For example, when a natural explanandum is shown weakly necessarily to depend counterfactually *only* on some law that is modally stronger than any ordinary law, such as a symmetry principle, conservation law, or coordinate transformation law, then you have one of these "super-nomic" explanations by constraint (Lange 2013b, 504). What to make of these "meta-laws" is beyond the scope of this book, though I will briefly return to strengths of necessity in Chapter 9.

counterfactually depends *only* on a mathematical fact, changes in *any* empirical fact have no effect on the explanandum. The explanandum is thus very modally robust.

Can NOCA satisfy the directionality desideratum? As argued in Chapter 2, both forward and reversed explananda *follow*[22] from mathematical facts. However, this does not imply that both forward and reversed explananda *counterfactually depend* on mathematical facts. For now, I focus on the non-modal forms of these explananda—explananda whose descriptions do not include any modal terms. I return to explicitly modal explananda later.

Forward explanandum: Terry failed to untie his trefoil knot. (Remember, we are only concerned with the narrowed[23] explanandum that presupposes that Terry's knot is a trefoil knot, because only by narrowing the explanandum can we satisfy the desiderata.)

Reversed explanandum: The knot Terry untied is not a trefoil knot. (Here we have similarly narrowed the explanandum, by including Reversed Trefoil Knot's empirical premise, that Terry untied his knot.)

Notice that both forward and reversed explananda follow from the relevant mathematical fact that the trefoil knot is distinct from the unknot (so, cannot be untied). The fact that both explananda follow from the mathematical fact shows again that an account according to which DMEs are *arguments*, and the explanatory relation of DMEs is entailment, like Baron's deductive-mathematical account, cannot satisfy the directionality desideratum.

However, NOCA gives the correct verdict on whether these explananda have DMEs. That is, NOCA correctly classifies the *forward* explanandum as having a DME and the *reversed* explanandum as not having one. Seeing why takes some work. First, consider the following two countermathematicals:

CP1: Were the trefoil knot isotopic to the unknot, Terry would have untied his trefoil knot.

CP2: Were the trefoil knot isotopic to the unknot, the knot Terry untied would've been a trefoil knot.

[22] Since "following" is strictly a relation between propositions or other contents of some kind, I should say that *descriptions* of both forward and reversed explananda follow from a *description* of the mathematical fact. For simplicity, I avoid this way of talking.

[23] In what follows, I will omit the qualifier "narrowed" when it is clear that it is the narrowed explanandum I have in mind.

These countermathematicals should be evaluated similarly to ordinary counterfactuals (Lewis 1973; Baron, Colyvan, and Ripley [2017] provide a framework for evaluating countermathematicals to which I return later and in Chapter 5). When evaluated at a world, *w*, we consider the worlds nearest to (i.e., most similar to) *w* where the antecedent is true and then consider whether the consequent is also true there (Lewis 1973). Thus, the truth or falsity of these countermathematicals depends on the world at which they are evaluated. (Note also that given that the antecedents involve variation in abstract objects, there will likely be many cases where it is simply indeterminate whether one such impossible world is nearer to the world of evaluation than another.) It turns out that any truth-value can be assigned to each of these countermathematicals in the appropriate world.

There are worlds where CP1 is true. For example, suppose Terry tries in vain for hours to untie his trefoil knot before declaring it a lost cause. In this world, it is plausible that, were the trefoil knot isotopic to the unknot, Terry would have untied his trefoil knot since, in the worlds nearest to this one, where the trefoil knot is isotopic to the unknot, Terry does untie his trefoil knot.

There are worlds where CP1 is false. For example, suppose Terry is about to begin his attempt at untying his trefoil knot when he is hit by a bus. Here, it is plausibly false that, were the trefoil knot isotopic to the unknot, Terry would have untied his trefoil knot. In the worlds nearest to this one, where the trefoil knot is isotopic to the unknot, Terry is still hit by a bus before he can untie his trefoil knot.

There are worlds where CP2 is false. For example, suppose Terry comes home from work, unties his Thistlethwaite knot (which is isotopic to the unknot), and makes dinner. In this world, it is plausibly false that, were the trefoil knot isotopic to the unknot, the knot Terry untied would've been a trefoil knot. In the worlds nearest to this one, where the trefoil knot is isotopic to the unknot, Terry's knot is still a Thistlethwaite knot.

There are worlds where CP2 is true. For example, suppose that Terry has a Thistlethwaite knot. Suppose further that he bought his Thistlethwaite knot from Knotmart because that is his favorite untie-able (i.e., able to be untied)[24] knot, though his favorite knot simpliciter is the trefoil knot—it beats out even the Thistlethwaite overall. Terry comes home from work, unties his Thistlethwaite knot, and makes dinner. In this world, it is plausible that, were

[24] Not "un-tieable," i.e., "unable to be tied"!

the trefoil knot isotopic to the unknot, the knot Terry untied would've been a trefoil knot. This is because, in the worlds nearest to this one, where the trefoil knot is isotopic to the unknot, the trefoil knot is Terry's favorite untieable knot, and, so, he would've bought a trefoil knot from Knotmart. So, the knot Terry untied would've been a trefoil knot.

At this moment, first-pass NOCA, according to which an explanation is a DME just in case it shows a natural fact to depend counterfactually *only* on a mathematical fact, seems out of luck. It says there are worlds or situations where the forward explanandum has no DME, and there are worlds where the reversed explanandum has a DME, violating the directionality desideratum. Thus, first-pass NOCA needs to be amended.

To see how NOCA should be amended, recall a point I made in Chapter 2 about the different kinds of explananda in DMEs. The explananda of Bridges and Trefoil Knot, for example, are "action-oriented"—these explananda are facts about someone's failing to do something (i.e., cross bridges and untie a knot). However, the explanandum in Pendulum is not like this—the explanandum is the fact that a certain object has a certain property (i.e., that a certain pendulum has at least four equilibrium configurations). Perhaps the former kind of explanandum is an event and the latter kind is a state of affairs—their exact metaphysical nature does not matter for our purposes, though "event" and "state of affairs" are the terms I will use to mark the distinction.[25] What matters is that they are different, and this gives us a clue about how to amend NOCA.

Let us see what happens if we make the explanandum in Trefoil Knot a state of affairs instead of an event. Let us make the explanandum the fact that Terry's knot is distinct from the unknot. The explanantia are the same: the empirical fact that Terry has a trefoil knot and the mathematical fact that the trefoil knot is distinct from the unknot. This case fits Lange's (2013b) criteria for DME: the explanantia are either modally strong facts, such as mathematical facts, or understood in the why-question's context to be constitutive of the physical arrangement or task at issue. If the original, event version of this case is a DME, then so is this state of affairs version. Presupposing the empirical fact creates the narrowed explanandum: the fact that Terry's trefoil knot is distinct from the unknot.

[25] I cannot here give an account of events or states of affairs or actions and each of their individuation conditions.

The reversal of the state of affairs version of Trefoil Knot is as follows. The explanandum is the fact that Terry does not have a trefoil knot. The explanantia are the empirical fact that Terry's knot is isotopic to the unknot and the mathematical fact that the trefoil knot is distinct from the unknot. Presupposing the empirical fact creates the narrowed explanandum: the fact that Terry's knot, which is isotopic to the unknot, is not a trefoil knot. Or, put more simply, that Terry's untieable knot is not a trefoil knot.

Now consider these countermathematicals:

CP1': Were the trefoil knot isotopic to the unknot, Terry's trefoil knot would have been isotopic to the unknot.

CP2': Were the trefoil knot isotopic to the unknot, Terry's untieable knot would have been a trefoil knot.

Unlike CP1, CP1' is (weakly) necessarily true. By that I mean that any world where the explanandum obtains or holds or exists (i.e., any world where Terry's trefoil knot is distinct from the unknot) is a world where CP1' is true. (CP1' is arguably false, or not true, in empty worlds.) CP2', however, is not (weakly) necessarily true. Our counterexample to CP2 above is also a counterexample to CP2'. Thus, this suggests that NOCA should be amended to say that an explanation is a DME just in case it shows a natural fact *(weakly) necessarily* to depend counterfactually *only* on a mathematical fact—it shows that every world where the explanandum holds is a world where it counterfactually depends only on a mathematical fact. NOCA thus correctly says that the forward state of affairs explanandum has a DME and the reversed state of affairs explanandum does not.

This is all well and good, but what about the event version of Trefoil Knot with which we started? My proposal is that the forward, but not the reversed, state of affairs explanandum is related to the forward, but not the reversed, event explanandum by a componency and necessitation relation. All four narrowed explananda are as follows:

Forward Event (FE): Terry failed to untie his trefoil knot.

Reversed Event (RE): The knot Terry untied is not a trefoil knot.

Forward State of Affairs (FSA): Terry's trefoil knot is distinct from the unknot.

Reversed State of Affairs (RSA): Terry's untieable knot is not a trefoil knot.

We have seen that FSA weakly necessarily counterfactually depends only on a mathematical fact; thus, according to NOCA, it has a DME. RE and RSA do not, as shown by the counterexamples to CP2 and CP2'. Furthermore, FSA necessitates FE: every world in which FSA is true is a world in which FE is true.[26] However, FSA does not necessitate RSA (or RE): not every world in which FSA is true is a world in which RSA (or RE) is true. In FSA-worlds, Terry has a trefoil knot; in RSA-worlds (and RE-worlds), he does not have a trefoil knot. Thus, FSA and RSA (or RE) cannot both be true (without contradiction) in the same worlds. We could continue examining whether further necessitation relations hold between any of these explananda, but this is all I need to complete NOCA. NOCA says that FSA has a DME, and we want it to say that FE does too, but that RSA and RE do not. Thus, we amend NOCA to say that an explanation is a DME just in case either a) it shows a natural fact weakly necessarily to depend counterfactually only on a mathematical fact, or b) it shows a natural event to be necessitated by a component natural fact that weakly necessarily counterfactually depends only on a mathematical fact. FSA meets condition a). FE meets condition b) since it is necessitated by FSA and FSA is a component of FE.[27] RE and RSA meet neither condition. Thus, NOCA gives the right verdicts.

Let me go through another example to allay the worry that the previous result is an artifact of that case specifically. Consider Bridges again. The narrowed explananda are as follows:

Forward explanandum (FE'): Marta failed an Eulerian walk across Königsberg's bridges (which we presuppose form a network of four

[26] Note three things about necessitation. First, the necessitation relation (of a given modal strength) is transitive: if *x* necessitates *y* and *y* necessitates *z*, then *x* necessitates *z*. Second, *x* makes impossible *y* iff *x* necessitates ~*y*. Third, "every *x*-world is a *y*-world" is logically equivalent to "no world is an *x*-world and not a *y*-world."

[27] By "component natural fact" I mean that the same object and property that constitute the natural fact are constituents of the natural event. A purely modal notion like necessitation leaves the account open to counterexamples, because the necessitation relation also holds between FSA and any strongly necessary natural events (see also Schaffer 2010). Thus, the appeal to componency is meant to capture the metaphysically intimate relation between FSA and FE. This is another place in my account where the ontic (viz., a componency relation) plays a role, more on which below. One way of avoiding the previously mentioned counterexamples is to give an account of natural events on which (strongly) necessary events are not natural. This may work, but I will not pursue that suggestion here. Even if I pursue the componency strategy, more would need to be said about natural events. For the componency strategy seems to require that natural events be natural in something like the Lewisian (1983) sense, so that conjunctive events are excluded (e.g., the event—if that's what it is—composed of FE and the fact that water is H_2O).

nodes, three of which have three edges and one of which has five—call this 'network structure P').

Reversed explanandum (RE'): Königsberg's bridges, across which Marta made an Eulerian walk, do not have network structure P. (In this narrowed explanandum, the empirical premise that Marta made an Eulerian walk across the bridges is presupposed; we do not, obviously, presuppose that Königsberg's bridges have network structure P.)

Notice, again, that both forward and reversed explananda follow from the relevant mathematical fact that an Eulerian walk cannot be made across a network with a certain topology: that Marta failed follows from the fact that Eulerian walks are only possible on some network topologies and that the bridges across which Marta made an Eulerian walk do not have a certain network topology follows from the fact that Eulerian walks are only possible on some network topologies.

Now consider the following two countermathematicals:

CP3: Had network structure P permitted an Eulerian walk, Marta would have made an Eulerian walk across Königsberg's bridges (which we presuppose have network structure P).

CP4: Had network structure P permitted an Eulerian walk, Königsberg's bridges (which, here, we do *not* presuppose have network structure P), across which Marta made an Eulerian walk, would have had network structure P.

As with CP1 and CP2, CP3 and CP4 have different truth-values in different worlds. We can construct such worlds on analogy with the worlds we constructed for CP1 and CP2. Thus, for example, CP3 is false at a world where Marta is hit by a bus before completing her walk, so first-pass NOCA says that case has no DME. Similarly, CP4 is true at a world where Marta builds her favorite Eulerian bridges and makes Eulerian walks across them. Her favorite bridges have network structure P, but, unfortunately, those do not permit Eulerian walks. However, had network structure P permitted an Eulerian walk, Marta would have built it and made an Eulerian walk across it.

The same strategy of converting event explananda into state of affairs explananda works here. Thus, the state of affairs version of Bridges is as follows. The explanandum in this case is the fact that Königsberg's bridges do not permit an Eulerian walk. The explanantia are the same as before: the empirical fact that Königsberg's bridges have network structure P and the mathematical fact that network structure P does not permit an Eulerian walk. The narrowed explanandum is the fact that Königsberg's bridges, which have network structure P, do not permit an Eulerian walk (FSA').

The reversal of the state of affairs version is this. The explanandum in this case is the fact that Königsberg's bridges do not have network structure P (this is false in the actual world, but we imagine a world where this is true). The explanantia are the empirical fact that Königsberg's bridges permit an Eulerian walk (this is true in the world we are imagining) and the mathematical fact that an Eulerian walk is not permitted on network structure P. The narrowed explanandum is the fact that Königsberg's bridges, which permit an Eulerian walk, do not have network structure P (RSA').

Now consider these countermathematicals:

CP3': Had network structure P permitted an Eulerian walk, Königsberg's bridges, which have network structure P, would have permitted an Eulerian walk.

CP4': Had network structure P permitted an Eulerian walk, Königsberg's bridges, which permit an Eulerian walk, would have had network structure P.

Unlike CP3, CP3' is weakly necessarily true—any world where Königsberg's bridges do not permit an Eulerian walk is a world where CP3' is true. CP4', however, is not weakly necessarily true. Thus, according to NOCA, the explanandum in the forward state of affairs version (FSA') of Bridges has a DME, but the explanandum in the reversed state of affairs version (RSA') of Bridges does not. Furthermore, FSA' necessitates the original forward event explanandum (FE') but not the original reversed event explanandum (RE') or RSA'. Thus, FSA' meets condition a) of NOCA, FE' meets condition b), and RSA' and RE' meet neither.

The reasoning through which I have gone in the previous examples can be straightforwardly extended to the other examples of DME. I won't repeat the reasoning, but here are the relevant countermathematicals for Strawberries and Pendulum:[28]

[28] Note that Pendulum already has a state of affairs explanandum. It thus meets condition a) of NOCA. One could construct an event version of Pendulum whose explanandum is the fact that Patty fails to do something that is made impossible by the setup. This explanandum would meet condition b) of NOCA.

CP5: Had 23 been divisible by 3, then Mary would not have failed to divide her 23 strawberries evenly among her three children.
CP6: Had 23 been divisible by 3, then Mary, who evenly divided her strawberries among her children, would have had 23 strawberries and three children.
CP7: Were a double pendulum's configuration space not a torus with at least four stationary points, then Patty's double pendulum would not have had at least four equilibrium configurations.
CP8: Were a double pendulum's configuration space not a torus with at least four stationary points, then Patty's pendulum, which does not have at least four equilibrium configurations, would have been a double pendulum.

In each case, the narrowed, forward explanandum, but not the narrowed, reversed explanandum, either weakly necessarily depends counterfactually on the relevant mathematical fact or is necessitated by a fact that weakly necessarily depends counterfactually on the relevant mathematical fact. Can we expect this always to be the case? I think so. In each case, the countermathematical that has a narrowed, forward explanandum statement as its consequent (i.e., CP 1, CP 3, CP 5, and CP 7) is doing something akin to modus ponens, and the countermathematical that has a narrowed, reversed explanandum statement as its consequent (i.e., CP 2, CP 4, CP 6, and CP 8) is doing something akin to affirming the consequent. This is due to the fact that Craver-Povich reversals are constructed by swapping and negating the empirical premise and explanandum statement of a forward DME.

Earlier I said that I would treat modal explananda separately, which I do now. First, let me make clear the difference between non-modal and modal explananda. Recall the forward and reversed explananda in the event version of Trefoil Knot:

FE: Terry failed to untie his trefoil knot.
RE: The knot Terry untied is not a trefoil knot.

I call these non-modal explananda because no modal terms appear in their description. The modal desideratum applies just as much, if not principally, to these non-modal explananda, since they are natural facts that possess a kind of necessity[29] even though they are not facts *about* necessity. The following are their modal counterparts:

Forward explanandum^M (FE^M): Terry could not have untied his trefoil knot.
Reversed explanandum^M (RE^M): The knot Terry untied could not have been a trefoil knot.

Now, according to NOCA, an explanandum has a DME just in case a) it weakly necessarily counterfactually depends only on a mathematical fact or b) it is necessitated by a natural fact that weakly necessarily counterfactually depends only on a mathematical fact. Thus, consider the following two countermathematicals:

CP1^M: Were the trefoil knot isotopic to the unknot, Terry could have untied his trefoil knot.

CP2^M: Were the trefoil knot isotopic to the unknot, the knot Terry untied could have been a trefoil knot.

There are worlds where CP1^M is false. For example, suppose that the only possible way for Terry to get access to his trefoil knot requires that he first untie a figure-eight knot, which is also distinct from the unknot. In this scenario, the fact that Terry could not have untied his trefoil knot does not counterfactually depend on the fact that the trefoil knot is distinct from the unknot: were the trefoil knot isotopic to the unknot, it still would have been impossible for Terry to have untied his trefoil knot, since he would first have to have untied a figure-eight knot.

There are worlds where CP2^M is true. The possible world above where Terry always buys his favorite untieable knot is obviously one where

[29] These explananda possess a kind of weak necessity (Kripke 1971)—truth in all possible worlds in which the individuals exist. Or, better, where what we might call the presuppositions of the fact hold. (Thanks to Arc Kocurek for this suggestion.) It is arguably false that necessarily Mary failed to divide evenly her 23 strawberries among her three children, because that fact does not obtain in worlds where Mary does not exist. It also arguably does not obtain in worlds where she exists but does not attempt such a division. But every world where she exists and attempts such a division is a world where she fails. "Necessarily, Mary *did not* divide her 23 strawberries evenly among her three children" gets around this, since this is arguably true in worlds where Mary exists and does not attempt such a division. I do not take this to imply that *no* explananda of DMEs are strongly necessary, though. Weakly necessary truths can be turned into strongly necessary ones by conditionalization. The following might be a strongly necessary explanandum that admits of DME: if Mary tries to divide her 23 strawberries evenly among her three children, she will fail.

CP2^{M} is true, since, in that world, were the trefoil knot isotopic to the unknot, the knot Terry untied would have been a trefoil knot, and *would* implies *could.*

Let us consider the countermathematicals associated with the state of affairs versions of these modal explananda, though.

CP1^{M*}: Were the trefoil knot isotopic to the unknot, Terry's trefoil knot could have been isotopic to the unknot.

CP2^{M*}: Were the trefoil knot isotopic to the unknot, Terry's untieable knot could have been a trefoil knot.

CP1^{M*} is weakly necessarily true—every world where Terry's trefoil knot could not have been isotopic to the unknot is a world where CP1^{M*} is true. Thus, the fact that Terry's trefoil knot could not be isotopic to the unknot (FSA^{M}; or must be distinct from the unknot) has a DME, according to NOCA. CP2^{M*} is not weakly necessarily true—not every world where Terry's untieable knot could not have been a trefoil knot (RSA^{M}) is a world where CP2^{M*} is true. For example, suppose Terry lives in a world where it is impossible to manufacture trefoil knots, because the only possible way to access the machines that manufacture trefoil knots requires the untying of a figure-eight knot. In such a scenario, were the trefoil knot isotopic to the unknot, Terry's untieable knot still could not have been a trefoil knot, because no one could have untied the figure-eight knot to gain access to the machines that manufacture trefoil knots. According to NOCA, then, the fact that Terry's untieable knot could not have been a trefoil knot does not have a DME.

Let us get back to the original modal explananda now: that Terry could not have untied his trefoil knot (FE^{M}) and that the knot Terry untied could not have been a trefoil knot (RE^{M}). As we have seen, the fact that Terry's trefoil knot could not have been isotopic to the unknot (FSA^{M}) meets condition a) of NOCA. FSA^{M} necessitates FE^{M}, so FE^{M} meets condition b) of NOCA: every world where Terry's trefoil knot could not have been isotopic to the unknot is a world where Terry could not have untied it. FSA^{M} does not necessitate RSA^{M} (or RE^{M}): not every world where Terry's trefoil knot could not have been isotopic to the unknot is a world where Terry's untieable knot could not have been a trefoil knot. In FSA^{M}-worlds, Terry has a trefoil knot; in RSA^{M}-world and (RE^{M}-worlds), he does not. Thus, FSA^{M} and RSA^{M} (or RE^{M}) cannot both be true (without contradiction) in the same worlds. Thus,

NOCA satisfies the directionality desideratum even for explicitly modal explananda.[30]

NOCA gives insight into how these modal facts can explain non-modal facts. For example, we saw that FSA (i.e., Terry's trefoil knot is distinct from the unknot) meets condition a) of NOCA. Assuming that FSA^M is a natural fact, FSA meets condition b) as well, for it is necessitated by FSA^M (i.e., Terry's trefoil knot could not have been isotopic to the unknot), which itself meets condition a). But the non-modal fact's being necessitated by the modal fact is only distinctively mathematically explanatory because the modal fact itself weakly necessarily counterfactually depends only on a mathematical fact. RE^M necessitates RE, but RE does not have a DME because RE^M does not meet condition a). Thus, if we focus on the necessitation relation and leave out the counterfactual dependence, we miss the real source of explanatory power of DME.

4.5. Ontic Demystification

I hope that I have shown that NOCA is a plausible account of DME. Yet, it is incomplete. The proponent of NOCA should have something to say about the nature of the relation of counterfactual dependence involved in DMEs. Otherwise, although the account meets all the desiderata, it remains mysterious what the relation is between mathematical facts and the natural facts that they explain. For counterfactual dependence is a relation that can hold for different reasons. *X* could counterfactually depend on *y*, because, for example, *x* and *y* are identical (e.g., were Mark Twain blond, then Samuel Clemens would have been blond), *y* constitutes *x* (e.g., were Lumpl made of marble, then Goliath would have been made of marble)[31], or *y* causes *x* (e.g.,

[30] I confess that my intuitions about these modal cases are not quite as strong as my intuitions about their non-modal counterparts. I do not think it would be much of problem if it turned out that NOCA did not satisfy the directionality desideratum for these modal cases. For that desideratum receives its plausibility from considering non-modal explananda, the directionality of which NOCA can account for, as we have seen. Note two things about our directionality desideratum (Craver and Povich 2017): first, it concerns only natural facts, and it is unclear whether modal facts are natural facts in the relevant sense. If modal facts are not natural facts (in the relevant sense), then the directionality desideratum arguably is not relevant for DMEs of modal explananda. Second, every one of our reversals examples has a non-modal explanandum. Carl Craver (personal communication) speculates that the modal explananda are more mathematical (i.e., closer to purely mathematical facts) than their non-modal counterparts. If that is right, then this would help explain why we do not need a directionality desideratum in these cases, since we would have one (quasi-)mathematical fact explained by another.

[31] Goliath is a statue and Lumpl is the lump of clay that constitutes it (Gibbard 1975).

were the flagpole taller, then its shadow would have been longer). In a DME, when a natural fact counterfactually depends only on a mathematical fact, why does that dependence hold? Arguably, the mathematical fact is not identical to, does not constitute, and is not a cause of the natural fact.

There are several options for ontic relations that could ground the relevant countermathematicals, any of which the proponent of NOCA may choose. I will briefly canvas two: the grounding relation and a structuralist-inspired instantiation/realization relation.

First, perhaps in DMEs, when a natural fact counterfactually depends on a mathematical fact, it could be because the former is (at least partially) grounded in the latter. Furthermore, such grounding is asymmetric: the fact that Patty's double pendulum does (or does not) have at least four equilibrium configurations is grounded in the fact that a double pendulum's configuration space is (or is not) a torus with at least four stationary points, but not vice versa; Mary's failure to divide her 23 strawberries evenly among her three children is grounded in the fact that 23 is not divisible by 3, but not vice versa.[32] Therefore, grounding seems like a good candidate relation to explicate the relevant counterfactuals: the previous grounding claims are plausible, the grounding relation is asymmetric, and grounding is already widely recognized to be a relation that bears explanatory force. However, we would need to know more about the nature of this grounding relationship, and I do not here have the space to wade into that extensive and controversial literature (see Correia and Schnieder 2012). Similarly, one might appeal to the *in virtue of* relation: the natural fact obtains *in virtue of* the fact that the mathematical fact does, but not vice versa. Again, this may be plausible but not very illuminating; it seems like a redescription of the grounding relation we want illuminated.

When thinking about what the nature of the relation of counterfactual dependence could be, it may be helpful to think about the nature of the relata. For different accounts of the ontology of mathematical facts may suggest certain relations. (I assume here that natural facts are unproblematic, but I will not assume any particular account. Note, though, that all the narrowed, natural facts that admit of DME that we have considered possess a certain kind of weak necessity—see note 29.) For example, on one prominent structuralist ontology, where mathematical objects are abstract structures or patterns, "the

[32] Whether this grounding claim is true depends on your philosophy of mathematics. A certain kind of empiricist/nominalist might reverse this and take natural facts to ground mathematical facts. For that reason, they are unlikely to think that putative DMEs are explanatory in the first place.

relationship between mathematics and material reality is, in part, a special case of the ancient problem of the instantiation of universals. Mathematics is to reality as universal is to instantiated particular" (Shapiro 1997, 248). The second option, then, is that in a DME, when a natural fact counterfactually depends only on, and is explained by, a mathematical fact, it is because the former is an instantiation (or perhaps a realization [Huneman 2010]) of the latter but not vice versa. This is especially plausible for DMEs with 'state of affairs' explananda. The natural fact instantiates/realizes the mathematical objects and properties/relations that compose the mathematical fact. Patty's double pendulum (the concrete object) is an instantiation or realization of the double pendulum (the abstract, mathematical object), and the double pendulum (the abstract, mathematical object) possesses the property of having at least four equilibrium configurations, so any instantiation of that mathematical object, such as Patty's double pendulum, will also instantiate the property of having four equilibrium configurations. The double pendulum (the abstract, mathematical object) is not an instantiation/realization of Patty's double pendulum (the concrete object), so instantiation is asymmetric, and this asymmetry can account for any explanatory asymmetry. We cannot use facts about Patty's double pendulum (the concrete object) to explain facts about the double pendulum (the abstract, mathematical object).

When we are dealing with DMEs for event explananda, the instantiation/realization relation combines with necessitation and componency relations. The natural fact that Terry's (concrete) trefoil knot is distinct from the unknot is an instantiation/realization of the mathematical fact that the (abstract) trefoil knot is distinct from the unknot. This natural fact is a component of, and necessitates, the event that Terry fails to untie his trefoil knot.[33] Another way to say the same thing: the mathematical fact is

[33] Going the instantiation route would make my account similar to Lyon's (2012) program account of DME and Pincock's (2015) abstract dependence account, which I discuss in Chapter 5. Lyon, following Jackson and Pettit (1990), takes a program explanation to be "one that cites a property or entity that, although not causally efficacious, ensures the instantiation of a causally efficacious property or entity that is an actual cause of the explanandum" (2012, 566). In general, I am sympathetic to Lyon's and Pincock's accounts, and I am happy to see NOCA as of a piece with theirs. One important difference between NOCA and the program account is that, on NOCA, the instantiated property needs to do more than cause the explanandum. To meet condition b), the instantiated property must be (instantiated in an object that is) a component of and *necessitate* the explanandum to count as a DME. Instantiated properties *cause* all kinds of things that do not thereby have DMEs. For example, the instantiation of network structure P in Königsberg's bridges ensures that causally efficacious properties are on the scene to cause a certain pattern of air flow, a rise in tourism, boats to crash, Marta to smile, and so on, none of which is *distinctively mathematically* explained by network structure P. Thus, NOCA is superior to Lyon's program account on this count.

instantiated *in* the explanandum-event, and that instantiation necessitates the explanandum-event.

Before concluding, I should like to reiterate the relation between the ontic aspect of NOCA and the counterfactual aspect. Relations of counterfactual dependence hold in virtue of relations of ontic dependence. Like supervenience, counterfactual dependence is a modal concept. Supervenience could hold in virtue of the holding of different relations of ontic dependence, including, among others, identity, constitution, and causal sufficiency (Heil 2003, 67). My emphasis on counterfactual dependence is essential, though, because it is only with information about counterfactual dependence that one can answer w-questions, as I argued in Chapter 3. Thus, counterfactual dependence is what unites different forms of ontic dependence (causation, constitution, grounding, etc.) and the different forms of explanation that describe them. According to the generalized ontic conception, explanation involves exhibiting ontic relations that support counterfactuals. Their ability to support counterfactuals is what unites these ontic relations as *explanatory* relations. I agree with Woodward (2003, 210–220), who holds that it is *in virtue of* conveying counterfactual information that causal relations are explanatory. Thus, perhaps one way of viewing what the two conditions of NOCA are showing is this: they are showing what kinds of counterfactual an ontic relation needs to support if it is to capture all of our intuitive judgments about DME. The ontic relation of instantiation seems to support the relevant kinds of counterfactual: abstract objects are necessary existents; thus, a change in an abstract object results in a change in all of its instances in every world where instances exist. So, we should expect instantiation to support exactly the kind of weakly necessary dependence I've appealed to.

4.6. Objections

I have argued that an ontic variety of counterfactualism, NOCA, can satisfy the three desiderata for an account of DME. I now consider some objections to my proposal.

First, consider the fact that, according to NOCA, the indivisibility of 23 by 3 explains why Mary failed to divide evenly 23 strawberries among her three children, since, had 23 been divisible by 3, then Mary would have succeeded. Arguably, had 26 been divisible by 3, then 23 would have been divisible by 3. Does this mean that Mary's failure counterfactually depends on the indivisibility of 26 by 3? If so, then this is a counterexample to NOCA, since, arguably, the indivisibility of 26 by 3 does not explain Mary's failure, although the latter counterfactually depends on the former.

As stated, this objection commits the counterfactual fallacy of transitivity (Lewis 1973, 32).[34] Transitive inferences are valid for material conditionals but not counterfactual conditionals. It could be true that had 23 been divisible evenly by 3, then Mary would have succeeded and that had 26 been divisible evenly by 3, then 23 would have been, but it does not follow from those truths that had 26 been divisible evenly by 3, then Mary would have succeeded.

Lewis (1973, 33) gives the following counterexample, due to Stalnaker, to this inference pattern:

> P1: If J. Edgar Hoover had been born a Russian, then he would have been a Communist.
>
> P2: If he had been a Communist, then he would have been a traitor.
> C: If he had been born a Russian, then he would have been a traitor.

However, Lewis (1973) is careful to note that transitivity fails when the antecedent of the first premise is more far-fetched than the antecedent of the second, and that does not seem true of the inference in the objection. And, of course, that the inference is invalid does not show that its conclusion (i.e., that had 26 been divisible by 3, Mary would have succeeded) is false. However, I do not see why we should believe it is true. At the very least, Baron, Colyvan, and Ripley (2017) show how to evaluate such a countermathematical in such

[34] The objection can be reformulated without going through a chain of counterfactuals, thus escaping the transitivity charge. One could use the indicative conditional that if 26 is divisible by 3, then 23 is divisible by 3. If we hold this indicative conditional fixed when we go to a world in which we "twiddle" 26, we should get a corresponding change to 23, making the problematic counterfactual (i.e., "had 26 been divisible by 3, Mary would have succeeded") true. Although this escapes the transitivity charge, it still runs afoul of the surgical strike rule for twiddling. See below. Now, you might reasonably worry about how we can twiddle 26 and hold everything fixed, including 23, without generating further contradictions. I do not think this is too much of a worry, though. As Baron, Colyvan, and Ripley (2017, 9) point out, this should not be any more worrisome than it is when we evaluate standard counterfactuals:

> But we do not need to resolve all the looming contradictions. We just need to resolve those relevant to assessing the counterfactual at hand. After all, that's all we do in the Suzy and the rock case. We do not go all the way back to the big bang or even to Suzy's birth in order to achieve consistency. We iron out the immediate inconsistencies and leave it there. But somewhere in the background there will be further inconsistencies looming. Suzy moved her arm in a throwing motion, yet the rock did not move? She willed her arm to move, but it didn't? We simply set these problems aside because they are not relevant to the assessment of the counterfactual of interest.

a way that it is false. (In Chapter 5, I will show how the normativist can evaluate countermathematicals.) Evaluating countermathematicals requires decisions about what and how much mathematics to hold fixed (just as evaluating an ordinary counterfactual requires decisions about what and how many empirical facts to hold fixed). Consider their (2017, 7) remarks on "twiddling" the number 13 by giving it the factors 2 and 6:

> We should not go too far, however; we still want to hold fixed as much as we can with respect to the natural numbers. What we're ultimately interested in, recall, are the ramifications of twiddling 13. We are not interested in the ramifications of twiddling any other number. In other words, we want to be able to carry out a "surgical strike" on 13 that enables us to gauge the consequences of altering this number for physical reality in as much isolation as possible from alterations to anything else within mathematics. (Baron, Colyvan, and Ripley 2017, 7)

Baron, Colyvan, and Ripley (2017, 7–9) show how to perform such a surgical strike by changing the multiplication function so that 2 × 6 = 13. Similarly, we want a "surgical strike" on 26 not to have consequences for 23 and for Mary's success or failure. Thus, Baron et al.'s procedure for evaluating countermathematicals allows me to say that it is false that, had 26 been divisible by 3, then Mary would have succeeded.

Next, according to NOCA, the fact that network structure P does not permit an Eulerian walk explains why Marta failed to make an Eulerian walk across Königsberg's bridges (which we presuppose have network structure P). Intuitively, Euler's general theorem that a network permits an Eulerian walk if and only if exactly zero or two of the nodes has an odd number of edges also explains why Marta failed to make an Eulerian walk across Königsberg's bridges (and, similarly, explains the state of affairs version of this explanandum, that Königsberg's bridges, which have network structure P, do not permit an Eulerian walk). However, arguably, there are worlds where it is false that had Euler's general theorem been false, then Marta would have made an Eulerian walk across Königsberg's bridges (or Königsberg's bridges, which have network structure P, would have permitted an Eulerian walk). Thus, we have a case of DME that does not meet either condition of NOCA.

It might seem that I am forced to accept the counterintuitive consequence that Euler's theorem does not explain why Marta failed to make an Eulerian walk across Königsberg's bridges (or why Königsberg's bridges, which have network structure P, do not permit an Eulerian walk).[35] For although from Euler's theorem it follows that Königsberg's bridges, which have network structure P, do not permit an Eulerian walk, had Euler's theorem been false, it might still have been the case that Königsberg's bridges, which have network structure P, do not permit an Eulerian walk (e.g., in a world where Euler's theorem is false because its sufficiency component is false, but its necessity component is still true). (Nor is the explanandum-fact an instantiation of the explanans-fact, to which I return below.) Euler's theorem necessitates the fact that Königsberg's bridges, which have network structure P, do not permit an Eulerian walk, but the latter fact does not weakly necessarily counterfactually depend on the former. Perhaps this is one of those misleading cases of necessitation without counterfactual dependence.

Let me first try to soften the counterintuitiveness of the claim that Euler's theorem is not explanatory and then give a tentative reason to think NOCA might be able to count it as explanatory.[36] The reason the intuition that Euler's theorem is explanatory may be wrong is that Euler's theorem is a conjunction of a necessity claim and a sufficiency claim, and the sufficiency claim is explanatorily idle. We can all agree that the fact that having exactly zero or two nodes with an odd number of edges is *sufficient* for permitting an Eulerian walk does not explain why Königsberg's bridges do not permit an Eulerian walk. Explanations can be destroyed by addition of irrelevancies (Salmon 1989). The conjunctive fact that 23 is indivisible by 3 and 3 is prime also doesn't distinctively mathematically explain why Mary failed to divide 23 strawberries evenly among her three kids. Other irrelevancies have the potential to cause problems for NOCA. "Were the trefoil knot isotopic to the unknot and 4 prime, Terry's trefoil knot would have been isotopic to the unknot" seems weakly necessary, but we don't want to count it as explanatory. Although the fact that Terry's trefoil knot is distinct from the unknot weakly necessarily counterfactually depends on the disjunctive fact that the trefoil knot is distinct from the unknot or 4 is composite, the latter doesn't explain

[35] Of course, as a last resort, one could restrict NOCA to giving sufficient conditions for DME, rather than necessary and sufficient conditions.

[36] This appears to be a general, unrecognized consequence of counterfactual theories of explanation, regarding the limited explanatory status of biconditionals or facts about material equivalence. For example, from the fact that being an eligible, unmarried man is necessary and sufficient for being a bachelor, it follows (i.e., necessitates) that Marta, a woman, is not a bachelor. However, were being an eligible, unmarried man not necessary and sufficient for being a bachelor, it would not necessarily follow that Marta would have been a bachelor. Whether this follows depends on how such counterfactuals are evaluating, a point to which I return when I discuss how NOCA might be able to count Euler's theorem as explanatory.

the former. Here I appeal to instantiation. Only the trefoil knot is explanatorily relevant because only it is instantiated in the explanandum.

Let me now give a tentative reason to think NOCA can count Euler's theorem as explanatory. If you look above at Reutlinger's dependency condition, you will see that it only requires, for a counterfactual to be true, that there is *some* way of making the antecedent true that makes the consequent true. Reutlinger (2016, 738) is explicit about this. On this understanding of what is required for the truth of a counterfactual, it is true that had Euler's theorem been false, then Königsberg's bridges, which have network structure P, would have permitted an Eulerian walk, so long as there is some way of making Euler's theorem false that also makes it true that Königsberg's bridges, which have network structure P, permit an Eulerian walk. Obviously, there is such a way: make Euler's theorem false by allowing networks with structure P to permit an Eulerian walk. Furthermore, this way of making the antecedent true that also makes the consequent true is available in every possible world where the explanandum obtains. Thus, the countermathematical is weakly necessary. Thus, Euler's theorem *does* distinctively mathematically explain why Königsberg's bridges, which have network structure P, don't permit an Eulerian walk. And since this necessitates the fact that Marta failed to make an Eulerian walk across Königsberg's bridges, that fact too is distinctively mathematically explained by Euler's theorem.

I am hesitant to commit to this response to the objection, though, because I am unsure what ramifications this understanding of what is required for the truth of a counterfactual will have on NOCA. For example, perhaps it will let in other reversals. Take the reversed, state of affairs explanandum of Trefoil Knot: that Terry's untieable knot is not a trefoil knot. The relevant countermathematical is: were the trefoil knot isotopic to the unknot, Terry's untieable knot would have been a trefoil knot. Is there a way of making the antecedent true that also makes the consequent true? It seems like there might be, in certain worlds. Imagine a world where Terry's untieable knot is a Thistlethwaite knot. Now, make the trefoil knot isotopic to the unknot by giving it the structure of a Thistlethwaite knot. Does this make Terry's untieable knot, which is a Thistlethwaite knot, a trefoil knot? If it does, then the counterfactual is true in this world. Obviously, this exact *way* of making the counterfactual true wouldn't work in every world where the explanandum obtains, because Terry's untieable knot is a not a Thistlethwaite knot in every world. However, in every world where the explanandum obtains there is *some* way of making the counterfactual true. Whichever untieable knot Terry has in some world, simply make the trefoil knot isotopic to the unknot by giving it the structure of the untieable knot he has; then, it seems, his untieable knot would have been a trefoil knot. Thus, it seems that the countermathematical for the reversal, on this understanding of what is required for its truth, is weakly necessarily true, and so the reversed, state of affairs explanandum has a DME.

Perhaps there is a way around this, though, if we adjust our quantifiers. Yes, in the reversal, it is true that every world where the explanandum obtains is such that there is some way of making the antecedent true that also makes the consequent true. But it is not the case that there is some way of making the antecedent true such that, in every world where the explanandum obtains, the consequent is also true. If by "weakly necessary" we mean the latter—i.e., that there is some way of making the antecedent true such that, in every world where the explanandum obtains, the consequent is also true—then we can keep our response to the objection, allowing Euler's theorem to be explanatory, while still ruling out the reversal. For our way of making "had Euler's theorem been false, then Königsberg's bridges, which have network structure P, would have permitted an Eulerian walk" true works in all worlds where the explanandum obtains. Our way of making "were the trefoil knot isotopic to the unknot, Terry's untieable knot would have been a trefoil knot" true only works in worlds where Terry's untieable knot is a Thistlethwaite knot. Even if this is right, there are other cases that we would like to exclude, and one way of excluding them is by appeal to the fact that their putative explanans is not the right kind of thing to be instantiated in the explanandum. And that claim, as we will see, seems to apply to Euler's theorem—it is not the right kind of thing to be instantiated in the explanandum. So, this pushes back against the claim that Euler's theorem is explanatory. Let's consider a case that we would like to exclude by appeal to the fact that its putative explanans is not the right kind of thing to be instantiated in the explanandum.

Take the reversed, state of affairs version of Bridges. Recall that in this version we imagine we are in world where, contrary to fact, Königsberg's bridges, which permit an Eulerian walk, do not have network structure P. That is our explanandum. Now consider the countermathematical: had Euler's theorem been false, then Königsberg's bridges, which permit an Eulerian walk, would have had network structure P. This is not weakly necessary for a similar reason that the previous countermathematical is not: had Euler's theorem been false, it might still have been the case that Königsberg's bridges, which permit an Eulerian walk, would *not* have had network structure P (e.g., in a world where Euler's theorem is false because its necessity component is false, but its sufficiency component is still true). Therefore, Euler's theorem does not distinctively mathematically explain RSA', which is good since that's a reversal. But now focus on the sufficiency claim. Surely, this countermathematical is weakly necessary: had permitting an Eulerian walk been sufficient for having network structure P, then Königsberg's bridges, which permit an Eulerian walk (or across which Marta made such a walk), would have had network structure P. It seems that the fact, supposing it were one, that it is not the case that permitting an Eulerian walk is sufficient for having network structure P distinctively mathematically explains why Königsberg's bridges, which permit an Eulerian walk (or across which Marta made such a walk), do not have network structure P.

Here an ontic story can be helpful. If, for example, the instantiation relation is the ontic relation that "grounds" the relevant, explanatory countermathematicals, then it can be used to exclude otherwise problematic countermathematicals that have no such grounding. The same thing is true of other ontic relations and the kinds of explanation they support. For example, there may be counterfactual dependence between one fact (or event or whatever) and another, but if that dependence does not hold in virtue of a causal relation between them, then the one fact does not causally explain the other. In this objection, the putative explanans-fact—i.e., the fact that it is not the case that permitting an Eulerian walk is sufficient for having network structure P—is a negative generalization and it doesn't seem like the right kind of thing to be instantiated, at least not in the way a simple mathematical fact composed of mathematical objects and mathematical properties/relations (e.g., the fact that the trefoil knot is distinct from the unknot) can be instantiated. This may be easier to see if we compare the logical structure of this explanans to that of a simple mathematical fact. As a universal generalization, it contains a *variable* that ranges over mathematical objects. No instantiable objects themselves are mentioned. The logical structure of this explanans is: it is not the case that for all *x*, if *x* permits an Eulerian walk, then *x* has network structure P (where "*x*" ranges over mathematical objects). The fact that Königsberg's bridges, which permit an Eulerian walk (or across which Marta made such a walk), do not have network structure P is not an instantiation of this negative universal generalization. (To connect this to the discussion above about Euler's theorem: the worry is that similar reasoning as that presented here forces us to say that Euler's theorem is not the kind of thing to be instantiated in the explanandum and, so, cannot explain.) This point still holds if we convert the negative universal generalization into a logically equivalent existential generalization: there is an x, such that x permits an Eulerian walk and x doesn't have network structure P.[37] The explanandum is not an instantiation of this existential generalization.[38]

I think this argument is correct, but did we reach it merely by a trick of logical notation or linguistic representation? We can remove the negative universal generalization altogether by simply changing our property-terms and object-terms like this: the Eulerian network does not have network structure P, where "the Eulerian network" refers to the network that permits an Eulerian walk. This seems to express the same fact expressed by the negative universal generalization, and it distinctively mathematically explains why Königsberg's bridges, which permit an Eulerian walk (or across which Marta made such a walk), do not have network structure P. For it is weakly necessary that, had the Eulerian network had network structure P, then Königsberg's bridges, which permit an Eulerian walk (or across which Marta made such a walk), would have had network structure P. Furthermore, the explanans-fact is instantiated in the explanandum-fact: Königsberg's bridges are an instantiation of the mathematical object *the Eulerian network* and they also instantiate the mathematical property *not having network structure P*.

I could object here to negative properties (e.g., *not having network structure P*), but I won't take that route. The trouble is that "the Eulerian network"—*the* network that permits an Eulerian walk—is not a network; it is a collection of different networks. This is not a point about multiple realization or abstractness; I'm not objecting to "the Eulerian network" because it is multiply realizable. Trefoil knots are multiply realizable; pendula are multiply realizable; etc. The problem is that networks are defined and

37 The form of this whole example is interesting. It basically has this form: "Why isn't my dog healthy?" "Some dogs aren't healthy." (Or "Not all dogs are healthy.") What I find interesting is that we sometimes *do* give such "it is what it is" explanations in everyday life, and that the explanandum *does* counterfactually depend on the explanans.

38 This is a claim about the proper relata of the instantiation relation. There is another analogy to Woodward's (2003) account of causation. For Woodward, causal relata are (or are represented by) variables taking values. It is variable x's taking value x_1 that causes variable y's taking value y_1. I am claiming that, for the instantiation relation, the first variable is an abstract object, its taking a value is its having some property, and that Euler's theorem is not an abstract object, thus not a proper relatum of the instantiation relation. Perhaps there is some way of shoehorning the explanatoriness of Euler's theorem into NOCA by allowing that, if abstract variable x's taking value x_1 distinctively mathematically explains variable y's taking value y_1, then anything that mathematically entails that abstract variable x takes value x_1 also distinctively mathematically explains variable y's taking value y_1. It seems to me that this would count far too many things as DMEs. For example, if z mathematically entails that abstract variable x takes value x_1, then so does z conjoined with the fact that $2 + 2 = 4$. Maybe relevance logic can be brought in to help, but I will not pursue this here.

individuated by their topologies or structures of nodes and edges. "The Eulerian network" is not defined by a topology of nodes and edges—it is a gerrymandered collection of many different networks made to fall under a singular term. The objector is the one who has made the linguistic trick. We can use a name in the logical calculus, say "*t*," to denote a mathematical object, say, the trefoil knot, and a predicate, D, to denote the property of being distinct from the unknot (or the set of objects to which the predicate applies). Thus, "*Dt*" expresses the proposition that the trefoil knot is distinct from the unknot. However, the name can be "converted" into a predicate, *T*, denoting the property of being a trefoil knot (or the set of objects to which the predicate applies). A proposition similar to the one expressed by "*Dt*" can then be expressed by "for all *x*, if *Tx*, then *Dx*" (with "*x*" ranging over mathematical objects). But this only works for an object and the property of being that object. One cannot sensibly turn the predicate "is red" into the name of an object. Being an Eulerian network is a property had by many mathematical objects. This is true even if the property in question is possessed by an object essentially. They are still very different kinds of thing. Excluding some reversals, then, requires NOCA firmly to commit to the idea that some mathematical objects exist, and others do not.[39] This means that NOCA is committed to a privileged mathematical ontology—not just anything goes. Below, I argue that other accounts of DME (Baron 2024; Pincock 2015; Reutlinger 2016) are also committed to a privileged ontology, and, in Chapter 5, I argue that normativism allows me to deflationarily reinterpret what it means to accept a privileged ontology.

In Chapter 2, I criticized Lange for assuming a privileged ontology because, to avoid our reversals, he must exclude the reality of certain mathematical objects (e.g., "the isotopic knot," a knot whose isotopy to the unknot is constitutive of it). It seems I must make the same move, insisting that networks are defined and individuated by their topologies of nodes and edges, so that "the Eulerian network" is excluded as a mathematical object that can be instantiated. Accepting a privileged ontology seems to be a bigger problem for Lange (2013b, 2018), though, whose account of DME has a psychological component: one of the empirical explanans-facts in a DME must be *understood in the why-question's context* to be constitutive of the physical task or arrangement at issue. Lange has placed no restrictions on what can

[39] Pincock (2023, 33) takes me to be objecting to the property of permitting an Eulerian walk and excluding it from mathematical ontology. That's incorrect. I'm only objecting to "the Eulerian network" conceived as a mathematical object.

be understood to be constitutive of what in a context. If both require a privileged ontology to exclude reversals, why prefer NOCA over Lange's account? The reason is the overall picture of explanation NOCA provides. Only NOCA delivers a unified picture of explanation, where DME and causal-mechanical explanation are species of a common genus, united by ontically backed counterfactual dependence.

Like Lange's account and NOCA, Pincock's (2015) abstract dependence account, Baron's (2024) Pythagoreanism, and Reutlinger's (2016) CTE all seem to need a privileged ontology that excludes mathematical objects like the isotopic knot and the Eulerian network in order to avoid these reversals too. Let me briefly explain Baron's new view, and then I'll show how he, Pincock, and Reutlinger need to exclude the Eulerian network from their ontologies. Baron calls his view "Pythagorean" or "partially Pythagorean" because he believes that there are mathematical objects, physical objects, mathematical properties, and physical properties, and that mathematical properties can be possessed by both mathematical and physical objects. The way a DME works is by showing that a physical system shares intrinsic mathematical properties with a mathematical object[40] and that these physically instantiated mathematical properties either guarantee the presence of other mathematical properties and the physical states that possess them, or rule out other mathematical properties and any associated physical states (2024, 664). So, for example, why does Terry fail to untie his trefoil knot? According to Baron, because untying it would put it in a physical state that requires it to have a mathematical property (i.e., being isotopic to the unknot) that is ruled out by its possessing another mathematical property (i.e., being a trefoil knot). This is similar to NOCA's claim that Terry's failure is necessitated by the instantiation of a mathematical object and property. Here is how it seems Pincock, Baron, and Reutlinger must exclude the Eulerian network. Why don't Königsberg's bridges have network structure P? (Recall that in this reversal we're imagining a world where the bridges don't have P, the structure they actually had in 1735.) Because the bridges instantiate the Eulerian network and the Eulerian network doesn't have P (à la Pincock).[41]

[40] I confess to not understanding how a concrete, spatiotemporally located object and an abstract, non-spatiotemporally located object could literally possess the same properties.

[41] Pincock could say that the explanandum in this reversal is not that a concrete object *possesses* a certain property, but that it doesn't. But Pincock should then explain why that matters. We could also just reframe the explanandum as the fact that Königsberg's bridges possess the property of not having network structure P. Pincock can avoid this only by accepting a privileged ontology that excludes negative properties.

Or because the instantiation in the bridges of the mathematical property of being an Eulerian network rules out the instantiation of the mathematical property of having P (à la Baron). Or because if Konigsberg's bridges weren't an Eulerian network, they would've had P (à la Reutlinger). This counterfactual is true because Reutlinger, recall, only requires that there is *some* way of making the antecedent true that makes the consequent true, which there obviously is. (Give the bridges their actual structure in 1735, which was not an Eulerian network and had P.) This is a problem for Reutlinger whether or not he excludes the Eulerian network from his ontology, for it also seems to count "if Konigsberg's bridges hadn't permitted an Eulerian walk, they would've had P" as true. Thus, unless Lange, Pincock, Baron, and Reutlinger can exclude the Eulerian network, it seems they all count this reversal as a DME. (Though, again, it seems Reutlinger would need to do more than exclude the Eulerian network.)

Finally, let me consider two objections regarding NOCA's use of narrow explananda. The first objection is that the narrowing procedure lifts a lot of mathematics into the explanandum, which results in the possibility that we don't have a DME, but rather an explanation of one mathematical fact by another.[42] I admit that the narrowing procedure makes the explananda of DMEs unique, but I don't think they are mathematical facts. (Note that this objection would seem to target Lange too, by whom my narrowing procedure was inspired.) The explananda are certainly not purely natural facts, facts featuring no mathematics whatsoever. But they are not purely mathematical facts either, facts featuring only mathematics. Purely mathematical facts feature only mathematics—they are composed only of mathematical objects and properties. Narrow explananda are not composed only of mathematical objects and properties. Therefore, narrow explananda are not purely mathematical facts. They are what you might call mixed natural-mathematical facts, natural facts that feature mathematics. All statements of applied mathematics refer to such facts, which frequently figure as explananda in scientific explanations.

Still, one might worry that narrow explananda seem different from these uncontroversial facts of applied mathematics. Here is another argument: narrow explananda are the result of combining the original *natural* explananda with their *natural* explanantia. It is not plausible that combining

[42] I thank an anonymous reviewer for raising this objection.

two natural facts results in a purely mathematical fact. Thus, my narrow explananda are not mathematical facts.

The second objection to narrow explananda is that they conflict with scientific practice (Holmes 2021). The thought is that some DMEs have explananda that are susceptible also to causal explanation, but this can't be true for narrow explananda. Narrow explananda depend only on mathematical facts. Change the causal structure of the world in any way you like and they would still hold, so they can't have causal explanations. There are a couple replies to this objection. First, on some extremely liberal views of causal explanation (e.g., Lewis 1986), all it takes for an explanation to be causal is for it to rule out some possible causal histories of the explanandum. On such a view, it seems that an explanation that reveals that the explanandum has no cause counts as a casual explanation! After all, such an explanation rules out many possible causal histories of the explanandum—all of them. Lewis (1986, 222) explicitly says that "it had no cause" is a causal explanation. On such a view, all DMEs are also causal explanations. It's hard to know what wouldn't be a causal explanation on such a view, so I'm hesitant to take this route. Second, I think the better reply is that when scientists are giving DMEs and causal explanations, they are actually thinking of slightly different explananda. DMEs explain narrow explananda, causal explanations explain unnarrowed explananda, and those explananda can be very similar. Also, note that "DME" is a philosophical term of art, and its concept is a highly theoretical one that I doubt practicing scientists possess. I predict that a close look at scientific practice and probing conversation with practicing scientists will show that there is nothing here inconsistent with scientific practice.

Holmes's own view of DME is an erotetic version of Baron's deductive-mathematical account, which I've already criticized. Holmes tries to avoid reversals, such as explaining why Mary doesn't have 23 strawberries, by saying that when the reversed explanandum is described modally, there is no problem; there is nothing problematic about there being a DME of the fact that Mary *couldn't* have 23 strawberries. Even if that is true, that doesn't explain why there isn't a DME of why Mary doesn't have 23 strawberries. Holmes (2021, 18) addresses this by saying that the modal character of the explanandum determines the type of explanation required. So, "Why *doesn't* Mary have 23 strawberries?" demands a causal explanation, and "Why *couldn't* Mary have 23 strawberries?" demands a DME. It isn't clear why that is, it is inconsistent with all the cases of DME in the literature that are not modal,[43] and it opens Holmes to the same objection he leveled against NOCA, for it entails that you cannot have causal explanations and DMEs of the same explananda.

4.7. Summary

Let us take stock. I argued that Baron's (2020) U-Counterfactual Theory does not meet the desiderata for an account of DME. Then, I showed how my counterfactual account of DME, the Narrow Ontic Counterfactual Account (NOCA), can meet the desiderata. I then briefly canvassed two asymmetric ontic relations that might hold between mathematical and natural facts: the grounding relation and the instantiation/realization relation.

By unifying ontic and modal explanations, NOCA shows the weakness of that distinction. Lange (2013b) presented DMEs not only as a challenge to the causal hegemony, but as a challenge to any ontic conception of scientific explanation. DMEs, Lange argued, are accommodable only by a modal, rather than an ontic, conception of explanation because of their strong modal import. However, NOCA is a monistic account of explanation. It says that all explanations follow a single pattern: they all exhibit relations of counterfactual dependence that hold in virtue of some ontic relation that holds between explanandum and explanans and in virtue of which they count as explanations. Thus, we see now why I said in Chapter 1 that NOCA portrays DME as a component in an intuitive typology of kinds of explanation that are individuated by the ontic relation in virtue of which the relation of counterfactual dependence between explanans and explanandum holds. Causation supports counterfactual dependence in causal explanations. A constitutive mechanistic relation supports counterfactual dependence in mechanistic explanations. Instantiation supports counterfactual dependence in DMEs. NOCA thus unifies causal and non-causal, ontic and modal.

While there are important differences between DMEs and non-DMEs, ultimately, I think, the distinction between ontic and modal *conceptions* of explanation is not a useful one.[44] There is no need to distinguish between

43 Barrantes (2023) also argues that only modal explananda have DMEs.

44 Of course, there is also the so-called epistemic conception of explanation (Salmon 1989), briefly mentioned in Chapter 1. To the extent that this conception is committed to the idea that explanations are deductive arguments, it is unworkable for DME, as we have seen in Baron's (2019) deductive-mathematical account, critiqued in Chapter 2.

ontic and modal conceptions of explanation for the same reason that there is no need to distinguish between causal and mechanistic *conceptions*, important differences between causal and mechanistic *explanations* there may be. All explanations—ontic and modal, causal and non-causal—work in the same basic way and inherit their explanatory power from the same basic source: ontically backed counterfactual dependence.

In Chapter 5, I will argue that NOCA can be normativistically deflated and that this doesn't deprive NOCA of its ontic status or explanatory power. Nothing in the present chapter will be negated; NOCA's platonistic language will simply be normativistically reinterpreted in ontologically noncommittal fashion. Carnap was not a platonist, but he thought he could justify using platonistic language (Carnap 1950). That is what I will try to do next.

5
Deflating the Narrow Ontic Counterfactual Account

5.1. Introduction

Distinctively mathematical explanations (DMEs) have been receiving a lot of attention recently (Baker 2005, 2009; Colyvan 1998; Craver and Povich 2017; Lange 2013b, 2016, 2018; Lyon 2012; Mancosu 2008; Pincock 2015; Povich 2019, 2020, 2023; Reutlinger 2016; Saatsi 2011, 2012, 2016; Steiner 1978). Some philosophers (e.g., Lange 2013b, 2016) take them to be inconsistent with ontic accounts of explanation.[1] I addressed this concern in Chapter 4 by presenting an ontic account of DME, the Narrow Ontic Counterfactual Account (NOCA). I also critiqued Lange's modal account in Chapter 2. Some philosophers (e.g., Baker 2005, 2009, contra Bangu 2008 and Saatsi 2011) take DMEs to play a crucial role in the enhanced indispensability argument (EIA), providing good evidence for the existence of the mathematical objects to which they appeal. This is my concern in the present chapter. It makes good on the claim I made in Chapter 1, that normativism undermines the ability of DMEs to serve as reasons for platonism—it blocks the EIA's inference from DMEs to platonism by showing how to accept the former while denying the latter. The normativist can even accept deflated versions of ontic accounts of DME, and I argue that deflated ontic accounts are just as explanatorily powerful, if not more, and still ontic. Note that I do not offer an argument for anti-platonism or against platonism. The goal is not to convince anyone to be an anti-platonist, but to convince them that anti-platonists can accept the existence of DMEs, thus blocking the EIA. Showing that the EIA is invalid only requires an argument for the consistency of anti-platonism and DME, not an argument for anti-platonism or against platonism.

[1] Lange here means "ontic accounts" in my sense.

Rules to Infinity. Mark Povich, Oxford University Press. © Oxford University Press 2024.
DOI: 10.1093/oso/9780197679005.003.0005

In Section 5.2, I introduce modal normativism and extend it to mathematics. In Section 5.3, I show how normativism and a semantic construal of instantiation as concept application deflate the ability of DMEs to serve as reasons for platonism in the EIA. I also explain two other accounts of DME (Pincock 2015; Baron 2024) in order to show how they can similarly be deflated. For my goal is not just to show how normativism undermines NOCA's ability to support platonism, but how it undermines any account's ability. Obviously, there are more accounts of DME out there, but hopefully a few examples will show how normativism's ability to undermine the EIA is generalizable to any account. In Section 5.4, I consider some objections. In Section 5.5, I argue that deflated ontic accounts are just as explanatorily powerful, if not more, and should still be considered ontic.

5.2. Modal Normativism

Modal normativism is similar to expressivism or non-descriptivism about modality with many metaphysical and epistemological advantages over descriptivist alternatives, advantages which I address shortly once the view is on the table (Blackburn 1993; Brandom 2008; Sidelle 1989; Thomasson 2019a, 2020a). According to modal normativism, metaphysically modal claims do not *describe* anything, but instead are object language *expressions* of conceptual/semantic rules or consequences thereof. A necessary claim such as "all bachelors are unmarried" is an expression of a semantic rule according to which "bachelor" is to be applied only where "unmarried" is applied. When we have an object language expression of a semantic rule, we are entitled to add a necessity operator: "necessarily, all bachelors are unmarried." Since "necessarily, all bachelors are unmarried" expresses a rule governing the concept of necessity, we are also entitled to add a necessity operator to that claim, resulting in "necessarily, necessarily, all bachelors are unmarried." So, the normativist can accept the characteristic axiom of S4 modal logic that if it is necessary that p, it is necessary that it is necessary that p (Thomasson 2020a, 88).

Since normativism denies that necessities *describe* semantic rules, it avoids many of the most (in)famous objections to conventionalism, objections that target the ideas of "truth by convention" and "truth in virtue of meaning." Conventionalism, a predecessor of normativism, was originally developed by the positivists to account for *logical* and *mathematical* necessity[2] (e.g., Ayer 1952; Schlick 1974; Wittgenstein 2013; see also the later Wittgenstein [956] 1978 and his followers, such as Baker and Hacker 2009 and Glock 1996, from all of whom the present account draws considerable inspiration; see also Friedrich 2011). According to them, all necessity—metaphysical, mathematical, and logical[3]—is analyticity, and analytic statements have no descriptive content. Against this, Boghossian (1997, 336) argues that since semantic rules or conventions are contingent, truth by convention makes "the truth of what is expressed contingent, whereas most of the statements at stake in the present discussion [logical, mathematical and conceptual truths] are clearly necessary." Furthermore, Boghossian argues, truth by convention and truth in virtue of meaning imply that we make necessary propositions true "by pronouncement." Sider (2003, 2011) reiterates both these arguments in his dismissal of conventionalism.[4] Both these problems are a consequence of the claim that mathematical (or logical) truths *describe* or are *made true* by semantic rules or conventions, and this claim is denied by normativism. As I mentioned in Chapter 1, I think Warren's (2020) conventionalism avoids these objections, and—for the purposes of this book—I view it as differing from normativism in emphasis only. I will address some minor problems with Warren's conventionalism in Chapter 8.

Before moving on to counterpossibles (i.e., counterfactuals with impossible antecedents), let me briefly mention the advantages of normativism over descriptivism. Descriptivism is the view, like that in metaethics, that the function of modal language is to describe (in a substantive, *synthetic* sense of that term) modal reality (in a substantive, *synthetic* sense of that term), similar to the way in which non-modal empirical language describes empirical reality, e.g., by tracking external, objective features. Normativism and descriptivism are functional theses, theses about the function of language. (I will discuss the distinctive functional claim of normativism in more detail in Chapter 6.) They are not semantic claims about what the meanings of terms are or metasemantic claims about how those meanings are established. Simplifying a bit, when combined with certain metaphysical views, descriptivism can lead to substantive realism or error theory. Normativism

[2] Thomasson (2020a) discusses some proposals for normativism about logical necessity and consequence. Kocurek and Jerzak (2021) offer a detailed formal account of logical expressivism—my account is of a piece with theirs.

[3] Leaving aside, perhaps, natural necessity.

[4] For discussion of the history of conventionalism and the reasons for its demise, see Thomasson (2020a).

is preferable to error theory in claiming that there is modal truth and that we can sometimes have knowledge of it. It is preferable to substantive or synthetic realism—platonism—in its metaphysics and epistemology. Platonism posits a realm of modal facts and properties knowledge of which becomes difficult to explain. Appeals to some kind of intuition are usually weak and naturalistically problematic. Normativism explains our knowledge of modal truths and its often a priori character in a naturalistically acceptable way, as knowledge of conceptual rules (see also Warren 2022a).

Modal normativism has been used to provide an account of non-vacuous counterpossibles with metaphysically impossible antecedents (Locke 2021) and of non-vacuous counterpossibles with (meta)logically impossible antecedents (Kocurek and Jerzak 2021). Consider the counterpossible: Were Goliath (the statue) to survive being flattened, it would be an abstract object. According to Locke, such counterpossibles have non-vacuous readings that express[5] the consequences of changing our semantic rules only as much as the antecedent demands.[6] This counterpossible expresses the claim that if the application conditions of statue names like "Goliath" were changed so as to continue to apply after flattening, Goliath would be an abstract object. Locke argues that this is false, because when we imagine changing the application conditions of "Goliath" only so much that it continues to apply after being flattened, we have not changed that part of the application conditions that ensures it only applies to concrete objects. Kocurek and Jerzak (2021) argue for the same idea regarding counterfactuals with (meta)logically impossible antecedents. According to them, a counterpossible such as "If intuitionistic logic were correct, the continuum hypothesis would be either

[5] It is important to note that expressing what would be the case if actual semantic rules had been different is not the same as expressing actual semantic rules. According to normativism, only necessities express actual semantic rules, so only if a counterpossible is necessary (and some may be; see Section 5.3) does it express actual semantic rules. One could simply avoid talk of "expressing" here by saying that non-vacuous readings of counterpossibles involve changing semantic rules. Thus, when I say "normativist account of counterpossibles," I do not mean normativism *about* counterpossibles, viz., the view that counterpossibles express actual semantic rules; I simply mean what the normativist says is going on in non-vacuous counterpossibles, viz., that we consider actually adopting different semantic rules. I thank an anonymous reviewer for pressing me to clarify this.

[6] This is the normativist analogue of "in the nearest possible world where the antecedent is true." In general, the normativist can give a semantic interpretation of Baron, Colyvan, and Ripley's (2017) account of the evaluation of countermathematicals—instead of conceiving ourselves as "twiddling" mathematical facts and thinking through the ramifications, we "twiddle" concepts, their application conditions, etc., and think through the ramifications. I discuss this below. This same normativist idea applies to Reutlinger's (2016) account of the evaluation of counterfactuals, discussed in Chapter 4, which doesn't rely on any notion of nearness and only requires that there is *some* way of making the antecedent true that also makes the consequent true.

true or not true" has a non-vacuous reading that expresses the consequences of accepting the intuitionist's semantic rules for "or" and "not". On this reading, it is false. Of course, on a standard Lewisian (1973) semantics of counterfactuals, all counterpossibles are vacuously true. One straightforward amendment to the Lewisian account is to introduce impossible worlds (Brogaard and Salerno 2013; see Kocurek 2021 for a survey of approaches to counterpossibles). One feature of normativism is that it can provide an account of countermathematicals that avoids both the extravagant ontological commitment to impossible worlds and the use of a contradiction-tolerant non-classical logic.

The following terms will be helpful. Einheuser (2011) called readings of counterfactuals on which we consider actually adopting different semantic rules "counterconceptual" readings[7] and readings on which we do not change our semantic rules "countersubstratum" readings.[8] Note that these do not refer to kinds of counterfactual but to ways of reading counterfactuals. Using this distinction, we can say that according to the normativist, counterpossibles are non-vacuous on counterconceptual readings.

In many instances of counterfactual reasoning, we automatically give countersubstratum readings of counterfactuals; that is, we continue to use our actual semantic rules (Kripke 1980; Wright 1985; see Kocurek, Jerzak, and Rudolph 2020 for cases where it is natural to give counterfactuals counterconceptual readings). It is plausible that this is how we naturally read so-called independence conditionals such as "even if our semantic rules had been different, the necessities would not have been different" (Thomasson 2007a, 2020a). The normativist can accept this: countersubstratum readings of that counterfactual are indeed true.

Normativism, as I have discussed it so far, is a view about specifically *metaphysical* and *logical* necessity. Here I extend normativism to mathematical necessity and extend the normativist treatment of counterfactuals with metaphysically and (meta)logically impossible antecedents to counterfactuals with mathematically impossible antecedents. Thus, the mathematical normativist says that claims like "2 + 2 = 4" or "The internal angles of (Euclidean) triangles sum to 180 degrees" express semantic rules governing

[7] This is similar to some two-dimensionalists' notion of considering a possible world as actual, especially, Stalnaker (2001). See the discussion in Chapter 8, note 34 of this chapter, and note 18 of Kocurek and Jerzak (2021, 683). Einheuser's distinction is also very similar to that used by some generality relativists in explicating the kind of modality they require (e.g., Studd 2019, 146–147).

[8] The normativist can agree with the Lewisian that all countersubstratum readings of counterpossibles are vacuously true. This is Kocurek and Jerzak's (2021) view.

the terms therein, and that countermathematicals like "If it had been that 2 + 2 = 5, then it would have been that I am a jazz musician" express the consequences of changing our semantic rules only as much as the antecedent demands.

5.3. The Normative Role of Mathematics in Scientific Explanation

I propose to extend the normativist treatment of counterpossibles with metaphysically and (meta)logically impossible antecedents to counterpossibles with mathematically impossible antecedents. Thus, I take non-vacuous countermathematicals to express consequences of changes in the rules governing mathematical concepts.[9] For example, return to the countermathematicals:

> Were the trefoil knot isotopic to the unknot, Terry's trefoil knot would have been isotopic to the unknot.
>
> Were the trefoil knot isotopic to the unknot, Terry's untieable knot would have been trefoil.

The normativist should interpret these as expressing something like:

> Were the semantic rules governing the application of the term "trefoil knot" such that, wherever it applied, "isotopic to the unknot" also applied, Terry's trefoil knot would have been isotopic to the unknot.
>
> Were the semantic rules governing the application of the term "trefoil knot" such that, wherever it applied, "isotopic to the unknot" also applied, Terry's untieable knot would have been trefoil.

where we consider actually adopting the semantic rule specified in the antecedent. These normativist interpretations should preserve the original countermathematicals' truth values. Thankfully, it seems that they do—the

[9] Here I will not rely on any particular account of the distinction between mathematical and non-mathematical concepts, which should not matter for my argument. The distinction may turn out to be disjunctive—a mathematical concept is either an arithmetical concept or a geometrical concept or. . . , where an arithmetical concept is a concept of quantity, a geometrical concept is a concept of space, etc. I do not think it is necessary for my argument that there should even be a clear distinction.

first counterfactual above is (weakly) necessarily true and the second is not. That is, in every world where Terry has a trefoil knot, the first counterfactual, but not the second, is true. Remember that we are to consider actually adopting the semantic rule specified in the antecedent: were we to imagine actually adopting the semantic rule that wherever "trefoil knot" applies, "isotopic to the unknot" applies, then "isotopic to the unknot" would have applied to the knot of Terry's to which "trefoil" applies; so, via semantic descent, Terry's trefoil knot would have been isotopic to the unknot.

I just characterized these countermathematicals *modally*: the first is (weakly) *necessarily* true and the second is not. The necessity involved here does not seem to be mathematical necessity, so the *mathematical* normativist *need* not say that it expresses a semantic rule, but I will suggest a way to say just that: the first counterfactual, but not the second, is a consequence of actual semantic rules governing the terms therein. Given that the first countermathematical is similar to a case of universal instantiation (i.e., if for all *x*, *x* is F, then *a* is F), I suggest that it follows from semantic rules governing the logical terms involved, such as "wherever."[10]

What about clause (b) of NOCA? This clause deals with necessitation, and though it is unclear whether this is *mathematical* necessitation, I will suggest a way to say that such necessitation claims express semantic rules. The fact that Terry's trefoil knot is distinct from the unknot necessitates that he will fail to untie his trefoil knot. This is usually cashed out as "necessarily, if Terry's trefoil knot is distinct from the unknot, then he will fail to untie his trefoil knot." That conditional is arguably an expression of actual semantic rules governing the terms therein—it expresses the analytic entailment of the consequent by the antecedent. Thomasson (2007b, 44–45) provides the following explanation of analytic entailment:

> Given the frame-level application conditions associated with singular and sortal terms, for any terms 'p' and 'q,' where the application conditions for 'p' are also sufficient conditions for 'q' to apply, claims such as '(A) p exists' analytically entail claims that '(a) q exists,' for example, the application conditions for 'house' in a situation are sufficient to ensure the application of 'building,' so 'There is a house' analytically entails 'There is a building.'

[10] Does this commit me to a kind of logicism? I do not think so. I would only be worried if I were committed to the claim that all purely mathematical truths are expressions of rules governing logical concepts. I certainly am not committed to that; and note that the countermathematical in question is not purely mathematical. I thank a reviewer for bringing this worry to my attention.

> While this guarantees that there are analytic interrelations between claims that there is something of a given sort and that there is something of the subsuming category, such analytic entailments hold generally for any terms with the relevant relation between their application conditions, whether or not these are terms of the same category.

Similarly, the application conditions for "is distinct from the unknot" are also sufficient conditions for "will fail to untie his trefoil knot" to apply. Thus, "Terry's trefoil knot is distinct from the unknot" analytically entails "Terry will fail to untie his trefoil knot." The final line of the Thomasson quote is important because these are not singular or sortal terms; "is distinct from the unknot" and "will fail to untie" do not even apply to the same object—one applies to Terry's trefoil knot, the other to Terry. But that is not a problem—the conditions for "is distinct from the unknot" to apply to Terry's trefoil knot in a situation are sufficient to ensure the application of "will fail to untie his trefoil knot" to Terry. Nothing in the above account of analytic entailment implies that the relevant terms must apply to the same object, and such "cross-object" analytic entailments are common. If one insisted that both apply to the same object we could simply rephrase the latter as "will fail to be untied by Terry," so that both apply to the knot.

Before concluding this section, let me show how normativism deflates two other accounts: Pincock's (2015) abstract dependence account and Baron's (2024) Pythagorean proposal. NOCA is quite similar to Pincock's account, though I narrow the explananda (i.e., the things being explained), and I elaborate the kinds of counterfactual that the ontic relation of instantiation supports, or must support to figure in a DME. Being ontic accounts of DME that rely on ontic relations of instantiation between abstract mathematical and concrete phenomena, NOCA and Pincock's account would be especially suited to the EIA—if either account is the right account of DME, then, it would seem, platonism straightforwardly follows.[11] However, my central argument is that normativism about mathematical necessity undermines this

[11] To be clear: I do not intend my main argument to apply only to explicitly counterfactual ontic accounts. Pincock's account, for example, though an ontic dependence account, never explicitly mentions counterfactuals. It is plausible that any ontic account will be a counterfactual account, at least partially, even if not explicitly billed as such, since ontic accounts posit a dependence relation between ontic explanans and ontic explanandum, and this dependence relation will undoubtedly support counterfactuals. Regardless, any account of DME according to which purely mathematical claims refer to platonistic facts and/or applied mathematical claims refer to instantiations of mathematical objects—that is, any ontic account of DME—is a target of my argument, whether it explicitly appeals to counterfactuals or whether it explicitly appeals to the specific relation of instantiation.

inference and, moreover, that proponents of ontic accounts can consistently accept normativism.

It is important to note that Pincock did not intend to give an account of DME. He wanted to argue 1) that there is a kind of explanation involving abstract entities, which he called "abstract explanation," 2) that abstract explanation is not causal, and 3) that causal explanation and abstract explanation both count as explanation in virtue of providing information about objective dependence relations. It is clear, though, that the examples usually given of DME, including Trefoil Knot, are abstract explanations in Pincock's sense.

Pincock motivates his abstract dependence account using the explanation of Plateau's three laws for soap-film surfaces and bubbles:

> First, a compound soap bubble or a soap film spanning a wire frame consists of flat or smoothly curved surfaces smoothly joined together. Second, the surfaces meet in only two ways: Either exactly three surfaces meet along a smooth curve or six surfaces (together with four curves) meet at a vertex. Third, when surfaces meet along curves or when curves and surfaces meet at points, they do so at equal angles. In particular, when three surfaces meet along a curve, they do so at angles of 120° with respect to one another, and when four curves meet at a point, they do so at angles of close to 109°. (Almgren and Taylor 1976, 82, quoted in Pincock 2015, 858)

The explanation of soap films' satisfying these laws relies on the mathematical fact that certain mathematical objects called *almost minimal sets* satisfy Plateau's three laws and that soap films instantiate almost minimal sets. As Pincock writes, "Many mathematical structures have concrete systems as instances. The almost minimal sets have soap films as some of their instances, and this is what makes facts about sets relevant to facts about soap films" (2015, 865–866).

Pincock suggests that the kind of explanation involved here—so-called abstract explanation—is akin to causal explanation on Woodward's (2003) interventionist account, though shorn of its interventionism. Woodward emphasizes that the ability to answer what-if-things-had-been-different questions (w-questions) regarding the explanandum—thus, knowledge of information about counterfactual dependence relations—is constitutive of explanation. Woodward even suggests that there could be non-causal explanations in cases where information about counterfactual dependence relations is provided, but those relations cannot sensibly be interpreted as involving interventions (2003, 221). Similarly, for Pincock, what makes both causal and abstract explanations *explanations* is that they reveal "objective dependence relations." The relation between almost minimal sets and soap films is not a causal one, but it is, Pincock argues, a kind of objective dependence relation—what he calls abstract dependence.[12] In the case at hand, Pincock suggests that the abstract dependence relation in question is instantiation. Thus, an abstract explanation (or at least one important kind of abstract explanation) seems to be an explanation in which a concrete object is shown to possess a certain property because it is an instantiation of an abstract object that possesses that property.

In Chapter 4, I also generalized Woodward's interventionism within an ontic account of explanation, and I also suggested that the ontic relation involved in DMEs is instantiation. I was specifically concerned, though, with giving an account of DME that satisfies the three desiderata, which, I argued, requires narrowing the explananda of DMEs. One important thing that helps the subsequent deflation of NOCA work is that platonism actually plays no role in NOCA's ability to satisfy the desiderata. I introduced mathematical objects and instantiation relations in order to provide truthmakers for the relevant countermathematicals. That platonism plays no role in NOCA's ability to satisfy the three desiderata can be seen by the fact that the two clauses of NOCA satisfy all three desiderata by themselves, without relying on any specific metaphysics of mathematics. Platonism is merely used to provide a metaphysics for the relevant countermathematicals. I argue that normativism can demystify the countermathematicals involved in DMEs without positing substantive mathematical facts or abstract instantiation relations. All the platonistic language of NOCA can remain, but it is shorn of its substantive ontological commitments.

Kostić and Khalifa (2021) pick up on the fact that the two clauses of NOCA satisfy all three desiderata by themselves and argue that this shows you can have a non-ontic account of DME, specifically, a non-ontic account of topological explanations like Bridges. Their counterfactual account (see also Kostić 2020), however, faces some of the same problems as Reutlinger's (e.g., problems with the distinctiveness desideratum and the Eulerian

[12] Pincock is not clear about the relation between abstract dependence and counterfactual/countermathematical dependence, but the very idea of a dependence relation, as well as the comparison with Woodward's account, seems to imply counterfactual dependence, regardless of whether the dependence relation in question can be *reduced* to or *analyzed* in terms of counterfactuals. Regardless, my argument that normativism renders invalid any inference from Pincock's account to platonism does not depend on this.

network), though, again, neither of those theories is intended as an account of DME generally. Kostić and Khalifa (2021) exclude many reversals by appeal to the context of the why-question. In typical contexts, when one asks a reversed why-question, one is more interested in something like a causal explanation, and Kostić and Khalifa bite the bullet for atypical contexts. That's fine; everyone ingests some lead—we just have to weigh it and compare at the end. Kostić and Khalifa exclude other reversals without appeal to the ontic by stipulating that in a topological explanation, the explanans (i.e., the thing that explains) has a topological property and the explanandum has a non-topological property. But if topological properties, non-topological properties, and the distinction between them are all non-ontic, then it seems that whether an explanation is topological is up to us. So, something ontic must still enforce directionality. Finally, if one is trying to avoid the ontic, it's hard to see the motivation for or the plausibility of the thesis that all of *that* is ontic (topological properties, non-topological properties, and the distinction between them), but there are no explanatory ontic relations between topological properties and non-topological properties, or no ontic basis for the counterfactuals relating them.

Although the two clauses of NOCA satisfy the three desiderata by themselves, instantiation can help NOCA exclude some problem cases, as I mentioned in Chapter 4. Obviously, Pincock's account also appeals to instantiation. How can normativism deflate instantiation? I argue that, for the normativist, instantiation should be seen not as an ontic relation but as a semantic one. To say that some concrete object instantiates a mathematical object is just to say that the relevant mathematical concept applies to it. Instantiation is concept application.[13] Or, more carefully, instantiation claims *express* facts about concept application. In some intuitive sense, "*a* is *F*," "'*F*' applies to *a*," and "*a* instantiates *F*-ness" "say the same thing". Instantiation claims don't express conceptual *rules of use*, so they are neither necessary nor analytic, but they express nonetheless.

Notice that the relation of concept application has features that are important for the explanatory aims of NOCA and Pincock's account. They both rely on the asymmetry of instantiation to buttress their theories'

[13] I cannot here specify what I take the relation of concept application to be (though I am sympathetic to Thomasson 2007b). I do not think my arguments require any particular account of that relation, though obviously an across-the-board deflationist (not merely a deflationist about mathematical objects) will want an account that does not appeal to substantive (i.e., synthetic) abstract objects. I discuss concepts more in Chapter 6.

explanatory credentials and exclude certain reversals and other potential counterexamples. Concept application too is an asymmetric relation:[14] "trefoil knot" (or "almost minimal set") applies to some concrete object, but that concrete object does not apply to "trefoil knot" (or "almost minimal set"). On NOCA, the mathematical fact that the trefoil knot is distinct from the unknot does not explain why the knot Terry untied is not trefoil because that mathematical fact is not instantiated in that natural fact.[15] According to the normativist interpretation of NOCA, with its construal of instantiation as concept application, the mathematical fact that the trefoil knot is distinct from the unknot does not explain why the knot Terry untied is not trefoil because the mathematical concept "trefoil knot" does not apply to anything in that natural fact (for the same reason that the trefoil knot is not instantiated in that natural fact—there is no trefoil knot there!). On Pincock's account, abstract explanations show that a concrete object is a certain way because it is an instantiation of an abstract object that is that way. According to the deflated, normativist interpretation of Pincock's account, in abstract explanations some predicate is shown to apply to a concrete object in virtue of the fact that its predication is analytically entailed by the predication of a mathematical predicate to it: soap films satisfy Plateau's laws because "almost minimal set" applies to them, and the application of "almost minimal set" to a concrete object analytically entails the application of "satisfies Plateau's laws" to it. Thus, neither NOCA nor Pincock's account by themselves—i.e., without anti-normativist premises—can be used in the EIA to support platonism.

Baron's (2024) new Pythagorean account of DME can also be deflated. Recall that on this view, the way a DME works is by showing that a physical system shares intrinsic mathematical properties with a mathematical object and that these physically instantiated mathematical properties either guarantee the presence of other mathematical properties and the physical states that possess them, or rule out other mathematical properties and any associated physical states (2024, 664). The trouble is that Baron doesn't

[14] At least in the relevant cases, such as in DMEs, where concept application is intended to take the place of the instantiation of an abstract object by a concrete object. As Earl Conee (personal communication) pointed out to me, perhaps the application of the concept *concept* to itself is not asymmetric. However, I do not think this is a case where we would say a concrete object instantiates an abstract object.

[15] As I have already noted, I do not need the instantiation relation to exclude this reversal—the counterfactual clauses of NOCA already do that. I suggested that the instantiation relation is what ontically grounds the counterfactual clauses of NOCA. In other cases below, appeal to instantiation seems required to exclude reversals.

explicate the metaphysics behind these "guaranteeing" and "ruling out" relations. NOCA does: in this context, guaranteeing and ruling out are forms of necessitation or, normativistically speaking, analytic entailment. *X* guarantees *Y* if and only if *X* metaphysically necessitates *Y*, and *X* rules out *Y* if and only if *X* metaphysically necessitates ~*Y*. Normativistically, *X* guarantees *Y* if and only if "*X*" analytically entails "*Y*", and *X* rules out *Y* if and only "*X*" analytically entails "~*Y*". Why are the mathematical property of being isotopic to the unknot and the physical property of having untied the knot ruled out by the mathematical property of being a trefoil knot? Because "being a trefoil knot" analytically entails "not having untied the knot" and "not being isotopic to the unknot".

Recall that, in Chapter 4, I had to exclude "the Eulerian network" from our mathematical ontology in order to avoid certain counterexamples. For normativistically deflated NOCA, a privileged ontology that doesn't include the Eulerian network is basically a conceptual scheme that doesn't include the concept of an Eulerian network. This idea is much less mysterious than that of an objectively privileged ontology in which the Eulerian network doesn't exist. Yes, we can possess the concept of an Eulerian network—that is how I am able to talk about the Eulerian network—but it is not one that mathematicians use, because they individuate networks by their structure of nodes and vertices. I concede that if mathematicians did use the concept of an Eulerian network, then this would be a DME within their conceptual scheme. Thus, in one respect, deflating NOCA brings it closer to Lange's view, according to which the empirical fact in a DME need only be *understood* to be constitutive of the physical task or arrangement at issue. One *could* understand a network's permitting an Eulerian walk as being constitutive of it, and we *could* have a scheme that includes the concept of an Eulerian network. This may seem like a problematic concession, but I think an objectively privileged ontology, according to which such a concept is not just useless, but useless *because* it does not latch onto anything in an objective mathematical reality, is worse.[16] My argument for why we should prefer NOCA to Lange's view and all others still holds: it is still the case that only

[16] I'm arguing that holding an objectively privileged ontology is worse than deflating NOCA. I am not arguing that abandoning an objectively privileged ontology directly leads to deflated NOCA or to normativism generally—it doesn't. So-called plenitudinous platonists have recognized the problems with an objectively privileged ontology and have abandoned it, instead holding that all possible (i.e., consistent) mathematical objects exist (Linsky and Zalta 1995; Balaguer 1998). Field (2022) argues that the differences between fictionalism, conventionalism, and plenitudinous platonism are relatively minor. I disagree, and I return to this in Chapter 8.

NOCA places DME within a picture of explanation, the generalized ontic conception, where all explanations are united by ontically backed counterfactual dependence.

Let us take stock so far. I explained modal normativism, extended it to mathematics, and showed how it can accommodate non-vacuous countermathematicals. I gave a semantic account of the instantiation relation as concept application. By adopting normativism and the semantic account of instantiation, NOCA, Pincock's account, and Baron's Pythagorean account are deflated and deprived of their ability to support platonism.[17] The EIA's inference from the existence of DMEs to platonism is rendered invalid—normativism allows one to accept the former and deny the latter.[18]

5.4. Objections

One objection to my normativist treatment of countermathematicals is that it only works for certain explananda, namely those that only depend on a mathematical fact, and not for cases like Cicadas or Honeycombs (Lyon and Colyvan 2008), whose explananda also depend on natural facts. Of course, if I am right, these explananda must also be narrowed so as only to depend on mathematical facts, if they are to be given DMEs. Regardless, the countermathematicals in these cases work the same way as the others.

We need a normativist evaluation procedure for countermathematicals. We could, like Baron, Colyvan, and Ripley (2017), hold fixed the "morphism" between mathematical structures and empirical structures, so that changes in mathematical structures have ramifications into empirical structures. For a normativist, this would mean holding fixed that the concept in question applies, ramifying into the world accordingly (i.e., we imagine that the world changes so that the changed concept still applies). I don't think there's anything wrong with that, but I think we can do something much simpler, without talk of worlds altogether, which seems to track how we actually reason through countermathematical scenarios. According to normativism, mathematical truths express semantic rules, which can be used as rules of

[17] Reutlinger's (2016) CTE was never intended as an account of DME, but normativism would obviously deprive it of any ability it might have to support platonism too.

[18] Obviously, I have not shown how every account of DME can be deflated, but normativism deflates mathematical necessity generally, so any account that appeals to mathematical truths or instantiation or countermathematicals—i.e., any account of DME—can be deflated. The specifics will obviously vary in each case.

inference, especially for transforming empirical descriptions.[19] Let's draw on that in our evaluation procedure: a countermathematical is true when and only when[20] the new rule of inference expressed in the antecedent licenses the derivation of the consequent from given empirical (and other unchanged mathematical) background premises. Obviously, other inference rules that have not been changed are also allowed in the derivation. This is similar to what Lewis (1973) called the metalinguistic theory of counterfactuals.[21]

This evaluation procedure works for the countermathematicals at issue in DMEs regardless of whether the explananda are narrowed. Take the countermathematical "If 13 hadn't been a prime number, then North American cicadas wouldn't have had 13-year life cycles." In the present case, we imagine actually adopting the rule that "prime" does not apply to anything "13" applies to. This can be seen as a rule of inference for descriptions containing "prime" and "13". Since the consequent follows from given background premises (e.g., that having a life-cycle period that minimizes intersection with other periods is evolutionarily advantageous and that prime periods minimize intersection) using the new rule of inference expressed in the antecedent, it is true on this evaluation procedure that the cicadas wouldn't have had 13-year life cycles. Let us examine the reasoning of Baron, Colyvan, and Ripley (2017, 11) regarding this countermathematical and show that this is exactly what they are doing—using the mathematical claim in the antecedent as an inference rule to reach the consequent via given background premises; their platonistic excesses are just that. They are concerned to show specifically the truth of the countermathematical, "If, in addition

[19] The fact that such inference rules can be used on descriptions of "non-physical" things—e.g., metamathematically—does not affect the point. I address metamathematics in Chapter 8.

[20] "When and only when" means just that—this is just your standard biconditional. I am not here giving semantic truth-conditions for countermathematicals. That would imply that I take countermathematicals to *mean* something about rules of inference and derivability, but I don't. Nor am I giving metaphysical truth-conditions, i.e., truthmakers, for countermathematicals. I discuss semantics and the importance of the distinction between truth-conditions and truthmakers in Chapter 6.

[21] Unlike most other defenders of metalinguistic theories, I do not prefer it because I have some problem with possible worlds. Carnapians let a thousand languages bloom. And I don't intend to commit myself to the linguistic ersatzist view that possible worlds *just are* sets of sentences or something of that sort, though what I say is consistent with such a view. (Even the modal realist will admit that to each world there corresponds a unique set of propositions describing it—the linguistic ersatzist simply claims that the correspondence is identity [Bennett 2003, 303].) I prefer this metalinguistic theory of countermathematicals only because it doesn't require the complication of holding fixed that the changed concepts apply, it seems to describe what we actually do when we evaluate countermathematicals, and I feel it just comports better with the idea that mathematical truths express rules of inference.

to 13 and 1, 13 had the factors 2 and 6, North American periodical cicadas would not have 13-year life cycles." Here is their reasoning:

> To evaluate this counterfactual, we start in the mathematics. [1] We hold fixed as much as we can by changing multiplication to behave like multiplication*. This leaves 13's factors as desired. This gives us a structure, S*, that is just like the natural numbers, except that 13 is not prime, and factorises via 2 and 6. [2] Because we are holding fixed the relationship between the mathematical and physical structures, the physical structure that is now being mapped onto S* must twist to keep up with the counterfactual change. [3] The result is that an interval of 13 years is now divisible into six two-year segments, or into two six-year segments. [4] It follows from this that a cicada with a 13-year life cycle will overlap with predators that have two-year and six-year life cycles and [5] thus that 13 is not an optimal way to avoid predation. [6] So cicadas won't evolve 13-year life cycles. [7] So [the countermathematical] is true. (11)

The first three claims, which I've collectively labeled [1], are, according to the normativist, simply telling us to imagine adopting a new inference rule according to which 13 has the factors 1, 2, 6, and 13, while leaving all other inference rules unchanged. Claim [2] is the morphism claim we discussed above, the normativist analogue of which would be holding fixed that the concept in question applies. Since we are here illustrating a different evaluation procedure that relies simply on descriptions and not on worlds, we can ignore claim [2]. Claim [3] is simply an application of our new inference rule: since 13 has the factors 1, 2, 6, and 13, an interval of 13 years is divisible into six two-year segments, or into two six-year segments. Claim [4] is inferred from [3] using normal inference rules that have not been changed, which is fine since [1] tells us that only one inference rule has changed. Similarly, claim [5] is inferred from [4], and claim [6] is inferred from [5] and empirical background premises (e.g., that nothing suboptimal will evolve), using normal inference rules that have not been changed. They conclude [7], that the countermathematical is true. Thus, they have concluded that the countermathematical is true, because its consequent can be inferred from given background premises using the inference rule specified in the antecedent (and any other unchanged inference rules).

The same points apply, mutatis mutandis, to Honeycombs and other cases. For example, if the structure that divides a planar region into regions of equal area using the least total perimeter were not a hexagonal grid, then the honeybees' combs would not have been a hexagonal grid. Here we imagine adopting the rule that "hexagonal grid" does not apply to anything "structure that divides a planar region into regions of equal area using the least total perimeter" applies to. Again, since the consequent follows from given background premises (e.g., that producing the largest honeycomb cells using the least wax is evolutionarily advantageous) using the new rule of inference expressed in the antecedent, it is true on my account that the combs would not have formed a hexagonal grid. Finally, take Strawberries. Mother fails to divide her 23 strawberries evenly between her three children. Why? Because 23 is indivisible by 3. Had 23 been divisible by 3, mother would not have failed. This countermathematical is true because on the normativist evaluation procedure the consequent can be derived from given background premises using the new rule of inference expressed in the antecedent. In general, whenever mathematical necessities appear ineliminably in a scientific explanation, they play the normative role of making explicit the conceptual norms linking the mathematical concepts applied in its empirical explanans-statement(s) to mathematical concepts applied in its empirical explanandum-statement. That is their function as expressions of rules of inference, rules for transforming empirical descriptions.

The metalinguistic theory of counterfactuals faces a notorious problem: the problem of cotenability (Goodman 1947). Consider the counterfactual "If this match had been struck, it would have lit." According to the metalinguistic theory, this is true if and only if "it lights" can be derived from "this match is struck." Obviously, this derivation doesn't work without further premises. But what further premises is it legitimate to include? Certainly allowed are laws of nature and premises that are implicit in the context of the conversation we are having. And equally certainly, we cannot allow the truth that the match was not struck. That would generate a contradiction and, assuming classical logic, every consequent would follow. Goodman argued that cotenability with the initial premise (i.e., "this match is struck") was a condition for inclusion into the further premises, where a sentence S is cotenable with the initial premise P if and only if it is not true that if P were true, then S would be false. Of course, he knew that this was circular, since the definition of cotenability was given in counterfactual terms. The problem of cotenability is to provide a definition that isn't in counterfactual terms.

My metalinguistic approach to countermathematicals may avoid this problem because we are only changing a rule of inference. We are not changing any premises; we are using actual, rather than counterfactual, premises. Obviously, we need to know what the given premises are, and there are decisions that need to be made about what premises and rules of inference to hold fixed in counterconceptual scenarios, but these decisions exactly parallel the decisions about what to hold fixed in any account of countermathematical reasoning (e.g., the decisions Baron, Colyvan, and Ripley must make about what ontic facts and morphic relationships to hold fixed). I want to emphasize that I am merely showing what the normativist must hold fixed to make the countermathematicals come out true. As Baron, Colyvan, and Ripley (2017, 12) note, "To ask whether it is reasonable to hold these facts fixed when evaluating counterfactuals is to call into doubt the truth of the counterfactuals at issue." However, even if this does not avoid the problem of cotenability, I am not trying to give a reductive account of counterfactuals generally, so I have no problem relying on counterfactuals to explicate countermathematicals. And, since I have no problem with possible worlds, I have no problem adopting Lewis' (1973, 69) possible worlds solution to the problem. According to Lewis, "χ is cotenable with an entertainable antecedent φ at a world *i* if and only if χ holds throughout some φ-permitting sphere around *i*." Defining cotenability this way makes the metalinguistic approach logically equivalent to the possible worlds approach (Lewis 1973, 69). Again, the only reason I prefer the metalinguistic approach is because it seems to me simpler and better describes our actual reasoning.

This leads nicely to another objection, that counterconceptual readings of countermathematicals incorrectly make the dependence of natural fact on mathematical fact into a dependence of the meaning of descriptions of natural fact on the meaning of descriptions of mathematical fact. I think there is something right about this objection, but it is obviously question-begging: it assumes anti-normativism—it assumes that pure mathematics offers descriptions of mathematical facts. What is right about it is something I do not take to be objectionable: that mathematical truths express rules of description—semantic rules—and there is nothing more to them. That is objectionable to many, but it is just normativism.

Another important objection is that mathematical normativism makes a mystery of why everyone in the world adopts the same semantic rules and why mathematics has any explanatory power (in the standard, "non-distinctive" sense not at issue in the DME debate). A complete answer to this objection would probe, among other things, the nature of proof, meaning, and their relation and can only be given in a separate book, but I think I can say enough here to show that these problems are not fatal, or at least not obviously so.

First, the objection would prove far too much if it were correct. I do not think either the agreement on, or the explanatory power of, mathematics is any less mysterious according to platonism or any other (non-empiricist)[22] anti-platonism. Take fictionalism, for example, which I discuss in Chapter 8. The objection applies equally to it—fictionalism makes just as much a mystery of why everyone in the world adopts the same fictions and why some of these mere fictions have explanatory power. Second, and more substantively, there are a few direct answers the normativist can give as to why mathematics has explanatory power and why everyone in the world adopts the same semantic rules—though, importantly, note that there does exist disagreement in mathematics, just as in logic (e.g., Balaguer 2017; Beall and Restall 2006; Davies 2005; Priest 2013, 2019). Some answers to the latter question can and have been given, mutatis mutandis, by the fictionalist. For example, as Colyvan (2011) notes, the fictionalist can appeal to constraints on writing the fiction of mathematics, such as that "new installments" (i.e., theories) in the fiction be self-consistent, consistent with past installments, and not introduce unnecessary "characters" (i.e., entities). The normativist can appeal to these as constraints on the creation of semantic rules as well. The normativist (and fictionalist) can also appeal to a shared (culture- or species-specific) aesthetic sense (see Steiner 1998 for a provocative discussion of the role of aesthetics in mathematical theorizing). Mathematicians whose proposed semantic rules fail to meet these constraints are sanctioned by the mathematical community, inducing further agreement. Finally, the normativist can also explain agreement, at least in basic arithmetic and geometry, in the way that the empiricist does—by appeal to empirical regularity.[23] This is an idea prominent in Wittgenstein, who argued that the propositions of basic arithmetic and Euclidean geometry were empirical generalizations "hardened into rules" (i.e., rules of inference) and "put in the archives" (i.e., made immune from empirical refutation) (Bangu 2018; Steiner 1996, 2009 Wittgenstein [1956] 1978, 1976).[24]

[22] The empiricist could explain (some of) the agreement of mathematicians by appeal to the empirical regularities to which all mathematicians have access and that, according to them, (at least basic arithmetic and geometrical) mathematical truths describe.

[23] If Maddy (1990) is right that we can perceive some sets, perhaps some of basic set theory can also be accounted for this way.

[24] Perhaps this accounts for Kant's judgment that "7 + 5 = 12" is synthetic a priori ([1781/1787] 1998, B15).

Regarding the standard, "non-distinctive" explanatory power of mathematics, it is perfectly consistent for the normativist to say that (many) mathematical concepts have empirical content and that applied mathematical propositions are straightforwardly descriptive. Normativism is a theory of mathematical modality, not of the content of mathematical concepts.[25] Normativism is thus compatible with the claim that mathematical concepts have (or can have, after suitable empirical interpretation) empirical, descriptive content[26] and that this content contributes to mathematics' (non-distinctive) explanatory power by mapping (Pincock 2011; Bueno and French 2018), indexing (Melia 2000), or representing (Saatsi 2011) explanatorily relevant quantities, magnitudes, etc. If this seems strange, consider a comparison. Normativism about metaphysical modality is compatible with the claim that empirical concepts with descriptive content can figure in necessary truths. "Bachelor" is a concept with empirical, descriptive content and "bachelors are unmarried men" expresses a semantic rule governing it. Similarly, "triangle" is a concept with empirical, descriptive content and "triangles have three sides" expresses a semantic rule governing it. Normativism about mathematical modality does not rob mathematical concepts of their explanatory power. Furthermore, mathematical semantic rules need not be "arbitrary," as evidenced by the Wittgensteinian idea mentioned above that basic arithmetic and geometric truths are empirical generalizations "hardened into rules."[27] Perhaps there remains for the normativist some version of Wigner's (1960) problem of the "unreasonable effectiveness of mathematics"—though I think the Wittgensteinian idea

[25] Is normativism thus compatible with the claim that mathematical concepts have *abstract objects* as their content and that such concepts sometimes successfully substantively refer, i.e., platonism? Yes—this kind of normativist platonism would say that mathematical concepts refer to abstract objects in applied mathematical propositions but not in purely mathematical propositions. This would be a strange, seemingly entirely unmotivated, but not contradictory sort of platonism (somewhat akin to what Rayo [2009] called "irrelevance theory"). (Consider also the fact that expressivist non-naturalism in metaethics is not a contradictory position. The former is a semantic thesis; the latter a metaphysical one.) Notice that the possibility of normativist platonism does *not* deprive normativism of its ability to block the EIA. As I emphasized at the beginning of this chapter, the main thrust of this chapter is not that anti-platonism is true nor that normativism entails anti-platonism (it doesn't) but that the EIA is invalid because normativism allows the anti-platonist to accept the existence of DMEs while denying platonism.

[26] Compare Waismann's ([1930] 1986, 66) description of Russell's position: "For Russell the propositions of mathematics are, to be sure, a priori—they are tautologies—but the concepts are empirical." I address the empirical content of mathematical concepts in Chapter 6.

[27] Paul Audi (personal communication) helpfully suggested another sense in which semantic rules generally are non-arbitrary: presumably, the *reason* that, e.g., "unmarried" applies if "bachelor" applies, is that the features of the *world* in virtue of which the former applies are a subset of those in virtue of which the latter applies. A similar point is made by Thomasson (2007b, 70).

goes a long way to dispelling this—but this is a problem for everyone, and here I can only refer the reader elsewhere (see, e.g., Bangu 2006; Bueno and French 2018; Clark 2017; Steiner 2009a).[28]

Finally, there is the worry that deflating instantiation by treating it as expressing facts about concept application results in too many things being counted as DMEs.[29] For example, we want to explain why Claire has 5 apples. Because she has 2 + 3 apples and 2 + 3 = 5. The narrow explanandum would be the fact that Claire, who has 2 + 3 apples, has 5 apples. This weakly necessarily counterfactually depends only on the mathematical fact that 2 + 3 = 5; if 2 + 3 were not equal to 5, then Claire, who has 2 + 3 apples, would not have 5 apples. Thus, we have a DME of why Claire has 5 apples. I can't appeal to instantiation qua concept application to exclude this case, since the concepts "5" and "2 + 3" both apply in this scenario. Thus, there are as many DMEs as there are equations.

This is a great example, but I think the objection misses the mark. Let me note four things. First, it is not obvious to me that explanations like this are always bad. It seems like this would be a good explanation for someone who didn't know that 2 + 3 = 5, although I admit that perhaps my intuitions are conflating explanation and evidence. Second, the truth of the relevant countermathematical doesn't depend on its being read counterconceptually nor on instantiation claims' expressing facts about concept application. For example, I don't see why it wouldn't be true according to Baron, Colyvan, and Ripley's (2017) evaluation procedure. Third, why might some say 2 + 3 can't be (inflationarily) instantiated? Presumably they would say it's because 2 + 3 is not a mathematical object. But why? Don't "2 + 3" and "5" both refer to the same object? After all, that's when an identity statement is true—when the expressions flanking the identity symbol refer to the same object. 2 + 3 is not a strange conjunctive object composed of 2 and 3; it *is* 5. 2 + 3 is instantiable, because 5 is instantiable and 2 + 3 is identical to 5 (via identity elimination or Leibniz's law—the indiscernibility of identicals, not the identity of indiscernibles). So, non-normativists will also have to accept the instantiability of 2 + 3.

[28] Some readers may be thinking that any view like normativism was decisively refuted by Gödel's incompleteness theorems, which, according to some (including Gödel himself), support platonism. Much ink has been spilled on this, and I merely point the reader to some ideas that might be helpful to the normativist (Awodey and Carus 2004; Berto 2009; Floyd and Putnam 2000; Lampert 2018; Moore 1998; and Sayward 2001). See also the references in Chapter 8, note 9.

[29] I thank an anonymous reviewer for raising this objection.

Could non-normativists argue that 5, and, so, 2 + 3, isn't instantiable? But then what is the relation between the number 5 and Claire's 5 apples? If it isn't instantiation, call it "shminstantiation." Clearly shminstantiation is a relation that can figure in DMEs, since many DMEs appeal to numbers to represent various quantities and magnitudes. Surely, we don't want to say there are no DMEs that appeal to numbers. Fourth, because of the last two points, many other accounts seem to render this a DME too. If Mary's having 23 strawberries is constitutive of the physical task or arrangement at issue in Strawberries, presumably having 2 + 3 apples is in this case, so Lange's account counts it as a DME. Perhaps Lange could say that having 5 apples can be constitutive of a physical task or arrangement at issue, but having 2 + 3 apples can't. It's hard to see how that could be, given that having 5 apples and having 2 + 3 apples are identical facts.[30] Pincock's (2015) abstract dependence account and Baron's (2024) Pythagorean proposal similarly seem to have to accept this as a DME. Claire has 5 apples because her apples instantiate the property of being 2 + 3 (in quantity), and 2 + 3 = 5 (à la Pincock). Claire has 5 apples because the instantiation in the apples of the mathematical property of being 2 + 3 (in quantity) guarantees the instantiation of the mathematical property of being 5 (in quantity) (à la Baron). This case also clearly fits Reutlinger's (2016) CTE, since if Claire hadn't had 2 + 3 apples, she wouldn't have had 5 apples. Reutlinger may be able to exclude this case by invoking a more general exclusion of self-explanations—since Claire's having 2 + 3 apples and her having 5 apples are the same fact, one cannot be used to explain the other. This is plausible, though remember that Reutlinger's was not intended as an account of DME, and it is unclear whether Lange, Baron, and Pincock can make the same move work. On Lange's account, the explanans and explanandum in this case are not the same fact—the explanans is the mathematical fact that 2 + 3 = 5, which is also an explanans on Pincock's account. The other explanans on Pincock's account is, crucially, a fact about *instantiation*—the fact that Claire's apples instantiate the property of being 2 + 3 (in quantity)—and it is unclear whether, for Pincock, this is identical to the fact that she has 5 apples. The same can be said of Baron's Pythagorean account.

[30] Lange (2016, xviii–xix) mentions identity explanations favorably: "that Samuel Clemens and Mark Twain are identical explains non-causally why they have the same height, weight, and birth dates." Similarly, Lange might accept that there is some context where the fact that Claire's 2 + 3 apples are identical to her 5 apples explains non-causally why they have the same mass, price, etc. However, Kim's (2011, 104–105) arguments against identity explanations in the philosophy of mind may be relevant here. See also note 33.

Finally, I may be able to rule this case out by arguing that it is a case of denying one of the why-question's presuppositions, which is something distinct from explanation. The narrowed why-question presupposes that Claire's having 2 + 3 apples and her having 5 apples are distinct facts, and the putative explanation undermines this. The why-questioner thus gains understanding, certainly, but this understanding is not explanatory. Furthermore, it is merely in virtue of learning that 2 + 3 = 5 that the why-questioner learns that Claire's having 2 + 3 apples and her having 5 apples are not distinct facts, so the putative explanation succeeds in undermining the presupposition regardless of whether the content of that knowledge (that 2 + 3 = 5) is interpreted normativistically. In other words, this move doesn't require any particular metaphysics of what the fact that 2 + 3 = 5 consists in. However, this move is not available to Baron and Pincock because for them the explanandum is not narrowed, i.e., the empirical explanans is not presupposed, so the why-question doesn't presuppose that Claire's having 2 + 3 apples and her having 5 apples are distinct.[31] I conclude that, if counting this case as a DME is a problem, it's a problem—like the Eulerian network—many of us seem to have. I think NOCA has fewer problems overall than other accounts, and it belongs to a unified theory of explanation, the generalized ontic conception.

5.5. The Ontic Status and Explanatory Power of Deflated Ontic Accounts

In this section, I argue that there is no loss of explanatory power or ontic status in going normativist. First, explanatory power. I argue that, for NOCA—and I suspect for other accounts too, especially for other counterfactual accounts—the goodness of explanations offered by deflated accounts corresponds to—or perhaps surpasses—the goodness of explanations offered by inflated accounts. In other words, there is no reason to think that explanations offered by deflated accounts are worse;

[31] The move is available to Lange, since he narrows the explananda of DMEs, but it would seem to be inconsistent with his approval of identity explanations. See note 32. He could still accept the legitimacy of identity explanations if he could show that there are contexts wherein non-identity is not presupposed. This seems implausible though. In his (2022, 388) debate with Roski (2021) over "really statistical" explanations (which I discuss in Chapter 9), he says that an indication that *p* is a presupposition of the question "Why is *p* the case?" is that it is pragmatically infelicitous to say "I do not want to assume that *p* is the case. But why is *p* the case?" However, it seems to me similarly pragmatically infelicitous to say "I don't want to assume that Samuel Clemens and Mark Twain are distinct. But why are they so similar?"

there is no loss of explanatory power in going normativist. Now, to argue that explanations offered by deflated accounts are just as good, one needs some account of what makes an explanation in general good. One prominent answer to this question—the one that motivates many ontic accounts but does not presuppose an ontic account—is that explanations are good to the extent that they can answer w-questions (Woodward 2003; Woodward and Hitchcock 2003). This account of explanatory goodness fits seamlessly with NOCA.

The reason I think explanations offered by deflated accounts are just as good is that they allow one to give all the same answers to w-questions that explanations offered by inflated accounts allow one to give. For example, the inflated ontic accounts answer "No" to the following w-question: "If the color of Terry's shirt had been different, would his trefoil knot have been isotopic to the unknot?" However, they answer "Yes" to the following w-question: "If the trefoil knot were isotopic to the unknot, would Terry's trefoil knot have been isotopic to the unknot?" Normativism does not prevent one from giving the same answers to these w-questions. The normativist can accept or deny all the same counterfactuals as the platonist, and thus—if explanatory power is gauged by the ability to answer w-questions—explanations offered by deflated accounts are at least equally explanatorily powerful.

Deflated ontic accounts might even be more explanatorily powerful, since the normativist can answer some w-questions that the platonist cannot. Recall the distinction between counterconceptual and countersubstratum readings of counterfactuals. Well, a w-question is merely an interrogative counterfactual. We can therefore distinguish between counterconceptual and countersubstratum readings of w-questions. For example, consider the w-question "Were the semantic rules governing the application of the term 'trefoil knot' such that, wherever it applied, 'isotopic to the unknot' also applied, would Terry's trefoil knot have been isotopic to the unknot?" The platonist answers "No." The normativist agrees, when the w-question is given a countersubstratum reading. But the normativist answers "Yes" when it is given a counterconceptual reading, and the platonist misses this. Thus, if the ability to answer w-questions, not only on countersubstratum readings but on counterconceptual readings too, is constitutive of explanatory power, then deflated ontic accounts are actually more explanatorily powerful. This seems like a reason to prefer deflated ontic accounts. I will not push too hard here, though. I am happy if I can convince the reader that there is plausibly no loss of explanatory power in going normativist.

Next, I argue that deflated ontic accounts should still be considered ontic. In fact, I think deflated ontic accounts have a better shot at ontic status than inflated ontic accounts. Let me explain. Kuorikoski (2021) has objected that platonistic accounts of DME, such as my inflated NOCA and Pincock's, cannot accommodate the Woodwardian "same-object condition," which requires that in counterfactual reasoning we really are reasoning about the *same* object under different conditions. According to Kuorikoski, when reasoning countermathematically we cannot distinguish whether we are conceiving of a change in a given mathematical structure or simply a different mathematical structure. As Kuorikoski puts the objection, "if there is no difference between changing a specific property of a mathematical object into something else and simply contemplating the properties of a different mathematical object, we lose the very distinction between explanatory and classificatory information" (2021, 197). The idea is that, in countermathematicals like "Were the trefoil knot isotopic to the unknot, Terry's trefoil knot would have been isotopic to the unknot," neither I nor Pincock have given a stipulation-independent reason to think that a 'trefoil knot' isotopic to the unknot would still *be* a trefoil knot. This is required for the counterfactual to express an explanatory relationship between antecedent and consequent. Such stipulation-independent reasons would basically amount to a theory of the essential and accidental properties of all mathematical objects involved in DMEs. Not only is this task daunting, but there is no guarantee that upon its completion, all the countermathematicals involved in DMEs will come out as same-object-satisfying, i.e., that they will involve countermathematicals whose antecedents state changes in the object's accidental properties. And even if by sheer luck all countermathematicals involved in *current* DMEs come out as same-object-satisfying, there seems nothing to prevent a DME that appeals to the essential properties of a mathematical object, failing to make the associated countermathematical same-object-satisfying. For example, suppose that being prime is an essential property of 3 – 3 wouldn't be 3 if it weren't prime. There's no guarantee that there are no DMEs that appeal to the fact that 3 is prime. The countermathematical in that case would be "if 3 weren't prime, . . ." which by assumption isn't same-object-satisfying.

Normativists have a way out: the same object is the term/concept, individuated syntactically, merely with a different meaning/content. Of course, this means that Kuorikoski is right that countermathematicals are importantly different from standard counterfactuals, and that there is *something* more "representational" about countermathematicals—this shouldn't be surprising since, after all, normativists take mathematical truths to express rules for the use of language—but also note how for the normativist countermathematicals are importantly *different* from the clearly *epistemic* counterfactuals with which Kuorikoski contrasts ontic counterfactuals, such as his Sisley example (2021, 196). We are to imagine that a museum has a policy that all and only Sisleys are hung in room 18. The counterfactual "If this painting were in room 18, then it would be a Sisley" is false when read ontically but true when read epistemically as a claim about what it would be rational to believe if the antecedent were true. But counterconceptual interpretations of countermathematicals are *not* epistemic claims like this, for what is true according to a convention is not an epistemic matter. The distinction between ontic and epistemic readings of counterfactuals cuts across the distinction between countersubstratum and counterconceptual readings of counterfactuals. The counterconceptual reading of, e.g., "Were the trefoil knot isotopic to the unknot, Terry's trefoil knot would have been isotopic to the unknot" does not concern what it would be rational to believe were the trefoil knot isotopic to the unknot, nor what it would be rational to believe were the semantic/conceptual rules governing the application of the term/concept "trefoil knot" such that, wherever it applied, "isotopic to the unknot" also applied. The counterconceptual reading concerns what would be *true* according to the convention specified in the antecedent. Neither of the epistemic questions involves a shift in conceptual scheme or convention; in that sense epistemic readings are akin to countersubstratum readings.

We have seen that counterconceptual readings of countermathematicals are not epistemic in Kuorikoski's sense; they do not concern what it would be rational to believe if such and such were the case. But the question still remains whether normativism deprives ontic accounts of DME of their ontic status. Here is why I think it does not. Let us simply think about Woodwardian (2003) interventionism from the normativist perspective, using the distinction between counterconceptual and countersubstratum readings of counterfactuals. Take the countermathematical "Were the trefoil knot isotopic to the unknot, Terry's trefoil knot would have been isotopic to the unknot." The normativist says we should interpret this as expressing something like "Were the semantic/conceptual rules governing the application of the term/concept 'trefoil knot' such that, wherever it applied, 'isotopic to the unknot' also applied, Terry's trefoil knot would have been isotopic to the unknot." Read in the usual, countersubstratum way, this is simply false. Read counterconceptually, it is true. But note that this can be interpreted in terms of Woodwardian interventions. Thus, imagine an intervention on the concept/term "trefoil knot" (individuated syntactically) that changes the semantic/conceptual rules governing it. I take it that such an intervention would amount to an intervention on people's brains or on their social conventions (an intervention which would again presumably have its intended effect via changes in people's brains) or something similar—maybe evolutionary history or learning history if you're a teleosemanticist. How exactly this could work depends on the metaphysics of concepts. (I defend a kind of inferentialism in Chapter 6, but that's not important here.) I will just note two important things about this suggestion: 1) Woodward does not require that interventions be physically possible, so difficulty in imagining what this would look like in practice is no objection to it. 2) I reiterate that we need to individuate terms/concepts syntactically or some other way such that changes in the rules governing the term/concept do not change the term/concept itself.[32] Otherwise, we won't have the same term/concept pre- and post-intervention and won't satisfy the same-object condition.

Our intervention would change which claims the people upon whom we intervened make and which beliefs they have—they would now assert that Terry's trefoil knot is isotopic to the unknot. Of course, we, the interveners, using our actual semantic rules, would not say that, post-intervention, Terry's trefoil knot is isotopic to the unknot. We would say that Terry's trefoil knot is still distinct from the unknot, and we would take our intervention merely to have demonstrated a causal or mechanistic relation between their brain states or social conventions or whatever and what they think and say. Of course, that is true, but the normativist can say more. If *we* were actually to adopt their post-intervention semantic rules, *we* would say that Terry's trefoil knot is isotopic to the unknot. Counterconceptual readings of interventionist counterfactuals show that there is a kind of "counterconceptual causal"[33] dependence here—a dependence that one can see only by switching conceptual rules. The idea here is that x counterconceptually depends on y just in case the counterfactual "were $\sim y$ the case, then $\sim x$ would be the case" is true on a counterconceptual reading. So, since the counterfactual "Were the semantic/conceptual rules governing the application of the term/

[32] Terms/concepts are individuated this way for Chalmers' (2004, 169–170) orthographic contextual intensions and Stalnaker's (1978, 2001) diagonal propositions.

[33] Craver (2007; Craver, Glennan, and Povich 2021) adjusts Woodward's interventionism to give an account of mechanistic/constitutive, rather than causal, relevance. Perhaps it would be better to say that there is a "counterconceptual mechanistic" dependence here, depending on what is intervened upon (e.g., the brain or social conventions).

concept 'trefoil knot' such that, wherever it applied, 'isotopic to the unknot' also applied, Terry's trefoil knot would have been isotopic to the unknot" is true on a counterconceptual reading, the fact that Terry's trefoil knot is distinct from the unknot counterconceptually depends on the semantic/conceptual rules governing the application of the term/concept "trefoil knot". And when we think of the antecedent as brought about by an intervention, à la Woodward—that's "counterconceptual causal" dependence. When we give the previous counterfactual a counterconceptual reading and conceive the antecedent as brought about by an intervention, it is true. Thus, the fact that Terry's trefoil knot is distinct from the unknot "counterconceptually causally" depends on the semantic/conceptual rules governing the application of the term/concept "trefoil knot". Distinctively mathematical explanation is counterconceptual causal explanation.

It is important to note that the view is *not* that Terry failed to untie his trefoil knot because the way the mathematical concepts "trefoil knot" and "unknot" are used. Whether that is true depends crucially on what we mean by "because." The normativist can recognize the falsity of that claim just as she can recognize the falsity of the standard reading of the counterfactual "If the concept 'trefoil knot' were used differently, Terry would've untied his trefoil knot." Nevertheless, the view is that "Terry failed to untie his trefoil knot because the way the mathematical concepts 'trefoil knot' and 'unknot' are used" is getting at *something* important in a *roundabout* way, a way which was the purpose of this section, and the concept of counterconceptual dependence, to explicate.[34] Suppose we want to explain why Terry failed to make his triangle four-sided or failed to make his sister a bachelor, say by widowing her. In these cases, I think it is uncontroversial that it would be *adequate* for an explanation of Terry's failure to cite *only semantic facts*. (See Donaldson 2020 for a defense of this kind of idea.) One could adequately explain Terry's failure by pointing out that "bachelor" only applies to men. But one *needn't* cite semantic facts; one could also explain his failure by appeal to the fact that bachelors are (necessarily) men. But that is simply an expression of a conceptual rule, and the explanation that cites these rules themselves is adequate on its own. I submit that any impression that DMEs are different is an illusion.

[34] I think the "something important" is also brought out by similar work on conventionalism and analyticity (e.g., Topey 2019; Donaldson 2020; and Warren 2020). These authors, each in their own way, argue that there are some non-linguistic facts (i.e., those expressed by analytic truths) that can be explained by convention, contra opponents of truth by convention (e.g., Boghossian 1997).

Note that accepting that counterconceptual dependence is explanatory seems not to require any significant revision in our ordinary concept of explanation. Kocurek, Jerzak, and Rudolph (2020, 7) point out that there are many times when we accept that counterconceptual dependence is explanatory. They give the following nice example. In 2006, the International Astronomical Union (IAU) revised the scientific definition of "planet". According to this new definition, Pluto is no longer classified as a planet. Kocurek et al. maintain that the following claims are literally true:

> Whether or not Pluto is a planet *depends* on what definition the members of the IAU agree on.
> Part of what *explains* why Pluto is not a planet is the IAU's decision in 2006 to redefine 'planet'.
> *Because* of the IAU's decision in 2006, Pluto is not a planet. (2020, 7, my emphasis)

Kocurek, Jerzak, and Rudolph consider a Gricean attempt to explain this away. According to the Gricean, these claims express literal falsehoods, and we should instead understand them as communicating something explicitly metalinguistic, e.g., "Part of what explains why Pluto is not classified as a planet is the IAU's decision in 2006 to redefine 'planet'" (2020, 7). Kocurek et al. argue in response that "[t]he defender of this line owes us a theory of how these utterances are transformed into explicitly metalinguistic ones. We think that the prospects for such a theory are not good because the exact nature of the transformation into an explicitly metalinguistic sentence is highly unsystematic" (7). They go on to defend this last claim, but we needn't continue it here. My point is just that accepting counterconceptual dependence as explanatory doesn't seem to do significant damage to our ordinary concept of explanation. One might try to argue that a proper philosophical explication of the ordinary concept should exclude counterconceptual explanation, but I have argued here we have good reasons for including it.

And I don't think there is any good reason to exclude counterconceptual explanations from being *ontic*. First, recall the point I made in Chapter 1: the definition of "ontic" shouldn't rule out the possibility of ontic explanation in the cognitive and social sciences, including sociology and linguistics. Second, there are three conceptions of explanation: the ontic, the modal, and the epistemic (Salmon 1989). Counterconceptual explanations certainly don't seem to fall into a modal or epistemic conception, for they don't show that their explananda had to occur, nor that they were expected to occur. As I mentioned in Chapter 1, by "epistemic conception," some just mean that explanation is a representational act. Nothing I've said here disagrees with that. For, by "ontic conception" I don't mean that explanations are themselves ontic; I just mean that they appeal to the ontic. Of course, this second argument relies on there being only three conceptions of explanation. I challenge those who don't think counterconceptual explanations are ontic to explain what they are and why.

Similar points apply to other accounts of DME that do not narrow their explananda, such as Pincock's. Although Pincock does not mention countermathematicals, he does call instantiation an objective dependence relation, which suggests the following countermathematical: "If almost minimal sets hadn't satisfied Plateau's laws, then soap films wouldn't have satisfied Plateau's laws." The normativist can interpret this as: "Were the semantic/conceptual rules governing the application of the term/concept 'almost minimal set' such that, wherever it applied, 'satisfies Plateau's laws' did not apply, then soap films wouldn't have satisfied Plateau's laws." If we read this counterconceptually and think of the antecedent as brought about by an intervention, then there is "counterconceptual causal" dependence between the semantic/conceptual rules governing the application of the term/concept "almost minimal set" and the fact that soap films satisfy Plateau's laws.

However, since on Pincock's account the explanandum is not narrow, a description of it is not analytic. But the normativist will say similar things about the mathematical premises in Pincock's account. Soap films satisfy Plateau's laws because they instantiate almost minimal sets and it is a mathematical fact that almost minimal sets satisfy Plateau's laws. The normativist can agree that the fact that soap films instantiate almost minimal sets (or that "almost minimal set" applies to them) is an empirical, non-conventional fact. However, for the normativist, the mathematical fact that almost minimal sets satisfy Plateau's laws is an expression of conceptual rules. The explanatory status of this fact has the same two-faced character as the one discussed above in connection with Terry's poor sister. The normativist 1) can accept that this mathematical fact partly explains the explanandum and 2) can hold that "soap films satisfy Plateau's laws in part because of how terms are used" is false on the standard reading of that claim, yet 3) can hold that it is true on a counterconceptual reading. For the normativist, DMEs on Pincock's account are no different from the following: Why is Bob an unmarried man? Because Bob instantiates the property of being a bachelor and bachelors are (necessarily) unmarried men. The fact that Bob is (or instantiates the property of being) an unmarried man is an empirical, non-conventional fact. "Bachelors are unmarried men" is an expression of conceptual rules. The explanation would be just as adequate if it appealed to a *semantic* fact here: because Bob is a bachelor and "bachelor" means *unmarried man.*

Now, one might claim that this isn't *really* an ontic account of DME. On ontic accounts, the explanandum, explanans, and the dependence relation between them are distinct, *ontic* things. Yet, what I described in the previous paragraph is merely a case where the *same* fact is *described* or *conceptualized* in two different ways. It is not a case where the explanandum ontically depends on some other fact(s): nothing about Terry's knot or the soap films really changed, only what people think and say about them. As I conceded in the previous section, I think there is something right about this, namely that the normativist views pure mathematics as expressing rules for the use of language. Still, I do not think the ontic proponent need fear. First, the hypothetical intervention into people's brains or social conventions or whatever clearly *is* one to which no ontic proponent would object—it plainly illustrates an *ordinary* ontic (causal or mechanistic) explanation of what people think and say. Second, according to the normativist, there *just is not anything else here to explain.* Mathematics is just a reflection of how people talk—a shadow of our syntax (Warren 2020). So, everything there *is* to explain can be explained ontically. No worry for the ontic proponent, then. One is simply metaphysically confused if one has in mind some more metaphysically robust explanandum. Compare the objection, "But you can't explain the *FACT* that Terry failed to make his sister a bachelor by appeal to only semantic conventions!" This betrays a confusion about the nature of the fact to be explained. (See again Topey 2019; Donaldson 2020; and Warren 2020.) I think those who would object that normativist accounts of DME are not really ontic are really objecting to normativism as a philosophy of mathematics—they are objecting that there must be something more to explain.

Things are slightly different on a normativist interpretation of Pincock's account. For views like Pincock's, the explanandum is not narrow, and so not analytic. Thus, it is not merely a fact about how something is conceptualized, and it cannot be explained *wholly* by convention. As I mentioned above, the fact that soap films instantiate almost minimal sets (or that "almost minimal set" applies to them) is an empirical, non-conventional fact. But, according to the normativist, the mathematical premises play the normative role of making explicit the conceptual rules linking the mathematical concepts applied in the empirical explanans(-statement) to mathematical concepts applied in the empirical explanandum(-statement). Compare again: Bob is an unmarried man because Bob is a bachelor and "bachelor" means *unmarried man.*[35]

5.6. Summary

I have shown how to deflate ontic accounts of DME, including NOCA. I explained modal normativism and extended it to mathematics. I proposed counterconceptual readings of countermathematicals, and I gave a semantic account of the instantiation relation as concept application. These resources show how one can accept the existence of DMEs while denying platonism. Thus, the EIA is invalid without anti-normativist premises.

The normativist can also disagree with the *critics* of the EIA who simply deny the existence of DMEs by arguing that the mathematics is merely playing a representational (Saatsi 2011) or indexing (Melia 2000; Daly and Langford 2009) role, not an explanatory one. It would be a serious mistake to say that normativistically deflating NOCA entails that mathematics plays a representational or indexing role. According to NOCA, in DMEs there is nothing other than the mathematics to provide the explanation—there are no empirical premises in which mathematics represents or indexes the "real" explanatory features. Nor is it the case that when we conceive of DMEs as "counterconceptual causal" explanations, the mathematics represents or indexes the "counterconceptual causes." The "counterconceptual causes" are conceptual rules, and those are not represented or indexed by mathematics; they are *expressed* by mathematics. The critics also mistakenly think that the existence of DMEs entails platonism, which is why they are keen to deny the existence of DMEs. The normativist can accept that the mathematics *is* doing something explanatory, and she can even accept ontic accounts of its explanatoriness, such as NOCA, suitably deflated. Furthermore, I argued that deflated ontic accounts are just as explanatorily powerful and ontic, if not more than inflated accounts.

Chapter 6 is all about semantics. I give an inferentialist account of the content of mathematical concepts that is consistent with normativism, and

[35] I thank an anonymous reviewer for pressing me to clarify this section.

I argue that normativism, deflationism, and inferentialism are consistent with truth-conditional semantics. This is because normativism is a functional thesis, not a (meta)semantic one, and truth-conditional semantics only requires a deflationary concept of truth that is not ontologically committing. Philosophers have for decades conflated semantic truth-conditions with metaphysical truthmakers.

6
Semantics, Metasemantics, and Function

6.1. Introduction

This chapter defends an inferentialist[1] account of mathematical conceptual content that is compatible with mathematical normativism. In Section 6.2, I argue for a broad, normative inferentialist (Brandom 1994, 2000; Peregrin 2014; Sellars [1963] 1991) account of the content of applicable mathematical concepts, according to which they have inferential as well as structural empirical content (or structural application conditions). This latter aspect of the view should be very clearly distinguished from the view that usually goes by "structuralism," according to which *pure* mathematics *describes* structures. Since broad, normative inferentialism is somewhat well-known, and I will not have anything new to say about it generally, I will concentrate on differentiating it from structuralism and connecting it to the normativist deflation of distinctively mathematical explanation (DME) presented in Chapter 5. I also argue that normativism is consistent with a form of realism about quantities and measurement. In Section 6.3, I argue that this metasemantic inferentialist account is compatible with truth-conditional semantics. This compatibility is possible, in part, because normativism is a thesis about the *function* of mathematical discourse; truth-conditional semantics is, obviously, a *semantic* thesis; and these are consistent with a variety of *metasemantic* theses, such as inferentialism.

6.2. Mathematical Concepts and Their Content

6.2.1. Broad Normative Inferentialism

Here I argue for a broad, normative inferentialist (Brandom 1994, 2000; Peregrin 2014; Sellars [1963] 1991) account of the content of applicable mathematical concepts, according to which they have inferential as well as

[1] See Warren (2020) for an impressive development of logical and mathematical inferentialism.

Rules to Infinity. Mark Povich, Oxford University Press. © Oxford University Press 2024.
DOI: 10.1093/oso/9780197679005.003.0006

structural empirical content (or structural application conditions). All mathematical concepts have formal inferential content that is determined by their rule-governed roles in a formal system. The axioms of a formal system implicitly define the terms therein.[2] Axioms can also be thought of as *inference rules* that serve as the basic inference rules for a mathematical language (Warren 2015a, 2020). The inferentialism I defend is *broad* because I interpret inferential rules broadly, to include empirical application conditions (Brandom 1994, 2000; Peregrin 2014; Sellars [1963] 1991).[3] I include within "application conditions" a term's co-application conditions—rules governing the re-application of a term—which determine the corresponding entity's identity and persistence conditions. Let us call that intralinguistic part of a term's inferential role its "narrow role." Those mathematical concepts that are empirically applicable have application conditions in addition to their narrow roles as determined purely by the axioms implicitly defining them. The empirical application conditions of those mathematical concepts that are applicable are *structural*. This will be explained below. The inferentialism I defend is *normative* because I think the way a word or concept *ought* to be used is what determines its meaning, and the way a word ought to be used is given by its rules of use, i.e., inference rules and, where empirically contentful, application conditions. However, unlike some normative inferentialists (e.g., Brandom 1994), I think such rules can be given a naturalistic explanation that will undoubtedly involve both evolutionary and social developmental components, including subtle and not-so-subtle forms of social reinforcement and punishment (e.g., Peregrin 2022; see also Haugeland 1998).

Let me unpack some of this. Inferentialism is best construed as a metasemantic thesis, rather than a semantic one. A semantic theory "assigns semantic values [i.e., meanings, referents, senses, etc.] to the expressions of the language, and explains how the semantic values of the complex expressions are a function of the semantic values of their parts" (Stalnaker 2003, 166). Notice that this says nothing about why semantic values are assigned to certain semantic primitives. This is the task of a metasemantic theory; it also explains why words are meaningful in the first place, what separates meaningful words from meaningless noise and marks. Normative inferentialism does not assign inferential rules to expressions as their semantic values. According to normative inferentialism, meaningful words are

[2] On implicit definition, see Chapter 5 of Hale and Wright (2001).

[3] Broad inferentialists also include connections to action, particularly for moral and evaluative concepts. This aspect can be put aside here.

distinguished from meaningless noise and marks by the fact that the former are governed by inferential rules, and the meaning of a word is distinguished from the meaning of another in terms of the different inferential rules governing them. This is usually and easily illustrated with the logical constants, say, conjunction and (inclusive) disjunction. The idea is that these have their distinctive meanings due to their distinctive inferential roles, as codified by their introduction (&I and ∨I) and elimination (&E and ∨E) rules (and perhaps De Morgan's Laws).[4]

&I: A,B ⊢ A&B &E: A&B ⊢ A; A&B ⊢ B
∨I: A ⊢ A∨B ∨E: A∨B,~B ⊢ A; A∨B,~A ⊢ B[5]

To use a mark or noise according to these rules is to use it as—to mean by it—conjunction or disjunction. Notice that unlike dispositional inferentialism, it is not the actual use of a term or the disposition to use a term that determines its meaning, but its rules of use—how it ought to be used. Dispositions may explain what it is to *follow* a rule—i.e., to follow a rule for a word may be to be disposed to use it in certain ways—and thus what it is to use a word in accord with its meaning, but dispositions are not the *source* of meaning. This may seem incorrect. Suppose that Cullen doesn't use or isn't disposed to use "and" in accord with &I and &E. We would say that he doesn't mean *and* by "and." Doesn't this show that his actual use, or disposition to use, "and" is what determines its meaning, a meaning that is different from *and*? I think that is the wrong conclusion to draw. What's going on here should also be explicated in terms of rules. To mean *and* by "and" is to use "and" in accord with &I and &E, just as to play chess is to play according to certain rules. If I don't play according to the rules of chess, I'm not playing chess, but we don't conclude that it's my actual play, or my disposition to play, that makes a game the game that it is or a piece the piece that it is. Instead, we use my actual play or disposition to play to determine what rules I am (not necessarily explicitly or consciously) playing in accord with. The way you play determines

[4] We needn't answer the question of which rules are meaning-determining or content-conferring here. Holists say all rules are meaning-determining; non-holists don't. For example, Brown (2007) makes a distinction between substantive and non-substantive rules, and Warren (2020) makes a distinction between basic and derivative rules, and both take only the former in these pairs of kinds of rules to be meaning-determining. See also Peregrin (2014). Note that non-holists needn't say that any concept can be acquired independently of any other; they can say that some concepts are (must be) acquired in bundles.

[5] This is often called "disjunctive syllogism," and "disjunction elimination" often refers to argument by cases. I follow Teller (1989) in calling disjunctive syllogism "disjunction elimination."

what game you are playing only derivatively. The rules are primary. Perhaps you learn from my actual play or disposition to play that I am using chess pieces while playing in accord with the rules of checkers. It's the rules that determine what is checkers and what is chess, and which rules I'm playing in accord with determines which game I am playing. Similarly, perhaps we learn from Cullen's dispositions to use "and" that he is using it in accord with ∨I and ∨E. It is those rules that determine the meaning of "or," and it is that he is using "and" in accordance with those rules that determines that he is using "and" to mean *or* instead of *and*. If we can't determine *any* rules he's following, we might be inclined to conclude he isn't using "and" meaningfully at all. Words are used in accord with their meaning—to mean anything—only insofar as they are used according to their rules, and this makes sense only if rules, not actual or dispositional usage, determine meaning.

Warren (2020) defends an inferentialism that emphasizes rules *and* usage, and it isn't always clear what he takes their relation to be. Sometimes he seems to imply that rules are meaning-determining; other times he seems to imply that usage is meaning-determining.[6] For example, he says, "Usage founds meaning, if anything does" (25) and "what gives these symbols content is the overall pattern of their use" (121). Yet, he also says that rules are "globally constitutive" (120), i.e., constitutive of meaning, and that "items have meaning because of the rules that are followed for their overall deployment" (121). Furthermore, Warren relies on rules' being meaning-determining in response to the circularity objection to inferentialism. According to the circularity objection, you can only infer to and from meaningful statements, so inference cannot be what *confers* meaning—inference *presupposes* meaning (see, e.g., Boghossian 2014). Warren's response uses the same chess analogy that Peregrin (2018) uses to rebut the circularity objection, though Peregrin is an openly normative inferentialist. According to Peregrin (2018), the objection rests on failing to distinguish inferences or inferrings from *rules* of inference. Of course, I move the rook as I do *because* it is a rook. So being a rook is prior to and explains the act of my moving it as I do. But what *makes* the piece a rook is the *rule* governing its movement. Similarly, I infer as I do because "and" means *and*. But what makes it mean *and* are the inference rules governing it. All we need to do to answer the objection is to recognize

[6] I take it that for Warren a certain kind of actual or dispositional usage determines rules, which determine meaning. See his (2020) discussion of Kripkenstein.

that "a rule-governed move presupposes rules that govern it" (Peregrin 2018, 451). Similarly, Warren (2020, 121, my emphasis) argues:

> "nobody doubts that the meaning of a piece—its role in the game—is *constituted by the rules of chess*. The rules must be in place for a piece of material to play the role of a knight, for example, and this is not at all mysterious. *Inferentialists think that something analogous is happening with language*, so see no need to deny that inferences are movements of thought that are naturally explained as operating on meanings or contents."

The objection is akin to objecting that implicit definitions can't work because a sentence must be meaningful before it can be used to say something true.[7] The implicit definition *endows* the implicitly defined terms with the meanings necessary to make the sentence true. Similarly, laying down rules of inference—i.e., stipulating their validity—is what endows the expressions with meanings necessary to make the inferences valid. Since answering the circularity objection seems to require that rules, not usage, be given meaning-determining power, that is the view we ought to take.

Let me now move on to application conditions, or what Sellars called "entry transitions." Recall that what makes the inferentialism I favor "broad" is that inferential rules need not be purely intralinguistic affairs (Brandom 1994, 2000; Peregrin 2014; Sellars [1963] 1991). For empirical concepts, it is important that their networks of inferential patterns are connected to the world. Thus, I include application conditions (and co-application conditions to provide identity and persistence criteria for sortal concepts) in the inferential rules governing empirical concepts. Not all concepts have application conditions—e.g., purely formal concepts—but all concepts, according to inferentialists, have a narrow role; this is what distinguishes applying a concept from mere labeling (Brandom 1994).

Supplying a formal concept with application conditions consists simply in specifying the conditions under which it applies correctly.[8] This can be done several ways, e.g., with an explicit specification, via ostension, or by using a meaning-, reference-, or denotation-claim. We may say, for example, in an explicit specification of the application conditions of some formal concept

[7] This was one of Frege's critiques of Hilbert (see Frege 1980, 34–38; Shapiro 2000, 155). Note that stipulating the validity of an inference (e.g., from "x" to "y") is equivalent to stipulating the (logical) truth of a sentence (e.g., "$x \rightarrow y$").

[8] The positivists called a specification of application conditions a "coordinative definition," "correspondence rule," or "correlative definition" (e.g., Reichenbach 1965; Carnap [1937] 2001).

"*x*," that "*x*" is to apply to something if and only if it possesses such and such properties. Or we may say that "*x*" is to apply or to refer to *this*, where our intentions make clear what *this* is. This method supplies application conditions in the same general way that a meaning-, reference-, or denotation-claim does. Note that although meaning and reference are distinct, often in these contexts to say that "*x*" is to *mean n* is the same as saying that "*x*" is to denote or refer to *n*. In such contexts, when we say that "*x*" is to mean *n* we do not mean that "*x*" is to mean "*n*", i.e., to be synonymous with "*n*." To say that would be to say that "*x*" is to be governed by the same inferential rules (including application conditions) as "*n*." To say that "*x*" is to mean, to denote, or to refer to *n* is to say (or express) that $x = n$, and, thus, that "*x*" is to have the application conditions of any concept "*y*" such that $y = n$.[9] To say, for example, that "*x*" denotes the evening star is to say that the application conditions for "*x*" are to include any criteria that can be used to identify the object that is the evening star. We shouldn't say that to say that "*x*" denotes the evening star is to say that "*x*" is to have the *same* application conditions as "the evening star," for those application conditions are different from the application conditions of, say, "the morning star" and "Venus," both of which also denote the evening star. If these terms didn't have different application conditions, then the identity of their referents would've been a priori. A meaning-, reference-, or denotation-claim also expresses the validity of the inferences allowable from an identity claim: if $x = y$, identity elimination allows me to infer "$P(x)$" from "$P(y)$" and vice versa. Thus, to say that "*x*" is to mean, to denote, or to refer to *n* is to say (or express) that certain inferences are valid (in truth functional contexts), namely those from "…*x*…" to "…*n*…" and vice versa. I discuss reference and denotation in greater detail in Chapter 7.

I don't think there are good reasons to distinguish metasemantically between ordinary empirical concepts (e.g., *honeycomb*) and applied mathematical concepts (e.g., *hexagon*): both have the content they do in virtue of their inferential rules, including their application conditions. And there is no *metaphysical* problem of the applicability of mathematics, no mystery about how or why our mathematical knowledge of hexagons (for example) is empirically useful: mathematical truths about hexagons help fix the concept *hexagon*, which, just like the concept *honeycomb*, applies to something in virtue of its satisfying the concept's application conditions. Unlike modal,

[9] This idea is inspired by Horwich's deflationary theory of reference, according to which—roughly and ignoring many complications—for all *x*, "*n*" refers to *x* if and only if $n = x$. See Horwich (1998a) for refinements.

moral, and other vocabularies that cause so-called placement problems[10] for philosophers, applied mathematical vocabulary is not especially philosophically troublesome. Balaguer has argued that this is not so for conventionalists. He argues that "conventionalists hold that the sentences of mathematics are analytic, or true by convention—and it is no less mysterious how a collection of factually empty sentences could be applicable to empirical science than how a collection of false sentences could be applicable to empirical science" (1998, 101). Thus, Balaguer thinks, with regard to applicability, conventionalism is no better off than fictionalism. (I discuss fictionalism in Chapter 8.) This is confused. Just because *pure* mathematical truths are factually empty doesn't imply that the concepts involved in those truths have no empirical content. "Bachelors are unmarried men" is analytic (i.e., "factually empty"), but obviously the concepts therein have empirical content.

However, special problems of applicability arise in part because of certain features of some mathematical concepts. Steiner (1998, 16), in a classic, wide-ranging discussion of different problems of applicability, presents the following argument:

(1) $7 + 5 = 12$.
(2) There are seven apples on the table.
(3) There are five pears on the table.
(4) No apple is a pear.
(5) Apples and pears are the only fruits on the table.
Hence, (6) There are exactly twelve fruits on the table.

Here there is a *semantic* problem of applicability: "7" in (1) is a singular term, but "seven" in (2) is a predicate (determiner), which renders the seemingly flawless argument formally invalid.[11] Frege's solution was to interpret numerals as singular terms in any context. Thus, (2) is better rendered (2') "The number of apples on the table = 7"; similarly for (3). Now, I have no problem with this solution—it is open to the normativist to accept it, for she would say that (2') and (2) are analytically equivalent. In a footnote, Steiner (1998, 17) notes, "One could, naturally, also solve the 'semantic' problem of the applicability of mathematics with a theory according to which all

[10] "The problem is that of 'placing' various kinds of truths in a natural world" (Price 2011, 6).

[11] There is evidence that historically and developmentally the determiner use of number-words comes first, and then they are nominalized into singular terms (Hofweber 2005, 2016; Thomasson 2024).

numerals are really predicates." This option—call it the predicative view—is also available to the normativist, who is free to explicate the argument's formal validity by reading (2), (3), and (6) as the numerical predications they appear to be (see, e.g., Kessler 1980; Lambros 1976; Oliver 1994) and instead rendering (1) as something like a universal generalization, e.g., $\forall x[(7x \,\&\, 5x)$ if and only if $12x]$[12] (cf. Ellis 1966, 14–15), where the numerals are predicates. One of Frege's main motivations for attacking the predicative view was to avoid Mill's empiricism, according to which the truths of pure mathematics are empirical generalizations. We can see now that empiricism does not follow from the claim that numerals are predicates: one can hold that numerical concepts apply to physical objects or aggregates or generally have empirical content without being a mathematical empiricist.

Of course, for the normativist, (2)–(6) is by itself *materially* valid, for (1) is an expression of a rule governing the concepts *7*, *5*, and *12* (and perhaps + and =), including as they occur in predicate positions, a rule which licenses the transformation of empirical descriptions, e.g., of (2)–(5) into (6). Regarding the argument's *logical* validity, the normativist is free to account for it in the Fregean or the predicative way, for she doesn't read any substantive, transconventional ontology into syntactic structure. The choice between them must be decided on the basis of whether it is pragmatically better to reinterpret the number-words in (2), (3), and (6) as singular terms or the numerals in (1) as predicates. Even if there are pragmatic reasons to prefer the Fregean view, that does not require us to abandon the idea that number-words and numerals have empirical content. That is, even if it is preferable to render (2) as (2') "The number of apples on the table = 7," we ought still to see that claim as an empirical application of the numeral "7" and, thus, see numerals as having empirical application conditions. In fact, the advantages that Millian empiricists and Aristotelian realists (e.g., Kitcher 1984; Franklin 2014; see also Michell 2021) claim for their accounts of the applicability of mathematics and measurement generalize straightforwardly to normativism, without the accompanying disadvantages of those views. Such views of applicability and measurement needn't conflict with the normativism I've espoused. I expand on this point next, but first I want to

[12] In predicative form, the argument may be more intuitively rendered in plural logic. Unfortunately, I can't consider here all the interesting implications plural logic may have on the philosophy of mathematics. See Florio and Linnebo (2021). I note only that, for the Carnapian, a plural logic is simply another framework, which may be more or less useful than other logical frameworks, given certain purposes, and this has no transframework ontological implications. "More useful" doesn't mean "more true" or "more reflective of the ontological structure of reality."

emphasize that what I've said about numerals having application conditions does not imply that a claim like "2 exists" or "numbers exist" places any demands on the world. To think otherwise is to think that any term with empirical content contributes that content to every proposition in which it occurs. I will expand on this below.

The two biggest advantages that empiricists claim for their view are 1a) that it offers an unmysterious, naturalistic epistemology of mathematics and 2a) that it makes clear sense of the applicability of mathematics, including measurement (measurement is Michell's main motivator; see 1994, 2021). The biggest disadvantages are 1b) that there are not enough physical objects to be truthmakers for truths regarding enormously large finite, infinite, and transfinite numbers and 2b) that mathematical knowledge seems a priori and necessary, properties not normally thought to be possessed by empirical knowledge. I argue that mathematical normativism has these advantages without the disadvantages. I take them in turn.

(1a) The normativist epistemology is also unmysterious and naturalistic for both pure and applied mathematics. Regarding applied mathematical knowledge, since the normativist accepts that mathematical concepts can have empirical content, knowledge of applied mathematical truths can be straightforwardly empirical. For example, we can know via perception that there are three objects on the table just as straightforwardly as we can know that there is a red object on the table.[13] We know this not only by subitizing—i.e., immediately recognizing the number of objects—but by counting. Obviously, not all knowledge of applied mathematical claims is so easily acquired, nor so straightforwardly empirical—i.e., not so devoid of theoretical and other extra-empirical considerations—in particular, many measurement claims (Chang 2004; Wolff 2020). I will not defend any particular theory of measurement, but I will argue in the next paragraph that normativism is compatible with a certain kind of simple realism about measurement according to which a measurand (i.e., the quantity being measured) exists independently of being measured.[14] The normativist epistemology of pure mathematics is also

[13] Maddy (1990) similarly argues that we can acquire numerical beliefs perceptually. She, inspired by Frege, takes such beliefs to be about sets.

[14] I have in mind standard, macroscale measurements, not quantum measurements, where such realism is less intuitive. As far as I'm aware, all agree that something disruptive of the measurand happens in quantum measurement, but they disagree over what happens (e.g., the wave function

unmysterious and naturalistic: such knowledge merely consists in knowledge of conceptual rules and their consequences (Thomasson 2020a). Obviously, far more must be said about the conventionalist epistemology of pure mathematics and proof, but here that is not my concern. See, e.g., Schroeder (2020), Shanker (1987), and Warren (2020).

(2a) That empiricism makes straightforward sense of the applicability of mathematics, including measurement, follows directly from the claim that mathematical concepts can apply to physical objects or aggregates. This claim is the basis of Michell's (1994, 2021) "realist theory of measurement," according to which the claim, for example, that a rigid rod is 3 meters long is a straightforwardly empirical claim about the relation of the rod to the standard meter. Empiricism itself—the claim that the truths of *pure* mathematics are empirical generalizations—plays no role in this account of measurement. The label "realist" is used by Michell to differentiate his view from once-prominent idealistic and verificationistic forms of operationalism that gave measurement a metaphysically constitutive role, which forced operationalists to deny that the measurand exists independently of being measured (Wolff 2020). The normativist is in no way committed to such an operationalism. The normativist can be a measurement realist in seeing "the rod is 3 meters long," "there are 3 rods," and "the rod is red" as being semantically similar, in that they are all straightforward empirical applications of concepts; what differs is the application conditions of those concepts. This is not to deny that conventions are involved in a claim such as that the rod is 3 meters long (Carnap 1966) or that there is some sense in which that claim is "more conventional" than the claim that there are 3 rods. The point is that such claims about conventionality describe the application conditions of the concepts involved; i.e., if the claim that the rod is 3 meters long is "more conventional" than the claim that there are 3 rods, then this is because conventions enter into the application conditions of the former in ways in which they do not enter into those of the latter. Carnapian metaontology is not committed to Carnap's own

collapses or the multiverse branches), which is why we don't observe superpositions of states of the measurand. I also ignore any complications that may arise from relativistic effects (e.g., contraction) in measuring lengths; I don't think they affect the semantic story I want to tell.

verificationistic, operationalistic account of measurement. Carnap (1966) writes throughout of "defining" concepts of measurable quantities in terms of measurement procedures, and he writes that "[t]he phenomenon [of weight] itself contains nothing numerical—only your private sensations of weight.... It is *we* who assign numbers to nature" (100, original emphasis). However, none of this detracts from the idea that the rod's being 3 meters long is an *empirical* reality that, as Carnapian metaontologists, we needn't read any *ontology* into. Recall from Chapter 1 the distinction between empirical reality and ontological reality—different ontologies of what it is for the rod to be 3 meters long are simply empirically equivalent, conceptually distinct languages for describing this empirical reality (its being 3 meters long). The normativist needn't deny that the world plays a role in the measurement process and in determining whether a property is quantitative or measurable. She will simply deny that there is one correct language (i.e., ontology) for discussing these matters. Thus, since the normativist accepts that (many) mathematical concepts have empirical content, she can accept the realist theory of measurement. Note that this gives normativism a clear advantage over other anti-platonist philosophies of mathematics, such as fictionalism, which must deny the literal truth of applied mathematical claims. (I return to fictionalism in Chapter 8.) According to the realist theory of measurement, the "representation theorems"[15] or axioms presented by so-called representational theorists of measurement (e.g., Luce et al. 1990), which describe the conditions under which quantities can be represented by numbers, should be seen as supplying empirical application conditions for our numerical concepts, as specifying the empirical (not ontological) structure the world must have for our numerical concepts to apply. The normativist can say the same thing. (The representational theory of measurement is closely connected to structuralism, which I discuss below.)

(1b) One famous objection to empiricism is that there are not enough physical objects to be truthmakers for truths regarding enormously large finite, infinite, and transfinite numbers. This objection arises because empiricism takes the truths of pure mathematics

[15] To make the points I want to make, it isn't necessary to get into the formalism.

to be empirical generalizations. This is denied by normativism. Importantly, the objection does not arise merely from the claim that (many) mathematical concepts have empirical content. For example, take the applied claim that there are Graham's number[16] of stars in the observable universe and the pure claim Graham's number is larger than 2. Empiricism can correctly account for the falsity of the applied claim, yet it has trouble accounting for the truth of the pure claim since (let us plausibly assume) Graham's number is not realized in (i.e., the concept does not apply in) the physical universe. The normativist, however, can easily account for its truth: it is an expression of actual conceptual rules.

(2b) While empiricism offers an unmysterious epistemology of mathematics, it has a hard time accounting for its methods and the fact that mathematical knowledge seems a priori and necessary. This objection also arises because empiricism takes the truths of pure mathematics to be empirical descriptions; it does arise merely from the claim that (many) mathematical concepts have empirical content. If knowledge of the proposition that 2 + 2 = 4 is acquired via empirical means, such as perception or testimony, then it is hard to see how such knowledge could be a priori and necessary. In fact, Mill bit the bullet on the contingency of mathematics. The a priori, necessary nature of mathematics is easily explicable on normativism. That conceptual analysis is sufficient for mathematical knowledge accounts for its a priori status. That mathematics is analytic and knowledge of it is a priori does not entail that such knowledge is always easy to acquire. All defenders of the a priori recognize that sometimes a priori knowledge is difficult to obtain. That mathematical truths express, but do not describe and are not made true by, conceptual rules accounts for their necessary status. When we consider counterfactual scenarios where our conceptual rules are different, the mathematical truths remain the same, because in counterfactual reasoning we continue using our actual conceptual rules (Thomasson 2020a). Hence, what Pincock (2004, 142) calls "Dummett's dilemma"—"It seems that we must either choose to have mathematical objects stand in a direct relation to the physical world [here Pincock is

[16] Graham's number once held the Guinness World Record for the largest finite number ever to appear in a mathematical proof (Padilla 2022, 2). Graham's number is unimaginably greater than even the number of particles in the observable universe.

> referring to mathematical empiricism], and thereby sacrifice the necessity of mathematical truth, or accept a tenuous link between the mathematical and the physical worlds in order to preserve the independence of mathematical truth"—is a false one. We can have the necessity of mathematical truth and the direct applicability of mathematical concepts, just as "bachelors are unmarried" is necessary, yet the concepts involved are empirically applicable.

As I mentioned in Chapter 5, I have no account of the distinction between mathematical and non-mathematical concepts. The distinction may turn out to be disjunctive—a mathematical concept is either an arithmetical concept or a geometrical concept or. . . , where an arithmetical concept is a concept of quantity, a geometrical concept is a concept of space, etc. But one important, apparent difference between mathematical and non-mathematical concepts that many have picked up on is that at least many mathematical concepts are structural (Hellman 1989; Parsons 2008; Resnik 1997; Shapiro 1997). However, I think this insight is misapprehended by the more platonistic structuralists.[17] They seem to make the same mistaken inference that empiricists make. Empiricists argue:

1. Mathematical concepts have empirical content.
2. Mathematical objects are empirical objects (e.g., physical aggregates).
3. Mathematics describes empirical objects.

Structuralists argue:

1. Mathematical concepts have structural content.
2. Mathematical objects are structures.
3. Mathematics describes structures.

I wouldn't have a problem with these claims if they were understood in Carnapian fashion. For example, if 2 were understood merely as a material mode expression of 1, and if 3 were understood merely as a material mode expression of the fact that mathematics consists of declarative sentences

[17] For example, when Shapiro (1997) says that "group theory *studies* not a single structure but a type of structure, the pattern common to collections of objects with a binary operation, an identity element thereon, and inverses for each element" (73, my emphasis). Instead, group theory determines the concept of a group.

containing terms with structural content. However, no extant structuralist I'm aware of is so deflationary. For them, these are substantive inferential moves, and they require argument that is often lacking. Millian empiricists and Aristotelian realists make the same error when they invalidly infer from the fact that mathematical concepts have empirical content that mathematical truths are empirical generalizations. Compare the following inference: "Bachelor" has empirical content; therefore, "Bachelors are unmarried" is a substantive (synthetic) empirical description of bachelors. The conclusion is controversial and can't be inferred from the premise without further controversial premises that beg the question against the normativist, such as that every declarative sentence is a substantive description or that every empirical concept contributes the same empirical content in the same way to every proposition in which it occurs.

There are many different forms of structuralism and many different things one might mean by "structural" and "structure" (Hellman and Shapiro 2018). For my purposes, when I say that (many) mathematical concepts have empirical-structural content, I mean that their empirical application conditions have nothing to do with the nature of individual objects and their relations. For example, Shapiro (1997, 115) writes, "For each natural number *n*, there is a structure exemplified by all systems that consist of exactly *n* objects. For example, the *4 pattern* is the structure common to all collections of four objects. The 4 pattern is exemplified by the starting infielders on a baseball team (not counting the battery), the corners of my desk, and two pairs of shoes." I agree, but recall from Chapter 5 that the normativist views instantiation (or exemplification) as concept application.[18] So, I think it is less misleading to say, for example, that the concept "4" applies to the corners of my desk, two pairs of shoes, etc. Such structural concepts are acquired unmysteriously via processes of perception, abstraction, and pattern recognition (Churchland 2012); structuralists like Resnik (1997) and Shapiro (1997) have said very helpful things about this, with which the normativist can agree (see also Maddy 1990). The problem is in moving from "mathematical concepts have structural content" to "pure mathematics describes structures."

What I've said about structural application conditions may be consistent with the prominent mapping account of the applicability of mathematics

[18] More carefully: the normativist views instantiation claims as expressing concept application claims.

(Bueno and Colyvan 2011; Bueno and French 2018; Pincock 2004, 2012). Mapping accounts of the applicability of mathematics require a mathematical structure to be mapped to an empirical system. But from my point of view, it is better to treat these views as offering application conditions for structural concepts. Many different kinds of mapping have been discussed (Bueno and French 2018; Da Costa and French 2003), and it is unnecessary to go over these here. A mapping must hold *between* structures, so the empirical system to which a mathematical structure is mapped must also be or instantiate a structure, or, I would rather say, a structural concept must also be applied to it.

But, just as many concepts can apply to an individual object, many structural concepts can apply to a system, so it doesn't make sense to talk of "the" structure a system instantiates—there are many different ways of "cutting up" a system into objects and relations, and the application of a structural concept will depend on this cutting (Frigg and Nguyen 2020; Pincock 2012). In a particular context, one will choose which structural concept to apply to a system depending on one's goals, which will require "cutting up" the system—i.e., dividing it into objects and relations between them—in a way appropriate for the structural concept one wishes to apply. Here is an example from Frigg and Nguyen (2020, 75) to illustrate this. A methane molecule consists of a carbon atom and four hydrogen atoms. We can treat each of these atoms as objects, which we denote by "*a*," "*b*," "*c*," "*d*," and "*e*." The set of these is the domain $U = \{a, b, c, d, e\}$. There is a covalent bond between each hydrogen atom and the carbon atom. We can treat the covalent bond as the relation, *r*, between the objects, which we specify extensionally as $r = \{\langle a, b\rangle, \langle b, a\rangle, \langle a, c\rangle, \langle c, a\rangle, \langle a, d\rangle, \langle d, a\rangle, \langle a, e\rangle, \langle e, a\rangle\}$. We thus have a structure $S = \langle U, r\rangle$, and we can say that *S* is "instantiated" by the methane molecule, which only means we have conceptually carved it in the way we have; the concept of structure *S* applies to it. However, we could just as well treat the covalent bonds as objects, which we denote by "*a*′," "*b*′," "*c*′," and "*d*′." The set of these is the domain $U' = \{a', b', c', d'\}$. We can treat 'sharing a node with another bond' as the relation, *r*′, between the objects, which we specify extensionally as $r' = \{\langle a', b'\rangle, \langle b', a'\rangle, \langle a', c'\rangle, \langle c', a'\rangle, \langle a', d'\rangle, \langle d', a'\rangle, \langle b', c'\rangle, \langle c', b'\rangle, \langle b', d'\rangle, \langle d', b'\rangle, \langle c', d'\rangle, \langle d', c'\rangle\}$. Two structures are isomorphic if and only if there is a mapping from one to the other that is bijective (i.e., a one-to-one correspondence) and relation-preserving (i.e., the objects that are mapped to each other stand in the relations that are mapped to each other). We thus have a structure $S' = \langle U', r'\rangle$, which is not isomorphic to *S*, that is also instantiated by the methane molecule, i.e., it is also an S' structure, or the concept of structure S' also applies to it.

I have suggested that what it is for an empirical system to instantiate a certain structure is for the concept of that structure to apply to the system, which requires the system to be conceptually carved into objects and relations in an appropriate way, a way that depends on which structural concept one wishes to apply to it. According to the mapping account, once this is done, a mapping must be established from a mathematical structure to the now-structurally-described empirical system. Here is one place where the metaphysical problem of applicability arises for platonists. If the mathematical structure is an abstract object and the structure instantiated by the empirical system is an abstract object, why would a mapping between them—two *abstract* objects—help to explain the *empirical* applicability of mathematics? Instead, it is less mysterious to say that when we say there is a mapping from a mathematical structure to a structure instantiated by an empirical system, we are expressing the fact that the object and relation terms of a structural mathematical description can be mapped (according to whichever morphism we wish to choose) to the object and relation terms of a structural description of the empirical system.[19] And there is nothing mysterious about the term "mapped" here—this just means the object and relation terms from each description can be correlated in the requisite way. This removes all mystery as to why mathematical structures are empirically useful: we are connecting a mathematical description to an empirical description of an empirical system.

Let me address two objections. First, am I saying that mathematical structures *are* descriptions or *metaphysically depend* on descriptions or that claims about them are *made true* by descriptions? I am emphatically not. I am merely trying to gesture at a deflationary way of thinking about what the structural application conditions of a structural concept express. Some philosophers might think that appeal to descriptions in the application conditions of the concept of a structure implies that the structure ontologically depends on descriptions. First, I did not say that the application conditions of structural concepts *describe* descriptions; I said they *express* something about descriptions. Like instantiation claims, they don't express conceptual rules, so they aren't necessary, but they express nonetheless. Carnap would say they are quasi-syntactical sentences of the material mode of speech. Second, to think that a thing ontologically depends on what the

[19] There are some similarities here to Nguyen and Frigg (2021), though they are not so deflationary.

application conditions of its concept describe is a serious confusion that is just a version of the conflation between truth-conditions and truthmakers I discuss in Section 6.3. This is all part of a broader philosophical conflation of metaphysics with semantics. Application conditions are semantic phenomena. Application conditions for the concept of *X* do not and are not intended to state the "real definition" of *X* or to describe the essence or nature of *X*, just as the truth conditions for a sentence do not and are not intended to state its truthmakers. Application conditions for the concept of *X* state—when statable at all!—the *empirical*, not *ontological*, conditions under which the concept is correctly applied, and there are many empirically equivalent, ontologically distinct ways to describe those conditions (Dyke 2007, 65; Thomasson 2014, 106–107). As a Carnapian, I have no problem with the more platonistic ways of describing the structural mapping account: let a thousand languages blossom, including platonistic ones, as long as their rules are clear. And it would be fine if there were *no way* of describing the mapping account or the application conditions of a structural concept without using platonistic language. That would simply be a fact about linguistic frameworks. Note that I am *not* using the putative ability to state, in a nominalistic language, what structural application conditions express as an argument for nominalism.[20] Here I am simply saying what the application conditions of a structural concept might express. I am giving an answer to a question akin to "If the application conditions of a structural concept are quasi-syntactical sentences of the material mode of speech, what are the syntactical sentences to which they correspond?"

The second, related objection is this. If the application conditions of mathematical concepts track the instantiation of mathematical properties or abstract structures, there will be no way to treat instantiation as concept application. Note that this is a worry for anti-platonism about properties generally. Consider an analogue: nominalism is false if the application conditions of the concept *red* track the instantiation of redness. I can take on board the responses of various property nominalists (Hellman and Shapiro 2018, 2). For example, a resemblance nominalist might say that the concept *red* applies to red things in virtue of a certain empirical resemblance between them (Rodriguez-Pereyra 2002; some trope theorists say basically the same thing [e.g., Heil 2003]). Similarly, I could say that the concept *trefoil knot*

[20] If I were, this would be an instance of what Dyke (2007) calls the representational fallacy: drawing ontological conclusions from linguistic facts.

applies to trefoil knots in virtue of a certain empirical resemblance between them. Furthermore, even if it were the case that the application conditions of mathematical concepts *track* the instantiation of mathematical properties or abstract structures—meaning just that they *correlate*—I do not think that that implies there is no way to treat instantiation as concept application. It would not imply that the application conditions of mathematical concepts must appeal to those abstract properties. Even if it were the case that whenever a mathematical concept applies to a concrete object, it instantiates a mathematical property, it is implausible that the abstract property itself plays a role in the act of application or of judgment—I judge that a concrete object is a trefoil knot based on certain empirical characteristics of it. That this concrete object instantiates a mathematical property is in that sense incidental to the act of application or judgment. Thus, there should be some way of conceiving of the application conditions of mathematical concepts that does not appeal to the instantiation of mathematical properties, only to the empirical characteristics in virtue of which they apply, even if the application of the former were to track (i.e., correlate with) the instantiation of the latter.

I have been discussing the applicability of mathematics and have found it unobjectionable to appeal to structures, suitably deflated. Many mathematical concepts have structural-empirical content, which just means that their empirical application conditions are structural. This is not at all to deny that mathematical concepts can sometimes be applied "non-empirically," for example, to ideas and abstract objects (e.g., "Zach has had 8 bad ideas today" or "There are at least 3 properties Jeremy and Kayla share"). (Though, in Chapter 8, I will deny that an important part of what is usually taken to be the application of mathematical concepts to mathematical objects, i.e., metamathematics, is really *application* at all.) Next, I want to discuss how metasemantic inferentialism interacts with my account of DME.

6.2.2. Mathematical Concepts and DMEs

In Chapter 5, I argued that when mathematical necessities appear ineliminably in a scientific explanation, they play the normative role of making explicit the norms linking the mathematical concepts applied in its empirical premises to mathematical concepts applied in its conclusion. In DMEs, the only premise is a mathematical truth expressing rules governing the concepts in the conclusion. Thus, when someone asks a why-question for which a DME is the answer, what she learns is conceptual information. In this section, I discuss how to think about this given inferentialism.

One thing I want to deny is that it is *always* the case that one who asks a why-question for which a DME is an answer is lacking conceptual competence. Sometimes that might be the case, but not always. That the questioner learns conceptual information need not imply that she is incompetent with the concept. For example, one can have competence with the concepts *node* and *edge* yet still not know why one always fails when one tries to walk a path that crosses each of Königsberg's bridges exactly once. Here the normativist need only say that one can grasp or be competent with *node* and *edge* without knowing Euler's theorem and that in learning Euler's theorem, one does not learn anything inconsistent with normativism. The normativist might say that one merely grasps better, or enriches one's ability with, concepts with which one is already competent. Any account of the possession conditions of mathematical concepts that is compatible with this—and all accounts of which I'm aware are—is compatible with my account of DME.

So, there are many routes one might go from here. Since according to normative inferentialism the content of a concept is determined by the inferential rules governing it, it is natural to connect the possession conditions of a concept to those inferential rules. Peacocke (1992, 6), for example, says (simplifying a bit) that to possess the concept of conjunction is to find &I and &E primitively compelling, where to find them primitively compelling is to find them compelling but not because they've been inferred from something else. On Warren's (2020, 87) account, basic understanding of an expression—which for our purposes we can take to be equivalent to possession of a concept—can be acquired by using it in accordance with its meaning-constituting rules of inference.[21] So, so long as Euler's theorem isn't involved in the rules one must find primitively compelling in order to possess the concepts *node* and *edge* or so long as Euler's theorem isn't involved in the rules in accordance with which one must use the expressions "node" and "edge" in order to understand them, then we can say that one can possess the concepts *node* and *edge* without knowing Euler's theorem. I have no account of what the meaning-determining rules governing *node* and *edge* are, but I know they don't involve Euler's theorem, because it would be absurd to

[21] Warren emphasizes that this is a sufficient but not necessary condition for basic understanding.

say that Euler didn't possess the concepts *node* and *edge* until he proved his theorem.

In other cases of DME, it may be more plausible that the questioner is lacking a concept or lacking conceptual competence and that the answer, if understood by the questioner, may result in acquisition of a concept. I think Strawberries is the closest example of this, but even there it is plausible that one can possess the concepts *23* and *3* without knowing that 23 is not divisible by 3. If Mary didn't know 3 is not divisible by 2, then I would start to question her conceptual competence.

This will all need to be determined on a case-by-case basis. Even if we have a general account of possession conditions, say, in terms of following meaning-determining rules, we will still need to investigate what exactly those rules are in each case. And it certainly isn't necessary to try to do that for all the concepts used in all the DMEs we've discussed. I merely mean to point out that whether a normativist has to say that a DME-questioner lacks conceptual competence or not will depend on her account of possession conditions.

6.3. Compatibility with Truth-Conditional Semantics

In this section, I argue that truth-conditional semantics (TCS) is compatible with inferentialism, normativism, and semantic deflationism. Call this general thesis "Compatibility." Call the compatibility of TCS and inferentialism "TI-Compatibility," TCS and normativism "TN-Compatibility," and TCS and semantic deflationism "TD-Compatibility." I address each of these in the following sections. Recall from Chapter 5 that while there are many ways to cash out semantic deflationism, the simplest is as the thesis that the truth concept is governed by the equivalence schema "'p' is true if and only if p" and nothing more. Compatibility is possible, in part, because normativism is a *functional* thesis, TCS is a *semantic* thesis, and these are consistent with a variety of *metasemantic* theses, such as inferentialism. I think one reason most have doubted Compatibility is that they have misunderstood the job of semantics and confuse it with the job of metaphysics. Before getting into TI-, TN-, and TD-Compatibility, let me first discuss one way to understand normativism as a functional thesis.

6.3.1. Normativism as a Functional Thesis

Throughout this book, I have described mathematical normativism as the thesis that mathematical claims express, or have the function of expressing, conceptual rules. There are two claims here: 1) that mathematical claims express conceptual rules, and 2) that that is their function. Following Donaldson and Wang (2022, 296), we could plausibly suggest that the first claim means that mathematical claims can be used by someone to manifest their understanding of the relevant rules and to impart that understanding to someone else. Note that the second claim isn't strictly required for normativism to be compatible with TCS and inferentialism. All that is required for their compatibility is the negative thesis that normativism *isn't* a semantic or metasemantic thesis. The functional claim is a way of cashing out what kind of thesis normativism is, if it isn't a semantic or metasemantic one. We could simply stop with the thesis that mathematical claims are analytic; that thesis is compatible with any semantics and metasemantics that allows for analyticities, which both TCS and inferentialism do. It would be nice, though, if we could say more than this—if we could say, for example, something about what the functional claim means and why, if it is right, mathematical language isn't exclusively in the formal mode.[22]

I want to start with the second question, because it will help to answer the first. If the function of pure mathematical claims is to express conceptual rules, then why don't we just *state* the conceptual rules that mathematical claims express? Why speak or write mathematically in the material mode if we are expressing something in the formal mode? I think the best answer to this question relies on the fact that, when a mathematical concept is empirically applicable, the conceptual rules that mathematical claims involving it express are rules that allow us to transform empirical descriptions. They are rules that aid us in empirical reasoning. As Wittgenstein said, "I am guided in practical work by the result of transforming an expression" ([1956] 1978, 357).[23] And our empirical reasoning is almost exclusively in the material mode. When making plans, none of us thinks things like "If 'raining' will apply tomorrow, then I ought to bring the thing to which 'umbrella' applies." So, if my empirical descriptions are in the material mode, mathematics can

[22] See Thomasson (2020a) for an account of the function of metaphysical modal language.

[23] Rayo's (2013) account of the cognitive accomplishment of mathematical knowledge is useful here. See also Yablo (2005) and Perez Carballo (2016).

help me reason with them better if it is in the material mode. The point about the cognitive ease of material mode reasoning is true, of course, about logical and mathematical reasoning too: material mode reasoning in general is simply easier for us. In our everyday dealings with the extralinguistic world, we reason in an object language, not a metalanguage. This may be because we acquire object language beliefs before we acquire metalinguistic beliefs. Perhaps it is possible that one could have no explicit metalinguistic beliefs at all. It seems conceivable that someone could have, e.g., the concept of a dog, but not the concept of the word or concept "dog."

What kind of claim is the claim that the *function* of pure mathematics is to express conceptual rules? Thomasson (2024) seems to take claims about the function of language to be synthetic claims, claims in the science of systemic functional linguistics. Of course, whether a function attribution is true depends on what exactly we mean by "function." If we think of functions as causal roles, then here is one way—admittedly not the only, and perhaps not the best—of making sense of linguistic function attributions. The causal roles, including the effects on behavior and reasoning, of the belief that *p* and the belief that *q*, where *p* is a pure mathematical proposition and *q* is a proposition stating the conceptual rule *p* expresses, are significantly and importantly similar[24]—the transformations of empirical descriptions that *p* allows are the same as, or are exact analogues of, those that *q* allows.[25] Let me illustrate this point with a simple non-mathematical example. Let *p* be the proposition that bachelors are unmarried, and let *q* be the claim that if "bachelor" correctly applies, then "unmarried" correctly applies. If one believes that *p* and believes that Dan is a bachelor, then one can conclude that Dan is unmarried; and if one believes that *q* and believes that "bachelor" correctly applies to Dan, then one can conclude that "unmarried" correctly applies to Dan. (Note that just because we rarely reason in the formal mode doesn't

[24] In fact, it is hard to imagine how one could acquire the belief that *p* without thereby acquiring the at least implicit belief that *q*; even if one doesn't accept the normativist thesis that *p* expresses *q*, it is arguable that even non-normativists must acquire the at least implicit belief that *q* upon acquiring the belief that *p*. I say "at least implicit belief" because, as I noted above, it seems possible that one could have no explicit metalinguistic beliefs at all. So, I am not claiming that these beliefs are the same belief or that *p* and *q* are synonymous. Clearly they are not, since they have different inferential roles.

[25] An expressivist deductivist could say basically the same thing: that "2 + 2 = 4" has the function of expressing the fact that "2 + 2 = 4" is deducible from the axioms, and that the fact that it has this function is evident from the similarity of the causal roles of the belief that 2 + 2 = 4 and the belief that "2 + 2 = 4" is deducible from the axioms. However, if "'2 + 2 = 4' expresses the fact that '2 + 2 = 4' is deducible from the axioms" doesn't just mean that "2 + 2 = 4" is analytic, then they need to explain what it means, and why we should believe it.

mean there's anything wrong with it.) Acquiring the belief that *p* effects my use of the terms "bachelor" and "unmarried" in the same way that acquiring the belief that *q* does. My suggestion is that this is (at least part of) what justifies the claim that *p* has the *function* of expressing *q*. It is a claim that has to do with the acquisition and maintenance of certain behavior, including reasoning.[26] The same points apply when, e.g., *p* is the proposition that 3 is prime and *q* is the proposition that if "3" correctly applies, then "prime" correctly applies.

Let me now turn to the compatibility of inferentialism, deflationism, and normativism with TCS.

6.3.2. TD-Compatibility

TCS is one of the most widespread and successful semantic theories in modern linguistics (Davidson 1967; Larson and Segal 1995; Lepore and Ludwig 2005, 2007; among countless others). For this reason alone, to be inconsistent with it is a strike against any theory. That's not to say that TCS can't be wrong. But for a thesis to be inconsistent with it is certainly a prima facie reason not to believe the thesis. Among the prominent philosophical theories thought to be inconsistent with TCS are inferentialism, semantic deflationism, and all versions of non-descriptivism or expressivism, to which normativism is related. I believe that TCS is compatible with all of them. Unfortunately, a complete defense of this claim would require a book of its own. I hope, though, to convince the reader that their inconsistency isn't as obvious as it may have seemed.

TCS is usually described in slogan form as the view that the meaning of a sentence is its truth-condition, or simply that meanings are truth-conditions. This must be understood carefully, though. Davidson's seminal paper beings with the sentence "It is conceded by most philosophers of language, and recently even by some linguists, that a satisfactory theory of meaning must give an account of how the meanings of sentences

[26] There is, of course, an entire field dedicated to investigating behavior and reasoning from exactly this functional perspective: behaviorist psychology. One needn't take on the implausible anti-mentalist claims to see that there might be something valuable in behaviorism. What's important is behaviorism's functional selectionist perspective, not its anti-mentalism. Behaviorism is perfectly compatible with systemic functional linguistics, and I'm sure Chomsky hates the latter as much as he hates the former. I won't pursue this any further though, because I can already see the pitchforks.

depend upon the meanings of words" (1967, 304). Davidson was thus after a *compositional* meaning theory, and TCS was his proposal. A compositional meaning theory would explain the productivity, systematicity, and learnability of language. Lepore and Ludwig (2005) call this Davidson's "initial project." How does Davidson's TCS provide a compositional meaning theory? Taking inspiration from Tarski, he proposes that the trick is turned by developing a Tarskian truth theory for a language L, the goal of which is to find a finite set of axioms that will entail all sentences, called "T-theorems," of the form:

S is true if and only if p.

where "S" is replaced by a structural description of a sentence of L and "p" is replaced by that sentence. The axioms are denotation or reference claims and truth-definitions for the logical connectives and quantifiers. Done right, the finite set of axioms will generate truth-conditions, i.e., meanings, for every possible sentence in the language, thus explaining the productivity, systematicity, and learnability of language. Much more can be said about TCS and objections to it, and I urge the interested reader to consult the references in this section, but for now, this is all we need.

The classic argument against TD-Compatibility is a circularity argument. The argument, briefly, is that TCS explains meaning on the basis of truth, and semantic deflationism explains truth on the basis of meaning. (The equivalence schema, "'*p*' is true if and only if *p*," assumes that "*p*" is meaningful.) Therefore, combining them results in a vicious circularity. There have been a number of convincing responses to circularity arguments against TD-Compatibility (Burgess 2011; Gross 2015; Henderson 2017; Horisk 2008; Kölbel 2002; Löwenstein 2012; Williams 1999, 2007). I briefly recount some of these.

Kölbel (2002), Löwenstein (2012), and Williams (1999, 2007), each in slightly different ways, pick up on the fact that, in TCS, truth is not used to *explain* meaning at all. TCS is a semantic theory, not a metasemantic one. The theory says what meanings are, not how they are acquired. The latter is an explanandum not of TCS but of Davidson's metasemantic theory of radical interpretation. The job of TCS is to assign meanings—which, according to the theory, and with which the deflationist can agree, are truth-conditions—to sentences in a way that can account for the productivity, systematicity, and learnability of language. This is accomplished in TCS by assigning meanings recursively. That's Davidson's "initial project." It does not explain how or why sentences and their semantically primitive parts have their meanings/truth-conditions in the first place. *That* is what Lepore and Ludwig call Davidson's "extended project."

Of course, for Davidson, the metasemantic theory of radical interpretation is connected to the semantic theory, in that the radical interpreter is an idealized truth-conditional field semanticist treating T-theorems as empirical semantic hypotheses. Roughly, Davidson's metasemantic theory says that semantic facts *consist in* facts about which T-theorems an ideal radical interpreter would empirically confirm; i.e., what explains why sentences have (their) meanings/truth-conditions is that an ideal radical interpreter would empirically confirm the relevant T-theorems. But the truth-conditional field semanticist *herself* is simply doing first-order semantics, recursively assigning denotations to sentential primitives and meanings/truth-conditions to sentences. She certainly isn't trying to explain the meaningfulness of language in general. If anything, she *assumes* the noises she's interpreting are meaningful, because she assumes they are truth-apt, able to figure in T-theorems. The assumption that the noises are meaningful is a prerequisite for her semantic job.

In fact, a truth-conditional field semanticist who had the concept of meaningfulness in general and lacked the concept of truth would be in the same semantic-*cum*-epistemic boat as a truth-conditional field semanticist who had both concepts. Call the former "the deflationary field semanticist." Davidson excludes from the admissible evidence available to a radical interpreter any information about the meanings of a speaker's expressions or the contents of her beliefs. If the deflationary field semanticist were told only that some foreign sentence means something that is the case, she would be as in the dark about its meaning (and the speaker's beliefs) as Davidson's radical interpreter if she were told only that the sentence is true. Deflationary TCS explains what Davidson wanted to explain, using admissible explanantia: a deflationary T-theory would explain how the meanings of sentences depend on the meanings of their parts, and knowledge of a deflationary T-theory for a language would suffice for a non-speaker to understand that language, without circularly building in any prior understanding.

It would be simple to construct a formal deflationary T-theory if one accepts something like Künne's (2003, 2005) so-called modest definition of truth:

$\forall x$ (x is true if and only if $\exists p$ ($x = [p]$ & p))

("[p]" denotes the proposition that p). Many find the definition's reliance on sentential or propositional (not substitutional!) quantification problematic, but I see no reason to object to it. I'm a tolerant Carnapian, after all (so I wouldn't find substitutional quantification problematic either, so long as its rules are clearly spelled out).

There are several ways Künne translates his definition into English. One is "x is true if and only if things are as x says they are." Another is "x is true if and only if x says that things are thus and so, and things are thus and so." I prefer "x is true if and only if x means something that is the case."

It is easy to show how to give recursive definitions of the connectives and quantifiers in a way completely analogous to standard TCS. Where "$[\![\phi]\!]$" is the denotation of ϕ,

$\exists p([\![Px]\!] = [p]\ \&\ p)$ iff $[\![x]\!] \in [\![P]\!]$
$\exists p([\![\sim A]\!] = [p]\ \&\ p)$ iff $\exists p([\![A]\!] = [p]\ \&\ {\sim}p)$
$\exists p([\![A\&B]\!] = [p]\ \&\ p)$ iff $\exists p([\![A]\!] = [p]\ \&\ p)$ and $\exists p([\![B]\!] = [p]\ \&\ p)$
$\exists p([\![A \vee B]\!] = [p]\ \&\ p)$ iff $\exists p([\![A]\!] = [p]\ \&\ p)$ or $\exists p([\![B]\!] = [p]\ \&\ p)$
$\exists p([\![\forall x\varphi]\!] = [p]\ \&\ p)$ iff for every value d, $\exists p([\![\varphi[x/d]]\!] = [p]\ \&\ p)$
$\exists p([\![\exists x\varphi]\!] = [p]\ \&\ p)$ iff for some value d, $\exists p([\![\varphi[x/d]]\!] = [p]\ \&\ p)$

Let us illustrate with a simple interpretation **I**, according to which:

$[\![a]\!]^{\mathrm{I}}$ = Alice
$[\![b]\!]^{\mathrm{I}}$ = Bob
$[\![F]\!]^{\mathrm{I}} = \{x: x \text{ is fabulous}\}$
$[\![a]\!]^{\mathrm{I}} \in [\![F]\!]^{\mathrm{I}}$
$[\![b]\!]^{\mathrm{I}} \in [\![F]\!]^{\mathrm{I}}$

Alice and Bob are the only objects in the interpretation, and according to the interpretation, Alice is fabulous, and Bob is fabulous. Restricting the domain of quantification to persons, in standard TCS one can derive the following T-theorem:

"$\forall xFx$" is true (in **I**) iff everyone is fabulous (in **I**)

We can similarly derive a deflationary T-theorem:

"$\forall xFx$" means something that is the case (in I) iff everyone is fabulous (in I)

Proof:

1. "$\forall xFx$" means something that is the case (in I) iff $\exists p([\![\forall xFx]\!]^{I} = [p] \,\&\, p)$
2. $\exists p([\![\forall xFx]\!]^{I} = [p] \,\&\, p)$ iff for every value d (in I), $\exists p([\![Fx[x/d]]\!]^{I} = [p] \,\&\, p)$
3. For every value d (in I), $\exists p([\![Fx[x/d]]\!]^{I} = [p] \,\&\, p)$ iff $\exists p([\![Fa]\!]^{I} = [p] \,\&\, p)$ and $\exists p([\![Fb]\!]^{I} = [p] \,\&\, p)$
4. $\exists p([\![Fa]\!]^{I} = [p] \,\&\, p)$ and $\exists p([\![Fb]\!]^{I} = [p] \,\&\, p)$ iff $[\![a]\!]^{I} \in [\![F]\!]^{I}$ and $[\![b]\!]^{I} \in [\![F]\!]^{I}$
5. $[\![a]\!]^{I} \in [\![F]\!]^{I}$ and $[\![b]\!]^{I} \in [\![F]\!]^{I}$ iff Alice is fabulous and Bob is fabulous.
6. Therefore, "$\forall xFx$" means something that is the case (in I) iff everyone is fabulous (in I).

A deflationary T-theory accomplishes everything Davidson wanted: by explaining how the meaning of a sentence depends on the meanings of its parts, it explains the productivity, systematicity, and learnability of language.

6.3.3. TI-Compatibility

We saw that TCS is Davidson's semantic theory, and the theory of radical interpretation is his metasemantic theory. Now, we needn't adopt Davidson's metasemantic theory. We might, for example, be metasemantic inferentialists or use-theorists. We could then say that a sentence has its meaning (= truth-condition) in virtue of its use-construction property (Horwich 1998a) or in virtue of the inferential rules governing it, as I argued above. Interestingly, Horwich actually takes Davidson's theory of radical interpretation to boil down to a use theory, but he doesn't adopt TCS because he—wrongly, I think—believes they are inconsistent for the circularity reasons we already addressed. Williams (1999, 2007) considers the theory of radical interpretation a form of inferentialism. Now, I am not saying there is no version of TCS, or no way of conceiving of TCS, that is inconsistent with inferentialism (or deflationism). I'm only saying that it is possible for there to be a version of TCS that is consistent with them and that explains everything Davidson (and semanticists) want TCS to explain.

But what about compositionality? This is one of the most prominent objections to TI-Compatibility. The whole point of TCS is to provide a compositional meaning theory, and it is widely assumed that inferentialism is not a compositional theory because inferential roles (or rules) don't compose (Fodor and Lepore 2001). There are a few things to say about this. First, it seems to confuse metasemantics with semantics. The semantic values of expressions need to compose, and inferentialism does not say that the semantic values of expressions are inferential roles (or rules). No inferentialist says that "dog" means an inferential role or rule.

Second, Horwich (1998a) argues that compositionality places no constraints are theories of *lexical* meaning. If we say that, for example, the meanings of semantic primitives are determined by their inferential rules, but the meanings of complexes of primitives (phrases, sentences, etc.) are determined by how the primitives are combined, there is no problem, according to Horwich. In such a theory, the meanings of complexes would not be determined by inferential rules governing the complexes as such, but simply by the specific combination of primitives whose meanings are determined by the rules governing them. Complexes whose meanings are compositionally determined don't have *their own* inferential rules. When there are inferential rules governing a complex, that complex has a meaning that isn't compositionally determined. For example, there are rules governing the use of "red" and rules governing the use of "herring," but there are also distinct rules governing the use of "red herring," which makes the meaning of "red herring" not compositionally determined. Horwich's claim is highly controversial, though, and it would be nice if we could account for TI-Compatibility without relying on it.

Third, Peregrin (2014) argues that compositionality is an intrinsic feature of inferentialism. As he puts it, "They [i.e., inferential roles] are contributions that individual expressions bring to the inferential potentials of the sentences in which they occur; and it is only the principle of compositionality that makes it possible to individuate such contributions" (61). Inferential rules, after all, are rules for inferring *sentences*. This seems to me reminiscent of Davidson's own holistic view when he writes, "If sentences depend for their meaning on their structure, and we understand the meaning of each item in the structure only as an abstraction from the totality of sentences in which it features, then we can give the meaning of any sentence (or word) only by giving the meaning of every sentence (and word) in the language" (1967, 308).

Thus, a proper understanding of the distinction between semantics and metasemantics allows for TI-Compatibility. I acknowledge that this is far from a complete defense, but I hope I have convinced you that TI-Compatibility isn't obviously wrong. Next, I argue that a proper understanding of the distinction between truthmakers and truth-conditions allows for TN-Compatibility.

6.3.4. TN-Compatibility

Benacerraf (1973) provides a classic statement of one argument against TN-Compatibility. His is a challenge to provide a homogeneous[27] semantics for mathematical and non-mathematical discourse. A homogeneous semantics would treat the following two sentences as both having the logical form of the third:

1) There are at least three large cities older than New York.
2) There are at least three perfect numbers greater than 17.
3) There are at least three FG's that bear R to a. (Benacerraf 1973, 663)

And, the thought goes, only a platonist can treat 2) as true and as having the logical form of 3). I believe Creath (1980) is right that Benaceraff begs a central question in demanding a substantive referential conception of truth for a homogeneous semantics, and also that the demand for homogeneity is overblown. While I do think the demand for homogeneity is overblown, I want to argue here that it is not at all obvious that normativism is incompatible with a homogeneous semantics based on TCS. The Carnapian normativist can agree that sentences 1) and 2) have the logical form of sentence 3). Carnapians and similar metaontological deflationists (Schiffer 2003; Thomasson 2014; see also Price 2011) have argued that, e.g., a proposition like "It is possible that *p*" analytically entails "There is a possible world where *p*," which analytically entails "There are possible worlds." Metaontological deflationists take such analytic entailments to have no substantive ontological implications;

[27] Note that there are (at least) two senses in which one's semantics might be inhomogeneous: one might, e.g., adopt TCS for non-mathematical discourse and a different semantic theory altogether for mathematical discourse, or one might adopt TCS for non-mathematical and mathematical discourse, but argue that non-mathematical and mathematical sentences with similar grammatical form actually have different logical form. I don't think our semantics needs to be inhomogeneous in either sense.

possible worlds are hypostatizations of our possibility-talk. Deflationists have made similar arguments for other kinds of entity. For example, "The ball is red" analytically entails "The ball has the property of being red," which analytically entails "There are properties." Again, such analytic entailments have no substantive ontological implications; properties are hypostatizations of predicates. The mathematical deflationist can similarly say that "There are three mice" analytically entails "The number of mice is 3," which analytically entails "There are numbers" (see Hale and Wright 2001 for similar arguments, and see Chapter 8 for a discussion of neo-Fregeanism). Thus, nothing prevents the normativist from saying that sentence 2) has the logical form of sentence 3). This is analytic; sentence 2) analytically entails sentence 3). In fact, "There are at least three perfect numbers greater than 17" analytically entails "Certain mathematical objects stand in a certain relation to each other," just as "There are at least three large cities older than New York" analytically entails "Certain cities stand in a certain relation to each other." This is just what Benaceraff demands of a homogeneous semantics. Normativism need not be a primitive expressivism that denies the surface grammar of sentences. Again, the normativist can speak of mathematical truths, reference, beliefs, knowledge, assertions, propositions, facts, and descriptions. She can even say that a true mathematical proposition describes a mathematical fact, as long as these terms are understood in suitably deflationary (analytic) senses, and as long as she doesn't say that the proposition is true *because* it describes a mathematical fact.

Here I think Creath (1980) hits the nail on the head: to demand more than this, to demand that the semantics invoke a *substantive* notion of reference (or truth), so that the ontology mirrors the semantics, is to beg the question. That demand also misunderstands the job of a semantic theory. Semanticists are not metaphysicians. The semanticist's truth-conditions are not the metaphysician's truthmakers (Bar-On 2019; Bar-On and Simmons 2018; Dyke 2007; Heil 2003), and it is not the job of the semanticist to find a proposition's truthmakers or determine whether it has or needs any in the first place. This might be the most pernicious confusion of contemporary philosophy, at least since Dummett's (1978) semantic construal of the distinction between realism and anti-realism. The semanticist's job is, primarily, to explain the productivity, systematicity, and learnability of language, and perhaps for the psychosemanticist, linguistic behavior, e.g., a person's patterns of assent and dissent to specific sentences in specific circumstances. This is completely orthogonal to metaphysics. To think otherwise commits one to absurd claims, such as that only metaphysicians understand language (or at least that all speakers are tacit metaphysicians), since to know the meaning of a sentence is to know its truth-condition and its truth-condition is its truthmaker, and to know the meaning of a sentence is to know its truthmaker, which only a metaphysician would know; that metaphysicians who disagree about a sentence's truthmaker (e.g., a trope theorist and an Armstrongian) disagree about its meaning;[28] that propositions with the same truthmaker have the same meaning;[29] and that unambiguous propositions only have one truthmaker, since they only have one truth-condition or meaning.[30] These are four powerful reasons not to confuse truth-conditions with truthmakers.

A truth-conditional theory of meaning for a language takes the form of a logically regimented recursive theory with a finite set of axioms because a theory of this form is compositional and easily explains the productivity, systematicity, and learnability of that language, *not* because a theory of this form limns the metaphysical nature of reality. Suppose the truth-conditional semanticist derives from her axioms the following T-theorem, that is, a specification of a truth condition: "There are at least three perfect numbers greater than 17" is true if and only if there are at least three perfect numbers that bear the greater-than relation to 17. There is nothing here for the normativist to balk at, for according to her, the sides of the biconditional analytically entail each other. The left-hand side can be read deflationarily as expressing an actual conceptual rule, and the right-hand side also expresses an actual conceptual rule (viz., the same rule), so the biconditional is true.[31] (Just as the normativist needn't balk when a concept's application conditions can only be stated in platonistic terms, for those terms will be read normativistically.) The move I'm making here is somewhat akin to the move the truthmaker B-theorist makes (see Dyke 2007). The truthmaker B-theorist accepts that no tensed sentences are synonymous with any tenseless sentences—the truth conditions of tensed sentences cannot be specified tenselessly—but tensed sentences have tenseless facts as their truthmakers. Similarly, I don't think that any platonistic sentences are synonymous with any nominalistic

[28] The fact that metaphysicians usually take themselves to be arguing about a certain *proposition's* truthmaker shows that on some level they know that a truthmaker is not a truth-condition. For, to disagree about the truthmaker of the *same* proposition requires holding its meaning fixed.

[29] Dyke (2007) argues, following Armstrong (2004), that nonsynonymous propositions can have the same truthmaker, e.g., "The rose is red" and "The rose is colored."

[30] Dyke (2007) argues, following Armstrong (1997), that some unambiguous propositions can have more than one truthmaker, e.g., "There exists at least one black swan."

[31] Obviously the biconditional would still be true if it specified the truth conditions for a mathematical falsehood since both sides would be false.

sentences—the truth conditions of platonistic sentences cannot be specified nominalistically—but we do not need platonistic facts to explain the truth of the former. However, we don't need nominalistic facts either. Here is where I part with the truthmaker B-theorist. Normativism explains why we don't need truthmakers for mathematical claims at all—they are expressions of conceptual rules.

According to the truth-conditional semanticist, to *know* a sentence's meaning is to *know* its truth condition. It is this *knowledge* claim, along with the fact that the *content* of what is known is given a recursively specifiable logical form, that is the basis of the explanation of the productivity, systematicity, and learnability of language—nothing about the metaphysics of what that content represents, or of the representation relation itself, enters the picture. I take this to be a general lesson of the following point of Davidson's (2001, 31):

> Even if we hold there is some important sense in which moral or evaluative sentences do not have a truth value (for example, because they cannot be verified), we ought not to boggle at "'Bardot is good' is true if and only if Bardot is good." . . . What is special to evaluative words is simply not touched: the mystery is transferred from the word 'good' in the object language to its translation in the metalanguage.

6.4. Summary

Let me sum up the main claims of this chapter. I defended a broad normative inferentialism about the content of (applicable) mathematical concepts. These concepts' content is determined by the inferential rules governing them, including empirical application conditions. There is no special philosophical problem of mathematical applicability: *hexagon* applies to a concrete hexagonal object for the same reason that *honeycomb* applies to a honeycomb—its application conditions are met. I agreed with structuralists that the content of a mathematical concept is structural, i.e., that it has structural application conditions. I disagreed that this implies that pure mathematics describes structures. I argued we can view the mapping account of application as supplying application conditions for structural mathematical concepts. Finally, I argued that distinguishing between the semantics, metasemantics, and function of a discourse, and between truth-conditions and truthmakers, allows us to see that normativism, inferentialism, deflationism, and TCS are compatible.[32] The semantic-metasemantic-functional strategy of this chapter is open to normativists and expressivists about any area of discourse.

I have only scratched the surface of these issues. A full exploration and defense of the ideas presented in this chapter is itself a book-length project. For now, we must move on. In Chapter 7, I discuss a similar topic—the content of models, including mathematical models of various sorts. Unsurprisingly, I defend an inferentialist theory there too.

[32] See also note 10 of Chapter 7.

7

The Content of a Mathematical Model

7.1. Introduction

What gives scientific representations or models[1] their meaning or content—how do they come to represent things in the world, and in what way do they represent them? In this chapter, we defend a novel inferentialist account of the content of mathematical models (and of models generally) that we call the fully inferentialist theory (FIT).[2] Previous inferentialist accounts have been "deflationary" (e.g., Suarez 2004); they say that inference affordance constitutes the content of representations but have been non-committal about how particular representations afford particular inferences. We provide a substantive account in this respect. According to FIT, the content of a model is determined by the inferences that are to be made from it, and the inferences that are to be made from it are determined by the form of the model and the denotational conventions surrounding it. (Note: throughout this chapter, we do not use "denotes" as a success term: one can stipulate that *X* denotes *Y* even though *Y* doesn't exist.) We argue for a normative role for denotation-claims as expressing the stipulated validity of what I call "rules of partial inference." (Note that just because they express rules doesn't mean denotation-claims are necessary. According to normativism, they would only be necessary if they expressed rules governing the use of the terms therein.) Denotations are stipulated, and stipulating a denotation is akin to stipulating the validity of an inference rule.[3] I say they express "rules of partial inference" because, typically, the form of the model and *several* rules of partial inference are required to determine any given inference from the model to the target system. We illustrate our account with several case studies of causal models,

[1] We use the terms "representation" and "model" interchangeably.

[2] This chapter is a slightly revised version of work with Dan Burnston that is currently under review. I will accordingly use first-person plural pronouns and possessives when drawing from that collaborative work and singular when the ideas are wholly mine. No claims I make in the appendix, nor regarding normativism and the generalized ontic conception, should be attributed to Dan.

[3] Given its reliance on denotative stipulation and its expressive-inferentialist way of cashing that out, Dan and I also considered calling our view "Gricean inferentialism."

Rules to Infinity. Mark Povich, Oxford University Press. © Oxford University Press 2024.
DOI: 10.1093/oso/9780197679005.003.0007

network models, oscillator models, and applied mathematical equations and argue that it accommodates the widespread use of idealization, and the many different styles of representation scientists use, better than non-inferentialist accounts. I also discuss how models provide explanations in a manner consistent with my generalized ontic conception and how FIT can account for the notions of model truth and accuracy.

Most current views of scientific representation are hybrids of one form or another. They admit that there are multiple factors that go into determining the content of a representation, and therefore how the representation shapes scientific endeavor. Usually, these include the intentions of scientists and the pragmatic context. We distinguish *inferentialist* from *referentialist* hybrid accounts. Inferentialist accounts identify content with the inferences that a representation affords a competent user. They cite intentional and pragmatic context to delimit the set of allowable inferences. Referentialist accounts identify content with some objective relation that obtains between a representation and its target—major versions include *similarity*, *morphism*, and *exemplification* accounts. They cite intentional and pragmatic context to specify the objective relation that holds in particular cases.

In this chapter, we argue that FIT gives a better answer than referentialist views to the problems of *idealization* and *style*. The problem of idealization is how to account for the fact that even successful representations misrepresent their targets in many ways, and that at best partial and complicated relations hold between them (Rice 2019). The problem of style is that there is an astounding *diversity* of types of scientific representation. A good account of representation should explain why this diversity is present, and why it is important to scientific practice. More generally, everyone party to the debate recognizes that a good account of representation should intelligibly connect the content of scientific representations to how they shape and direct the practice that employs them.

The basic problem for referentialist accounts is that they have to sift through the many complex relations between representations and their targets to determine the precise objective relation that obtains between them. It is very doubtful that the intentions and pragmatic contexts they cite are fine-grained enough to specify these relations, without being attributed to the scientists post hoc. With regard to idealization, they implausibly presume that scientists have a precise relation in mind when employing a representation. With regard to style, they implausibly presume that all stylistic differences must ultimately bottom out in referential differences.

Inferentialism, on the other hand, does *not* postulate that some specific objective relation constitutes the content of a representation, and hence has compelling answers to both problems. Idealizations are employed when they afford the inferences that scientists need to make about the target. Different styles of representation are employed because they afford different inferences.

We proceed as follows. In Section 7.2, we describe extant accounts in more detail. In Section 7.3, we outline our fully inferentialist theory (FIT), and in Section 7.4, we illustrate it by analyzing three different kinds of commonly used scientific representation: causal models, network models, oscillator models, and applied mathematical equations. In Section 7.5, we argue that inferentialism fares better than referentialism at accounting for idealization and style. In Section 7.6, we discuss model truth and accuracy, model explanation, and a limited potential role for similarity and morphism in securing model success.

7.2. The Lay of the Land

There are three types of hybrid referentialist account—similarity accounts, morphism accounts, and exemplification accounts—which differ in the objective relation they posit as a partial determiner of content. On similarity accounts, representations bear some type and degree of similarity relation to their targets. On morphism accounts, both representation and target instantiate a shared set-theoretic structure. On exemplification accounts, representations exemplify features of their targets.

To a significant degree, the hybrid nature of these accounts is motivated by needing to solve the problem of idealization.[4] Referentialist accounts posit an objective relation between representation and target—however, if we admit that idealization is both widespread and necessary, then describing that relationship is not straightforward, since idealization simply is a mismatch between the features of the representation and those of what it represents. The most sophisticated forms of referentialist views thus employ their hybrid aspects in helping specify the objective relation.

So, for instance, on Weisberg's (2013) influential similarity view, it is not similarity full stop that underlies representation, but similarity with respect

[4] Another motivation is to account for purported logical problems in specifying the relation—namely showing how the representation relation can be asymmetric and irreflexive. Since these problems have been widely discussed (Suarez 2004), we do not discuss them in depth here.

to certain features and to certain degrees.[5] The respects and degrees are determined by the purposes of the user—the scientist employing the representation sets the "fidelity conditions" that they take to obtain between representation and target, which underlie using the former to uncover things about the latter. On da Costa and French's (2003) "partial morphism" account, a representation implements a partial structural mapping with its target, where again which mapping is relevant depends on the aims of the representer.

Recently, Frigg and Nguyen (2020) have incorporated Goodman's (1976) and Elgin's (2009) view of exemplification into a sophisticated hybrid account of representation. On their "DEKI" account, representation is determined by Denotation, Exemplification, Keying-Up, and Imputation. On this view, a scientist uses a representation to denote a target. While both the representation and the target have many features, the exemplification relation is specified by the scientist's "interpretation" of the representation—they specify that the properties of the representation exemplify properties of the target in a particular respect. This interpretation is then encoded into the "key" of the representation, which, analogously to the key on a map, allows the user to apply or "impute" those features of the representation to the target.

So, referentialist accounts attempt to theorize around a purported mismatch between the representation and its target, by relying on the purposes and intentions of the user to specify the particular relations that determine the representation's content. On inferentialism, the intentions of the user specify the target of the representation—i.e., what it denotes or refers to (cf. Callender and Cohen 2006; Ruyant 2022). Then the content of the representation is constituted by the inferential allowances that it provides about that target. One can see this structure even in the earliest formulations of inferentialism. In Suarez's (2004, 773) original formulation of the view, "A represents B only if (i) the representational force of A points towards B, and (ii) A allows competent and informed agents to draw specific inferences regarding B," where the "representational force" is a function of the aims and intentions of the scientist.

Prima facie, inferentialism has an easier path with regard to idealization, because it does not require a particular objective relation to hold

[5] There is some debate about how exactly to flesh out this idea of a metric, e.g., whether it is only quantitative or also qualitative similarity (Parker 2015), or whether similarity can be assessed only holistically (Fang 2017). We do not think these extensions matter for our arguments against similarity below, so we will gloss over them here.

between representation and target. Inferentialism, however, faces two major problems of its own. The first is the problem of surrogate inference. Since inferentialism says nothing about the substantive relations that hold between representation and target, it doesn't explain why it is that particular inferences about the target are afforded by the representation—i.e., why one can use the representation to reason surrogatively about the referent. One part of this challenge has been to suggest that inferentalists in fact "smuggle in" more substantive representation-target relations without realizing it (Contessa 2013). The second, related problem is that inferentialism is "too deflationary." "Affording inference" is a very nebulous notion. What is it for a particular representation to afford particular inferences about its target? Why does it afford some and not others? While the deflationary nature of inferentialism is sometimes touted as an advantage (Suarez 2015), one might reasonably want a more substantive account, particularly when the goal is to explain scientific practice (Frigg and Nguyen 2020; Poznic 2018).

In a recent and important paper, Khalifa, Millson, and Risjord (2022) have made significant progress with regard to the problem of surrogative reasoning (cf. Fang 2019). On their view, A represents B if it plays a part of an accepted scientific practice licensing the interpretation of derivations from A in terms of testable conclusions about B. This licensing, on their view, requires no specific structural relationship to obtain. Rather, when scientists reason with a representation, they rely on its "inferential pedigree"—its history of success in allowing us to draw testable inferences about its target. Since this reference to inferential pedigree does not require positing objective relations, inferentialism can account for surrogative reasoning without smuggling any in. We think that Khalifa et al.'s view is on precisely the right track with regard to the problem of surrogative inference. However, their view faces a rather serious version of the deflationism worry. This is because they are inclined to say that a representation only has content—i.e., denotes or represents a specific target—subsequent to the establishment of an inferential license. They say, "A model M represents a target T if and only if justified surrogative inferences about T can be drawn from M" (265). They make a similar claim about denotation (283).

This cannot be the right account of content, at least in a non-deflationary sense, because positing content at the end of a licensing process ignores the fact that content is part of establishing the license in the first place. Representations must afford particular inferences in order to establish the history of successful inference that underlies justification, so the theory of content must not presume successful licensing. Moreover, representations frequently fail to attain inferential license. That is, they fail to provide successful inferences. But presumably, the way that failure is discovered is precisely by using it to draw inferences about the target, which then are not borne out. So, even if the account of surrogative inference is right, we still need an account of why particular representations afford the inferences they do.

According to our version of inferentialism, which we cash out in detail below, the form of a representation and its representational conventions determine which inferences we are allowed to make. Note that this does not imply that the conclusions of those inferences—the claims about the target—are justified, true, or accurate. In contrast to Khalifa, Millson, and Risjord, we think denotation is prior to and meant to constrain inference. Denotation, along with the other conventions, helps to determine which inferences we are allowed or entitled to make (and those we are not allowed to make). It is then a substantive question whether those inferences are true or justified. The next section fleshes out our version of inferentialism.

7.3. The Fully Inferentialist Theory

As noted, inferentialism says that a representation's meaning is its contribution to an agent's inferences about a referent. In our view, representations shape scientific inquiry by affording certain kinds of inferences rather than others. As discussed in Chapter 6, inferentialism takes the use of a representation to be explanatorily prior to its meaning (Brandom 2000). On this kind of view, the meaning of a representation is the result of a (perhaps implicit, rule-governed) disposition to use it in certain ways. The challenge of the inferentialist approach is to explain how these implicit tendencies result in explicit claims that can be true or false. We argue that the correct use of a representation depends on the conventions surrounding the representation, where these include conventions about the representation's form, what (parts of) the representation denote(s), and how that representation is to be manipulated in drawing inferences from it.

So, here is a formulation of our view. We begin with an analysis of representing, which we take to be explanatorily prior to the representation itself:

Representing: An intentional act of using a representation with conventions c, involving form f and referents p. These components together determine the inferential set, i, of the representation.

Representation: The meaning of a representation is its inferential set.

The hybrid aspect of our view is captured in the notion of "representing." Representing is, as with early versions of inferentialism, an intentional act to use the representation for a specific purpose. It is this intention which determines the referent or referents of the representation. These referents, combined with the form of the representation and the conventions surrounding its use, determine the inferences that can be drawn from the representation, which we call its inferential set. As noted above, this falls short of saying that successful surrogative reasoning is enabled simply through creating a representation. The inferential set is the set of inferences that the representation affords; it is then a separate question whether they are true or justified.

Let us begin by talking through a standard example: maps. The semantics of maps has been discussed in some detail recently (Camp 2018), and we do not plan to engage with every aspect of this debate. Moreover, maps are often cited in the literature on scientific representation (Boesch 2019; Van Fraasen 2008), and we don't want to argue here that our view is the best or only reading of the semantics of maps. Instead, we simply want to provide an intuitive, quotidian set of examples to illustrate the aspects of our inferentialist view. This will set up our description of the semantics of specific scientific representations in Section 7.4, and our arguments about idealization and style in Section 7.5.

On our view, a map is a representation of a geographic area in virtue of an agent intentionally representing that area using conventions (c), involving referents (p) and form (f). Together, these determine which content-constituting inferences (i) can be drawn from the map. Maps are used to denote geographical particulars and their spatial relations using symbols which index them. Maps represent lakes and rivers, subway stations, demographic populations, voting districts, hiking trails, etc. These symbols and indices, along with the selection of a geographic scope for the map, determine p, the referents of the representation. The model affords inferences in virtue of the referents being represented by way of a particular form and set of conventions.

Conventions interact with and take advantage of the form of a representation to shape allowable inferences. Most maps represent a three-dimensional surface of the world in a two-dimensional display and have several common conventions. For instance, spatial proximity of two icons on the map is standardly interpreted as portraying spatial proximity between the objects they denote. Lines on maps that connect icons are generally taken to portray some navigable route between them, where that route is respectful of the spatial relations conveyed. In using a representation, we interpret the physical form of the representation according to the conventions to infer things about the referent(s). So, if I am looking at any map, I can interpret distance and direction in the map in terms of distance and direction in the world, due to the conventions that all maps share. Any map, for instance, will portray Boston as higher and to the right of New York, and therefore any map will allow me to infer that navigating from New York to Boston will involve going northeast.

However, a quick glance at different types of maps shows that differences in conventions tracks differences in allowable inferences. A famous example is the difference between subway maps and street maps—while street maps represent spatial relations at a constant scale, these relations are often warped in a subway map to emphasize navigability in the subway. So, while two equal distances in a road map are always the same distance in the world, one cannot infer this in a subway map. There are many other examples. Consider the difference between a hiking and a subway map. On a hiking map, any time two trails intersect, one may infer that they can switch between one and the other. This is not the case on a subway map—the ability to change from one line to another can be inferred only when the lines intersect at a station. Or consider a hiking map versus a demographic map. When I intersect a new feature in a hiking map, something about my surroundings will change. I will have to cross a stream, go uphill, etc. In a demographic map, no such change is entailed when one crosses a border.

The focus on conventions and form is firmly supported by work in the cognitive sciences. For instance, Hegarty and colleagues (Hegarty 2011) have extensively studied the way in which both students and experts learn to employ different forms of representation, and what forms make certain kinds of representations useful (Hegarty, Stieff, and Dixon 2013). They argue compellingly that, for instance in introductory organic chemistry classes, learning a domain involves using the right representational tools in the right ways. Importantly, these ways must be taught, either explicitly or implicitly. In our view, this means that students' ability to solve problems in a given domain requires using the representations with the proper conventions. Similarly, research has shown that experts do better at integrating different forms of representation, for instance data graphs and equations, to solve more complex problems (Stieff, Hegarty, and Deslongchamps 2011). Such research has also inspired normative analysis of what the most useful forms and conventions are for certain purposes (Sheredos 2017).

Let us now expand on our claim that the meaning of a representation is its inferential set. We define the inferential set as comprising three subsets. First, there is the set of inferences that are entailed by the representation, without any additional information. Call this the "entailment set." In a scale map, this will largely consist of distance-proximity relations. For example, if the dot labeled "Boston" is two inches from the dot labeled "New York" on the map, and the scale is 150 miles per inch, then one can infer that Boston is 300 miles from New York, etc. Second, there is the "disallowed set," which is the set of inferences I cannot make when reasoning in the representation. So, given that Boston is up and to the right from New York, I cannot infer that traveling southwest from New York is a way to get to Boston. Last, there is what we call the importation set. This is the set of inferences that is not in the entailment set, but would be entailed given the conventions and form of the map plus background information. The differences between distinct representations, and types thereof, are due to differences in their inferential sets—i.e., different representations constrain and afford reasoning in different ways.

The entailment set and disallowed set are relatively straightforward. The importation set is a novel proposal, and requires some fleshing out and justification. Suppose I locate myself on a road map exactly between New York and Boston. The entailment set includes that if I travel southwest I will be closer to New York than to Boston, and vice versa if I move northeast. The importation set combines this information with background knowledge about the referents. So, the importation set allows the inference that if I move southwest, I will be closer to good pizza than to good chowder, and vice versa if I move northeast. While this is a quotidian example, it is meant to capture something important about representations, namely that they are reasoned with by agents for purposes. It is highly artificial to think that an actual agent reasons "purely inside" a representation. What we use a map for is not simply to extract entailments from it, such as that Boston is closer to New York than to Tampa (although of course we may do that), but to reason about situations. Do I have enough gas to make it to Boston? Do I have enough time for all the changes I'd need to make to get to the Met before the exhibition opens? It is these kinds of scenarios that invite background knowledge relevant to our purposes.

So, why include importation in the content of a representation, rather than tying the content to the entailment set and leaving importation as a separate reasoning process? Aside from the foregoing, it is vital to note that different forms and conventions allow for and encourage the importation of different types of information, because there are standard kinds of purposes to which they are put. The amount of gas in my car is relevant in a road map, but not so much in a hiking map. The kind of shoes I am wearing is very relevant when using a hiking map, but not a subway map. We think that any substantive use of a representation employs importation of this type, and hence that structuring what kind of inferences can be imported and combined with its entailments is a vital function for any representation. Hence, we think any view of the semantics of representations has to include a role for something like importation.

There are two major, related objections one might have to including the importation set in the content of a representation. The first is that it leaves the content open-ended. The second is that, given that background knowledge will differ between individuals, its content will be idiosyncratic. Our response is to introduce a distinction between "social" and "individual" content (cf. Povich 2021a).[6] The key to this distinction is to recognize that representations are public artifacts, with surrounding accepted practices of use and shared knowledge about the targets. But representations are often employed and reasoned with by individuals who have their own (more or less idiosyncratic) purposes and knowledge.

For instance, we all agree about the standard conventions for road maps and the kinds of things one can represent with them, but this leaves open the importation of distinct information in distinct contexts.

[6] In a different context, Ruyant (2022) has given a similar view with which we are largely sympathetic. Ruyant, following Grice, distinguishes between "contextual use" of a representation (or utterance) and its "general status." The difference is that a particular contextual use of a representation is dependent on the mental states of the user, while its general status is the result of communal norms of appropriateness.

A motorist and a general will both use a roadmap according to its standard conventions, but their aims and differing background knowledge will shape what inferences they draw from it. In either case, a subway map would simply not afford the same kinds of imported inferences that the road map does.

Our claim is that when scientists employ representations, they utilize a combination of social and individual content in their deliberations. Social content comprises the standard representational conventions and shared background knowledge about the target. Individual content is shaped by one's own background knowledge. Both contribute to the inferential set of the representation, including its importation set. Consider two different scientists from different experimental backgrounds, using the same diagram or model of a system. These scientists will be like the motorist and the general—while they employ the same conventions and referents in the representation, the upshot of the inferences drawable from the model will be different. They will expect, for instance, different experimental outcomes in virtue of the same represented entities and relationships (Burnston [2013] gives a case study illustrating this kind of outcome).

So, our view is that the content of representations is both open-ended and idiosyncratic, but that this is a fact about representational practice that we should capture rather than avoid. Further, these features are not inexplicable. We can think of them as intelligible and specific within particular contexts of reasoning and particular representational purposes. Last, recall that any hybrid view refers, at certain points and for certain purposes, to the pragmatic context surrounding the use of a representation in explaining its content. So, invoking these in our discussion of social content is in no way illegitimate; this is simply where we employ that resource, whereas a referentialist view employs it in fixing the appropriate kind of relation between representation and target. In the next section, we will show how our account explains the content of different types of representations, both in general and in neuroscientific applications.

7.4. Case Studies

We now illustrate how FIT explains the content of several kinds of scientific model: causal models, network models, oscillator models, and applied mathematical equations.

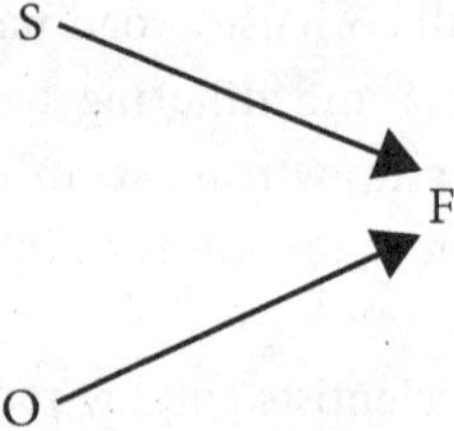

Figure 7.1 A simple causal model. From Woodward (2003, 45, Fig. 2.2.2).

7.4.1. Causal Models

Causal models consist of variables, often symbolized by capital English letters and arrows between them. In the simplest case, a causal model represents causal relationships between binary (event-type) variables. Such models are prized for their potential explanatoriness and the opportunities for counterfactual analysis they offer (Pearl 2000). Consider the simple example in Figure 7.1 from Woodward (2003, 45).

The representational conventions, c, are as follows. The diagram has a form, f, consisting of the English letters "S", "O", and "F", and arrows pointing from each of "S" and "O" toward "F". Each variable denotes an event-type whose occurrence is denoted by the variable taking the value "1" and whose non-occurrence is denoted by the variable taking the value "0". The referents, p, include the S variable denoting a short circuit, O denoting oxygen, and F denoting fire. Thus, S = 1 denotes the occurrence of a short circuit, and so on. Arrows denote causal difference-making relations between the events denoted by the variables, meaning that a change in the value of one variable would change the value of the other, for some fixed values of the other variables in the graph. This relation is usually called "direct causation." Assume that the variables are related by the following equation: F = S x O. Importantly, as can be seen by both the equation and the definition of direct causation, an arrow does not denote the relation of causal sufficiency—that is, the conventions involve interpreting the arrows as causal contributors but not as causally sufficient for F to occur.

With these conventions in place, we can explore the inferential set, i. First, there are the entailed inferences, e.g., that the presence of a short circuit and oxygen are jointly, but not individually, causally sufficient for the occurrence of fire. (Since F = S x O, F = 1 when and only when S = 1 and O = 1.) Second, there are disallowed inferences, e.g., that oxygen is individually causally sufficient for the occurrence of fire. Here we include not only inferences that are inconsistent with the entailment set or are inconsistent with the conventions, but certain inferences that are not supported by, or "go beyond," the conventions. For example, the conventions say nothing about the specific lengths of arrows, so an inference from the length of a given arrow to a claim about the target system is in the disallowed set. Third, there are the imported inferences, e.g., that I ought to be alert to wear and tear on the electrical wires in my garage, since I know that wear and tear increases the probability of a short circuit and I don't want a fire.

Let us move on to an applied example. Consider the dual-route cascade (DRC) model of reading, shown in Figure 7.2 (Coltheart 2005; Coltheart et al. 2001).

The conventions, c, are as follows. The form, f, consists of labeled boxes, ellipses, and arrows arranged in a specific way. The referents, p, include that arrows denote excitatory connections, and lines ending in dots inhibitory ones. Ellipses refer to inputs from the environment to the reading system in the form of printed texts, as well as its output of speech. Boxes refer to cognitive modules. The conventions for this kind of representation involve thinking of modules as distinct processing units that exchange information via their connections. These modules are also standardly construed as having distinct information stores, e.g., for "letter units," which are then processed into the orthographic and phonemic units stored at other modules.

We can now explore the inferential set, i. First, there are the entailed inferences, such as that there are distinct paths through the system—e.g., there is a route from the letter units module to speech that goes unidirectionally through the grapheme-phoneme rule system and the phoneme system, and another, more complicated route that goes through the orthographic and phonological lexicons. Second, there are the disallowed inferences, such as that information can pass directly from the grapheme-phoneme rule system to the orthographic lexicon. Finally, there are the imported inferences. For instance, if I know that injury to a particular part of the brain affects the grapheme-phoneme rule system, then I can infer that injury to that part of the brain will affect the route to the phoneme system but not the route running through the orthographic and phonemic lexicons.

These inferences are used to explain specific phenomena surrounding reading, such as dyslexia. For instance, an interruption to the route through the lexicon would interrupt more demanding processing based on stored

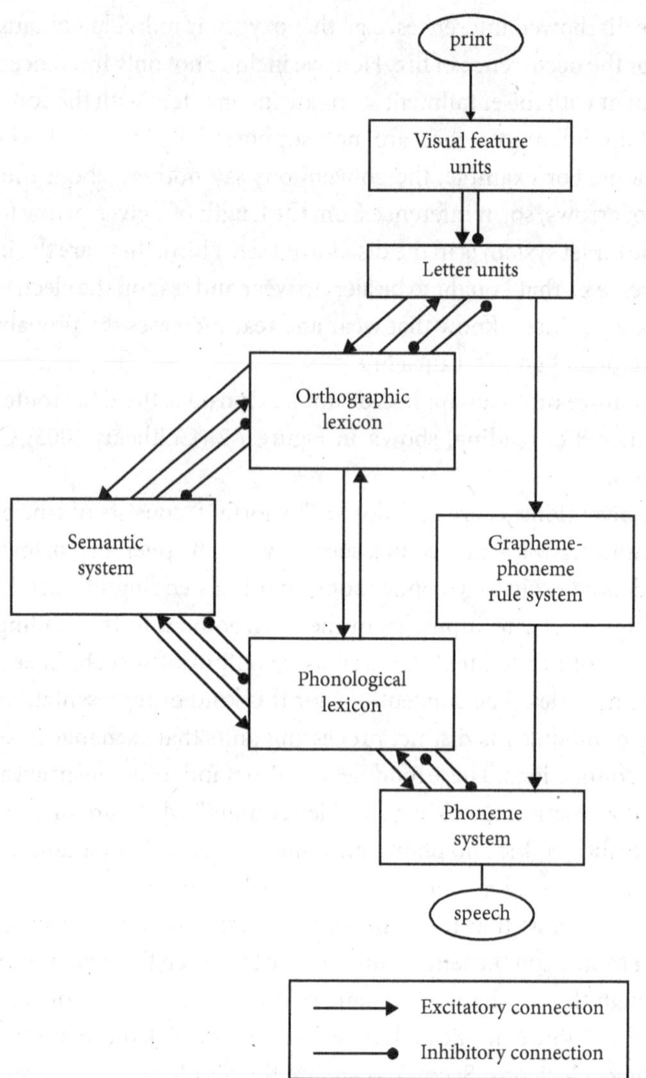

Figure 7.2 The DRC model. From Coltheart (2005, p.12, Figure 1.2). Reprinted with permission from OUP.

orthographic and phonemic knowledge (e.g., knowledge of exceptions), while leaving intact processing of phonemes that could be interpreted by a strict grapheme-phoneme rule. This predicts some of the differential deficits shown in dyslexia, such as that reading of non-words or "regular" words (e.g., "market") can remain intact while processing of irregular words (e.g., "yacht") is interrupted. Irregular words require the lexical pathway because they have no grapheme-phoneme correspondence rules.

Importation can extend these inferences. Suppose, for instance, that developmental deficits in phonological awareness specifically affect the grapheme-phoneme rule system. If that is the case, then one may predict that children with those developmental deficits will develop forms of dyslexia opposite of those above; i.e., they will have trouble reading non-words while being better at regular and irregular words. This kind of explanation is one that is put forward for the etiology of distinct forms of dyslexia.

7.4.2. Network Models

A network model is a representation consisting of nodes (or vertices) and edges (connections between nodes). The nodes and edges denote different things in different network models. One significant fact about network models is that one can make generalizations across networks of similar structure, regardless of what the nodes and edges are taken to represent. For example, one can make generalizations across all networks that are "small-world," i.e., that have high clustering but a small characteristic path length (Watts 2000; Watts and Strogatz 1998). This means that most nodes are in close communication with their local community, but also that it is easy to get from any node to any other node. Consider the small-world network shown in Figure 7.3, adapted from Barabási (2002, 71).

The representational conventions, c, are as follows. The form, f, consists of nodes and edges in a particular arrangement. For referents, p nodes denote large American airports, and edges denote the existence of direct flights between them; the large node denotes O'Hare International Airport in Chicago. Given its many connections, it is called a network hub.

We can now explore the inferential set, i. First, there are the entailed inferences, e.g., that from Chicago we can get to any other airport with just a few direct flights. Second, there are disallowed inferences, e.g., that there is a direct flight from every airport to every other airport. Third, there are the imported inferences; e.g., if I know that there is good deep-dish pizza in Chicago, then I know that from any airport I am a few direct flights away from good deep-dish pizza.

Similar kinds of network model, including small-world models, are constructed in neuroscience. For example, network models of schizophrenia

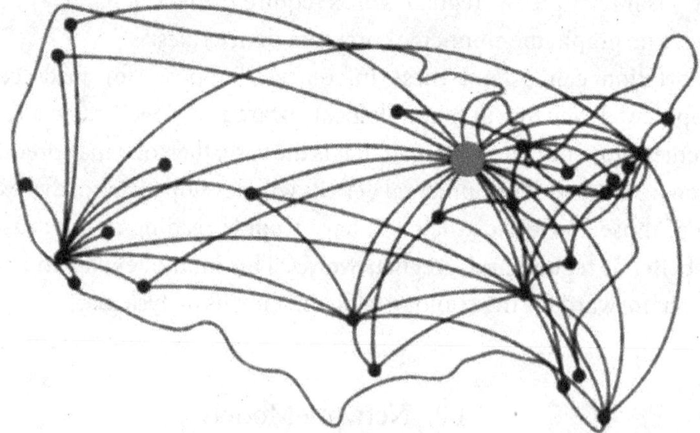

Figure 7.3 Network structure in airport connections. Adapted from Barabási (2002, p.71, Figure 6.1). Reprinted with permission from Albert-László Barabási.

are influential, where studies have repeatedly found fewer and less-central hubs in frontal association areas in persons with schizophrenia (for an overview, see Rubinov and Bullmore 2013). There are several measures of centrality, the most common being based on degree (the number of edges between a node and other nodes). Regional efficiency is a similar measure of the connectivity of a node to all the other nodes. Thus, nodes with high regional efficiencies and high centrality are hubs, which, in the neural context means they are brain areas that can communicate efficiently with many other areas (Wang et al. 2012, 1089). Wang et al., among others, have characterized schizophrenia as a disruption of the brain's small-world properties.

In their network model, portrayed in Figure 7.4, the representational conventions, c, are as follows. The form, f, comprises nodes of varying sizes and edges connected in a specific way. The referents, p, are that nodes denote particular functional brain areas, and that edges denote connections between them. In this case, the edges denote anatomical connectivity—i.e., the presence of white matter tracts connecting two areas of the brain. Black and gray nodes denote comparisons of regional efficiency in schizophrenic versus control patients; black nodes have decreased efficiency in clinical patients compared to controls, while gray ones do not. Regional efficiency is based on the average length of shortest paths from a node to all other nodes (Rubinov and Bullmore 2013, 342), and hence regionally efficient nodes can

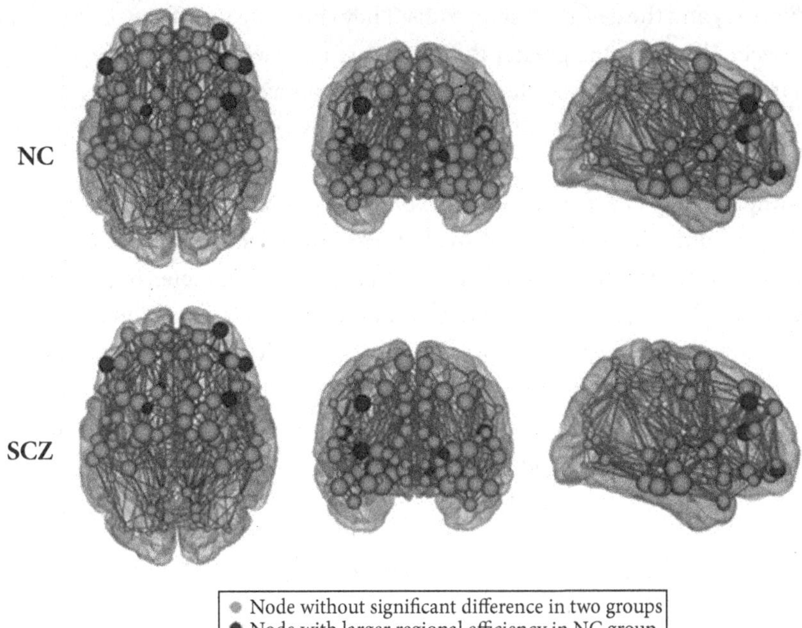

Figure 7.4 The network structure in schizophrenia. From Wang et al. (2012, p.1090, Figure 3). Reprinted with permission from Elsevier.

be considered hubs; black nodes denote regions with larger regional efficiency in the control group; gray nodes denote regions without significant difference between control and schizophrenic groups; the size of a node is proportional to its mean regional efficiency.

We can now determine the inferential set, i. First, there are the entailed inferences, e.g., that schizophrenia is associated with a disruption of the brain's small-world properties, as can be seen by the presence of nodes representing smaller hubs in schizophrenic patients (i.e., regions of reduced regional efficiency). Second, there are disallowed inferences, e.g., that some region represented by a gray node has smaller regional efficiency in schizophrenic patients, or that control patients have smaller, less-central hubs. Third, there are the imported inferences; e.g., knowing the location and function of particular hub regions with reduced efficiency allows imported explanations of clinical symptoms.

In using the model to explain symptoms of schizophrenia, the researchers searched for a quantitative relationship between the degree of decreased efficiency and the degree of symptoms. They showed a significant correlation between the two—the greater the decrease in efficiency among the subjects in the study, the more significant their symptoms as measured by psychiatric evaluation. This suggests that network features are predictive of symptoms in a fine-grained way.

Importation can extend these explanatory inferences. Explanations of clinical symptomatology are provided by knowledge of the location of the hubs affected, the function of those areas, and the character of symptoms. For example, there are disrupted hubs in multimodal association areas, and these areas are known to facilitate the integration or binding of perceptual stimuli into unified percepts (Wang et al. 2012, 1090; Rubinov and Bullmore 2013, 346). The network model thus has a straightforward imported explanation of perceptual symptoms of schizophrenia.

7.4.3. Oscillator Models

Oscillator models are one of the most common model types in physics and have a wide range of applications in both biological and engineering sciences. Most basically, an oscillator is any system subject to a restoring force that is proportional to the displacement of the system from an equilibrium. Such a system can be described as existing on a phase plane, and its position at any given moment is described by its location in phase space. A simple representation of this kind of cycle is shown in Figure 7.5.

One can use oscillator models for a wide range of physical systems, e.g., displacement of objects on springs or of simple pendulums, wherein the former involves representing the mass of an object attached to the spring, and the latter involves representing the pendulum's moment of inertia. Other referents can include electrical circuits or ocean tides, which in turn involve interpreting the variables in terms of different physical quantities. Models can be made more complicated by representing the oscillation as driven by an external force and damped by friction.

Suppose we use the simple representation to refer to an object on a spring. The conventions, c, are as follows. The form of the model, f, consists of a phase space description or diagram of the state of the system. Location in the phase space denotes the referent, p, the positional state of the object. In a simple spring system, the equation governing the system is that its position $x(t) = A\cos(wt + \Theta)$, where A is the peak amplitude of the oscillation, w is

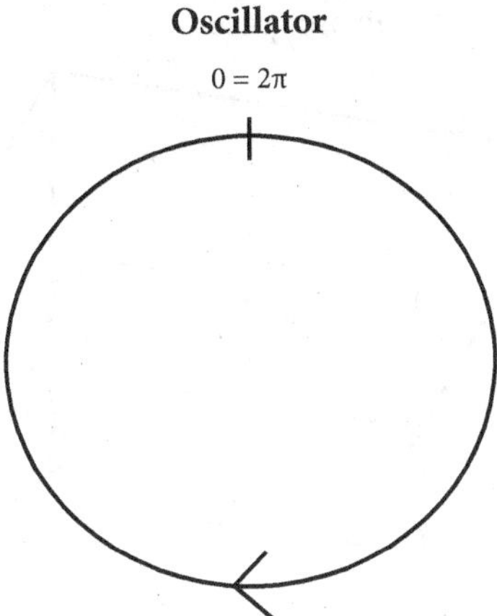

Figure 7.5 A basic oscillator. Adapted from Stiefel and Ermentrout (2016, p.2951, Figure 1). Reprinted with permission from the American Physiological Society (APS).

the rate of change (determined by the mass of the object and the restorative force), and Θ is the phase.

We can now explore the model's inferential set, i. First, there are the entailed inferences, e.g., that given a certain amplitude and phase, the object will be in position *x*. The entailment set will include position values for any given time and phase. Second, there are the disallowed inferences, e.g., that the position of the system will be somewhere else at the same parameter values. Finally, there are the imported inferences; e.g., if I know that an object is attached to the spring, then I know that, given these parameter values, the object will be in position *x*.

Oscillators have also been used to model neural activity—most mathematical models of neuron behavior implement oscillators, including the classic Hodgkin-Huxley model as well as the many lower-dimensional versions that have been developed. Theorists have stressed the mathematical importance of thinking of this class of models as implementing the abstract structure of an oscillator (Stiefel and Ermentrout 2016). One such representation of the phase space of a neuron is shown in Figure 7.6.

The representational conventions, c, are as follows. The form, f, of the representation is a plotting of membrane voltage against the conductances of two ion channels. In regard to referents, p, V denotes the membrane voltage of the neuron, and the values along the axes n and h represent the conductances

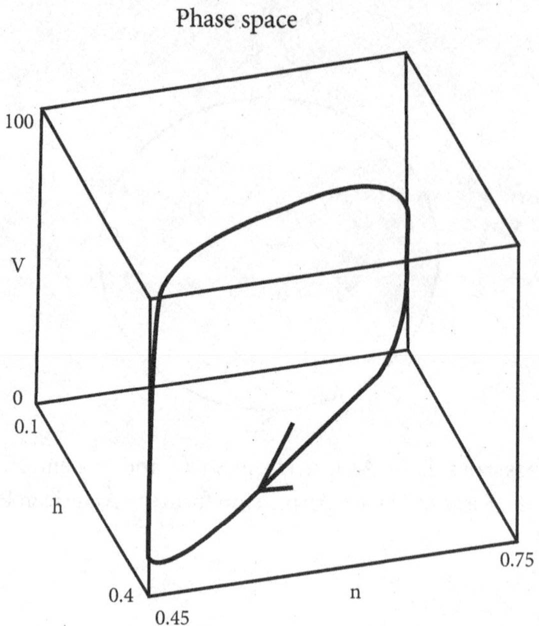

Figure 7.6 The phase space of a neuron. Adapted from Stiefel and Ermentrout (2016, p.2951, Figure 1). Reprinted with permission from the American Physiological Society (APS).

of potassium and sodium channels, respectively. The conventions for use involve the implementation of the coupled differential equations governing the relationships between membrane voltage and channel conductance from the Hodgkin and Huxley model of the neuron. We see then how the simple cycle can represent a neural spike and interspike interval. The spike interval will be the period of high membrane voltage, V, and interspike intervals will be periods of low membrane voltage.

The inferential set, i, is then as follows. First, there are the entailed inferences, determined by the model's form and denotation-claims, e.g., that the modeled neuron engages in regular voltage spikes, or that the action potential ceases as the conductance of h and n decrease. Second, there are disallowed inferences, e.g., that a neuron near the bottom of the cycle is currently spiking. Third, there are the imported inferences, e.g., that such a neuron, in the presence of a depolarizing current, will be providing regular inputs to other neurons with which it communicates.

Such models are often employed in explaining how certain important physiological behaviors come about. Stiefel and Ermentrout (2016), for instance, use them to explain processes of neural synchrony. They do this by first deriving a "phase response curve" (PRC) for individual neurons. Such curves represent how an oscillator will be advanced or delayed on its cycle by input, in this case synaptic input. PRCs, importantly, are part of the entailment set of this expanded model—the model shows that an input of a certain magnitude, at a certain time in the neuron's cycle, will modify the cycle by some amount. Given different physiological assumptions, different PRC types can be derived, including ones that can be advanced only by input ("type I" PRCs), or ones that can be either advanced or delayed ("type II" PRCs). One can then model "coupled" neurons where the outputs of one are inputs to another, to see when and under what conditions they will synchronize by their respective inputs bringing them into phase with each other. A variety of results can then be shown, including that coupled oscillators with type II PRCs are more likely to synchronize, and to a greater degree, than ones with type I PRCs.

Importation can extend these inferences. For instance, Stiefel and Ermentrout (2016) cite previous evidence that the presence of acetylcholine can shift individual neurons from a type II to a type I PRC. That imported knowledge, along with the knowledge that acetylcholine fluctuates during sleep stages, is offered as a potential explanation of the observation that neural synchrony varies during the different stages of sleep. As the authors note, it would not be possible to derive this explanation without the knowledge of PRCs provided by the oscillator models. But it is also worth noting that the oscillator models themselves do not suggest this hypothesis either. It is the oscillator models plus imported knowledge about acetylcholine that produces the inferred hypothesis. Other theorists might import different knowledge to account for other phenomena surrounding neural synchrony, including its contributions to plasticity and to neural communication.

7.4.4. Mathematical Equations

Many mathematical models take the form of one or more equations of some kind. These equations, suitably interpreted, are claims about the world—empirical generalizations—not the analytic, a priori, metaphysically necessary truths of pure mathematics. Mathematical equations differ in important ways from the previous kinds of model discussed, but not in any ways FIT can't handle. The most important difference is that none of the models considered so far is linguistic in form. It makes sense to ask whether the models considered so far are *accurate*, but they don't have the sentential or propositional form that we usually associate with *truth*-evaluability. Certainly, none of the previous models can intelligibly literally appear as lines in proofs, whereas equations can. Thus, it would be natural to suspect that the metasemantic inferentialism I defended in Chapter 6 will explain the content of equations. That's partly true, but we still need to account for denotation-claims.

Consider the following equation:

$$T = 2\pi\sqrt{l/g}$$

The conventions, c, are as follows. The form, f, consists simply of a string of symbols, some of which have given meanings (as determined by the inferential roles those symbols have in pure mathematics). The referents, p, include the period of a simple pendulum, denoted by "*T*," its length, denoted by "*l*," and acceleration due to gravity denoted by "*g*." The inferential set, i, consists of entailed inferences, such as that the period of a simple pendulum is equal to 2π times the square root of its length divided by acceleration due to gravity; disallowed inferences, such as that the period of a simple pendulum is equal to 2π times the square root of its length divided by the number of particles in the Standard Model; and imported inferences, such as that Caitlyn's pendulum has a period of 2 seconds, since I know it is 1 meter long.

Without an interpretation, the equation is not an empirical generalization—it doesn't yet "say" anything. As I said above, the mathematical symbols—"=," "2," "*π*," "$\sqrt{\ }$," "/"—already have meanings, as fixed by the rules governing their use in pure mathematics. The equation then has its standard English translation: *T* is equal to 2π times the square root of *l* divided by *g*. The function of denotation-claims for equations is simpler to understand than for non-linguistic models. Here, to say, e.g., that "*T*" denotes the period of a simple pendulum is simply to say that it means *the period of a simple pendulum*, in other words, that it means the same as "the period of a simple pendulum." For an inferentialist, then, to stipulate that "*T*" denotes the period of a simple pendulum is just to stipulate that "*T*" and "the period of a simple pendulum" are to be used according to the same inferential rules.[7] In fact, most presentations of equations like this won't even use the word "denotes" but simply "is" or "equals" or "=," as in "*T* is the period of a simple pendulum." From the equation we can then straightforwardly infer by simple substitution of synonyms a claim about the world in the form of an empirical generalization: that the period of a simple pendulum is equal to 2π times the square root of its length divided by acceleration due to gravity.

7.5. Idealization and Style Revisited

In this section, we revisit the problems of idealization and style, comparing referentialist accounts to our novel version of inferentialism.

7.5.1. Idealization

As noted in Section 7.1, referentialists respond to the problem of idealization by referring to intentions and pragmatic contexts. We think that these moves are insufficient and therefore that inferentialism has a better account of idealization. Let's begin by briefly reviewing how this strategy works on the leading accounts.

On similarity accounts, the idea is to specify a similarity *metric* that quantifies the relation between the representation and target, such that the representation instantiates that relation. It is up to scientists to specify, in Weisberg's (2013) terminology, the "degree of fidelity" to the target that the representation must exhibit. The core commitment, though, is that some quantified similarity relationship holds between representation and target in any successful instance. On morphism views, the idea is that morphisms are partial, and that which aspects of the representation and target need to stand in the relevant relation depends on what scientists are trying to do. So, while many details of the model and target may fail to map, the aspects which do are the ones which are relevant to the pragmatic aims of the scientist.

On the DEKI account, the strategy plays out with regard to the notion of exemplification. Models do not literally instantiate the properties of

[7] In cases like this, the function of denotation-claims seems to be to express abbreviations of the kind Quine (1951) found unobjectionable.

their targets, in many cases. Following Goodman (1976) and Elgin (2009), Frigg and Nguyen (2020) suggest that this requires a switch to a notion of "metaphorical exemplification"—on this view, instantiation is not literal, but relies on an interpretation of both the model and the target, according to which they share some kind of feature. The key of the model specifies which features one may impute from representation to target, and this key is specified by the scientists constructing the representation. To begin our analysis, consider this quote from Giere: "[W]hen, through observation or experimentation . . . particular models are judged to be well-fitting, we are justifiably confident that the world itself exhibits a structure similar to that of our models" (1999, 241).

The thing to note about this quote is that it infers *from* successful representation to a particular degree of similarity. But this cannot be a good strategy for the referentialist, because it is ineluctably post-hoc (Downes 2009)—according to the referentialist, it is precisely the specification of a relation by the scientific context that *underlies the content of the representation in the first* place. As we noted above, the content of the representation is prior to its success, and hence cannot be described by the philosopher only on the back end of a successful practice.

To avoid being post-hoc, referentialist views that rely on specifying degrees or types of relations must show that (i) precisely a particular degree or type of relation is driving the use of a model before its success is established, and (ii) that the scientists employing the representation are employing it with that relation in mind. We submit that these requirements are unlikely to hold in all, or even very many actual representational contexts. The relations between a representation and its target are often obscure even to the scientists employing it. The relations of which scientists are likely to be cognizant are insufficient to explain why the representation contributes what it does for inferring things about the target.

Let us take a network model as an example. In defining a "node" in a neural network, we must make informed but underdetermined choices about how to spatially draw a circle around a particular neural population. Despite morphological features that differ between parts of the brain, there is no independently agreed-upon fact of the matter about where and how precisely to draw these lines. Whichever lines one draws are unlikely to conform to standing, constant anatomical/functional divisions in the brain.[8] Further,

[8] As Bechtel (2015) has noted, the activity of a part of the brain may be affected by activity in other parts, both at long timescales and at long distances, and we are often unaware of these effects.

once one has defined a node, one treats the activation of this node as a singular quantity. But of course, any neural population will exhibit a complicated internal dynamic, with spatial and temporal variations among its parts.

The point here is that in order to employ these representations, one *doesn't need*, and frequently *doesn't have*, access to the independent facts about the system which one is idealizing (cf. Matthiessen 2022). Hence, specifying a particular type or degree of relation between target and representation cannot be a prerequisite for using the representation to draw inferences about the system. Similar things could be said about the other models that we have discussed. This is not to say that scientists *never* have specific ideas about relations in mind. Sometimes, as with maps and concrete models, the physical features of the target are very well understood, and so representation users can supply rather straightforward relations. But it is a mistake, we have argued, to make these a central part of the content and conditions for use of a representation.

Inferentialism, in particular our hybrid inferentialism, accounts for idealization nicely. On inferentialism, denotation is an intentional act on the part of the scientist, and the representation is chosen to denote the target based on its inferential set. So, when one employs a network representation in neuroscience, one employs it to denote parts of the brain because it allows for inferences about the topological relations between those parts, and further because it will allow us to make testable predictions—e.g., that decreases in hub efficiency will correlate with the severity of symptoms in schizophrenia. While this is informed by what we think is really there—i.e., what we think the parts of the brain are—this does *not* require that the scientist employing the representation specify some particular precise relation between representation and target. If representations are primarily employed because of their inferential allowances, we should precisely expect that there should be significant, ineluctable, and often unspecifiable differences between the form of the representation and the structure of the target.

7.5.2. Style

Referentialist views have to account for the problem of style via differences in the substantive relation they posit. So, different representations will have to be similar to the target in different respects, be morphic with different features of the target, or exemplify distinct features of the target. Again, at a superficial level this has some degree of plausibility. One uses oscillator models to represent oscillatory features, network models to represent network features, etc. Similarly, hiking maps refer to trails, subway maps to subway lines, etc. Put briefly, for the referentialist, distinct styles of representation must refer to distinct features or properties of the system.

There are two primary problems with this approach. The first is that it does not do a good job of accounting for what Hughes (1997) called "demonstration," and the second is what we call the "problem of representational overlap." We take these two issues in turn.

Hughes defined demonstration in terms of the "resources" of a representation, which allow the derivation of "results," which can then be applied to a target. Basically, demonstration is using the structure of the model to drive the model's use—for instance, Galileo's using the geometrical properties of his representations to derive things about the acceleration of objects. Representations thus have a kind of "internal dynamic"—once one has specified the targets of the representation, there are a series of properties of the representation that drive the kinds of conclusions one can draw from it, without having to "go back" to the target, as it were. Hughes is non-committal about what actually shapes this process, but presumably it is closely bound up with the problem of style, since we would expect different styles of representation to have distinct resources for demonstration.

The referentialist strategy of appealing to referential differences, arguably, cannot account for distinct kinds of demonstration in a non-circular way. Suppose we ask why, for instance, causal and network models have distinct demonstrative affordances. The referentialist must account for these purely in terms of the properties of the system that they refer to—content is, after all, comprised of referential relations. But the description of the referential differences between different kinds of representations is hard to cash out in an informative way. It is not informative, for instance, to say that network representations have their distinct demonstrative capacities because they represent network features, and causal models have theirs because they represent causal features. The precise question in the problem of style is *why* representing the target one way or another allows us to demonstrate different things about the target. Simply re-describing the system features in terms of the purported content of the representation does nothing to explain its distinctive demonstrative capacities.

Of course, one might try to insist that there really *are* such distinct features in the target—i.e., that systems really come divided up into causal features, network features, oscillatory features, and so on. The problem with this is that it runs right up against the problem of idealization. Given that we often do not precisely know the features of the target we are representing, it is post-hoc, in the sense discussed above, to just assume that the system has distinct and separate features corresponding to the descriptions in particular types of representations.

These considerations can be illustrated via another problem for referentialist views, which has not seen significant discussion—call this the "problem of representational overlap" (Burnston n.d. fleshes this problem out in much more detail). The referentialist's response to the problem of style is to distinguish between distinct system features referred to by distinct types of representation. But if different styles of representation can be used to represent precisely the *same* entities and relationships in a target, then their stylistic differences cannot be explained in this way.

Imagine a group of three neurons with synaptic connections between them. We might choose to represent those neurons as implementing a network motif (Green et al. 2018), as a set of coupled oscillators, as a directed causal graph, or all of those things. But the system itself is not discretely organized into those different features. It is the *very same* entities and relations in the system—the cells and the synaptic interactions between them—that we represent via arrows in a causal graph, via a coupling parameter in a paired oscillator model, etc. These distinct representations have significant differences in the inferences that they allow, but the distinctions between the features of the system that they represent are, arguably, not rich enough to describe those different affordances. Again, attempting to describe the system in such a way that each of the representations refers to different features would risk being post-hoc, or would run up against the problem of idealization.

Again, inferentialism—and again, specifically FIT—easily handles these cases. Recall that on our account, the content of a representation is partially determined by the form of the representation and its conventions of use. These forms and conventions will differ between different types of representations, *even when their references significantly overlap*. So, the form and convention of a particular representation explain why one can use it to demonstrate (i.e., infer) particular things about the target, and different forms and conventions surrounding different styles of representation explain their different demonstrative uses. Since denotation is intentional on our hybrid view, we should expect that scientists will often intentionally use different representations to represent the same targets, and that they will do so because of the different inferential affordances those representations allow. Such cases, we submit, are common (see Burnston n.d.).

7.6. Truth, Accuracy, and Explanation

Anecdotally, many philosophers of science are extremely uncomfortable with the idea of representations not being explicated in terms of objective relations. We think the crux of this intuition is concerns about success and accuracy. How can a representation ever be successful if it doesn't bear some exploitable relation of similarity, etc. to its target? This connects further to concerns about accuracy and truth. While we can't hope to fully address these issues here, we want to give some ways for the inferentialist to respond, and point out how doing so would further theorizing within the inferentialist position.

The first thing to note about the success/accuracy argument is that it trades on an ambiguity. We can distinguish the following two claims: (i) a representation that was completely dissimilar to its target would be unlikely to be successful; (ii) a specific objective relationship must be in place in order for the representation to be successful. Clearly, these are two very distinct claims about how objective relations relate to the content of a representation. One might broadly endorse claim (i), at least as a point of principle, and still deny claim (ii). Claim (i), on its own, doesn't tell us much about the nature of specific representations. Claim (ii) would certainly do so, but runs into all of the problems we have discussed in trying to specify the content of a representation. So, we suggest that, even if one wants to support claim (i), that should not motivate one to endorse referentialist views of content.

Moreover, construed this way, the inferentialist is free to admit that, first, similarity/morphism *can* be a good-making feature of representations. That is, similarity/morphism can be one way in which a representation might enable inferences about its target to be afforded. Inferentialists just deny that it is the only or a necessary way, at least if construed as a particular objective relation being in place. Second, and relatedly, the inferentialist can admit that, in some circumstances, scientists do intentionally try to implement a similarity-morphism relation to take advantage of those good-making features. They just deny that any of these are constitutive of the content of a representation.

Eventually, the inferentialist will have to say something about what constitutes truth and accuracy on their view, and we do not have space to pursue this in detail here. We want to end by noting, however, that there are a number of resources available in the literature that the inferentialist can appeal to here. In general, these strategies deny that a representation or model is true or accurate simpliciter, or in virtue of its content. For instance, Bailer-Jones (2003) argues that there is no fact of the matter which model of the electron is true full stop. Instead, we use models to *generate* (in our view, *infer*) propositions which themselves are true or false. More recently, Andersen (2023) has argued that the notion of "true" should be replaced with the notion of "trueing," where model and world are brought into a kind of alignment for relevant purposes. Just like truing a bike wheel allows for the wheel to succeed for certain road conditions without coming to resemble the road, truing of models would involve coordinating the model and world (e.g., through experimental conditions) so as to allow inferences from the model that are useful for the particular pragmatic aims of the scientist. Our view is compatible with either of these approaches.

Last, the inferentialist might adopt the increasingly popular view that representations are *tools*. Proponents of the representations-as-tools view often claim it is a non-representational account of models, but that is because they think of representation as the referentialist does (Knuuttila 2011). There is an appealing position available on which one thinks of representations as tools for generating inferences about the target. A tool can have many potential successful uses, but not infinite ones. A hammer can be used to hammer nails, as a paperweight, to put a hole in drywall, to slide a wrench to a friend, etc. It can't be used, for instance, to file documents or scoop water. Successful use requires the world, tool, and user to cooperate in the right way, but it does not require that some specific set of relations between hammer and world obtain—the relationships between hammer and world are too multifaceted, diffuse, and complicated for that to be a requirement—nor does it require a metaphysical realism inconsistent with deflationary metaontology like Carnapianism.

Finally, a full philosophical account of the practice of modeling would take an account of model content and use it to address the nature of explanation. How do models contribute to explanation (Bokulich 2011)? And does this answer constrain one's views of what explanations fundamentally do? FIT gives a natural account of how models enable explanations—by allowing inferences about the target system that answer the questions scientists have about how the system works. Although I hold the generalized ontic conception of explanation, FIT is beneficially neutral on the second question of what explanations do. To see this, note that the account explains the content of the model, and says that explanations take advantage of the content. This is compatible with the notion that only certain kinds of inferences, or certain kinds of denotata referenced in those inferences, constitute explanations. One philosopher might say that a model is explanatory if and only if a proposition citing a regularity governing the target system's explanandum is a member of the set of outcomes of inferences. Another might say that a model is explanatory if and only if a proposition citing a cause or mechanism of the target system's explanandum is a member of the set of outcomes of inferences. Our account of content is compatible with any further restrictions on what kinds of inferences are required for a model genuinely to explain. FIT can even accommodate pragmatist accounts of explanation. A pragmatist might say that a model is explanatory when and only when it is useful, i.e., when it entails propositions that answer the questions the modeler has about the explanandum. Thus, FIT is beneficially compatible with a wide range of views about explanation.

7.7. Summary

We argued that the content of a model is determined by the inferences that are to be made from it, and the inferences that are to be made from it are determined by the form of the model and the denotational conventions surrounding it. The denotational conventions have the normative-expressive role of expressing the validity of rules of surrogative inference. We used FIT to explain the content of causal models, network models, oscillator models, and applied mathematical equations. FIT is compatible with a variety of views on truth, accuracy, and explanation. Further work within the inferentialist perspective might continue to flesh out these ideas.

Appendix A: Surrogative Logic

None of the claims made in this chapter hinges on the success of the following formalism or of any formalism. I just think this formalism will help explain what exactly partially valid rules of surrogative inference are, and it will help to show the exact normative-expressive role of denotation-claims.

Let "success" be a concept of getting things right that encompasses the concepts of truth and accuracy. Surrogative validity is not truth-preserving but success-preserving in the following sense: if the premise, which is a claim about a model, of a surrogatively valid inference is accurate, then the conclusion, which is a claim about the target, must be true. The premise of a surrogative inference always has the form of a true claim about a model, and the conclusion is always a claim about the target. Although the premise always has the *form* of a true claim about a model, we are not treating it *as* a truth-evaluable claim *about* a model. We will be treating it as representing a *fact* about the model that is *accuracy*-evaluable. For example, say we have a map that has a large red dot on it. "The red dot is large," which can be the premise of a surrogative inference, is a true claim about the model, but the *fact* that the red dot is large is either accurate or inaccurate, depending on what that fact is supposed to represent and the state of the target in the world.

A model's entire set of denotation-claims then expresses the stipulated validity of certain rules of surrogative inference. I distinguish "complete" and "partial" surrogative validity. These are not absolute notions. The use of a surrogative rule typically only results in a surrogatively valid inference when it is used in conjunction with other such rules. I call the set of rules required to derive a conclusion from a premise "completely valid," and I call each such rule "partially valid." Thus, which rules are completely valid or only partially valid depends on the inference. For example, if two rules are required to derive a conclusion from a premise, each is partially valid, and they are jointly completely valid.

Let us distinguish model names and predicates from target names and predicates with subscripts "M" and "T," respectively. Variables also receive subscripts depending on whether we are quantifying into model name positions or target name positions (and similarly if we are quantifying into predicate positions). Formulas containing only model names and predicates ("model formulas") are accuracy-evaluable. Formulas containing only target names and predicates ("target formulas") are truth-evaluable. No formulas containing both model names or predicates and target names or predicates ("mixed formulas") are success-evaluable (i.e., either truth- or accuracy-evaluable). To make a surrogatively valid inference, we must pass through mixed formulas.

Let me illustrate. Let's imagine that we have a map with a large red dot and a small blue dot. We stipulate that the red dot denotes Chicago, the blue dot denotes Peoria, being small denotes (represents, signifies) being unpopulous, and being large denotes being populous. These four denotation-claims express the stipulated partial surrogative validity of four corresponding inference rules.

Notation and interpretation: "(. . . s . . .)" is any well-formed formula containing the name "s." "(. . . R . . .)" is any well-formed formula containing the predicate "R." The interpretation of names and predicates is as follows: "a_M" names the red dot, "a_T" names Chicago, "b_M" names the blue dot, "b_T" names Peoria, "F_M" is a predicate applying to small things, "F_T" is a predicate applying to unpopulous things, "G_M" is a predicate applying to large things, and "G_T" is a predicate applying to populous things. (PSV = partially surrogatively valid, i.e., valid when used in conjunction with any other rules required to derive a target formula from a model formula.) Thus:

D_1. "The red dot denotes Chicago" expresses that the inference rule $\dfrac{(\ldots a_M \ldots)}{(\ldots a_T \ldots)}$ is PSV.

D_2. "The blue dot denotes Peoria" expresses that the inference rule $\dfrac{(\ldots b_M \ldots)}{(\ldots b_T \ldots)}$ is PSV.

D_3. "Being small denotes being populous" expresses that the inference rule $\frac{(\ldots F_M \ldots)}{(\ldots F_T \ldots)}$ is PSV.

D_4. "Being large denotes being unpopulous" expresses that the inference rule $\frac{(\ldots G_M \ldots)}{(\ldots G_T \ldots)}$ is PSV.[9]

The inference rules are simple symbol substitutions. The form of the well-formed formulas in which the relevant names or variables occur is irrelevant for the use of the rules. We add what I call the variable match principle (VMP): variable and quantifier subscripts must match the subscripts of the predicates applied to them.

We can now illustrate a surrogative inference. We begin with a premise that has the form of a true description of the model: the red dot is large. We show that from this we can derive that Chicago is populous.

1. $F_M a_M$ (Premise)
2. $F_M a_T$ $(1, D_1)$
3. $F_T a_T$ $(2, D_3)$

Since we converted a formula containing only model names and predicates into a formula containing only target names and predicates using only partially valid inference rules, this surrogative inference is valid, meaning that if that part of the model that the premise describes is accurate, the conclusion is true. For this particular inference, the partially valid inference rules D_1 and D_2 were jointly completely valid. This seems to be the right verdict. Since the red dot denotes Chicago and being large denotes being populous, if the red dot's being large, or the fact that the red dot is large, is accurate, then Chicago is populous.

Let me make some comments on the positive features of this proposal. It requires no substantive denotation relation, and it explicates the normative-expressive import of denotation-claims. It seems to comport well with our intuitive notion of valid surrogative inference. We cannot use the inference rules to make intuitively surrogatively invalid inferences. For example, from "$F_M a_M$" we cannot derive "$G_T b_T$" (i.e., "if the red dot is large, then Peoria is unpopulous" is not surrogatively valid). The proposal also handles quantified surrogative inferences. For example, we can derive the conclusion that something in the target is populous from the premise that something in the model is large, as follows:

1. $\exists x_M F_M x_M$ (Premise)
2. $\exists x_T F_T x_T$ $(1, D_3)$

VMP says that variable subscripts match the subscripts of the predicates applied to them, so when the subscript of "F" changes from line 1 to line 2, the subscript of the variable to which "F" applies also changes, as does the subscript on the quantifier. We could easily add another variable match rule for second-order quantification.

[9] If we wanted, we could add that these denotation-claims also express the validity of the associated target-to-model inferences, so that we can derive model formulas from target formulas. The definition of surrogative validity as necessary success-preservation would still hold.

Recall that model formulas should not be interpreted as making truth-evaluable claims about models. We are not interested in the truth of the claim "the red dot is large" with respect to the model it describes; we are interested in the accuracy of the fact that that claim describes: the red dot's being large, or the fact that the red dot is large. We could make this explicit, and perhaps less likely to mislead, by adding a fact operator to all model formulas. Let "[X]" denote the fact that X. Then we write the above surrogative inference as:

1. $[F_M a_M]$ (Premise)
2. $F_M a_T$ $(1,D_1)$
3. $F_T a_T$ $(2,D_3)$

Now it is clear that premise 1 is not truth-evaluable, but accuracy-evaluable. It is facts that are accuracy-evaluable: it does not make sense to say that the fact that the red dot is large is true or that the red dot's being large is true, but it does make sense to say that it is accurate. We add the syntactic rule that fact-operator brackets attach to all and only model formulas, thus brackets are dropped in the transition from line 1 to line 2. Brackets are irrelevant to the application of partially surrogatively valid inference rules, thus we are allowed to transform bracketed formulas into non-bracketed formulas, as in line 1 to line 2, and non-bracketed formulas into other non-bracketed formulas, as in line 2 to line 3. The above inference illustrates that if the fact that the red dot is large is accurate, then Chicago is populous—just the inference we wanted. This is how denotation-claims express the partial surrogative validity of rules of inference.

The formalism I've presented is intended for models that are not linguistic in form. This feature of many models is not shared by mathematical equations, which *are* linguistic in form, as noted above. There is nothing counterintuitive about conceiving of the success-evaluability of equations as *truth*-evaluability. When it comes to equations, then, conceiving of the premise of a surrogative inference as a *fact* about the model with accuracy-conditions isn't necessary, so the premise needn't take the form "[X]" where "X" is a true description *of* the equation;[10] instead, the premise can simply *be* the equation.

[10] There is an apparent parallel between FIT and truth-conditional semantics which I will only briefly discuss, since 1) I'm not sure whether the apparent parallel amounts to anything significant, and 2) whether the apparent parallel amounts to anything significant affects nothing that I argue in this book. According to FIT, the content of a model is determined by the inferences that are to be made from it, and the inferences that are to be made from it are determined by the form of the model and the denotational conventions surrounding it. A description of the model is transformed into a description of the target via the rules of inference expressed by denotation-claims. If your description of the target is false, you conclude that the model—at least that part of it that warranted the specific claim you made—is inaccurate; you don't conclude that your description of the model was false. We use denotation-claims and the form of the model to generate claims like "M is accurate if and only if T." But this is exactly how truth-conditional semantics (TCS) works. It is important to note that in TCS, truth-conditions for sentences in a language L take the form "S is true if and only if p," where "S" is replaced by a structural description of a sentence of L and "p" by that sentence (Davidson 1967; Lepore and Ludwig 2007). "S" is *not* a quote-name of a sentence; it is a structural *description*, which describes the sentence "as a concatenation of elements drawn from a fixed finite list (for example of words or letters)" (Davidson 1967, 18n25). A truth-conditional theory, then, is an inferential mechanism for transforming descriptions of sentences into descriptions of the world. From a FIT perspective, TCS treats languages as models of the world. Furthermore, the denotation axioms in TCS have the same normative function as the denotation-claims I described above—they express rules for transforming descriptions of sentences into descriptions of the world. Fleshing this idea out and investigating whether TCS implicitly makes metasemantic claims in addition to its explicit semantic claims is far beyond the scope of this book.

For that reason, we don't need names for things *in* the model either; the equation already has terms we can use. The normative-expressive role of denotation-claims remains the same. Let me illustrate with the pendulum equation used above. Let the logical constant "p" name the period of a simple pendulum, "q" name its length, and "r" name acceleration due to gravity. The denotation-claims express validity as follows.

E_1. "'*T*' denotes the period of a simple pendulum" expresses that $\frac{(\ldots T \ldots)}{(\ldots p \ldots)}$ is PSV.

E_2. "'*l*' denotes its length" expresses that $\frac{(\ldots l \ldots)}{(\ldots q \ldots)}$ is PSV.

E_3. "'*g*' denotes acceleration due to gravity" expresses that $\frac{(\ldots g \ldots)}{(\ldots r \ldots)}$ is PSV.

The surrogative inference then goes as follows.

1. $T = 2\pi\sqrt{l/g}$ (premise)
2. $p = 2\pi\sqrt{l/g}$ ($1, E_1$)
3. $p = 2\pi\sqrt{q/g}$ ($2, E_2$)
4. $p = 2\pi\sqrt{q/r}$ ($3, E_3$)

Translating the conclusion into English yields: the period of a simple pendulum is equal to 2π times the square root of its length divided by acceleration due to gravity.

Before concluding, let me consider an important objection. According to the objection, the premises I've appealed to are assumed to denote accuracy-evaluable facts about models. Thus, the models are assumed to already have content. Thus, this inferentialism cannot explain the content of models. Similarly, in the equation example, the premise must be empirically interpreted already, so inferentialism cannot explain its empirical content. This objection is actually quite similar to the circularity objection to metasemantic inferentialism addressed in Chapter 6. Recall that there the solution was to distinguish inferences or inferrings from *rules* of inference. The objection could similarly be put in terms of truth-evaluability or truth-conditions: you can only infer to and from truth-evaluable statements, so inference cannot be what confers truth-evaluability—inference presupposes truth-evaluability. The same response applies: stipulating the validity of rules of inference endows expressions with the meanings and truth-conditions necessary to make the inferences valid.

This response is also available to me. The objector conflates acts of surrogative inference with rules of surrogative inference. What endows the fact that the red dot is large with the content and accuracy-conditions it has is precisely the stipulated validity of the surrogative inference rules. So, yes, the fact that the red dot is large already has content and accuracy-conditions at the beginning of the surrogative inference (as does the equation have truth-conditions), but it has that content and those accuracy-conditions (truth-conditions) precisely because of the stipulated validity of the PSV inference rules. Stipulating the surrogative validity of inference rules is what *endows* a model with content and accuracy-conditions necessary to make those rules surrogatively valid. I surrogatively infer as I do because the denotation-claims have endowed the model with content and accuracy conditions, and denotation-claims have this ability *because* they express the stipulated validity of surrogative inference rules.

8

Normativism and Its Rivals

8.1. Introduction

In this chapter, I compare normativism to three similar views in the philosophy of mathematics: conventionalism, fictionalism, and neo-Fregeanism.[1] Note that I will use "normativism" to refer to the philosophy of mathematics as well as the Carnapian metaontology. Although I am most sympathetic to Warren's (2020) conventionalism, and I don't really see it as a rival, I note some important points of disagreement regarding the nature of explanation (in Section 8.2.1), the (non)conventionality of metamathematics (in Section 8.2.2), and how we follow the ω-rule (in Section 8.2.3). Field (2022) has recently argued that conventionalism is equivalent to fictionalism. I raise several objections to this idea in Section 8.3.1. Then I discuss Plebani's (2018) take on a recent debate between Contessa (2016) and Thomasson (2013, 2014, 2017b), and I offer a Carnapian way forward in Section 8.3.2. Part of that debate is mirrored in a debate between Linnebo (2018) and Rayo (2013), and I offer a Carnapian way forward there too in Section 8.4.

8.2. Warren's Conventionalism

In Sections 8.2.1–8.2.3, I explain Warren's explanatory version of conventionalism and note some important points of disagreement regarding the nature of explanation (in Section 8.2.1), the (non)conventionality of metamathematics (in Section 8.2.2), and how we follow the ω-rule (in Section 8.2.3).

[1] The material in this chapter is drawn from several works in progress.

Rules to Infinity. Mark Povich, Oxford University Press. © Oxford University Press 2024.
DOI: 10.1093/oso/9780197679005.003.0008

8.2.1. Warren's Conventionalism and Explanation

Warren distinguishes three versions of conventionalism: descriptive, non-cognitivist, and explanatory.[2] Warren's conventionalism is explanatory conventionalism. According to descriptive conventionalism, mathematical truths describe linguistic conventions. We have already seen the problems with this: it is inconsistent with the epistemic and modal character of mathematical claims. Descriptions of conventions are a posteriori and contingent; mathematical claims are a priori and necessary (i.e., necessarily true, if true, and necessarily false, if false). Normativism is clearly not a form of descriptive conventionalism. According to non-cognitivist conventionalism, mathematical claims are literally rules. This is non-cognitivist because, since rules can't be true or false, neither can mathematical claims. Warren's two objections to this idea are that mathematical claims are obviously truth-evaluable, and it faces the Frege-Geach problem familiar from metaethics. We saw already that, given semantic deflationism, normativism can say that mathematical claims are truth-apt, so normativism is not flatly non-cognitivist. But does normativism escape the Frege-Geach problem? Here is the problem as applied to non-cognitivism about mathematics. Let's say that "3 is prime" is a command to use a certain linguistic convention, or an expression of approval of a certain linguistic convention. Now consider the conditional: "If 3 is prime, then Francis was right." The antecedent does not command the use of, nor express the approval of, a convention. Does that mean "3 is prime" has a different meaning when embedded in the antecedent of a conditional? We certainly don't want to say that, because that destroys the validity of common inferences, such as:

1. If 3 is prime, then Francis was right.
2. 3 is prime.
C. Francis was right.

This wouldn't be valid since "3 is prime" means something different in premises 1 and 2. The lesson is that the claim that "3 is prime" expresses approval of a convention can't be understood as a metasemantic claim; it can't be that

[2] Warren's conventionalism concerns *logical* as well as mathematical truth. I will not be concerned with logical truth here, though I think everything I've argued in this book should generalize to logical truth pretty straightforwardly.

the meaning of "3 is prime" consists in or is determined by the fact that it expresses approval of a convention.

As we saw in Chapter 6, normativism, while somewhat similar, is not traditional non-cognitivism, precisely because it holds a broad inferentialist metasemantics. Normativism is a functional claim, not a metasemantic one. This allows it to escape the Frege-Geach problem (Thomasson 2020a).[3] Broad inferential role determines the meanings of mathematical terms, and these meanings are constant across different (e.g., embedded) contexts. So, normativism is not a form of non-cognitivist conventionalism and faces neither objection to it.

According to explanatory conventionalism, the conventions of a language fully explain mathematical truth in that language. This is Warren's version of conventionalism. The truth of a synthetic claim like "snow is white" is partly explained by convention (which determines that "snow is white" *means* that snow is white) and partly explained by the way the world is (the fact that snow is white). Mathematical truth, on the other hand, is *fully* explained by convention. Before we can compare explanatory conventionalism and normativism, we need to get clearer about what being "fully explained by convention" is.

According to Warren's conventionalism, conventions fully explain mathematical truth. Conventions (i.e., the basic inference rules) fully explain a mathematical truth when it can be derived solely from those conventions (i.e., the basic inference rules). We convert the axioms of first-order Peano arithmetic (PA) into inference rules which serve as the basic inference rules for our mathematical language. The exact details aren't relevant here, but these inference rules tell us things such as that we can conclude that zero is a number at any point in a proof; that we can conclude that the successor of a number is also a number; and that we can conclude that zero is not the successor of any number (Warren 2015a). These rules implicitly define our arithmetical terms and are automatically valid. To say, then, that an arithmetical truth is fully explained by convention is to say that it is derivable from the Peano rules.

So, it seems then that Warren is committed to the claim that "2 + 2 = 4" is true because it is derivable from the Peano rules. Being derivable from the Peano rules fully explains why "2 + 2 = 4" is true. But many—though

[3] Mark Warren (2015) shows how inferentialism about moral terms avoids the Frege-Geach problem.

certainly not all—philosophers, including myself, take explanation to imply dependence.[4] So, if "2 + 2 = 4" is true because it is derivable from the Peano rules, then if it weren't derivable from the Peano rules (i.e., if our conventions had been different), "2 + 2 = 4" would've been false. But that counterfactual is false, as Warren recognizes in his response to the contingency objection (2020, 172). Recall that according to the contingency objection, conventionalism makes necessities contingent, since conventions are contingent. Warren denies that if "2 + 2 = 4" weren't derivable from the Peano rules, "2 + 2 = 4" would've been false. Instead, if "2 + 2 = 4" weren't derivable from the Peano rules, we would have had a different language where a sentence of the syntactic form "2 + 2 = 4" is false, but "2 + 2 = 4" in that language wouldn't mean 2 + 2 = 4.

I think all of this is right. However, that means more needs to be said about the sense of "explanation" at issue in Warren's explanatory conventionalist thesis. He says that conventions fully explain mathematical truth, yet he denies the dependence of the latter on the former. I think the kind of dependence at issue in explanatory conventionalism is counterconceptual dependence (Einheuser 2006, 2011). Warren seems to be sympathetic to this idea when he writes (2020, 172, original emphasis):

> When properly understood, the contingency objection is no more serious than the claim that since the words "dog" and "galaxy" could be systematically swapped in an imagined language, it is possible for a dog to be many light years across. The standard ways to read these counterfactuals evaluates them with respect to our existing linguistic conventions, rather than with respect to the conventions of our counterparts in the given counterfactual. We could, of course, define such a reading of the counterfactual. But these so-called counter*conventional* conditionals don't undercut the standard necessity of the logical truths.

So, I don't disagree with explanatory conventionalism, but I think that in order for it to be compatible with dependence accounts of explanation, we need to recognize counterconceptual dependence as a kind of explanatory dependence, an idea for which I argued in Chapter 5. Conventionalists (e.g., Sidelle 2009; Topey 2019; Warren 2020) have convincingly argued that the

[4] At least when there are no overdetermining or preempting explanantia (see note 1 in Chapter 1), which we can assume don't occur in this case since derivability from the basic inference rules is supposed to be the full explanation, i.e., the only explanans.

independence of necessity from convention does not contradict conventionalism, but I think more can be said about how, then, conventions explain necessities. This is the purpose of the concept of counterconceptual dependence. I think that if counterconceptual dependence is explanatory, then normativism needn't disagree with Warren's explanatory conventionalism.[5]

A similar concern about Warren's use of the concept of explanation comes up in his discussion of metaphysical analyticity and what he calls "the master argument" against conventionalism (2020, 173–175).[6] Recall that according to the metaphysical sense of analyticity, analytic truths are those owing their truth to the meanings of their constituent concepts alone; they are true *because* the concepts therein have the meanings they do and not because of the way the (extra-linguistic) world is. That certainly sounds like an explanatory claim. The putative rejection of metaphysical analyticity figures in the master argument against conventionalism, which Warren (2020, 175) formalizes as:

1. (sentence S is true $\leftrightarrow \exists p(p$ is a proposition $\wedge$ S means that $p \wedge p))$
2. $\forall p \neg$linguistic conventions make it the case that p
3. So: $\neg$linguistic conventions make it the case that sentence S is true (1, 2).

Premise 1 states a necessary connection between a sentence's truth and its expressing a proposition that is the case. We encountered this idea in Chapter 6, which I support. In fact, it seems analytic to me! (But see Donaldson 2020.) Premise 2 is just a denial of (a particular understanding of) metaphysical analyticity. The conclusion is a denial of (a particular understanding of) conventionalism.

Warren points out that the argument needs to be adjusted in order to target his explanatory version of conventionalism, which would look like this:

1. (sentence S is true $\leftrightarrow \exists p(p$ is a proposition $\wedge$ S means that $p \wedge p))$
2. $\forall p \neg$linguistic conventions explain why p
3. So: $\neg$linguistic conventions explain why sentence S is true (1, 2).

Warren then argues that now premise 2 looks much less plausible. However, how would someone who holds a dependence account of explanation, as

[5] Sidelle (2009) ably addresses the explanatory issue as well.

[6] The argument has been levied by Boghossian (1996, 1997), Sider (2003, 2011), and others.

many do, deny premise 2, when all agree that none of the relevant facts[7] counterfactually depends on convention? Just as I argued above, defenders of a dependence account of explanation must recognize counterconceptual dependence as an explanatory relation, and metaphysical analyticity, if it is to be understood as an explanatory claim, should also be understood counterconceptually. Warren says much more in response to the master argument with which I take no issue.[8]

Let me take this opportunity to discuss briefly metaphysical analyticity more generally. Kocurek, Jerzak, and Rudolph (2020), who are modal normativists (they say "expressivists") sympathetic to Einheuser's work, argue that there is still something unsatisfying about cashing out metaphysical analyticity and the dependence of necessity on convention in terms of counterconceptual dependence.[9] For, according to them, the idea of counterconceptual dependence articulates something that nobody should deny: "that if we had spoken differently, different claims would *count* as necessary on that way of speaking" (22, original emphasis). That, however, is not what Einheuser said. Here is the Einheuser quotation on which they are commenting:

> Conventionalists about abstract objects do not claim that since [the sentence $\Box$(there are numbers)] depends on contingent conventions, [the sentence $\Diamond\neg\Box$(there are numbers)] is true. Rather, they claim that, against the conceptual background of our *actual* practices, the existence of numbers is necessary. Had these practices been suitably different, they would have generated a different set of metaphysically possible worlds relative to which the existence of numbers would not be necessary. (2006, 477, original emphasis)

[7] By "relevant facts" I mean the facts—e.g., about necessity—conventionalism is intended to explain. Perhaps some convention annoys me, and my annoyance counterfactually depends on the convention. No one disputes the dependence on convention of this kind of fact.

[8] Specifically, he argues 1) that the master argument misses explanatory versions of conventionalism according to which our conventions don't make *p* the case, but instead explain why *p*; 2) that even if it's not the case that our conventions explain why *p*, it wouldn't follow that they don't explain why a sentence *S* that means that *p* is true, even if necessarily, *S* is true if and only if *S* means that *p*, and *p*, because explanatory contexts are hyperintensional; and 3) that if one got around this by accepting a special principle according to which if *C* explains why *S* is true, then *C* explains why *p*, then this would just be to accept a view of propositions that every conventionalist would reject on metasemantic grounds. See also Asay (2020), Donaldson (2020), and Topey (2019) for more criticisms of the master argument.

[9] Kocurek, Jerzak, and Rudolph (2020) accept normativism's functional thesis, and they think that's what's required to make Einheuser's point satisfying.

Notice that Einheuser nowhere talks about what would "count" as necessary. Perhaps nobody should deny that if we had spoken differently, different claims would *count* as necessary on that way of speaking, but for Einheuser what is distinctive about conventionalism (including normativism) is the claim that there is *nothing else* to necessity. What Einheuser says is that if we had spoken differently, different claims would *be* necessary on that way of speaking, i.e., from *within* that way of speaking, actually adopting its rules. Not only would we *count* different claims as necessary, but we wouldn't be getting anything *wrong*—in a transconventional or transframework sense—in so doing. There is no such sense of getting things wrong. This point is one stressed often by Wittgenstein and Carnap when discussing language[10] choice or framework choice. To choose a linguistic framework is to choose a set of necessities, and framework choice is pragmatic. There is no such thing as getting things wrong in choosing a framework. The very possibility of getting things wrong—i.e., of saying anything at all—requires that one already possess a framework with its set of necessities. Much the same can be said by Warren to explicate the sense in which analytic truths make no demands on the world. For him, a sentence is analytic in a language just in case it is derivable from the basic inferential rules of the language. This is not an overtly epistemic characterization of analyticity—whether a sentence is so derivable is not an epistemic fact, even if it has epistemic implications—but it also doesn't quite explicate why analytic truths make no demands on the world. I think this is achieved by adding Warren's unrestricted inferentialism, the thesis—similar, I think, to Carnap's principle of tolerance—that *any* basic inferential rules are epistemically permissible and automatically valid. Carnap's frameworks, Wittgenstein's grammars, and Warren's basic inferential rules are completely theoretically unconstrained—there is no *sense* in their being theoretically (as opposed to practically) right or wrong. This complete unconstrainedness by the world helps to explicate why analyticities make no demands on said world.[11]

The notion of counterconceptual dependence, like that of metaphysical analyticity or a sibling notion, can also help us understand why analytic truths make no demands on the world in ways consistent with the just-mentioned point about unconstrainedness. The notion of counterconceptual

[10] Wittgenstein would often say "grammar" choice—grammar cannot be true or false, cannot get things right or wrong.

[11] See again Sidelle (2009) on different semantic rules' not getting things metaphysically wrong.

dependence can be used to characterize a notion of dependence on meaning that analytic truths alone have. There are several ways to bring this out using sibling notions developed primarily by two-dimensionalists. For we will need to be able to separate analytic truths from a posteriori necessities—it won't work merely to say that analytic truths depend on meaning alone in the sense that they would still be true no matter what the world were like, for that is also true of a posteriori necessities, which clearly do make demands on the world. I have already briefly discussed how normativists account for a posteriori necessities, and I will discuss this again in Chapter 9; recall that normativists explain posteriori necessities by appeal to the fact that some conceptual rules include variables the values of which can only be determined empirically. What certain two-dimensionalists (e.g., Chalmers) have said about a posteriori necessity seems quite consistent with what the normativist says about it.

Here is a first pass at using the concept of counterconceptual dependence to make out the sense in which analytic truths make no demands on the world. If we adopt Chalmers's two-dimensionalist notion of epistemic possibility, where *p* is epistemically possible just in case it is not ruled out a priori, then we can see that analyticities are the *only* truths that depend on meaning alone (in the now several senses of "depend"). For it is generally agreed that a posteriori necessities are not epistemically necessary, i.e., that it is (or was) epistemically possible that, e.g., water isn't H_2O. Thus, an a posteriori necessity is true in all standardly possible worlds (i.e., in all countersubstratum worlds, or as Chalmers puts it, all worlds considered as counterfactual), but not in all epistemically possible worlds and not in all counterconceptually possible worlds, thus there is epistemic and counterconceptual dependence exhibited by a posteriori necessities; an analyticity is true in all standardly possible worlds and in all epistemically possible worlds, but not in all counterconceptually possible worlds, thus there is *only* counterconceptual dependence exhibited by analyticity. This result is simply that reached by two-dimensionalists wishing to characterize a posteriori necessity for certain Fregean purposes (e.g., Chalmers 2004; Jackson 1998), with the addition of the notion of counterconceptual dependence to characterize analyticity.[12]

However, since this characterization of analyticity relies on the notion of *epistemic* possibility, which Chalmers makes use of in a largely *epistemic*

[12] It seems to me that the same could be said using Chalmers' orthographic contextual intensions in place of counterconceptual dependence.

project linking modality, meaning, and reason, it seems that we end up with an *epistemic* notion of analyticity that can't do for us what we wanted metaphysical analyticity to do, viz., to explicate the sense in which analytic truths make no demands on the world. Whether this is true is controversial, however, for Chalmers also thinks that all epistemically possible worlds are centered metaphysically possible worlds, where a centered world represents "the perspective of the speaker within the world" (Chalmers 2004, 160). It seems like this will work so long as the notion of a centered world can be explicated in a way that doesn't undermine our task of elucidating the sense in which analytic truths make no demands on the world. I think it can, but elaborating on that would unfortunately take me too far afield. The points I wish to emphasize are 1) that it is quite common now to admit that a posteriori necessities exhibit *some* kind of dependence on the world, even if Chalmers' way of explicating that dependence isn't right,[13] and 2) that to explicate the sense in which analyticities make no demands on the world it is sufficient to point out that they *don't* exhibit even *that* kind of dependence on the world and that they *only* depend on what they (their orthographic strings) mean. Any further doubts about whether analyticities place demands on the world can be answered by the appeal to unconstrainedness above.[14]

To conclude this subsection, I think normativism and explanatory conventionalism mainly differ in emphasis, so long as one takes counterconceptual dependence to be explanatory. The difference in emphasis comes from normativism's functional thesis, that the function of mathematical language is to express conceptual rules.

8.2.2. Warren on Metamathematics

In this section, I discuss what the normativist/conventionalist should say about metamathematics. Warren argues that metamathematics is not conventional but applied mathematics. I argue that it is conventional (Friederich

[13] The normativist claim that a posteriori necessities are products of conceptual rules that include variables the values of which can only be determined empirically is one explication of this dependence, and note that this explication does not seem epistemic in a way that would threaten the explanation of why analyticities place no demands on the world.

[14] I noted in note 12 of Chapter 1 that Nyseth (2021) argues that normativists should not say that analyticities have no truthmakers, but should instead say that in analyticities the application conditions of the concepts involved are "fulfilled no matter what the world is actually like" (280). This also seems like a way of cashing out the idea that analytic truths make no demands on the world and is compatible with everything I say here.

2010; Mühlhölzer 2012). When discussing conventionalism and metamathematics, one immediately thinks of Gödel, for many think his metamathematical work on the incompleteness theorems destroyed conventionalism, and he himself argued against it (see the references in note 29 in Chapter 5). But the current question is not about Gödel's incompleteness theorems. I agree with Warren's arguments that Gödel's incompleteness theorems pose no problems for conventionalism (see Section V of Chapter 12, among others, of Warren 2020). I briefly recount just part of one of Warren's arguments, because I think it is as convincing as it is simple. One of Gödel's basic worries—the worry leveled against Carnap—was this: if mathematics is true by convention, no empirical statement follows from its basic inference rules. Mathematics should not imply anything empirical—it would directly contradict conventionalism for putatively analytic statements to imply a synthetic statement. If the basic rules did imply an empirical statement, that would make the basic rules empirical, not analytic. This means that the basic rules must be consistent, for in an inconsistent language everything follows, including every empirical statement. Now, by Gödel's second incompleteness theorem, no consistent formal system containing elementary arithmetic can prove its own consistency. So, to prove the basic rules consistent, we must appeal to mathematics not implied by those rules. So, mathematics must not be true solely by convention. Warren's response is that inferentialism implies that an inconsistent language has no empirical content.[15] If the basic rules were inconsistent, every inference rule in the language would be valid, and every sentence would be analytically true (because derivable from the basic rules). Such an inconsistent language could prove the syntactic string "pigs fly," but it wouldn't be an empirical statement that means that pigs fly. With this I agree.

Where I disagree with Warren is where he argues that metamathematics is applied mathematics. This is certainly a common and intuitive way of thinking about metamathematics, which is often said to be the area of mathematics in which the properties of mathematical theories are investigated, e.g., what is provable and what isn't in which theories, which theories are consistent, etc. David Hilbert, the father of metamathematics, was quite explicit that metamathematics was applied mathematics or, as he put it, contentual (i.e., having content):

[15] Warren has another response that I won't elaborate in detail. The gist of it is that proving the basic rules consistent is not required for justifiedly believing they are consistent.

> In addition to this formalized mathematics proper, we have a mathematics that is to some extent new: a metamathematics that is necessary for securing mathematics, and in which—in contrast to the purely formal modes of inference in mathematics proper—one applies contentual inference, but only to prove the consistency of the axioms. In this metamathematics we operate with the proofs of mathematics proper, and these proofs are themselves the object of the contentual investigation. (Hilbert 1923, quoted in Mühlhölzer 2012, 107)

The famous (meta)mathematician Abraham Robinson characterizes the topic of his metamathematics of algebra as "the analysis and development of Algebra by the methods of Symbolic Logic. . . . Instead of formulating and proving individual theorems as in orthodox Mathematics, we may consider statements *about* theorems in general" (1951, 1, my emphasis). So, the idea that metamathematics is applied mathematics is a natural one. But Epictetus taught always to be wary of first impressions.

Let us examine what Warren has to say about metamathematics being applied mathematics. Unfortunately, there isn't much argument for this claim. Warren (2015a, 1357) writes:

> Whether or not a certain sentence is derivable in a given formal system is a matter of fact. Similarly, whether or not a given sequence of expressions is a sentence (according to our grammatical conventions) is a matter of fact. In general, syntax concerns matters of fact that can't be made true or false simply by convention or stipulation. And this is true even if the rules of proof and grammar are themselves a matter of convention—cf. the rules of chess are conventional but whether or not a mate is possible with two knights and a king is a matter of fact.

He later writes, "Given that a community follows the Q-rules,[16] it will be a matter of fact, not convention, whether or not the sentence '0 = 1' is provable using the rules" (2020, 303). These points seem to me reiterations of the claim that metamathematics is applied mathematics rather than arguments for it. And I don't find them plausible. We're not told why whether or not a mate is possible with two knights and a king is a matter of fact. That seems to

[16] These are the rules of Robinson arithmetic, which are basically the Peano rules minus the induction schema.

me conventional. Surely, whether that is possible is determined by the rules of chess, and whether the sentence "0 = 1" is provable in Q is determined by the rules of Q, and the claim that it is provable would follow from the rules of Q along with the rules of the formal system in which we are investigating Q. We saw above in the discussion of Gödel that we cannot have conventional rules implying factual statements. So, if we want to remain conventionalists, we better deny that metamathematics is factual, for its results seem to follow from conventional rules.

Perhaps metamathematics seems factual because if I lay down some random rules, it takes investigation to determine whether they are consistent. And then the claim "those rules are consistent" (or, using a definite description instead of a demonstrative, "the rules are consistent") seems like an empirical claim. And, indeed, *that* claim is empirical—it is certainly not a priori, for it depends on what *those rules* (or *the rules*) are. Whether it is necessary or contingent depends on whether you are interpreting "those rules" rigidly. If you interpret the phrase rigidly, then it refers to whatever those actual rules are in every possible world, so "those rules are consistent" will be necessarily true, if true, and necessarily false, if false. Does thinking of "those rules are consistent" as an a posteriori necessity help support the idea that metamathematics is factual? No, because the actual metamathematical part of the investigation into the truth of that claim is *not* empirical—what is empirical is determining what *those rules actually are.* Once that is determined, it is an a priori matter to determine whether they are consistent. Compare: I randomly write a very large odd number. Is "that number is prime" factual? It is not a priori—certainly, it will take some empirical investigation to determine what number I wrote. It will be necessary if "that number" refers rigidly to the number I actually wrote. But, then, determining whether *that* number is prime is wholly a priori. This certainly wouldn't show that mathematics is factual.

If claims like "those rules are consistent" and "that number is prime" are taken to be a posteriori necessities, then the conventionalist can "factor" or "decompose" them into wholly factual and wholly conventional components (Sidelle 1989; Thomasson 2020a): it should be factored into "those rules are R_1, R_2, etc.," where R_1, R_2, etc. state what the rules are, which is wholly factual, and "R_1, R_2, etc. are consistent," which is wholly conventional (i.e., analytic). I discuss Warren's (2022b) theory of a posteriori necessity below. We will see that Warren's theory of a posteriori necessity doesn't support the claim that metamathematics is factual.

Metamathematics makes no claims that require any empirical investigation; it is, like mathematics, wholly a priori.

Warren writes that once the rules of a formal system are laid down, its consistency "isn't something that we can control via stipulation or convention" (2015a, 1358). That's right, but that doesn't make the consistency of the formal system non-conventional. Once we lay down the Peano rules, whether 2 + 2 = 4 (or whether "2 + 2 = 4" is true) isn't something that we can control via stipulation or convention either, but Warren accepts that "2 + 2 = 4" is true by convention. Warren has mistaken what the force of something's being outside our control via stipulation or convention means in this case. A formal system's consistency is outside our control via stipulation or convention not because it is a matter of fact but because if we were to change it, we would no longer be talking about the same formal system. The consistency of PA is outside our control in the same sense that the primeness of 3 is, and that sense is perfectly compatible with conventionalism—and Warren agrees that the primeness of 3 is outside our control and that it is conventional.

In fact, the conventionality of metamathematics fits seamlessly into the rest of conventionalism. The results of metamathematics express conceptual rules just as the results of mathematics do. It is just that the results of metamathematics express rules governing concepts of formal systems. "PA is consistent" expresses a rule governing the concept of PA. And just as in mathematics, metamathematical concepts (i.e., consistency, provability, concepts of formal systems, etc.) can be applied in empirical statements. For example, "Shannon studies consistent systems," "Mackenzie's favorite system is PA," etc. But results within metamathematics are not results of applied metamathematics.

These considerations suggest the existence of distinctively *meta*mathematical explanations (DMmEs), such as the following: Why did Rob fail to derive a contradiction in his system? Because the system he is working in is PA (an empirical premise), and PA is consistent (a metamathematical premise). The Craver-Povich reversal would be: Why isn't Rob working in PA? Because he derived a contradiction in his system (empirical premise) and PA is consistent (metamathematical premise). The narrow explanandum (i.e., the thing to be explained) would be the fact that Rob failed to derive a contradiction in PA. The explanans (i.e., the thing that explains) is the metamathematical fact that PA is consistent. The following countermetamathematical is true: if PA weren't consistent, Rob would have derived a contradiction in it. And we can interpret this countermetamathematical counterconceptually. Thus, NOCA and its deflated sibling apply equally to DMmEs. As this example shows, metamathematical concepts *can* be applied, just as mathematical concepts can; you can make factual claims using metamathematical concepts, just as you can with mathematical concepts. That makes neither the results of pure metamathematics nor of pure mathematics factual.

Could Warren try to save the claim that metamathematics is factual by arguing that it is necessary a posteriori? That would flatly contradict what the practice of metamathematics is like, which differs in no philosophically important respects from the a priori practice of mathematics (Friederich 2010). But let's ignore that for a moment. According to Warren's (2022b) account of a posteriori necessity, such truths can be broken down into a factual claim and an analytic linking conditional. For example, the truth of "water is necessarily H_2O" is accounted for by breaking it into the factual claim that water is H_2O and the analytic linking conditional that if water is H_2O, then water is necessarily H_2O (529). I support a somewhat similar view of a posteriori necessity (Sidelle 1989; Thomasson 2020a), but this begs the question. First, note that in Warren's theory, a posteriori necessities are explicit necessity claims that are a posteriori, e.g., "water is necessarily H_2O." The non-modal claim that water is H_2O is, according to Warren, wholly factual.[17] So, Warren's theory wouldn't get us the a posteriori necessity of "PA is consistent" but of "PA is necessarily consistent." Second, we would need to account for the a posteriori necessity of "PA is necessarily consistent" by breaking it into the (putatively) factual claim that PA is consistent and the analytic linking conditional that if PA is consistent, then PA is necessarily consistent. But this precisely assumes that "PA is consistent" is a factual claim. I have argued that Warren hasn't supported this and that there are good reasons to deny it. This would be no different from claiming that "3 is necessarily prime" is an a posteriori necessity because "3 is prime" is factual and "if 3 is prime, then 3 is necessarily prime" is analytic.

Why does Warren make the claim that metamathematics is factual? Let us look in some detail at the case which prompts this claim:

[17] How can "water is H_2O" be both necessary and wholly factual? Perhaps Warren has in mind the following comment from Sidelle: "While, for colloquial purposes, we may go along speaking in the material mode, the real empirical import of, say, 'Water is H_2O' can be found in 'Most (enough) of the samples that we call 'water' are composed of H_2O'" (1989, 44). So, perhaps Warren intends his analytic linking conditional to read, "If most (enough) of the samples that we call 'water' are composed of H_2O, then water is necessarily H_2O."

> Imagine that we encounter a Plutonian community whose arithmetic includes all of the axioms of Q in addition to the sentence "¬Con(Q)" [i.e., Q is not consistent], so that, in effect, Plutonian arithmetic is the theory Q + ¬Con(Q). We know, in our arithmetic, that the theory Q + ¬Con(Q) is consistent if and only if Q is consistent. Also, from the way that consistency sentences are constructed, Q + ¬Con(Q) ⊢¬Con(Q+¬Con(Q)), so assuming that Q is consistent (a safe bet!), Plutonian arithmetic is based on a consistent theory that proves its own inconsistency sentence! Hardcore realists will say that the Plutonians have a false theory, since their "¬Con(Q)" axiom is false. Conventionalists cannot say this, since . . . the Plutonians' basic rules are automatically valid in the Plutonian language. (2020, 304–305)

Warren's response to this worry is that it is not the case that something true for us is false for them (or that both "Con(Q)" and "¬Con(Q)" are true), but simply that "¬Con(Q)" means something different for them than it does for us. I think that's right, but the question is what that has to do with the claim that metamathematics is factual. The response certainly doesn't imply that metamathematics is factual. It is a response that works just as well in mathematical (rather than metamathematical) cases, and it doesn't imply there that mathematics is factual. Suppose the Plutonians have a different arithmetic in which "2 + 2 = 5" is true. The worry is exactly the same: that the conventionalist is committed to saying that something true for us is false for them. And the response is exactly the same: that "2 + 2 = 5" means something different for them than it does for us. If this response implies that mathematics is factual, Warren is in trouble. Thankfully, it doesn't, and it doesn't in the metamathematical case either.

Warren continues:

> Arithmetization [i.e., the coding of syntactic properties with arithmetical predicates] is a bit of applied arithmetic, and in ω-inconsistent[18] theories this application goes haywire. In models of Plutonian arithmetic, predicates like "Wff_Q" and "Prf_Q" will be satisfied by nonstandard elements that don't really code for actual well-formed formulas or proofs in the Plutonian language. (2020, 305)

[18] A theory is ω-inconsistent if and only if it proves of every natural number that it has some property, and it proves that it is not the case that all natural numbers have that property.

So, the claim that metamathematics is factual is used to explain what is going on in the example of Plutonian arithmetic. But that claim is not necessary to explain what is going on. All that's required is the realization that "¬Con(Q)" means something different for them than it does for us. That follows straightforwardly from inferentialism; the claim that metamathematics is factual isn't required to understand why we and the Plutonians mean different things. Also note that we still don't have an argument for the claim that metamathematics is factual. Warren's final claim about the Plutonian predicates "Wff_Q" and "Prf_Q" begs this question, for it requires treating claims about what is a well-formed formula and what is a proof in a formal system, which are metamathematical claims, as factual, and we still haven't been told why to think that. There is no reason to conceive of the satisfaction of the Plutonian predicates "Wff_Q" and "Prf_Q" by nonstandard elements as a *factual application* of those predicates. I don't disagree with Warren that the Plutonian predicates will factually apply to different things than our predicates—they mean different things, after all. I disagree with Warren about what counts as factual application. While it is important to recognize the factual applicability of mathematical and metamathematical concepts, it is very important to recognize that what can seem like factual application might not be. For example, "there are 4 gauge bosons in the Standard Model" is a factual application of "4"; "there are 4 primes less than 10" is not; it is analytic, a priori, conventional. "The number of particles in the Standard Model is prime" is a factual application of the predicate "is prime"; "17 is prime" is not. Similarly, metamathematical claims like "'2 + 2 = 4' is a well-formed formula of PA" are not factual applications of the well-formed formula predicate; they are analytic, a priori, conventional.[19] You can call that the application of the well-formed formula predicate if you want, as long as you recognize that it isn't *factual* application and doesn't contradict the analyticity, a priority, and conventionality of metamathematics. As above, the well-formedness of "2 + 2 = 4" in PA is outside our control in the same sense that the primeness of 3 in PA is, and that sense is perfectly compatible with conventionalism.

[19] We could give DMmEs involving these metamathematical predicates. For example: why is Lucy's formula well-formed (in PA)? Because her formula is "2 + 2 = 4" (empirical premise) and "2 + 2 = 4" is a well-formed formula of PA (metamathematical premise). Reversed: why isn't Lucy's formula "2 + 2 = 4"? Because her formula is not well-formed (in PA) (empirical premise) and "2 + 2 = 4" is a well-formed formula of PA (metamathematical premise). NOCA and its deflation can apply in the usual way.

Furthermore, arithmetization is simply a way of "saying" these kinds of metamathematical claim in arithmetic. Arithmetizing the non-factual doesn't make it factual.[20]

Perhaps the seeming factuality of these metamathematical claims results from a comparison to natural language. It seems like I must empirically investigate a natural language to determine what counts as a grammatical sentence in it. We have to be careful here, though. Formal systems are plausibly individuated by their syntactic rules, including their formation rules for well-formed formulas. Natural languages have grammatical rules, but they also have that philosophically most inconvenient thing: semantics. Let us not let semantics get in the way—we will assume English words have their actual standard meaning. Then, is "'Dogs run' (with its actual standard meaning) is a grammatical sentence of English" conventional, i.e., analytic? That depends on how English is individuated. If it's individuated, among other things, by its grammar, then yes, and the appearance that our investigation was empirical is an illusion. The empirical part would have been learning what the grammatical rules were; using the rules to determine what is grammatical wouldn't have been empirical. It's the same as determining whether the number on the chalkboard is prime. Such determination first requires something empirical—looking at the number on the chalkboard; nothing else is empirical. So, we shouldn't think claims about what is or isn't a well-formed formula in a formal language are empirical. The metamathematical properties of formal systems are essential to them in the same way that the mathematical properties of numbers are essential to them. For the same conventional reasons, if it isn't prime, it just isn't 3, and if "2 + 2 = 4" isn't a well-formed formula in it, it just isn't PA. Those are analytic truths.

Warren hasn't given us good reasons to suggest that metamathematics is factual, and he has not reconciled his conventionalism with the claim that it is. As I mentioned above, whether the sentence "0 = 1" is provable in Q follows from the rules of Q, along with the rules of the formal system in which we are investigating Q, and a conventionalist cannot have conventional rules implying factual statements. Thus, I think Warren must extend conventionalism to metamathematics.

[20] That is, using arithmetic to say something analytic doesn't make it synthetic.

8.2.3. Warren on the ω-Rule

The last disagreement with Warren I want to address concerns the ω-rule. Warren (2020) discusses the ω-rule in part of his defense of mathematical determinacy, which is part of a larger response to the claim that Gödel's incompleteness theorems show that mathematical truth cannot be a matter of derivability from basic rules. Unlike most philosophers, I agree with Warren that we follow the ω-rule, but I disagree about what is involved in following it.[21]

According to Warren's (2020, 263) natural deduction form of the ω-rule,

$$\frac{\varphi(0), \varphi(1), \varphi(2), \ldots}{\forall x(\mathrm{N}x \rightarrow \varphi(x))}$$

In other words, it is valid to infer that all natural numbers possess some property, if 0 possesses it, 1 possesses it, 2 possesses it, and so on.[22] The relevance of the ω-rule to Gödel's incompleteness theorems is that addition of the rule as an axiom schema to the axioms of, say, PA results in a complete theory that decides all arithmetical truths, i.e., for every arithmetical statement, PA + ω-rule will either prove the statement or prove its negation. For Warren, then, including the ω-rule as a meaning-constituting rule of inference will help to explain mathematical determinacy, the apparent fact that every (non-vague) mathematical statement is either true or false. However, actual use of the ω-rule seems to require a kind of infinite reasoning ability, for any application of the rule seems to require acceptance of infinitely many premises. Hence, the problem. Warren argues that we do have the relevant kind of infinite reasoning ability and that it has a naturalistic explanation (see also Warren 2021). Warren's defense of these claims relies on a dispositional account of implicit belief. When the infinite beliefs required to follow the ω-rule are understood in an implicit, dispositional fashion, there is nothing naturalistically objectionable about them, according to Warren. We all hold infinite beliefs of this dispositional kind. For example, I believe that $1 > 0$, that $2 > 0$, that $3 > 0$, and so on, on the basis of the fact that, among other things, I am disposed to answer "Yes" to "Is $1 > 0$?," "Is $2 > 0$?," "Is $3 > 0$?," and so on.

[21] Carnap ([1937] 2001) also accepted and appealed to the ω-rule.

[22] The ω-rule (i.e., the omega rule) is so-called because ω is the first ordinal number after all the natural numbers.

I think there are two ways to conceive of the disagreement I will register. On the strong reading, one could think of my argument as claiming that following the ω-rule doesn't require infinite reasoning ability of the kind to which Warren appeals. On the weak reading, one could think of my argument as claiming merely that such-and-such additional things need to be said to demystify the claim that following the ω-rule requires infinite reasoning ability and to make that claim consistent with conventionalism. I think the strong reading would be anti-Carnapian, as I explain below, so I prefer the weak reading.

To explicate my disagreement, I draw on an (as always) somewhat cryptic passage of Wittgenstein's. Note that in any presentation of the ω-rule, infinite premises are *not* written, nor is a single infinite conjunction of premises, but several premises followed by the *symbol* ". . . ," which we often express in English as "and so on." About such symbols and such natural language expressions, Wittgenstein writes:

> The expression "and so on" is nothing but the *expression "and so on"* (nothing, that is, but a sign in a calculus which can't do more than have meaning via the rules that hold of it; which can't say more than it shows). That is, the expression "and so on" does not harbour a secret power by which the series is continued without being continued. . . . For the sign "and so on," or some sign corresponding to it, is essential if we are to indicate endlessness—through the rules, of course, that govern such a sign. That is to say, we can distinguish the limited series "1, 1 + 1, 1 + 1 + 1" from the series "1, 1 + 1, 1 + 1 + 1 and so on." And this last sign and its use is no less essential for the calculus than any other. (1974, 282–283, original emphasis)

Although he is here talking about infinite series of numbers, Wittgenstein's thought, I think—or least the thought that the passage elicited in me—is that to understand a claim such as that $\varphi(0)$, $\varphi(1)$, $\varphi(2)$, and so on, one needn't understand infinitely many things, or at least that we must be careful about what we mean when we say that in understanding that claim someone thereby understands infinitely many things. For "and so on" is part of the claim, the final expression of the claim. Not the final expression in the *series of premises*—that series has no final expression, as indicated by "and so on." But "and so on" is just another expression, whose meaning we learn like any other. And when " . . . " is part of the language of a formal system, it must be governed by strict rules like everything else in the language, regardless of whether those rules are made explicit. "[W]e calculate with the sign '1, 1 + 1, 1 + 1 + 1 . . . ' just as with the numerals, but in accordance with different rules" (Wittgenstein 1974, 285). Just so, we infer with the sign "$\varphi(0)$, $\varphi(1)$, $\varphi(2)$, and so on" just as with the components, but in accordance with different rules. The ω-rule is one such rule; it is a " . . . "-elimination rule (and perhaps also a ∀-introduction rule).

Warren writes, "We tell a child that God didn't create squared circles on the first day, nor the second day, nor the third, and so on. The child "gets it," forms infinitely many beliefs about particular days, and on this basis, concludes that on all days, God did not create squared circles" (2021, 403–404). I think the example is perfect and illustrates the naturalness and ubiquity of our use of the ω-rule.[23] However, in what sense does the child's "getting it" require that she form infinitely many beliefs? Isn't it enough that she gets the meaning of "and so on," whose meaning is partly constituted by the ω-rule? She believes the generalization simply and directly on the basis of understanding "and so on." The ω-rule, being *meaning-constituting*, sets up an analytic connection between the "and so on"–statement and the generalization; "and so on" and "all" are thereby semantically connected. And I think it is obvious that we in fact use "and so on" in accordance with the ω-rule. Someone who didn't follow the ω-rule would mean something else by "and so on" (or by " . . . "), just as the intuitionist who doesn't follow double negation elimination means something else by "not." (And if the ω-rule is also partly constitutive of the meaning of "all," they would mean something else by "all" too.)

To be clear, I am not saying that " . . . " doesn't "really" mean an infinite series or sequence. It does; but it does—just like every meaningful sign—in virtue of being governed by certain rules, including the ω-rule. The ω-rule is one of our rules to infinity. Similarly, I am hesitant to say that the child doesn't "really" have infinitely many beliefs. I think that would be anti-Carnapian, since we seem to have clear enough rules for the use of such language. The child meets the dispositional criteria for having infinitely many beliefs, so she has infinitely many beliefs. However, I think these rules of use are intimately tied to the rules governing "and so on" and that understanding such ties helps to answer questions like "How can her finite brain house infinitely many distinct beliefs?" My suggestion is that the brain state that is the categorical basis of the dispositions criterial for her possessing the relevant

[23] I think it is much more convincing than the example involving a supertask computer checking Goldbach's conjecture, to which Nyseth (2023) plausibly objects.

set of infinitely many beliefs is the brain state that realizes her finite "and so on"–belief. In other words, the neural realizer of her "and so on"–belief is what disposes her to behave in ways that make it correct to attribute to her the relevant set of infinitely many beliefs. And this "and so on"–belief is a finite belief composed of finitely many concepts. "And so on" is *not* merely an expression *we* use just to abbreviate the infinitely many beliefs we attribute to her; it expresses a *concept* she possesses. That it expresses a concept is revealed by our distinctive and rule-governed use of it.[24]

That she possesses the "and so on"–belief *explains why* it is correct to attribute to her the relevant set of infinitely many beliefs or the belief of the relevant infinite conjunction. It is in virtue of possessing the former belief that she possesses the latter belief(s). But why think that the "and so on"–belief has this kind of explanatory priority over the relevant set of infinitely many beliefs and the belief of the relevant infinite conjunction? Especially since what I said in the previous paragraph about criterial dispositions seems to indicate that the "and so on"–belief, the relevant set of infinitely many beliefs, and belief of the relevant infinite conjunction all have the same causal roles. There are at least two reasons to accept the explanatory priority claim. The first is the abovementioned fact that it helps us to answer questions about infinitely many beliefs in finite brains. One might object that Warren already accepts that the relevant set of infinitely many beliefs has a single neural realizer, and thus he seems to be able to answer such questions just fine. But if what gives the child the dispositions criterial for having the relevant set of infinitely many beliefs is her acquisition of the "and so on"–belief, then the realizer of that belief is the natural candidate for the single realizer that Warren acknowledges. The second reason to accept the explanatory priority claim is that it makes the account of following the ω-rule more consistent with conventionalism. A conventionalist like Warren (and myself) is a deflationist about propositions. Warren writes, "I usually prefer to talk about accepting and rejecting sentences rather than propositions. . . . [A]ccepting and rejecting a sentence amounts to having certain behavioral dispositions, including but not limited to dispositions toward the sentence itself (*or some related sentence*—for instance, a translation of the sentence in question)" (2020, 35, my emphasis). But there are not infinitely many sentences

[24] Note that this does not imply that every use of the phrase "and so on" or symbol " . . . " expresses the same concept or expresses a concept at all. Such expressions may have homonyms. I am talking specifically about their use in mathematics as putative abbreviations of infinite series of symbols.

and there are not infinitely long conjunctions of sentences, so I can have no dispositions toward them. The only relevant *related sentence* toward which I have any dispositions is the "and so on"-sentence. I think Warren ought to say that having certain behavioral dispositions toward *that* sentence amounts to having the relevant set of infinitely many beliefs or amounts to believing the relevant infinite conjunction. It thus seems that to make conventionalism and the claim that we follow the ω-rule consistent, we should accept that "and so on" expresses a concept whose content is partly constituted by the ω-rule and that the "and so on"-belief explains why we have the relevant set of infinitely many beliefs.

Now on to fictionalism.

8.3. Fictionalism

In Sections 8.3.1–8.3.2, I discuss what Field and Plebani, respectively, have recently said about fictionalism.

8.3.1. Field on Fictionalism and Conventionalism

We have seen that normativism and explanatory conventionalism are roughly equivalent, so long as counterconceptual dependence is explanatory. Field (2022) has recently wondered whether conventionalism is fictionalism by another name.[25] I argue that it isn't.

There are many different versions of fictionalism (see Balaguer 2023), so I must write at a very general level. Mathematical fictionalists are nominalists of a certain sort—they deny the (both synthetic and analytic) existence of mathematical objects. They also think pure mathematics purports to describe mathematical objects. Since pure mathematics purports to describe things that don't exist, all of pure mathematics is false. Fictionalists have different strategies for accommodating common sense. For example, they may distinguish between literal and fictional truth and falsity, so that they can say that "2 + 2 = 4" is literally false but fictionally true, i.e., true in or according to the fiction of mathematics, just as we can say that it's literally false that Sherlock Holmes lived on Baker Street, but true according to the fiction.

[25] Or is fictionalism conventionalism by another name?

Conventionalism seems at first glance quite different from fictionalism. However, Field isn't so sure. He writes, "After all, a fictionalist grants that sets exist *according to the fiction of ZFC*, so hasn't the conventionalist just substituted 'convention' for 'fiction', and 'exists by'/'true by' for 'exists according to'/'true according to'?" (2022, 819, original emphasis). I will add: hasn't the conventionalist substituted "analytic"/"synthetic" for "fictional"/"literal"?

There are many things to say about this. First, it seems to me that the *fictionalist* has substituted "fictional"/"literal" for "analytic"/"synthetic". My sense is that, whenever metaontological deflationists eschew analyticity, their analyticity-replacement will always be worse (i.e., more philosophically problematic) than analyticity, and that their analyticity-replacement will always just be analyticity by another name to the normativist or that the best account of the analyticity-replacement will be in terms of analyticity. This seems to be the case with fictionalism and Linnebo's (2018) abstractionism, which I discuss in Section 8.4.

How do fictionalists account for mathematical truth and existence without (explicit) appeal to analyticity? With the notions of truth and existence according to the fiction of mathematics, and these notions must be such as to account for the (apparent)[26] a priority and necessity of mathematical truth and existence. Scrutinize how this is cashed out and you will find analyticity or something best understood in terms of it. According to Field's (1989) account of mathematical truth, the difference between "2 + 2 = 4" and "2 + 2 = 5" is analogous to the difference between "Sherlock Holmes lived on Baker Street" and "Sherlock Holmes lived on Knox Avenue." This suggestion alone doesn't account for the a priority and necessity of mathematical truth and falsehood. It's plausible that it isn't necessary or a priori that Sherlock Holmes lived on Baker Street—the story could've been different, after all—and if it *is* necessary and a priori, it would only be because we wouldn't count someone who lived on Knox Avenue as Sherlock Holmes; i.e., it would only be because "Sherlock Holmes lived on Baker Street" is analytic. Presumably the fiction of mathematics could've been different as well. What is special about the actual fiction of mathematics that accounts for its a priority and necessity? Balaguer (2001) appeals to the intuitive obviousness of its axioms.

[26] The a priority and necessity of mathematical truth is merely apparent for fictionalists, but they need an explanation of the illusory appearance. For the normativist, mathematical truth really is a priori and necessary in the only senses those terms have.

But the explanation of the intuitive obviousness of our axioms has always been a central object of dispute between platonists and conventionalists. The conventionalist explains the intuitive obviousness of axioms by appeal to the fact that they are implicit definitions, i.e., analytic. It's not clear what Balaguer takes intuitive obviousness to consist in, but in some places (2001) it appears to be radically contingent and somehow to bottom out in mathematical practice, which will not account for the apparent a priority and necessity of mathematics. Elsewhere, he says that the intuitive obviousness of an axiom of set theory suggests that it is "built into our conception of set" (Balaguer 2009, 151). If that doesn't mean the axiom is analytic, I'm not sure what it could mean. Balaguer seemingly eschews analyticity but appeals to something—viz., the idea of an axiom's being built into our conception of a mathematical object—that is best understood in terms of analyticity.[27]

Second, there are very big picture differences between conventionalism and fictionalism: fictionalists believe in a trans- or extra-fictional concept of truth. There is truth outside the fiction. In fact, there, and only there, is where the real truth lies. "Truth according to the fiction F" implies some notions of truth and falsity that apply inside F and outside F. We use the transfictional concept when we say the claims made in the fiction are false. Conventionalists, at least of my Carnapian variety, do not believe in a trans- or extra-conventional concept of truth. Conventions are required for there to be truth-aptness in the first place. Truth without convention is truth without meaning.

Third, Thomasson (2014) has argued that (one version of) the fictional/literal distinction faces insurmountable difficulties. I return to this in Section 8.3.2.

However, Field (2022, 821) thinks that Warren's explanatory conventionalism "does appear to be genuinely different" from fictionalism. Field's primary criticism has to do with the nature of the existence of mathematical entities according to conventionalism. According to conventionalism, the existence of mathematical entities is somehow "lightweight." But what is this lightweight/heavyweight distinction? Curiously, Field doesn't mention the analytic/synthetic distinction once, which seems to me the obvious way for the conventionalist to make the lightweight/heavyweight existence distinction. Lightweight existence is analytic existence (i.e., Xs have lightweight

[27] The same problems beleaguer Balaguer (2009), which also relies on the notion of intuitive obviousness.

existence if and only if "Xs exist" is analytic); heavyweight existence is synthetic existence (i.e., Xs have heavyweight existence if and only if "Xs exist" is synthetic). I think Field suspects this account of the lightweight/heavyweight existence distinction, though, because he then brings up an objection frequently leveled against defenders of analytic existence claims: if "there is an all-powerful creator" were derivable from our basic rules, such a being wouldn't come to exist, so something is amiss with the very idea of analytic existence claims. We know Warren's response: in a language in which "there is an all-powerful creator" is derivable from its basic rules, "there is an all-powerful creator" wouldn't mean that there is an all-powerful creator. Field (2022, 822 n13) addresses Warren's response in a footnote: "But if their use of 'powerful', 'create' etc. was otherwise like ours?" That still wouldn't justify translating their "there is an all-powerful creator" to mean that there is an all-powerful creator, because "[w]hen translating language L into English, we should reject any translation that maps a provable (via basic rules) sentence of L to a non-provable sentence of English, or vice versa" (Warren 2020, 129). "There is an all-powerful creator" is provable from the basic rules in their hypothetical language, but it isn't in English, so we should reject the translation. It would seem, in the language where "all," "powerful," and "creator" are *otherwise* used exactly like ours, that the meaning of "there is an all-powerful creator" is not compositionally determined—its meaning is not a function of the meanings of "all," "powerful," and "creator." In that language, "all" would mean *all*, "powerful" would mean *powerful*, and "creator" would mean *creator*, since those words are used as they are in English, but "all-powerful creator" wouldn't mean *all-powerful creator*. There's nothing mysterious about that. There are many phrases in English whose meanings aren't compositionally determined, such as "red herring." The meaning of "red herring" is not a function of the standard meanings of "red" and "herring." We can easily imagine a language that uses "red" and "herring" in the ways that we do, so that we should homophonically translate those, but where they do not use "red herring" the way we do, we should *not* homophonically translate that. They don't mean *red herring* by "red herring." We can imagine them not even possessing the concept of a red herring. Thus, in that language, "red" means *red* and "herring" means *herring*, but "red herring" doesn't mean *red herring*.

Thus, I don't think Field's objection has bite. Now I want to discuss Plebani's take on a recent debate between fictionalists and metaontological deflationists and argue for a Carnapian way of settling it.

8.3.2. Plebani on Fictionalism

There is currently a debate between fictionalists and normativists. According to Thomasson's (2013, 2014) deflationary metaontology, called "easy ontology," we can make trivially valid inferences to ontological conclusions such as those in the following argument:

(1) There are exactly three exams this semester.
(2) The number of exams this semester is three (from 1).
(3) There is a number that is the number of exams this semester (from 2).

Hermeneutic fictionalists such as Yablo (2001) dispute the inference from (2) to (3). According to hermeneutic (as opposed to "revolutionary") fictionalists, we don't (or shouldn't) take premise (2) literally.[28] Yablo's objection thus requires a distinction between what he calls the "real" and the "literal" content of a claim. The real content of (2) is that there are three exams this semester, which carries no ontological commitment to numbers, and its literal content is that the number of exams this semester is three, which does carry ontological commitment to numbers. Furthermore, ordinary speakers assert only the real content, and the real content does not entail the literal content. Thomasson doesn't think this is coherent. On her deflationary, easy ontological view, (1) analytically entails (2), and (2) analytically entails (3) (i.e., "if the number of exams this semester is three, then there is a number that is the number of exams this semester" is an analytic truth); you can't be committed to the real content of (2) and not be ontologically committed to numbers. Furthermore, since the entailment is analytic, accepting (1) and denying (the literal content of) (2) betrays conceptual incompetence, like accepting that someone is an unmarried man and denying that he's a bachelor. Thomasson challenges the fictionalist to say what more it would take for there to be numbers than for the real content of (2) to be true. Contessa (2016, 771) thinks the challenge is easily met: what it would take

[28] Balaguer (2023) criticizes hermeneutic fictionalism for being an implausible empirical hypothesis about what mathematicians intend, but he doesn't think Yablo intends his view to be about what mathematicians intend. Balaguer criticizes many views for implying implausible empirical hypotheses. Recall that normativism is not and does not imply any empirically hypotheses about what mathematical terms mean or what people intend by their use of them. However, as I mentioned in Chapter 1, normativism *does* seem to imply an empirical hypothesis about the *function* of a class of terms (Thomasson 2022), though I think one could also read normativism normatively, as suggesting that regardless of the actual function of a class of terms, its function ought to be such-and-such.

is for there to be numbers, i.e., "mind-independent, non-spatiotemporally located, causally inert abstract objects that make arithmetical truths true." But on Thomasson's easy ontology, the existence of numbers is not an ontological extra; it comes for free given the truth of uncontroversial claims like "there are three exams this semester."

Plebani (2018, 306) suggests that we've reached an impasse: "it is difficult to say who is begging the question here: in order to answer the challenge posed by the deflationist, the fictionalist seems to presuppose the incorrectness of the deflationist account and in order to reject the fictionalist reply the deflationist seems to presuppose the correctness of her account." And he provides a way forward. He aims to distinguish real from literal content without explaining what the difference would be between a world in which the literal content of a claim is true and a world in which only the real content is true. His proposal is intended not to be question-begging; it should work even if Thomasson were correct. To be clear: he is not giving an argument for fictionalism.

For Plebani, the difference between real and literal content is simple: they concern different subject matter. The real content of (2) concerns exams; it "addresses the issue" of exams, as Plebani puts it. The literal content of (2) concerns numbers; it addresses the issue of numbers. Since I am not[29] concerned with numbers when I utter (2), what I utter is its real content, and I do not commit myself to the existence of numbers. When I infer (3) from (the real content of) (2), I shift subject matters.

This is all very plausible, but what exactly is subject matter? According to Plebani, each sentence S is associated with a directed proposition <|S|>. A directed proposition <|S|> consists of a proposition |S|, conceived as a set of worlds where it is true, and a subject matter <S>, which itself consists of S's truthmakers <S+> and falsemakers <S–>. Plebani conceives of possible truthmakers and falsemakers as propositions. (Note that already we seem to be running afoul of Plebani's promise not to beg the question, since Thomasson [2020b] doesn't deal in truthmakers and falsemakers.) This gives us a notion of subject matter that is distinct from simple truth at a world. For example, "I am either tall or not tall" and "I am either rich or not rich" are true in the same worlds, but have different subject matters because they have different truthmakers: the proposition that I am rich is a truthmaker for the

[29] At least I am typically not concerned with numbers. It seems that on Plebani's account one *couldn't* utter (2) and be concerned with numbers.

latter sentence but not the former. (This is an unfortunate example, because even if Thomasson believed in some truthmakers, her modal normativism precludes her from thinking these logical truths have any.)

Ignoring concerns about the notion of truthmaking mentioned above, I think Plebani achieves his goal: since a trivial inference involves a shift in subject matter, it becomes intelligible how one can accept its premise without accepting its conclusion, without begging the question against the deflationist. I think this points toward a better and more Carnapian way for the deflationist to respond to the fictionalist. For—again ignoring Plebani's appeal to truthmaking—a subject matter seems a lot like a linguistic framework, and introducing a new subject matter seems a lot like introducing a new framework. In fact, the comparison is unintentionally suggested when Plebani uses his notion of subject matter to describe another argument between Contessa and Thomasson. Contessa (2016, 766) presents a dilemma to Thomasson: either her "trivial" inferences (e.g., from (1) to (2)) are ampliative—meaning (2) contains information that (1) doesn't contain—or they aren't. If they are ampliative, then they aren't trivial. If they aren't ampliative, then their conclusions can't contain any new information about a new kind of thing (e.g., numbers). So, we can't get the existence of numbers from uncontroversial premises. Thomasson (2017b) accepts that conclusions reached via trivial inferences don't contain new information. But if (1) and (2) contain the same information, then either (2) isn't committed to numbers or (1) implicitly is. Thomasson (2017b) accepts that (1) is implicitly committed to numbers. For her, the move from (1) to (2) is not an increase in information, but an increase in conceptual scheme—we add a new concept. Call this "being ampliative with respect to conceptual scheme." Plebani explicitly responds to this disagreement with the claim that trivial inferences are ampliative with respect to subject matter—they bring in new subject matters. Obviously conceptual schemes are not identical to Plebani's subject matters, but it seems plausible that being ampliative with respect to subject matter is necessary and sufficient for being ampliative with respect to conceptual scheme.

Regardless, I think a focus on linguistic frameworks or conceptual schemes can help the deflationist in this debate. I agree with Plebani that there is something wrong with saying that accepting (1) and denying (2) betrays conceptual incompetence, and I agree with Contessa that there is something wrong with saying that (1) is implicitly committed to numbers. And I think there are good Carnapian reasons to agree with them. For the Carnapian, there's nothing unintelligible about refusing to use a certain framework, nor does such refusal betray any incompetence, at least not *conceptual* incompetence. Refusing to use a certain framework might be practically irrational (say, because the framework is much more efficient), but there's nothing necessarily *theoretically* or *conceptually* wrong with accepting (1) and denying (2).[30] Thomasson is right, of course, that the number framework is used by ordinary English speakers. But that fact can't be used to saddle refusers of the number framework with incompetence. What makes the fictionalist's position odd, though not betraying conceptual incompetence, for the Carnapian, is 1) that they make explicit claims (e.g., that there are no numbers) that could only intelligibly mean that they refuse to use the number framework, yet they continue to use the number framework (maybe Field 1980 can be excepted), and 2) that none of their arguments gives (legitimate, practical) reasons for why we shouldn't use the number framework. It is akin to someone saying they refuse to use hammers, while using them and justifying it by insisting they aren't real hammers, because real hammers would be made of non-existent ectoplasm.

It is for similar Carnapian reasons that we shouldn't say that (1) is implicitly committed to numbers, at least if that implies, as Thomasson seems to intend it to, that in believing (1) one is committing oneself to the existence of numbers. There are two reasons to deny this implicit commitment. First, as I just explained, there is nothing theoretically or conceptually wrong with accepting (1) and denying the existence of numbers. That is just adopting one framework and refusing to adopt another. Second, if (1) is implicitly committed to numbers simply because it analytically entails a claim in the number framework, then it seems we are constantly committed to the claims and ontologies of other, perhaps extremely bizarre frameworks whenever we speak. Whenever we talk about cars, we are unknowingly committed to Hirsch's (2011) incars and outcars, and countless other unusual ontologies.[31] The point is not that there is anything wrong with the incar ontology. The point is that it is implausible that we are committed to everything our claims analytically entail in other frameworks. Ontologies are frameworks, and to be committed to an ontology is to be committed to a framework, but in general we are not committed to frameworks we aren't using. Fictionalists

[30] This allows Thomasson to avoid Hofweber's (2016, 190) objection that denying "if there are simples arranged tablewise, then there is a table" doesn't betray any conceptual incompetence.

[31] An incar (outcar) is the (sometimes improper) part of a car that is inside (outside) a garage.

are only committed to the number framework (thus, the number ontology) when they use it, and there is nothing theoretically wrong with refusing to use it. (Though it's strange to use it while verbally refusing to.)

Interestingly, the debate between Contessa and Thomasson has an analogue in the neo-Fregean literature, to which I now turn.

8.4. Linnebo on Analyticity and Sufficiency

Neo-Fregeanism is a modern revival of Frege's logicist platonism—the theses that mathematics is about independently existing objects and that mathematical truths are analytic in virtue of being logical truths derivable from logical laws and suitable definitions (Hale and Wright 2001, 1).[32] It may seem odd to combine platonism with the claim that mathematical truths are analytic, but neo-Fregeans bill themselves as platonist in quite a lightweight sense. In fact, Thomasson (2014) and Warren (2020) are both generally sympathetic to neo-Fregeanism, with Warren (2020, 198, 203) calling it "conventionalist-adjacent," and it is often grouped with metaontological deflationisms or minimalisms. This is obviously a purely terminological disagreement, but I would hesitate to call neo-Fregeanism platonist for the same reason I don't call normativism or conventionalism platonist: the merely analytic existence of numbers is something to which no nominalist should object. (But note that, like a good Carnapian, I have also nowhere called normativism or conventionalism nominalist.) Nominalists may object to the analytic/synthetic distinction, but that's not the issue.

Neo-Fregeanism is sometimes called (a version of) "abstractionism" because of its reliance on so-called abstraction principles (Ebert and Rossberg 2016; Linnebo 2018). The general form of an abstraction principle is:

$$\S\alpha = \S\beta \leftrightarrow \alpha \S \beta$$

where "§" is a term-forming operator, and ~ is an equivalence relation. Here is one of Frege's non-mathematical examples of an abstraction principle:

(d): The direction of line *a* = the direction of line *b* if and only if lines *a* and *b* are parallel.

[32] I'm ignoring the fact that often neo-Fregeans are (as Frege himself was) only concerned with arithmetic and real analysis.

Here "the direction of" is "§," "the direction of line *a*" being a term, and the relation of being parallel is the equivalence relation. The relation of being parallel is an equivalence relation because it is reflexive, symmetric, and transitive: a line *a* is parallel to itself; if line *a* is parallel to line *b*, then line *b* is parallel to line *a*; and if line *a* is parallel to line *b*, and line *b* parallel to line *c*, then line *a* is parallel to line *c*.

What is the philosophical significance of (d)? For Frege, terms that figure in abstraction principles must refer to objects. So, "the direction of line *a*" refers to an object, a *direction*. The principle tells us when any two such objects are the same—it offers criteria of identity for directions. Criteria of identity determine when objects are identical or distinct, and many philosophers hold that objects must have criteria of identity, in agreement with Quine's (1958) slogan, "no entity without identity." Furthermore, neo-Fregeans hold that it is only by grasping an object's identity conditions that we are able to grasp the concept of that object and have thoughts about it. So, that (d) provides criteria of identity for directions is what allows its terms to refer to directions, conceived as objects—clearly *abstract* objects, not physical or mental concrete objects. Objecthood, reference, and criteria of identity are linked, in what Linnebo (2018, 21) calls the Fregean triangle.

What makes this so radical is this. Imagine that we had no concept of direction in Frege's sense. Then Frege comes along and gives us principle (d). With (d), we can grasp a new concept and refer to a new object—new in the sense that we couldn't refer to it before, not new in the sense that Frege brought it into existence. Furthermore, all it takes, metaphysically speaking, for directions to exist is for lines to exist—the truth of the left-hand side of (d) requires no more, metaphysically speaking, than the truth of the right-hand side. Thus, we seem to have an unmysterious picture of the metaphysics and epistemology of at least some abstract object, *directions*.

This picture is transferred into the philosophy of mathematics with abstraction principles like Hume's principle:

(HP) The number of Fs = the number of Gs if and only if F and G are equinumerous (i.e., can be one-to-one correlated).

Let us engage in a similar thought experiment. Imagine that we had no concept of number. Then Hume comes along and gives us principle (HP). With it, we can now grasp the concept of number and use that concept to refer to new abstract objects: *numbers*. Furthermore, the truth of the left-hand side of (HP) requires no more, metaphysically speaking, than the truth of the right-hand side. Neo-Fregeans like Hale and Wright (2001) take (HP) to be analytic, implicitly defining the number concept. This gives us an unmysterious metaphysics and epistemology of numbers, for we gain access to facts about numbers via facts about one-to-one correlations.

I won't object to anything I've said so far. From a Carnapian point of view, abstraction principles are devices for introducing new concepts into a framework. One might take issue with the nature of such devices, whether they are really suitable for introducing a concept (e.g., debates about impredicativity and bad company), and so on. Some abstraction principles are impredicative, meaning that they quantify over objects some of which fall under the concept being defined, and there is debate over whether this seeming circularity is harmful. Frege's abstraction principle Basic Law V is impredicative and (combined with other plausible principles) famously leads to contradiction in Russell's Paradox. Basic Law V says:

The extension of F = the extension of G if and only if F and G are coextensive.

Think of extensions as sets, and ask whether the set of all sets not members of themselves is a member of itself. Contradiction quickly follows. The bad company problem (sometimes put in the form of an objection) is the problem of distinguishing "good" abstraction principles (i.e., those that successfully introduce a new concept) from "bad" (i.e., those that fail, like Basic Law V). Thomasson (2014, 138–139), who is otherwise sympathetic to neo-Fregeanism, also raises concerns about the need for criteria of identity when introducing a new concept. She's not certain neo-Fregeans take criteria of identity to be necessary when introducing a new concept, though, and Linnebo (2018, 33) is explicit that he takes criteria of identity only to be sufficient for introducing a new concept. Unlike Hale and Wright, Linnebo rejects the analytic/synthetic distinction, which makes his position quite different from mine. So, I will spend the rest of this section examining Linnebo's version of neo-Fregeanism, which he calls abstractionism.

Linnebo's (2018, 2023a, 2023b) abstractionism is a deflationary metaontology similar to neo-Fregeanism in that it relies on abstraction principles, but it eschews analyticity. Thus, Linnebo needs some other way of cashing out the thin, lightweight, insubstantial existence of abstract objects. The way he does this is with his concept of *sufficiency*. This is his analyticity-replacement, and, as above in the discussion of fictionalism, we will see that the best account of this notion is in terms of analyticity.

Linnebo uses his notion of sufficiency to explicate abstraction principles and to account for the kinds of inference that Thomasson takes to be trivial analytic entailments, such as "if there are exactly three exams this semester, then the number of exams this semester is three." For Linnebo, the truth of the antecedent suffices, in the relevant sense, for the truth of the consequent. This notion of sufficiency is used to explicate similar kinds of claim, such as "all it takes for the number of exams this semester to be three is for there to be exactly three exams this semester." Linnebo rejects using analyticity to analyze these kinds of inference and claim because he is concerned about analytic existence and *de re* analyticity (2018, 13–14). We have already addressed analytic existence. In *de dicto* sufficiency statements, only formulas with no free variables flank the sufficiency operator; in *de re* sufficiency statements, formulas with free variables flank the sufficiency operator. Take the claim that there are thin objects, expressed as the sufficiency claim $\exists x(\top \Rightarrow Ex)$, where Ex is an existence predicate, and $\top$ is a tautology. The problem, according to Linnebo, is not that this is an existence claim or that it uses an existence *predicate*, but that a formula with a free variable Ex flanks the sufficiency operator. (Linnebo means that x is free in 'Ex', not that it is free in '$\exists x(\top \Rightarrow Ex)$'.) Linnebo assumes that the defender of analyticity must *define*[33] the claim that there are thin objects to mean $\exists x \mathrm{A}(\top \rightarrow Ex)$, where 'A' is the analyticity operator "it is analytic that." However, Linnebo writes, "it is only *sentences* that are analytic, not open formulas relative to variable assignments. Analyticity is meant to be an entirely linguistic phenomenon, whereas variable assignments typically involve non-linguistic objects" (2018, 13, original emphasis). (See also Thomasson [2020a] and Donaldson and Wang [2022] on normativism and *de re* modality.)[34]

[33] "Frege proposed to *define* $\phi \Leftrightarrow \psi$ as $\mathrm{A}(\phi \leftrightarrow \psi)$" (Linnebo 2018, 13, my emphasis). Linnebo then raises the objection from *de re* analyticity.

[34] I think the necessity of identity and the substitutivity of identicals into modal contexts are easier for normativists to secure than Donaldson and Wang (2022) think. The substitutivity of identicals into modal contexts follows straightforwardly from the necessity of identity. Those who deny the substitutivity of identicals into modal contexts deny the necessity of identity (e.g., Gibbard 1975). When an identity claim is necessary, it expresses a rule according to which the expressions flanking the identity sign must be applied to the same individual. Suppose that necessarily, *Fa*. This expresses the rule that the name "*a*" must be applied to an *F*. (I follow Thomasson 2020a and Donaldson and Wang 2022 in talking of names *applying*. Perhaps we could also specify the rule as: the name "*a*" must [be used so as to purport to] refer to an *F*.) By "'*a*' must be applied to an *F*," I obviously don't mean

However, I don't think there is anything wrong with the normativist characterizing the claim that there are thin objects as *expressing* the claim that some things exist analytically, though it is important how we logically regiment this. We must do it in a way that avoids predicating analyticity of non-linguistic objects and quantifying into modal contexts. For, an immediate thought is to regiment the claim that some things exist analytically as the claim that there is an x such that "x exists" is analytic. But here we are quantifying into a quotational context, which is nonsensical (Burgess 1997; Quine 1953).

One thing you might try is to stipulate a context which is like quotation but into which we can quantify. Since there is already some precedent in the literature on truth-conditional semantics for using quotation marks not to create an expression-name but to indicate a "structural description" of an expression that "describes the expression as a concatenation of elements"

that avoiding conceptual impropriety requires constantly applying "*a*" to every *F* you encounter or requires applying "*a*" to some particular *F* every time you encounter it or some such thing. I mean that, to avoid conceptual impropriety, if you apply "*a*" to anything in any scenario, real or imagined, it had better be an *F*. You could read "'*a*' must be applied to an *F*" as shorthand for "'*a*' may not be applied to a non-*F* in any scenario, real or imagined" (cf. Donaldson and Wang 2022, 300). Now, assuming "*a*" and "*b*" are rigid, if $a = b$, then this is a (perhaps a posteriori) necessary truth expressing the rule that "*a*" and "*b*" must be applied to the same individual. From these two rules—that "*a*" must be applied to an *F* and that "*a*" and "*b*" must be applied to the same individual—it follows that "*b*" must be applied to an *F*, which is expressed by "necessarily, *Fb*." Thus, the substitutivity of identicals into modal contexts is accommodated. This presupposes an account of the necessity of identity. The necessity of identity follows from the fact that names are rigid designators, i.e., that they refer to the same individual in every possible world or, less metaphysically, every counterfactual situation (Fitch 2004, 36), in which that individual exists. (Sidelle [1989, 1992, 1995] has convincingly argued we can understand rigidity and its reliance on transworld identification in a way consistent with conventionalism.) Suppose the name "*a*" actually refers to *a*, and suppose we learn (perhaps a posteriori) that the name "*b*" also actually refers to *a*. These aren't expressions of rules; they are just (often empirical) facts about what words refer to. But if names are rigid, then if name "*a*" actually refers to *a*, then name "*a*" necessarily refers to *a*. (Two quick notes: First, I do not mean that certain *sounds* and *strings* could not have referred to something else. They could have, but then they wouldn't have counted as the same *name* [cf. Kripke 1980, 77]. Second, this way of characterizing rigidity might be a bit controversial, but it is not uncommon [cf. McGinn (1982, 97): "[a rigid designator] necessarily designates what it actually designates"], and I think for the normativist account of the necessity of identity to work, rigidity must be characterized as, or taken to imply, a necessary claim that expresses a rule like the one next discussed.) This expresses the conditional rule that if name "*a*" actually refers to *a*, then name "*a*" must be applied to *a*. I think this comports well with Kripke's (1980, 49) test for rigidity: "*x*" is rigid if and only if "*x* might not have been *x*" is false. This seems to me equivalent to "x" is rigid if and only if *x* is necessarily *x*; and "'*x*' must be applied to *x*" seems a good candidate for a rule expressed by "*x* is necessarily *x*." (Though there are debates about Kripke's tests for rigidity.) Now, since "*a*" and "*b*" are both rigid names that actually refer to the same individual, they must be applied to the same individual. As above, this rule finds expression in "necessarily, $a = b$." Hence, the necessity of (perhaps a posteriori) identity. (Thomasson 2020a presents a different explanation of the substitutivity of identicals into modal contexts and the necessity of identity, but I think my explanation is more intuitive and better avoids the objections brought by Donaldson and Wang 2022.) Deniers of the necessity of identity (e.g., Gibbard 1975) are explicit that they reject rigidity. A full defense of these claims is outside the scope of this book (see Povich forthcoming-b).

(Davidson 1967, 321), to which truth is then ascribed, I stipulate that *Davidsonian* quotation marks work as follows: the open sentence $\mathrm{A}^{\mathrm{D}}Ex^{\mathrm{D}}$ is satisfied by an object if and only if it possesses the property of creating an analytic sentence when concatenated with the existence predicate. This open sentence is satisfied by names of 2.[35] If truth is allowed to be predicated of such concatenations, then I don't see why analyticity shouldn't be. On this proposal, the claim that there are thin objects expresses the claim that there are names whose concatenation with the existence predicate is analytic, or, equivalently for all intents and purposes, it expresses the claim that there are analytic existence sentences.[36]

I doubt this proposal can be made to work due to issues regarding substitutional quantification, among others. I think the right thing for the normativist to do is to appeal to schemas and rigidity. For a normativist, we will judge "It is necessary that *n* is *F*" to be true when and only when "*n* is *F*" expresses an actual rule of ours, or a consequence of an actual rule of ours, including consequences that only follow with the inclusion of empirical information, to handle a posteriori necessities (Sidelle 1989; Thomasson 2020a). We can thus say that "It is necessary that *x* is *F*" will be true of an object *o* just in case "*n* is *F*" expresses a rule (or rule-consequence, possibly empirically derived), where "*n*" rigidly refers to *o*. We can think of the claim that there are thin objects as thus expressing the claim that there is an *x* such that "*n* exists" is analytic (or expresses a rule), where "*n*" rigidly designates *x*.

But how could "*n* exists," where "*n*" is a rigid designator, ever be analytic? Aren't rigid designators contentless? Here the normativist needs something like Sidelle's (1992, 1995) neglected account of rigidity (Povich forthcoming-b). The basic idea is that if an expression is rigid, then it is governed by a rule according to which it must be applied[37] in every possible world to the individual that satisfies or fulfills the transworld identity criteria analytically associated with it.[38] That is Sidelle's account of rigidity put in explicitly rule

[35] Analyticity is relative to some language, L, so you should read "in L" as implicit in the previous examples.

[36] The ideas presented here bear some similarity to Carnap's (1947) conceptual interpretation of quantified modal logic in which quantifiers range over concepts instead of objects. However, unlike him, I do not take what I've said to be an explication of what sentences of (objectual) quantified modal logic "really mean".

[37] By "must be applied" here, I mean that it may be applied to a certain individual and may not be applied to anything else.

[38] This seems consistent with the idea that transworld identity can be stipulated (Kripke 1980; Salmon 1996; Fiocco 2007). *This* stipulation is not of the identity of individuals between *possible* worlds, but the worlds simpliciter under consideration. Accounts of modal epistemology that accept

form; it ties the criteria of counterfactual application of an expression, i.e., criteria for its application in another world, to satisfaction or fulfillment of relevant transworld identity criteria.

The transworld identity criteria associated with an object depend on the kind of sortal under which the object falls.[39] Transworld identity criteria are sortal-relative and can be specified in general as follows: $\forall x \forall y$ (if x is an S in w_1 and y is an S in w_2, then $x = y$ iff $R_S xy$). For example, $\forall x \forall y$ (if x is a person in w_1 and y is a person in w_2, then $x = y$ iff x and y have the same biological origin). We can then give an account of the satisfaction of an open modal formula as follows:

> (*Normativist Satisfaction*) "F*x*" is true of or satisfied by *o* just in case the claim that G*n* expresses a rule or rule consequence.[40]

This should be read as an open-ended schema. Permissible instances of the schema can be generated by replacing "F" with any predicate of the object language, "G" with the translation of "F" in the metalanguage, "*o*" with any referring term of the metalanguage, and "*n*" with any rigid designator of *o* in the metalanguage, i.e., any term that must be applied in every scenario, actual or counterfactual, to the individual that satisfies the transworld identity criteria of a sortal under which *o* falls. Open-endedness allows the normativist to avoid worries regarding, e.g., the fact that there are more real numbers than expressions in our language that can denote them.[41] This would seem to imply that some real numbers aren't necessarily real numbers, since for some real numbers there isn't a name "*n*" such that "*n* is a real number" expresses a rule; thus those real numbers don't satisfy "□(*x* is a real

that transworld identity can be stipulated must answer the question of what distinguishes possible worlds from impossible worlds, for the latter are just as stipulable as the former. The normativist has a straightforward solution: what is stipulated is some content. That content is possible if and only if it is consistent with actual semantic rules—including identity criteria or criteria that play the same essential-property-specifying role—and their consequences. Since we can be ignorant or incorrect about the actual semantic rules and their consequences, we can be mistaken about whether what we've stipulated is possible. Normativism is thus consistent with haecceitism, or at least what Salmon (1996) means by "haecceitism."

[39] Those conventionalists/normativists who think objects themselves are sortally individuated can simply talk of the transworld identity criteria of object o, rather than those of a sortal under which o falls.

[40] As mentioned in Chapter 1, I follow Thomasson (2020) and Ludwig (n.d.) in taking analyticity to be a property of meaningful claims or statements rather than strings.

[41] See Warren's (2020) argument from open-endedness for the categoricity of arithmetic. If open-endedness can do what Warren and others (e.g., Lavine 2006; McGee 2000) say it can for the foundations of mathematics, then there should be no problem for *Normativist Satisfaction*. Whether the antecedent of the previous sentence is true is unfortunately beyond the scope of this chapter.

number)."[42] However, open-ended rules hold in any consistent expansion of the language. It seems obvious that many rules relevant to *de re* necessity are open-ended, and the open-endedness of *Normativist Satisfaction* is justified by that fact. When a person is born and a new person-name is introduced into the language, it too is governed by the open-ended rule according to which any person-name must be applied to a person. That person is thus necessarily a person. Similarly, the normativist might plausibly suggest that there is also an actual open-ended rule (or rule consequence) according to which any name for a real number must be applied to a real number. Since the rule is open-ended, it governs any coherent expansion of the language.

Let us examine an instance of *Normativist Satisfaction*. "$\Box$(x is person)" is true of or satisfied by Socrates just in case the claim that Socrates is person expresses a rule or rule consequence. Here "Socrates" must be applied in every possible world to the individual that satisfies the transworld identity criteria of a sortal under which Socrates falls (the relevant sortal being "person"). The rule that the claim that Socrates is person expresses is that "Socrates" (and any other name of Socrates) must be applied to a person (Povich n.d.-a; Thomasson 2020a).[43]

One might worry that reference to "a sortal" in *Normativist Satisfaction* could cause problems. Is satisfaction relative to which sortal is chosen? This is not a problem. All sortals that apply to a given object share their transworld identity criteria. An object can only fall under one category, and every sortal within a category shares its identity criteria (Dummett 1973; Lowe 1989, 2007).[44] Suppose that o falls under sortals with different identity criteria. Things falling under sortals with different identity criteria cannot be identical. Therefore, o cannot be identical with itself. That's absurd. So, o cannot fall under sortals with different identity criteria.

[42] I thank a reviewer for pressing this worry.

[43] One might object as follows. Socrates also falls under the sortal "collection of cells." Since "n is a person" does *not* express a rule or rule-consequence, where "n" must be applied in every possible world to the individual who satisfies the transworld identity criteria of "collection of cells," "$\Box$(x is a person)" is *not* true of or satisfied by Socrates. Contrary to what I said above, choice of the sortal under which an object falls matters! This is confused from the beginning. Socrates is a person, *not* a collection of cells. The collection of cells composing Socrates at a time is an object not identical to Socrates, precisely because they have different identity criteria (see Lowe 1989, especially Chapter 7). If "Schmocrates" names a collection of cells composing Socrates at t, then "$\Box$(x is a person)" isn't true of or satisfied by Schmocrates, but Schmocrates is not identical to Socrates.

[44] Dummett and Lowe were talking about *intra*world identity criteria, but the arguments clearly generalize to transworld identity criteria. I am, of course, assuming that there are such things as transworld identity criteria and that counterpart theory, e.g., is false. But this is not because counterpart theory is inconsistent with normativism. Lewis was adamant that the counterpart-determining similarity relation is context-dependent and it is easily construed as conventional.

The claim that there are thin objects can be taken to express that there is an *x* such that "*n* exists" expresses a rule or rule consequence, where "*n*" must be applied in every possible world to the individual that satisfies the transworld identity criteria of a sortal under which *x* falls. This is the normativist precisification of the claim that there is an *x* such that "*n* exists" is analytic, where "*n*" rigidly designates *x*.

Let us look at an existentially instantiated thinness claim. The natural number 2 is thin; its existence makes no demands on the world. For the normativist, this should be understood to mean that the claim that 2 exists expresses a rule or rule consequence, where "2" must be applied[45] in every possible world to the individual that satisfies the transworld identity criteria of a sortal under which the natural number 2 falls (e.g., "natural number"). Now, I have no account of the transworld identity criteria associated with the sortal "natural number." One might need a specific account of the nature of natural numbers before such criteria can be suggested, or perhaps they are given by the Peano axioms (see below for more on this thought). Regardless, 1) Sidelle's (1992, 1995) argument that determinate reference requires transworld identity criteria suggests that *some* such criteria are required, and 2) I think I can say enough here to make plausible that the normativist has an account of *de re* necessary existence claims like this even without a specific account of the transworld identity criteria for natural numbers.

Why, for the normativist, isn't the existence of Socrates necessary? Because fulfilling the relevant transworld identity criteria in a world isn't guaranteed—there are worlds where nothing shares actual Socrates' biological origin, so in those worlds Socrates doesn't exist. It is consistent with those criteria that nothing fulfills them. A *de re* necessary existence claim is true when something fulfills the relevant transworld identity criteria in every world. In such a case, there is an individual in every world that is identical to the actual individual, so the individual exists necessarily. So, the normativist can say that the necessary existence of 2 reflects the fact that fulfillment of the relevant transworld identity criteria—whatever they are—is guaranteed in every world.

It would be nice, though, if the normativist can say more about *why* the transworld identity criteria are guaranteed to be fulfilled in every world. Here is a suggestion. Warren (2020) has argued that the Peano axioms can

[45] To ward off a confusion, I must emphasize that when I say "apply" in this context, I do not mean what is often called the application of mathematics. So, when I talk of the application of "2," I mean its use to pick out the number 2; I don't mean its use in, for example, counting.

be thought of as the rules governing our natural number concepts (see also Friederich 2011). Perhaps it is these rules that determine the transworld identity criteria for "natural number." And the Peano axioms simultaneously imply the existence of things that fulfill the transworld identity criteria in any world in which they are true (i.e., in any world in which the rules are in force). (Several relevant axioms are: 0 is a natural number; the successor of any natural number is a natural number; if the successor of a natural number m = the successor of a natural number n, then m = n.) Now, it is already part of the normativist/conventionalist position that in counterfactual reasoning we hold fixed our actual rules (see, e.g., Sidelle 2009; Thomasson 2020a; Wright 1985). So, we go from world to world "looking" for something that fulfills the relevant transworld identity criteria. As we go from world to world, we are holding fixed the Peano axioms, our rules governing our natural number concepts, which simultaneously supply the relevant transworld identity criteria and imply the existence of things that fulfill them. So, as we go from world to world looking for something that fulfills the relevant transworld identity criteria, we are guaranteed to find it. The *de re* necessary claim that 2 exists thus expresses a rule-consequence—a consequence of the rule that "2" (in fact, *any* name of 2) must be applied in every possible world to the individual that satisfies the transworld identity criteria of a sortal under which 2 falls and the fact, just explained, that in every world it is guaranteed that there exists something that fulfills the criteria. In other words, that any name of 2 applies in every world, i.e., every scenario, real or imagined, actual or counterfactual. This, I suggest, is the rule-consequence expressed by the *de re* necessary claim that 2 exists.[46]

So, I don't think Linnebo has yet ruled out understanding thin existence in terms of analyticity, so long as this doesn't require the thesis that thin existence claims are synonymous with or logically equivalent to analyticity claims—and I don't think any current defenders of analyticity and conventionalism (e.g., Warren) would think their view committed to that. Here, I've argued that claims of thin existence, including relative thin existence, *express* conceptual rules or their consequences. This allows the normativist to escape the objections of Quine and Burgess. Another important relation between thin existence (claims) and analyticity (claims) that isn't synonymy

[46] What I've argued for the natural number 2 obviously applies to every natural number and, presumably, to other kinds of number (e.g., real numbers), mutatis mutandis (e.g., by substituting in the axioms of real analysis for the Peano axioms). A similar story might be told for *de re* necessary existence claims for other kinds of abstract objects, though the details await future work.

or logical equivalence is counterconceptual dependence. Given that thin existence claims express conceptual rules, the former will counterconceptually depend on the latter. As noted above, the following counterfactual seems true read counterconceptually: "if there were no analytic existence sentences, then there would've been no thin objects." Similarly, "if there were no analytic entailments, then there would've been no relatively thin objects" seems true read counterconceptually. Let's now examine how Linnebo conceives sufficiency.

What exactly is sufficiency in Linnebo's sense? It is a relation that is supposed 1) to be less demanding than analytic entailment, 2) to be more demanding than strict (i.e., necessary) implication, 3) to imply metaphysical explanation (so that if φ suffices for ψ, φ metaphysically explains ψ), 4) to be ontologically ampliative (so that if φ suffices for ψ, the ontological commitments of ψ exceed those of φ), and 5) to imply that it is possible to know that φ implies ψ (Linnebo 2018, 14–17).[47] What relation could possibly do all these things? Analytic entailment is a plausible candidate (ignoring the first criterion, of course). Call this sufficiency-as-analytic-entailment claim "SAE."

The second criterion means that we shouldn't define $\varphi \Rightarrow \psi$ as the strict conditional $\Box(\varphi \rightarrow \psi)$. Linnebo's (2018, 15) reasons are 1) that it would count a necessarily existing God, if They exist, as a thin object since $\Box$(T→God exists); 2) that it would run afoul of the third criterion, because no tautology metaphysically explains God's existence; and 3) that it would run afoul of the fifth criterion, because it is not possible to move from knowledge of a tautology to knowledge of God's existence.[48]

This seems to be a problem for SAE, since I argued in Chapter 5 that necessitation (i.e., strict implication) is analytic entailment, so if analytic entailment is sufficiency, then necessitation is sufficiency. If necessitation is sufficiency, then I need to answer these three objections. I will address the second objection below when I discuss metaphysical explanation. The solution to the first and third objections is to recognize that only *metaphysical* necessitation is analytic entailment. Thomasson (2020a, 115) considers whether the claim that God exists is a counterexample to normativism. The

[47] This is the simplified criterion he uses in Linnebo (2023a). The full criterion is "If $\varphi \Rightarrow \psi$, then it is possible to know $\varphi \rightarrow \psi$; and if additionally φ is known, then this possible knowledge is compatible with continued knowledge of φ" (Linnebo 2018, 16). All this criterion is supposed to do is ensure that if $\varphi \Rightarrow \psi$, it is possible to move from knowledge of φ to knowledge of ψ.

[48] Defenders of a priori arguments for God's existence might disagree.

thought is that if it's true, it's metaphysically necessary, but not an expression of conceptual rules. Thomasson suspects that some other kind of necessity is at play here than metaphysical necessity—perhaps nomological necessity—and I agree. Lange (2009) suggests that there are various strengths of nomological necessity. Perhaps the necessity at play is the strongest kind of nomological necessity. (I briefly discuss strengths of necessity in Chapter 9.) But what if there *were* a metaphysically necessary God? Again, the only way I can make sense of this question is by imagining a being with the strongest kind of nomological necessity. If you stipulated that it is metaphysically necessary that God exists, you'd be making "God exists" analytic and, thus, changing its meaning.

What about objects that *are* metaphysically necessary? Consider $\Box(\top \rightarrow 2$ exists). Is it possible to move from knowledge of a tautology to knowledge of 2's existence? Yes, you can move from knowledge of anything to knowledge of 2's existence, because 2's existence is analytic and a priori. Linnebo includes the epistemic criterion to account for knowledge of abstract objects. How do we acquire knowledge of directions? Somehow, knowledge of lines must suffice for knowledge of directions. Supporters of analyticity have an easy answer: knowledge of lines suffices for knowledge of directions because claims about lines analytically entail claims about directions. Thus, Linnebo's second criterion, that sufficiency be more demanding than strict implication, is unnecessary when you have analyticity and recognize that only metaphysical necessitation is analytic entailment.

We saw above when discussing the debate between Contessa and Thomasson that trivial inferences are ontologically ampliative—which, for the normativist, just means ampliative with respect to conceptual scheme—when the conclusion contains a noun term not contained in the premise. Thus, the fourth criterion is met so long as we stipulate that the analytically entailed consequent contain a noun term not contained in the antecedent. Let us say that *X* analytically entails* *Y* if and only if *X* analytically entails *Y*, and "*Y*" contains a noun term not contained in "*X*." According to SAE, sufficiency is analytic entailment*.

The debate between Contessa and Thomasson is mirrored in a debate between Linnebo and Rayo. Linnebo calls his abstractionism "asymmetric" because of the third and fourth criteria: the two sides of a sufficiency claim differ in explanatory priority and ontological commitment. He also adds subject matter: the two sides are about different objects. He contrasts this with Rayo's (2013) trivialism, which is akin to a symmetric form of abstractionism

(Linnebo 2018, 79). However, instead of relying on abstraction principles, Rayo relies on "just is"-statements. Some examples, which are akin to trivial inferences, are (Rayo 2013, 3, original emphasis):

> For Susan to instantiate the property of running *just is* for Susan to run.
> For there to be a table *just is* for there to be some things arranged tablewise.
> For the number of the dinosaurs to be Zero *just is* for there to be no dinosaurs.

Linnebo calls trivialism symmetric, because Rayo intends the two sides of "just is"-statements to make the same demands on the world. Rayo thus doesn't think either side can be used to metaphysically explain the other. To accept a "just is"-statement is to close a theoretical gap between its sides, which makes it incoherent to ask whether one side metaphysically explains another. Thus, trivialism looks a lot like SAE: it seems like "just is"-statements are analytic entailments*, and both eschew metaphysical explanation. Furthermore, which "just is"-statements one accepts structures one's "logical space" in the same way that which conceptual rules one adopts structures one's conceptual space. Once the "just is"-statements are accepted, and a logical space is in place, the truth of mathematical and logical claims is determined and requires no demands of the world, hence their truth-conditions are trivially satisfied. Rayo makes this comparison with Carnapianism explicitly and says that his notion of a "just is"-statement is his replacement for analyticity (2013, 36). I'm not convinced that Rayo has really eschewed analyticity. Is there really a way of conceiving *how* acceptance of "just is"-statements structures a logical space—makes certain claims intelligible and others unintelligible—*without* conceiving of them as analytic? Perhaps the differences will end up being largely terminological, or perhaps they result from foundational disagreements in (meta)semantics. But let us get back to where we were. It will be helpful to examine Linnebo's objections to Rayo, since they will also be objections to SAE.

Linnebo's objections point to the three putative asymmetries, ways in which the two sides of an abstraction principle can differ: explanatory priority, ontological commitment, and subject matter. Curiously, the last two objections are the same as Contessa's objections to Thomasson. Let us start with ontological commitment. Linnebo presents Rayo with roughly the same dilemma that Contessa presents to Thomasson regarding whether trivial inferences are ontologically ampliative. And Rayo chooses the same horn as Thomasson: "there are three exams this semester" is implicitly committed to numbers. Linnebo's (2018, 85) responses to this are, first, that any notion of ontological commitment according to which both sides of a "just is"-statement share ontological commitments is a notion not worth having; and, second, that Quine's criterion of ontological commitment, according to which "to be is to be the value of a variable" (Quine 1948, 34),[49] "is an entirely worldly matter" (Linnebo 2018, 84). Since the two sides of a "just is"-statement obviously differ in ontological commitment by Quine's criterion, they must make different demands on the world. My response here is the same as my response to Thomasson, but first I want to note something about this last point. It seems quite controversial to say that Quine's criterion is an entirely worldly matter. Linnebo says, "The Quinean notion is concerned with what objects reality must contain for a certain sentence to be true" (2018, 85), but that is very different from what Quine said. Linnebo's claim sounds much more like what truthmaker theorists say, and many of them vehemently deny Quine's criterion (e.g., Cameron 2010; Heil 2003). Regardless, I think Linnebo is right that there is something wrong with saying that both sides of a "just is"-statement share ontological commitments. Being ontologically ampliative *just is* being ampliative with respect to conceptual scheme! So, of course they differ in ontological commitment. But there is nothing anti-Carnapian about that. A similar point can be made about the asymmetry of subject matter: being ampliative with respect to linguistic framework will entail an asymmetry in subject matter. But here is where Linnebo would appeal to the "worldly matter" of ontological commitment. That just doesn't hold for a Carnapian. As I mentioned in Chapter 1, ontologies are languages, so while one philosopher may say that tables exist and another may say that only particles arranged tablewise exist, they are merely talking about the same thing in different languages (Dyke 2007; Heil 2003; Hirsch 2011; Putnam 1981, 1987; Rayo 2013; Thomasson 2014). That the two sides of a "just is"-statement differ in ontological commitment does not entail that they make different demands on the world. They present the same information about the world, thus make the same demands, but in different ways (Thomasson 2017b, 774). Thus, the asymmetries of ontological commitment and subject matter are already built into analytic entailment*.

[49] That is, "a theory is committed to those and only those entities to which the bound variables of the theory must be capable of referring in order that the affirmations made in the theory be true" (Quine 1948, 33).

This leaves the asymmetry of explanatory priority. It certainly does seem like there being some things arranged tablewise metaphysically explains there being a table, rather than vice versa. And it is not generally the case that if *X* analytically entails* *Y*, then *X* metaphysically explains *Y*. For example, in some cases, analytic entailment* is symmetric where metaphysical explanation isn't. That Jeremy is a bachelor analytically entails* that he is an unmarried man, and vice versa, but it doesn't seem like metaphysical explanation similarly goes in both directions. So, I agree with Linnebo that metaphysical explanations are usually asymmetric—one side of a sufficiency claim usually does have explanatory priority—but what is the motivation for requiring that sufficiency imply metaphysical explanation? About this requirement, Linnebo (2018, 16–17) writes:

> A second promised benefit of thin objects is a response to the worry about the seeming ontological extravagance of modern mathematics and certain other bodies of knowledge, such as classical mereology. How can these sciences get away with postulating such an abundance of objects when ontological economy is otherwise regarded as a virtue? Again, the minimalist has an answer, namely that the generous ontologies in question either make no substantial demand on the world (in the case of pure abstract objects such as numbers and sets), or their demands on the world do not substantially exceed demands that have already been met (in the case of impure sets or mereological sums). This answer motivates another constraint on $\Rightarrow$. Assume that $\varphi \Rightarrow \psi$. Then any metaphysical explanation of ϕ must also explain ψ, or at least give rise to such an explanation.

Thus, what allows sufficiency to function as Linnebo's analyticity-replacement is precisely the requirement that it imply metaphysical explanation, something, I think, far more philosophically problematic than analyticity. According to the normativist's SAE, the claim of insubstantial demand is justified by appeal to analyticity. The formal sciences get away with postulating an abundance of objects because their demands are insubstantial, which means the existence of their objects is analytic. So, for the normativist, the requirement that sufficiency claims imply metaphysical explanation is unnecessary. Recall that the philosophical appeal of abstraction principles is that they explain how we can grasp a new concept and use that concept to refer to a "new" object. From a Carnapian point of view, they answer the question of how legitimately to introduce new concepts to our scheme. (Though I've already noted that we might think identity conditions aren't required to introduce new concepts to our scheme legitimately [Thomasson 2014].) Metaphysical explanation is irrelevant to that question. If we had the concept of a table but not the concept of things arranged tablewise, we could use an abstraction principle to introduce the concept of things arranged tablewise, even though tables do not metaphysically explain things arranged tablewise. So, explanatory priority is irrelevant when introducing a new concept. Linnebo would say that this introduction of the concept of things arranged tablewise is illegitimate because it doesn't track the direction of metaphysical explanation, but remember that he says that only because he eschews analyticity; he thinks appeal to metaphysical explanation is required to explicate the notion of insubstantial demand. Since tables do not metaphysically explain things arranged tablewise, we can't be sure that our introduction of the concept of things arranged tablewise hasn't substantially increased the demands we make on the world. This is not a worry when you have analyticity and accept that there being tables analytically entails* there being things arranged tablewise. So, although analytic entailment* does not imply metaphysical explanation, that isn't a problem.

I'm not sure what motivation there would be for the following, but if one accepted analyticity and still insisted on the requirement of metaphysical explanation, the normativist *can* accommodate it. Locke (2020), whose work on the normativist interpretation of counterpossibles inspired my account of countermathematicals in Chapter 5 (Locke 2019), has recently given a normativist interpretation of metaphysical explanation. Let us call metaphysical explanation from a normativist perspective "analytic explanation." This seems to me unmotivated, but one could then formulate SAE as: sufficiency is analytic entailment**, where *X* analytically entails** *Y* if and only if *X* analytically entails *Y*, "*Y*" contains a noun term not contained in "*X*," and *X* analytically explains *Y*. I will only give a brief overview of Locke's account here, since I don't think abstraction principles or sufficiency claims need to track metaphysical explanation.[50]

Locke (2020) argues that in metaphysical explanations we are expressing some kinds of asymmetric relation between our concepts. Metaphysical explanations are a motley, and just because some philosophers might say,

[50] Obviously, the normativist needs an account of what is going on in metaphysical explanations. I'm just saying that that account isn't necessary for an account of abstraction principles or sufficiency claims.

e.g., that all metaphysical explanations represent grounding relations doesn't change that fact. For grounding relations are also a motley. There is considerable disagreement over which cases actually are metaphysical explanations and why they are metaphysical explanations. So, we shouldn't be concerned if the asymmetric conceptual relations expressed in metaphysical explanations are themselves a motley. Here is one example. According to (Locke 2020, 42), a claim like "*x* grounds *y*" expresses the following:

(i) the use of "*y*" is conceptually warranted primarily by the use of "*x*" (along with the relevant conceptual laws); and
(ii) "*x*" conceptually precedes "*y*"; and
(iii) the relevant empirical conditions have been satisfied, if there are any.

Note that (i) and (ii) appeal to asymmetric conceptual relations, so they account for the asymmetry of grounding claims. To illustrate, consider the claim that the existence of Socrates grounds the existence of singleton Socrates (i.e., the set {Socrates}). How is the use of "singleton Socrates" conceptually warranted primarily by the use of "Socrates" (along with the relevant conceptual laws)? The application conditions of "Socrates" warrant the introduction and use of "the set {Socrates}" (perhaps along with rules governing the introduction of set theoretic terms). How does "Socrates" conceptually precede "singleton Socrates"? Competent use of "singleton Socrates" requires competent use of "Socrates," but not vice versa. This is because the application conditions of "singleton Socrates" require the satisfaction of the application conditions of "Socrates," but not vice versa (Locke 2020, 43). Condition (iii) is meant to accommodate some grounding claims that involve a posteriori necessities, which aren't relevant here.

It doesn't matter whether Locke's (2020) normativist account of metaphysical explanation is exactly right. What matters is that the normativist has plausible things to say about metaphysical explanation if she wants to include it in her account of abstraction principles.

8.5. Summary

In this chapter, I discussed conventionalism, fictionalism, and neo-Fregeanism. I registered some important points of disagreement with Warren (2020) regarding the nature of explanation in his conventionalism, the (non)conventionality of metamathematics, and how we follow the ω-rule. I argued that Warren's explanatory conventionalism is compatible with normativism, so long as counterconceptual dependence is explanatory. I argued that metamathematics is conventional—metamathematical claims express rules governing concepts of formal systems. Finally, I argued that, to make conventionalism consistent with our following of the ω-rule, we should hold that it implicitly defines " . . . " (and "and so on") and that our beliefs involving these concepts explain how we are able to possess infinitely many of the relevant corresponding beliefs. I then discussed Field's (2022) argument that conventionalism is equivalent to fictionalism. I criticized this and defended Warren's conventionalism from Field's objections. Then I discussed Plebani's (2018) take on a recent debate between Contessa (2016) and Thomasson (2013, 2014), and I offered a Carnapian way forward. I argued that the Carnapian can agree that denying a trivial inference doesn't reflect conceptual incompetence and that acceptance of a trivial inference's premise doesn't saddle one with the ontological commitments of its conclusion. Finally, I examined Linnebo's (2018) abstractionism, and I argued that the normativist can explain how abstraction principles work without appeal to metaphysical explanation.

9
Conclusion

9.1. Summary

We've come a long way. Let me briefly summarize the main sights along the journey. I started off by presenting prominent examples of distinctively mathematical explanations (DMEs). I laid down three desiderata that any account of DME should satisfy. I argued that many other accounts fail to satisfy one or more of them. I argued that renormalization group (RG) explanations are not DMEs, contra Reutlinger (2014). They are ontic explanations, contra Batterman and Rice (2014).

I presented my own account of DME, the Narrow Ontic Counterfactual Account (NOCA), according to which an explanation is a DME just in case either a) it shows a natural fact weakly necessarily to depend counterfactually only on a mathematical fact, or b) it shows a natural event to be necessitated by a component natural fact that weakly necessarily counterfactually depends only on a mathematical fact. I argued that several problem cases for NOCA (such as those appealing to isotopic knots or Eulerian networks) are problems for many other accounts of DME too. But NOCA faces fewer, less severe problems overall, and it comes in a unified ontic package of scientific explanations generally. I then argued that there is nothing inherently platonistic about NOCA; it can be normativistically deflated and retain its explanatory power and ontic status. Importantly, all ontic accounts of DME can be normativistically deflated, thus rendering invalid the enhanced indispensability argument.

I argued that the content of mathematical concepts is determined by their inferential rules—their narrow rules, when they have no empirical application, and their broad rules, including application conditions, when they do. This is consistent with the idea that when one learns a DME one acquires conceptual information. I then argued that the package of views I defended—semantic deflationism, normativism, inferentialism—is

Rules to Infinity. Mark Povich, Oxford University Press. © Oxford University Press 2024.
DOI: 10.1093/oso/9780197679005.003.0009

consistent with truth-conditional semantics. This is possible in part because inferentialism, truth-conditional semantics, and normativism concern different things: metasemantics, semantics, and function, respectively. I then presented the fully inferentialist theory (FIT) of the content of scientific models. According to FIT, denotation-claims are content-conferring in virtue of expressing the validity of rules of surrogative inference. Finally, I compared normativism to conventionalism, fictionalism, and neo-Fregeanism and concluded that normativism is the superior.

There are many independently moving parts in this book. Take NOCA, normativism about mathematics, and FIT. I want to emphasize that an argument against one is not an argument against all. Any combination of these views could be true. In the next two sections I discuss areas of future work. These include but are certainly not limited to the strengths of different kinds of necessity, including natural necessity, and DME-adjacent explanations.

9.2. Future Directions: Strengths of Necessity, including Natural Necessity

In this book I defended normativism about mathematics. But normativism is also a view about metaphysical modality (Thomasson 2020a). Similarly, conventionalism, a predecessor of normativism, was originally developed by the positivists to account for logical and mathematical necessity[1] (e.g., Ayer 1952; Schlick 1974; Wittgenstein 2013; see also the later Wittgenstein [1956] 1978 and his followers, such as Baker and Hacker 2009 and Glock 1996). According to them, all necessity—logical, mathematical, and metaphysical—is analytic, and analytic statements have no descriptive content. I take that claim to mean that the norms such necessities express are *conceptual* norms.

A normativist about a certain kind of necessity need not say that the norms it expresses are conceptual norms,[2] but, given the plausible link between meaning and logical, mathematical, and metaphysical necessity, I think she should for those kinds of necessity. However, an account is then needed for

[1] Thomasson (2020a) discusses some proposals for normativism about logical necessity and consequence. See also Kocurek and Jerzak's (2021) logical expressivism—my account is of a piece with theirs.

[2] Consider normativism about moral, epistemic/rational, and natural necessity, according to which those necessities might express norms governing planning (Gibbard 2009), belief formation (Chrisman 2012), and measurement (Roberts 2008), respectively.

the possibility that these varieties of necessity possess different strengths. Can normativism account for the potentially different strengths of logical, mathematical, and metaphysical necessity? This is an area of future work, but I will briefly canvass two ways to address this possibility.

I think Lange (2009) is right that strengths of necessities can be gauged by their collective perseverance under counterfactual suppositions consistent with them. Nested subsets are formed by the ranges of counterfactual supposition under which sets of (necessary) truths hold. For example, the set of logical necessities holds under the widest range of counterfactual suppositions that are consistent with that set. If the set of metaphysical necessities holds under a narrower range of counterfactual suppositions that are consistent with it, then logical necessity is stronger than metaphysical necessity.

I disagree with Lange (2009), though, that the truthmakers for the counterfactuals that constitute the necessities' necessity are brute subjunctive facts. Instead, building on the idea from Chapter 5 that countermathematicals express what would be the case if certain conceptual rules had been different, I suggest that Lange's hierarchy of counterfactual perseverance has a conceptual-normative analogue. Here's how this idea might work. Logical necessity is the strongest species of necessity; the set of logical necessities holds under the widest range of counterfactual suppositions that are consistent with that set. This strong necessity is an expression of the nature of logical concepts. Logical concepts have the widest range of applicability, and the norms that govern them govern every conceptual scheme. Perhaps they are constitutive of concept-use as such (MacFarlane 2000).[3] Nothing that didn't have them would count as a *conceptual* scheme at all. The metaphysical necessities are less strong than the logical necessities. Perhaps they express concepts peculiar to our own conceptual scheme, which have a narrower range of applicability; the norms that govern them are peculiar to our scheme.[4] Expressions of norms that govern every conceptual scheme are logical necessities. Expressions of norms that govern our conceptual scheme are metaphysical necessities.[5] Here, then, is the conceptual-normative analogue of Lange's hierarchy of counterfactuals—that the logical necessities

[3] This Kantian-Fregean idea is arguably consistent with logical pluralism, at least of the Carnapian variety (Steinberger 2017).

[4] Are our peculiar conceptual rules collectively *constitutive* of our conceptual scheme? Thomasson (2020a) argues that the normativist should not assert this, because, among other reasons, it makes disagreement between people using slightly different concepts impossible.

[5] So, metaphysical necessity depends on conceptual scheme? Only counterconceptually, not counterfactually.

would have still held, if the metaphysical necessities had not, is an expression of the fact that the norms governing concepts required for any conceptual scheme would have still held, if the norms governing the concepts peculiar to our conceptual scheme had not. Whereas Lange's explanation of necessity and its different strengths bottoms out in primitive subjunctive facts, this one (and the next) goes one step further.

Instead of explaining the strength of logical necessity by appeal to what is constitutive of concept-use as such, the explanation might similarly be told in terms of the familiar idea that logical truths are true under any interpretation of non-logical terms, because only syntactic-inferential considerations enter into norms of use for logical concepts. (In either case, the normativist explains the strength of logical necessity in terms of features of logical concepts and their relations to non-logical concepts.) The logical truths hold under any changes in the meanings of constituent non-logical terms—which, for the normativist, just means that the logical truths hold under any changes in the norms of use for non-logical terms, object language expressions of which just are the metaphysical necessities. Thus, that the logical necessities would have still held if the metaphysical necessities had not[6] is an expression of the fact that the norms of use for logical concepts would have still held if the norms of use for non-logical concepts had not.

The normativist explanation of strengths of necessity illustrates a kind of conceptual or semantic independence of logical from non-logical concepts, an independence that may hold wherever there are different strengths of necessity. Some conceptual rules can change without others changing, and this is reflected in our judgments of modal strength.[7]

So far, I have only contrasted logical with metaphysical necessity in terms of strength. Where to locate the *mathematical* necessities is a philosophically and historically complex question, a complete discussion of which would require delving into the debate over logicism. They are sometimes placed alongside the logical necessities and sometimes between the logical and metaphysical necessities.[8] Perhaps the logical truths would have still held if the

[6] Lange (2009) takes the set of metaphysical necessities to contain the set of logical necessities and takes it that the metaphysical necessities *would not* have held, if the logical necessities had not, which has a similar normativist interpretation.

[7] This gives the normativist reason not to be a radical semantic holist, since the holist thinks a change in the meaning of any term affects the meanings of every term, thereby seemingly denying the kind of semantic independence expressed here.

[8] Of course, different branches of mathematics may themselves possess different strengths of necessity.

mathematical truths had not; perhaps the logical truths would not have still held. The normativist will explain whichever is true by appeal to the same kind of consideration offered above. If the logical truths would have still held if the mathematical truths had not, this would be an expression of the fact that the norms of use for logical concepts would have still held if the norms of use for mathematical concepts had not. And some explanation would need to be given for this fact—if it is one—about our logical and mathematical concepts. Thankfully, my arguments in this book do not require an answer to the question of where to place the strength mathematical necessities—I only need the idea that mathematical necessities express conceptual rules.

I have been discussing what the normativist could say about the possibility of different strengths of logical, mathematical, and metaphysical necessity. What could the normativist say about natural necessity, especially if Lange (2009) is right that even within natural necessity there are different strengths? This too is an area ripe for future work. An account of natural necessity is important not only for a complete picture of the world but also because I have throughout this book appealed to notions that are closely related to natural modality, such as counterfactuals and causation. Here are some ways a normativist might locate natural necessity in the modal hierarchy.[9]

Because natural necessities are not plausibly analytic, they should not be taken to express *conceptual* norms. Perhaps they are expressions of norms governing measurement (Roberts 2008) or norms governing prediction and explanation (Ward 2003). Since measuring, predicting, and explaining are practices carried out within a given conceptual scheme, the norms governing that scheme must be in place before those practices can begin. The norms governing our conceptual scheme would still have held if the norms governing those practices within it had not. Thus, expressions of rules governing those practices possess a necessity weaker than metaphysical necessity. Note that if my argument in Chapter 6 is correct, these normativist accounts of laws are fully compatible with truth-conditional semantics.

The normativist could also be a dispositional essentialist about the laws. Dispositional essentialists appeal to the powers or dispositions that properties bestow on their objects to explain the laws. Since, for them, the causal powers a property bestows on its object are bestowed necessarily, they believe that the laws are metaphysically necessary (e.g., Ellis 2001; Heil 2003,

[9] I will, where irrelevant, ignore the distinction between laws of nature—the regularities themselves—and law-descriptions.

2012; Bird 2007). An electron, for example, is "governed" by certain laws (e.g., Coulomb's law) because its properties necessarily confer powers or dispositions upon it (e.g., to repel and attract other objects in certain ways) consistent with those laws. On such a view, an electron simply doesn't count as being negatively charged—and therefore simply doesn't count as an electron, if being negatively charged is essential to it—if it doesn't behave in the ways described by Coulomb's law (for example).

Dispositional essentialists usually take the laws to be necessary a posteriori. Just as, for example, "Water is H_2O" is necessary, yet took empirical investigation to discover, so are the laws. This view could be combined with normativism using the normativist's account of the necessary a posteriori (Sidelle 1989, 2002; Thomasson 2020a). According to the normativist's account of the necessary a posteriori, some conceptual rules include variables the values of which can only be determined empirically.[10] For example, the necessary a posteriori status of the truth that water is H_2O is explained by appeal to the analytic truth that nothing counts as water in any situation unless it has the same deep explanatory features (if any) as the stuff we call "water" and the empirical truth that the deep explanatory feature of the stuff we call "water" is being composed of H_2O (Sidelle 1989, 2002).[11] One objection (among many) to dispositional essentialism is that it mistakenly puts natural necessity on par with metaphysical necessity (Lange 2009; see Sidelle 2002 for more objections). While that is true, I don't think it is true that dispositional essentialism-cum-normativism simply collapses all necessity into a single layer. It seems that the dispositional essentialist-cum-normativist can still recognize different strengths of metaphysical necessity, as determined by the truth of various counterlegals/counterpossibles. Some laws may be more counterfactually resilient, and thus more metaphysically necessary, than others. Some laws may have held if others had not. In other words—parallel to what was suggested above with respect to logical, mathematical, and metaphysical necessity—there may be conceptual stratification among the metaphysically necessary laws of nature, which results

[10] I see the normativist account of a posteriori necessity as helping to explain features of the two-dimensionalist account of a posteriori necessity, such as why it is not just that if the XYZ-world is actual, then water is XYZ, but if the XYZ-world is actual, then water is *necessarily* XYZ.

[11] Brandom (2015, 153) argues that modal normativism requires the idea that it takes empirical investigation to discover what is contained in the content of (some) concepts. Brandom thinks this idea is required to reconcile the claim there are a posteriori necessities with the claim that all necessity is conceptual. The Sidelle-Thomasson approach shows how this might work.

in certain counterpossibles being true, which results in some laws being more metaphysically necessary than others. That metaphysical necessity can come in different strengths is something dispositional essentialism–cum–normativism can explain (by appeal to conceptual stratification or independence) that I'm not sure dispositional essentialism alone can.

Note that, as with all ontological theses, the Carnapian will take dispositional essentialism to be a suggestion to use a certain conceptual scheme (viz., one in which the laws themselves are analytic or there are the relevant analytic principles containing empirical variables), and thus, the only legitimate arguments one could give in favor of dispositional essentialism are pragmatic arguments in favor of the use of this conceptual scheme.

Of course, the normativist needn't take the laws to express anything, let alone conceptual norms. For example, normativism is consistent with Humeanism, according to which laws are just regularities with nonmetaphysical features that distinguish them from accidental regularities, features like their figuring in our best (i.e., simplest and strongest) theories (Lewis 1973). This is the Best Systems Account of lawhood (Lewis 1973; Dorst 2019). The idea is that laws have the kind of counterfactual resilience Lange discusses, but not for the reason he thinks. They are resilient simply because we hold them fixed, for very good epistemic and practical reasons, in our counterfactual reasoning; holding them fixed helps us with our practical endeavors in the *actual* world (Dorst 2022). Let me briefly explain with an example from Dorst (2022). Suppose we are at the scene of a car accident, and we want to know how fast the car was going. The driver claims they were going 30 miles per hour. We can look at the length of the tire tracks and ask, "Would the tire tracks have been this long if the car had been traveling 30 miles per hour?" To answer this question, we imagine a time before the accident with the car traveling 30 miles per hour, keeping everything as similar as possible to what we know, including holding fixed the laws of nature. Then we run the clock forward and see what length the tire tracks would be. Why did we hold everything else, including the laws of nature, fixed? As Dorst (2022, 554, original emphasis) explains, "We have a hypothetical state of the past, and we are trying to figure out whether it would have led to the evidence we have observed. What we need, then, are principles that accurately describe how actual-world systems evolve over time. And *the laws of nature are precisely such principles*."

Lange (forthcoming) has objected to this pragmatic Humeanism on the grounds that, although it may account for why a law's truth is counterfactually resilient, it cannot account for why its lawhood is counterfactually resilient. That is, although it may explain why we hold a law's truth fixed in counterfactual reasoning, it cannot explain why we hold fixed the fact that it is a law, i.e., naturally necessary, in counterfactual reasoning. Let me give an example from Lange (forthcoming) to illustrate. When I assert, "Had there been nothing except two electrons, they would have mutually repelled in a manner directly proportional to the product of the magnitudes of their charges and inversely proportional to the squared distance between them," I hold fixed the *truth* of Coulomb's law, but not necessarily its lawhood, its necessity. When I assert, "Had there been nothing except two electrons, then Coulomb's law would still have been a law," I hold fixed the lawhood (and, a fortiori, the truth) of Coulomb's law. That we hold fixed the laws' necessity, Lange argues, shows up in the fact that we accept many nested counterfactuals. In other words, since we accept counterfactuals like "Had there been nothing except one electron, then Coulomb's law would still have been a law," we also accept nested counterfactuals like "Had there been nothing except one electron, then had there been a second electron, they would have mutually repelled in a manner directly proportional to the product of the magnitudes of their charges and inversely proportional to the squared distance between them." Since Coulomb's law is still a law in some counterfactual world, it is counterfactually resilient in *that* counterfactual world, so many of our nested counterfactuals are true. Note that Lange (2009, 2016) takes counterfactual resilience to be the mark of lawhood, whereas Humeans don't.

I think Lange (forthcoming) is right about the fact that we often hold the laws' lawhood fixed in counterfactual reasoning. The question is whether there is a way of accounting for this that doesn't appeal to substantive modal or counterfactual facts. The fact that we often hold the laws' necessity fixed is a problem for Humeans because they think that the laws in a world are determined by the "vast mosaic of local matters of particular fact" (Lewis 1986, ix) in that world. Thus, in worlds that differ substantially from ours in these facts, such as the lone electron world, the laws are different. The Humean might try to account for the fact that we hold fixed the laws' necessity or lawhood in the same way that she accounts for the fact that we hold fixed their truth: by appeal to pragmatic or epistemic convention. Perhaps we hold fixed the truth of the laws in all iterations of counterfactual reasoning for the same pragmatic reasons we hold the laws' truth fixed in non-nested counterfactual reasoning (Dorst personal communication). We hold the laws' truth fixed when we reason about a counterfactual world, and we continue to hold it fixed when we reason counterfactually from *that* counterfactual world. That would make our laws counterfactually resilient in *that* counterfactual world. As Dorst (personal communication) explains, building on the previous car accident case, "Then someone says, 'But what if it was raining? Couldn't that have made it skid more and thus produce longer tire tracks even if it were traveling slower?' Then we have to evaluate a counterfactual of the form: 'If the car had been traveling 30mph, then if it had been raining, the car would have produced tire tracks of length *y*.'" So, the same kinds of pragmatic considerations explain why we continue to hold fixed *our* laws' truth when reasoning counterfactually within a counterfactual world, rather than hold fixed the truth of the laws *in that* counterfactual world, determined by *its* local matters of particular fact.

This doesn't quite get us the laws' lawhood in counterfactual worlds, though. If we take counterfactual resilience to be the mark of necessity or lawhood, then our laws would be laws in those worlds. But remember that a Humean can't say that because she doesn't take counterfactual resilience to be the mark of lawhood. She takes being part of the best system (for example) to be the mark of lawhood. She would say that our laws have counterfactual resilience in other worlds, but that that doesn't make them laws there. Perhaps that's ok. Perhaps the Humean can account for everything she needs to account for with counterfactual resilience, rather than lawhood, in other worlds (Dorst personal communication).

But perhaps there's a way to have it all—to accept that we hold fixed the laws' truth, their counterfactual resilience, *and* their lawhood in counterfactual worlds. Perhaps it will help us simply to give up the idea that the laws at world *w* are determined by local matters of particular fact at *w*. This would be to give up the Humean part of pragmatic Humeanism, but maybe we can retain its pragmatic spirit as follows. Let's accept Lange's idea that counterfactual resilience is the mark of lawhood and let the laws at *w* be determined by what we hold fixed when we consider *w* as actual and reason counterfactually. Since in all our counterfactual reasoning, regardless of what world is considered as actual, we hold fixed the truth of our actual laws, and since this is all that is required for lawhood, our actual laws will be the laws at those worlds.[12] The question of why in all our counterfactual reasoning, regardless of what

[12] Note the similarity to the normativist's and conventionalist's response to the contingency objection: neither the truth of necessities nor their necessity depends counterfactually on our conventions because it is one of our (meta)conventions to hold our actual conventions fixed in counterfactual reasoning (Sidelle 2009; Thomasson 2020a; Warren 2020).

is considered actual, we hold fixed the truth of our actual laws is given the pragmatic answer concerning nested counterfactuals above. You could still be a kind of Humean or hold a Best Systems Account, but the account would no longer function as an account of *lawhood*. Now it would function as an account of which truths we hold fixed when we reason counterfactually. The lawhood of these truths is now explained simply by the fact that we hold them fixed when we reason counterfactually. Their lawhood consists simply in the fact that we hold them fixed, and why we hold them fixed is explained by the Best Systems Account (specifically, Dorst's [2019] predictive version, since it captures the pragmatic Humean explanation). Note that the dispositional essentialist doesn't seem to have this problem, since for her the laws are metaphysically necessary. The actual laws are still laws in counterfactual worlds. Had there been nothing except one electron, then Coulomb's law would still have been a law, because it would still have been in the essential nature of the one electron to behave in accordance with the law.

How might a normativist distinguish different strengths of necessity *within* the natural? I already discussed the possibility that dispositional essentialism–cum–normativism can do this when responding to Lange's objection to dispositional essentialism. Even if all the laws are metaphysically necessary, it could still be the case that some are more metaphysically necessary than others, as reflected in the truth of various counterpossibles. The normativist would explain this in terms of the stratification of our concepts. The normativist could also appeal to the relativized or constitutive a priori (Friedman 2001; Reichenbach 1965). A law is said to be constitutive a priori when it is constitutive of the (concept of the) phenomenon it concerns. For example, according to Friedman (1999, 59):

> "the entire spatiotemporal framework of Newtonian physics—what we now call the structure of Newtonian space-time—belongs to the pure part of natural science [i.e., is constitutive a priori]. The empirical part then consists of specific laws of nature formulated within this antecedently presupposed framework: for example, and especially, the law of universal gravitation and, more generally, the various specific force laws that can be formulated in the context of the Newtonian laws of motion."

The constitutive a priori laws are modally stronger than the force laws because the former constitute the framework within which the latter are formulated.

There are different ways of understanding what it means for certain laws or principles to be constitutive a priori. Perhaps they are implicit definitions. Perhaps, for example, Newton's laws of motion are constitutive of the concepts of Newtonian force, mass, etc. (Samaroo 2022). On this understanding of the constitutive a priori, those modally loftiest natural laws are analytic, expressions of conceptual rules. A natural law's being an implicit definition would explain why it is more necessary than other natural laws formulated in the terms defined by it. If this is right, the stratification of natural necessity is an expression of the stratification of the conceptual structure of scientific theories. Obviously, there are similarities between the constitutive a priori view and the dispositional essentialism–cum–normativism view: both see natural laws as expressing conceptual rules (or conceptual rules combined with empirical truths). However, dispositional essentialists tend to apply their view to all natural laws, whereas defenders of the constitutive a priori tend to apply their view to a proper subset of natural laws.

In this section, I merely floated some ideas about what the normativist could say about laws of nature without necessarily endorsing any of them. I suspect that different laws are best accounted for in different ways. Perhaps some laws—those of the lowest grade of natural necessity—are given the pragmatic Humean treatment; perhaps other laws—those of a higher grade of natural necessity—are a posteriori necessary as dispositional essentialism(–cum–normativism) says; and perhaps those laws of a higher grade still are constitutive a priori or analytic. All of this remains to be seen.

9.3. Future Directions: DME-Adjacent Explanations

In this final section, I want to discuss some DME-adjacent explanations. Some of these are like DMEs in that they show their explananda (i.e., the things to be explained) to be necessary—these are Lange's (2016) explanations by constraint, of which DME is a species. Others are more like RG explanations in that they centrally involve mathematics and appear to be non-causal, though they do not work by showing their explananda to be necessary—these are Lange's (2013a, 2016, 2022) really statistical (RS) explanations (among many others). RS explanations, I think, are accommodable by my generalized ontic conception, but I cannot fully defend that claim here. Finally, there are dimensional explanations (Lange 2016; see also Pexton 2014), some of which are explanations by constraint and others of which are not. Let us begin with explanations by constraint.

Like DMEs, explanations by constraint reveal their explananda to be necessary by appeal to a truth modally stronger than ordinary natural law. Unlike DMEs, this modally strong truth is not a mathematical truth but a natural one, though still modally stronger than *ordinary* natural law. Recall above that some natural laws are more necessary than others. According to Lange, these more necessary natural laws can explain by constraint the others. The former likely[13] include conservation laws, symmetry principles, and Newton's laws of motion, among others. The symmetry principles could in fact explain the conversation laws, if they are modally stronger than the conservation laws. The issues here are immense, and a full treatment of them requires careful scientific investigation as well as solutions to the problems of natural necessity posed in the previous section. Here I can only say this: I think many explanations by constraint can be assimilated to NOCA. These laws of high-strength necessity can play the same role in explanations by constraint that mathematical truths play in DMEs. When a natural explanandum is shown weakly necessarily to depend counterfactually *only* on some law that is modally stronger than any ordinary law, such as a symmetry principle, conservation law, or coordinate transformation law, then it is an explanation by constraint. And if the normativist can find an account of the different strengths of natural necessity, perhaps such explanations by constraint can be deflated too.

Let me illustrate with an example of such an explanation by constraint (Lange 2016, 132). Why does a carriage remain roughly in place when the baby inside starts bouncing? Because the carriage is in conditions C, in which it is at rest on a flat surface with negligible horizontal forces, and momentum in a given direction is conserved. That the carriage is in conditions C is a contingent, empirical fact that we can shift into the explanandum, just like in a DME. That momentum in a given direction is conserved is a constraint—an especially high-strength natural necessity. The narrowed explanandum would be that a carriage in C doesn't move around much when the baby starts bouncing. This weakly necessarily depends only on the momentum conservation law. (Of course, the "necessarily" here is of a different strength than that in a DME.) The reversal would be as follows. Why isn't a carriage in C? Because it doesn't remain roughly in place when the baby starts bouncing, and

[13] Lange takes it to be an empirical question which laws are constraints.

momentum in a given direction is conserved. The reversed narrowed explanandum would be that the carriage that doesn't remain roughly in place isn't in C. This seems not to depend weakly necessarily only on the momentum conservation law. Thus, NOCA seems to handle this explanation well. Whether a normativist can too depends on what she says about conservation laws and their specific strength of necessity. I've given some options above.

Let me now consider RS explanations. RS explanations reveal their explananda to be results of or instances of characteristically statistical phenomena (Lange 2016, 2022). Consider the following example. Why do students with the lowest (or highest) scores on the first exam tend not to be the students with the lowest (or highest) scores on the second exam? Because there is an imperfect correlation between the outcomes of the two exams, and when there is an imperfect correlation between two variables, extreme values of one variable tend to be followed by less extreme values of the other variable—a statistical fact or principle known as "regression toward the mean." Craver and I (2017, 2018) have argued that such explanations can be "reversed." Why isn't there an imperfect correlation between the outcomes of the two exams? Because the students with the lowest (or highest) scores on the first exam tend to be the students with the lowest (or highest) scores on the second exam, and when there is an imperfect correlation between two variables, extreme values of one variable tend to be followed by less extreme values of the other variable. An account of RS explanation should illuminate why one explanation succeeds and the other fails. I assume that Lange will say that the reversal doesn't count as an RS explanation because it doesn't reveal its explanandum to be an instance of a characteristically statistical phenomenon. For an RS explanation to reveal its explanandum to be an instance of a characteristically statistical phenomenon, it must appeal only to a generic arrangement of chances, such as that there is an imperfect correlation between two outcomes, and the reversed explanation doesn't do that. This seems plausible, and I will not object to it. What seems less plausible is that RS explanations are non-causal or non-ontic explanations. (Lange certainly thinks they are non-causal. I'm not sure if he thinks they are non-ontic. He certainly doesn't think they are modal explanations in the sense that explanations by constraint are.) I think RS explanations can be accounted for by my generalized ontic conception. The regression toward the mean case seems to pass prominent tests for causal explanation.[14] For

[14] Roski (2021) argues that all RS explanations are either non-explanations or causal explanations. See Lange (2022) for a response.

example, recall that according to Woodward's (2003) interventionism, *x* is causally relevant to *y* if and only if an intervention on *x* would change *y*, and it isn't necessary that the relevant intervention be physically possible. It is certainly not metaphysically impossible to change whether there is an imperfect correlation between the outcomes of the two exams, and this would change whether the students with the lowest (or highest) scores on the first exam tend not to be the students with the lowest (or highest) scores on the second exam. Lange is certainly right that this explanation abstracts away from nearly all causal details, but there are many causal explanations that do that, as he acknowledges (Lange 2016). Even if the relation between the explanans and explanandum in the regression toward the mean case isn't causal, I don't see how it could be non-ontic. There is some objective connection, even if you don't want to call it "causal," between the explanans and the explanandum that accounts for the explanans's ability to explain the explanandum.

Note that, although RS explanations are not DMEs or explanations by constraint, you could easily turn RS explanations into DMEs, and I think NOCA can account for such DMEs. Simply narrow the explanandum by assuming the empirical explanans (i.e., that there is an imperfect correlation between the outcomes of the two exams), and then the narrow explanandum (i.e., that on the two exams the outcomes of which are imperfectly correlated, the students with the lowest [or highest] scores on the first exam tend not to be the students with the lowest [or highest] scores on the second exam) depends necessarily only on the statistical explanans. The reversed narrow explanandum (i.e., that there isn't an imperfect correlation between the outcomes of the two exams, on which the students with the lowest [or highest] scores on the first tended to be the students with the lowest [or highest] scores on the second) does not depend necessarily only on the statistical explanans. The relevant weakly necessary countermathematical (counterstatistical?) would thus be: if it weren't the case that when there is an imperfect correlation between two variables, extreme values of one variable tend to be followed by less extreme values of the other variable, it wouldn't have been the case that, on the two exams the outcomes of which are imperfectly correlated, the students with the lowest (or highest) scores on the first exam tend not to be the students with the lowest (or highest) scores on the second exam. I think normativism can handle this too, since the statistical principle of regression toward the mean seems analytic, an expression of conceptual rules.

You might think that RS explanations can't be turned into DMEs because DMEs show their explananda to be necessary, whereas the explananda in RS explanations are by their nature not necessary but probabilistic. This rests on a confusion. There is a difference between these two explananda: that students with the lowest (or highest) scores on the first exam *tend* not to be the students with the lowest (or highest) scores on the second exam, which is a fact involving a *tendency*, and that the students with the lowest (or highest) scores on the first exam *aren't* the students with the lowest (or highest) scores on the second exam, which does not involve a tendency. When properly narrowed, the first explanandum, but not the second, depends *necessarily* only on the statistical explanans. Thus, there is only a DME-RS explanation of the first explanandum (when narrowed). This DME-RS explanation reveals its explanandum to be necessary, where the necessary explanandum involves a tendency—what is revealed to be necessary is not merely some fact *p*, but the fact that *p* is likely. (Lange [2016, 2022] almost always speaks of the explanandum of an RS explanation as involving a tendency, and it is unclear whether he thinks the explanandum that doesn't involve a tendency has an RS explanation, but I assume he doesn't.) Thus, I think RS explanations can be accommodated by my generalized ontic conception as either causal or non-causal but still ontic explanations, and that relevantly narrowed RS explanations can be DMEs accommodable by NOCA. However, I think a full investigation of this would require delving into the metaphysics of tendencies, probability, and chance, so I must leave all of this to future work.

Another type of DME-adjacent explanation is dimensional explanation. Some dimensional explanations are explanations by constraint and others are not. Those that are not are still, according to Lange, non-causal. According to Lange, the explanans in a dimensional explanation is dimensional homogeneity, i.e., the fact that a dimensionally homogeneous relation holds between the relevant quantities, where a relation R is dimensionally homogeneous "exactly when it is a broadly logical truth[15] that if R holds in one system of units, then R holds in any system of units for the various fundamental dimensions (e.g., length, mass, time) of the quantities so related" (Lange 2016, 206). Suppose my height in centimeters to be roughly equal to my weight in pounds. This relation (of rough equality) only holds when the relevant quantities are measured in those units. For example, my height in

[15] "Broadly" logical necessity encompasses "narrowly logical necessity, metaphysical necessity, mathematical necessity, conceptual necessity, moral necessity, and so forth" (Lange 2016, 208).

centimeters is not roughly equal to my weight in grams. So, the relation between these quantities is not dimensionally homogeneous. When a relation between quantities is dimensionally homogeneous, it is "a relation among those quantities themselves, not among them as measured in some particular way" (206).

As an example of dimensional explanation, Lange (2016, 210) gives the following. The period T of a circular orbit of radius r of a planet of mass m around a star of mass M is proportional to $r^{3/2}$. Why? We know T is proportional to $m^{\alpha}M^{\beta}G^{\gamma}r^{\delta}$, T's dimension is T, m's dimension is M, M's dimension is M, the gravitational constant G's dimensions are $L^3M^{-1}T^{-2}$, and r's dimension is L. Since the dimensions of T and $m^{\alpha}M^{\beta}G^{\gamma}r^{\delta}$ must balance (since T stands in a dimensionally homogeneous relation to some subset of m, M, G, and r), their exponents give us $0 = 3\gamma + \delta$, $0 = \alpha + \beta - \gamma$, and $1 = -2\gamma$. Solving for δ yields 3/2. Thus, T must be proportional to $r^{3/2}$. For Lange, the primary explanans here is the fact that T stands in a dimensionally homogeneous relation to some subset of m, M, G, and r. This argument demonstrates that the proportion follows from these other facts. But does this demonstration constitute an explanation? Craver and I (2018) have argued that this too is susceptible to a "reversal." Given the proportionality of T to $r^{3/2}$, the proportionality of T to $m^{\alpha}M^{\beta}G^{\gamma}r^{\delta}$, and the dimensionalities of the variables, including that G has dimensions $L^xM^{-1}T^{-2}$ (excluding the exponent of L), it follows from dimensional homogeneity that the exponent of G's L dimension is 3. But the fact that the exponent of G's L dimension is 3 (rather than some other exponent) would appear to be a natural fact calling out for some ontic (perhaps causal) explanation. An account of dimensional explanation should elucidate why one explanation succeeds and the other fails. If it cannot, this is reason to believe we do not have a genuine type of explanation here. Note that the reversal also appeals to the fact that T stands in a dimensionally homogeneous relation to some subset of m, M, G, and r. So, if appeal to a dimensionally homogeneous relation is the mark of a dimensional explanation, then the reversal is one.

The nature of dimensional explanation is much less clear to me than even the nature of RS explanation, assuming dimensional explanation is a genuine type of explanation. The kind of explanation a dimensional explanation is depends on what kinds of fact it appeals to and on what kinds of relation hold between explanans and explanandum. Recall that, according to Lange, the explanans in the above example is the fact that T stands in a dimensionally homogeneous relation to some subset of m, M,

G, and *r*. This means that *T* stands in a relation R to some subset of *m*, *M*, *G*, and *r*, for which it is a broadly logical truth that if R holds in one system of units, then R holds in any system of units for the various fundamental dimensions (e.g., length, mass, time) of the quantities so related. Note that it is not a broadly logical truth that *T does* stand in such a relation R to some subset of *m*, *M*, *G*, and *r*. That is a contingent fact (Lange 2011, 2016). The notion of broadly logical truth is used to characterize the relation of dimensional homogeneity itself, not its holding between particular relata. Could this contingent fact then be a cause of explanandum proportionality? Although Lange emphasizes that this explanation "does not work by describing the world's causal nexus" (2017, 214), the Woodwardian test seems applicable. If *T*'s standing in a dimensionally homogeneous relation to some subset of *m*, *M*, *G*, and *r* is not metaphysically necessary—and Lange (2011, 2016) states clearly that it is not—then it is metaphysically possible to change this fact, and some such changes would change the explanandum proportionality. Thus, I am not convinced that we have a non-causal, much less a non-ontic, explanation.

Finally, there are dimensional explanations that are explanations by constraint. These work just like DMEs do. The explanantia "function in the dimensional explanation just as mathematical facts do in the distinctively mathematical scientific explanations" (Lange 2016, 207), i.e., by showing their explananda to be necessary. Here is an example (Lange 2016, 205). If *d* is the distance traversed in the first interval by a body falling freely from rest, then it traverses 3*d*, 5*d*, 7*d*, 9*d*, . . . in succeeding intervals. This is Galileo's odd-number rule, and it is in fact true. Honoré Fabri proposed that a body traverses 2*d*, 3*d*, 4*d*, 5*d*, . . . in succeeding intervals. Why is Fabri's proposal false?[16] Because it is not dimensionally homogeneous; it cannot hold in all units of time. Suppose that Fabri's proposal holds for some unit of time. Now let's use a new unit twice as long. The body should traverse the distance 1*d* + 2*d* (since the unit is twice as long) in the first time interval, 3*d* + 4*d* in the second, 5*d* + 6*d* in the third, and so on. But these sums, 3*d*, 7*d*, and 11*d*, do not stand in the ratio of 1 to 2 to 3. Thus, Fabri's proposal is false and necessarily so. Furthermore, this impossibility is stronger than natural impossibility. Lange (2016, 207–208) writes, "For the relation among the distances traversed in successive equal time intervals by a body falling freely from rest

[16] This is different from the question "Why is Galileo's proposal true?," which does *not* have a dimensional explanation by constraint.

to accord with Fabri's proposal is just as impossible as for someone to untie a trefoil knot, to cross the Königsberg bridges, or to distribute 23 strawberries evenly among 3 children without cutting any."

Why is Fabri's proposal as impossible as untying a trefoil knot? Lange says, "That is because there is no way for those bodies to be that would fit the proposal in every unit for measuring time, yet the proposal purports to specify a relation among the distances and times themselves (i.e., a dimensionally homogeneous relation)" (2016, 207). There are two explanantia here: "the fact that any relation among these quantities themselves is dimensionally homogeneous and that Fabri's proposal does not give a dimensionally homogeneous relation," both of which "possess a stronger variety of necessity than ordinary natural laws do" (207). The explanandum is that Fabri's proposed relation isn't a relation among the distances and times themselves. This kind of dimensional explanation also seems subject to reversals. Can we explain why a proposed relation is dimensionally homogeneous by appeal to the fact that it is a relation among the distances and times themselves and the fact that any relation among these quantities themselves is dimensionally homogeneous? Can we explain why a proposed relation is dimensionally inhomogeneous by appeal to the fact that it isn't a relation among the distances and times themselves? Absent answers to these questions, I'm skeptical of the existence of dimensional explanations. Note that the resources Lange used to exclude reversals to DMEs, discussed and critiqued in Chapter 2, are not available to him here. There he excluded reversals by appeal to the fact that their contingent explanantia were not understood to be constitutive of the physical task or arrangement at issue. (Let's abbreviate this phrase as simply "constitutive.") The contingent explanantia in genuine DMEs, in contrast, are understood to be constitutive. However, in this dimensional explanation there are no contingent explanantia and nothing is understood to be constitutive. That Fabri's relation is dimensionally inhomogeneous is not understood to be constitutive; it is a crucial part of the explanans discovered by an analysis of Fabri's proposal. That any relation among quantities themselves is dimensionally homogeneous is also not understood to be constitutive. It is a principle appealed to, along with the fact that Fabri's relation is dimensionally inhomogeneous, to get us the result that Fabri's relation isn't a relation among the distances and times themselves. So, it is unclear how Lange can exclude reversals of dimensional explanations such as this.

9.4. Conclusion

I began this book with a brief discussion of functional pluralism and related themes. Recall that functional pluralism is the thesis that not all declarative sentences have the function of describing or representing the world, in any substantive sense (Price 2011). We must keep this in mind in all our philosophical analyses if we want to avoid confusions. Scientific explanation and the employment of mathematics therein are social practices in which certain rational animals engage. Engaging in these social practices requires the production of many types of declarative sentence. What are these animals doing when they produce such sentences? I hope to have made plausible that the right answer to this question does not require a commitment to traditional platonism. The right answer requires the application of the functional pluralist perspective, and that perspective applied to the question at hand is normativism.

References

Almgren, Frederick J., Jr. and Jean E. Taylor. 1976. "The Geometry of Soap Films and Soap Bubbles." *Scientific American* 235: 82–93.

Andersen, Holly K. 2023. "Trueing." In *The Pragmatist Challenge*, edited by Holly K. Andersen and Sandra D. Mitchell, 67–102. Oxford: Oxford University Press.

Aristotle. 1936. *Minor Works: On Colours. On Things Heard. Physiognomics. On Plants. On Marvellous Things Heard. Mechanical Problems. On Indivisible Lines. The Situations and Names of Winds. On Melissus, Xenophanes, Gorgias.* Translated by W. S. Hett. Loeb Classical Library 307. Cambridge, MA: Harvard University Press.

Armstrong, David M. 1997. *A World of States of Affairs.* Cambridge: Cambridge University Press.

Armstrong, David M. 2004. *Truth and Truthmakers.* Cambridge: Cambridge University Press.

Asay, Jamin. 2020. "Truth(making) by Convention." *American Philosophical Quarterly* 57(2): 117–128.

Awodey, Steve, and A. W. Carus. 2004. "How Carnap Could Have Replied to Gödel." In *Carnap Brought Home: The View from Jena*, edited by Steve Awodey and Carsten Klein, 203–223. Chicago: Open Court.

Ayer, Alfred J. (1936) 1952. *Language, Truth and Logic.* New York: Dover.

Azzouni, Jody. 2004. *Deflating Existential Consequence: A Case for Nominalism.* Oxford: Oxford University Press.

Badia Rodríguez, Santiago, Francisco Manuel Guillén González, and Juan Vicente Gutiérrez Santacreu. 2011. "An Overview on Numerical Analyses of Nematic Liquid Crystal Flows." *Archives of Computational Methods in Engineering* 18: 285–313.

Bailer-Jones, Daniela M. 2003. "When Scientific Models Represent." *International Studies in the Philosophy of Science* 17(1): 59–74.

Baker, Alan. 2005. "Are There Genuine Mathematical Explanations of Physical Phenomena?" *Mind* 114: 223–228.

Baker, Alan. 2009. "Mathematical Explanations in Science." *British Journal for the Philosophy of Science* 60(3): 611–633.

Baker, Alan. 2012. "Science-Driven Mathematical Explanation." *Mind* 121(482): 243–267.

Baker, Gordon P., and P. M. S. Hacker. 2005. *Wittgenstein: Understanding and Meaning: Volume 1 of an Analytical Commentary on the Philosophical Investigations, Part I: Essays.* Oxford: Blackwell.

Baker, Gordon P., and P. M. S. Hacker. 2009. *Wittgenstein: Rules, Grammar and Necessity: Volume 2 of an Analytical Commentary on the Philosophical Investigations, Essays and Exegesis §§ 185–242.* Oxford: Blackwell.

Balaguer, Mark. 1998. *Platonism and Anti-Platonism in Mathematics.* Oxford: Oxford University Press.

Balaguer, Mark. 2001. "A Theory of Mathematical Correctness and Mathematical Truth." *Pacific Philosophical Quarterly* 82(2): 87–114.

Balaguer, Mark. 2009. "Fictionalism, Theft, and the Story of Mathematics." *Philosophia Mathematica* 17(2): 131–162.

Balaguer, Mark. 2017. "Mathematical Pluralism and Platonism." *Journal of Indian Council of Philosophical Research* 34(2): 379–398.

Balaguer, Mark. 2021. *Metaphysics, Sophistry, and Illusion: Toward a Widespread Non-factualism.* Oxford: Oxford University Press.

Balaguer, Mark. 2023. "Fictionalism in the Philosophy of Mathematics." In *The Stanford Encyclopedia of Philosophy* (Spring Edition), edited by Edward N. Zalta and Uri Nodelman. https://plato.stanford.edu/archives/spr2023/entries/fictionalism-mathematics/.

Bangu, Sorin. 2006. "Steiner on the Applicability of Mathematics and Naturalism." *Philosophia Mathematica* 14(1): 26–43.

Bangu, Sorin. 2008. "Inference to the Best Explanation and Mathematical Realism." *Synthese* 160(1): 13–20.

Bangu, Sorin. 2018. "Later Wittgenstein and the Genealogy of Mathematical Necessity." In *Wittgenstein and Naturalism*, edited by Kevin M. Cahill and Thomas Raleigh, 151–173. New York: Routledge.

Barabási, Albert-László. 2002. *Linked: The New Science of Networks*. Cambridge, UK: Perseus.

Bar-On, Dorit. 2019. "Neo-expressivism: (Self-)Knowledge, Meaning, and Truth." *Royal Institute of Philosophy Supplement* 86: 11–34.

Bar-On, Dorit, and Keith Simmons. 2018. "Truth: One or Many or Both?" In *Pluralisms in Truth and Logic*, edited by Jeremy Wyatt, Nikolaj J. L. L. Pedersen, and Nathan Kellen, 35–61. Cham: Palgrave Macmillan.

Baron, Sam. 2016. "Explaining Mathematical Explanation." *Philosophical Quarterly* 66(264): 458–480.

Baron, Sam. 2019. "Mathematical Explanation by Law." *British Journal for the Philosophy of Science* 70(3): 683–717.

Baron, Sam. 2020. "Counterfactual Scheming." *Mind* 129(514): 535–562.

Baron, Sam. 2024. "Mathematical Explanation: A Pythagorean Proposal." *British Journal for the Philosophy of Science* 75(3): 663–685.

Baron, Sam, Mark Colyvan, and David Ripley. 2017. "How Mathematics Makes a Difference." *Philosophers' Imprint* 17: 1–29.

Barrantes, Manuel. 2023. "Structural Explanations: Impossibilities vs Failures." *Synthese* 201(4): 1–15.

Batterman, Robert. 2000. "Multiple Realizability and Universality." *British Journal for the Philosophy of Science* 51: 115–145.

Batterman, Robert. 2002a. "Asymptotics and the Role of Minimal Models." *British Journal for the Philosophy of Science* 53: 21–38.

Batterman, Robert. 2002b. *The Devil in the Details: Asymptotic Reasoning in Explanation, Reduction, and Emergence*. Oxford: Oxford University Press.

Batterman, Robert, and Collin Rice. 2014. "Minimal Model Explanations." *Philosophy of Science* 81: 349–376.

Beall, J. C., and Greg Restall. 2006. *Logical Pluralism*. Oxford: Oxford University Press.

Bechtel, William. 2015. "Can Mechanistic Explanation Be Reconciled with Scale-Free Constitution and Dynamics?" *Studies in History and Philosophy of Science Part C: Studies in History and Philosophy of Biological and Biomedical Sciences* 53: 84–93. doi:10.1016/j.shpsc.2015.03.006

Benacerraf, Paul. 1973. "Mathematical Truth." *Journal of Philosophy* 70(19): 661–679.

Bennett, Jonathan. 2003. *A Philosophical Guide to Conditionals*. Oxford: Clarendon Press.

Berto, Francesco. 2009. "The Gödel Paradox and Wittgenstein's Reasons." *Philosophia Mathematica* 17(2): 208–219.

Bird, Alexander. 2007. *Nature's Metaphysics: Laws and Properties*. Oxford: Oxford University Press.

Bird, Graham. 2003. "Carnap's Internal and External Questions." In *Language, Truth and Knowledge: Contributions to the Philosophy of Rudolf Carnap*, edited by Thomas Bonk, 97–131. Dordrecht: Kluwer Academic.

Blackburn, Simon. 1993. *Essays in Quasi-realism*. New York: Oxford University Press.

Boesch, Brandon. 2019. "Scientific Representation and Dissimilarity." *Synthese* 198(6): 5495–5513.

Boghossian, Paul. 1996. "Analyticity Reconsidered." *Noûs* 30(3): 360–391.

Boghossian, Paul. 1997. "Analyticity." In *A Companion to the Philosophy of Language*, edited by Bob Hale and Crispin Wright, 331–368. Oxford: Blackwell.

Boghossian, Paul. 2014. "What Is Inference?" *Philosophical Studies* 169: 1–18.
Bokulich, Alisa. 2011. "How Scientific Models Can Explain." *Synthese* 180: 33–45.
Bokulich, Alisa. 2016. "Fiction as a Vehicle for Truth: Moving beyond the Ontic Conception." *The Monist* 99(3): 260–279.
Brandom, Robert. 1994. *Making It Explicit: Reasoning, Representing, and Discursive Commitment.* Cambridge, MA: Harvard University Press.
Brandom, Robert. 2000. *Articulating Reasons.* Cambridge, MA: Harvard University Press.
Brandom, Robert. 2008. *Between Saying and Doing.* Oxford: Oxford University Press.
Brandom, Robert. 2015. *From Empiricism to Expressivism: Brandom Reads Sellars.* Cambridge, MA: Harvard University Press.
Brogaard, Berit, and Joe Salerno. 2013. "Remarks on Counterpossibles." *Synthese* 190: 639–660.
Bromberger, Sylvain. 1966. "Why Questions." In *Mind and Cosmos*, edited by R. G. Colodny, 86–111. Pittsburgh, PA: University of Pittsburgh Press.
Brown, Harold I. 2007. *Conceptual Systems.* London and New York: Routledge.
Bueno, Otávio, and Mark Colyvan. 2011. "An Inferential Conception of the Application of Mathematics." *Noûs* 45(2): 345–374.
Bueno, Otávio, and Steven French. 2018. *Applying Mathematics: Immersion, Inference, Interpretation.* Oxford: Oxford University Press.
Burgess, Alexis. 2011. "Mainstream Semantics + Deflationary Truth." *Linguistics and Philosophy* 34(5): 397–410.
Burgess, Alexis, Herman Cappelen, and David Plunkett, eds. 2020. *Conceptual Engineering and Conceptual Ethics.* Oxford: Oxford University Press.
Burgess, John P. 1997. "Quinus ab Omni Nævo Vindicatus." *Canadian Journal of Philosophy Supplementary* 23: 25–65.
Burnston, Daniel C. 2013. "Mechanistic Diagrams as Search Organizers." Paper presented at the annual meeting of the Cognitive Science Society, Berlin.
Burnston, Daniel C. n.d. "The problem of representational overlap."
Callender, Craig, and Jonathan Cohen. 2006. "There Is No Special Problem about Scientific Representation." *THEORIA. An International Journal for Theory, History and Foundations of Science* 21(1): 67–85.
Cameron, Ross P. 2010. "How to Have a Radically Minimal Ontology." *Philosophical Studies* 151(2): 249–264.
Camp, Elisabeth. 2018. "Why Maps Are Not Propositional." In *Non-propositional Intentionality*, edited by Alex Grzankowski and Michelle Montague, 19–45. Oxford: Oxford University Press.
Carnap, Rudolf. (1937) 2001. *Logical Syntax of Language.* London: Routledge.
Carnap, Rudolf. 1947. *Meaning and Necessity.* Chicago: University of Chicago Press.
Carnap, Rudolf. 1950. "Empiricism, Semantics, and Ontology." *Revue internationale de philosophie* 4(11): 20–40.
Carnap, Rudolf. 1955. "Meaning and Synonymy in Natural Languages." *Philosophical Studies* 6: 33–47.
Carnap, Rudolf. 1966. *Philosophical Foundations of Physics: An Introduction to the Philosophy of Science.* New York: Basic Books.
Chalmers, David. 2004. "Epistemic Two-Dimensional Semantics." *Philosophical Studies* 118(1–2): 153–226.
Chang, Hasok. 2004. *Inventing Temperature: Measurement and Scientific Progress.* Oxford: Oxford University Press.
Chirimuuta, Mazviita. 2014. "Minimal Models and Canonical Neural Computations: The Distinctness of Computational Explanation in Neuroscience." *Synthese* 191: 127–153.
Chirimuuta, Mazviita. 2018. "Explanation in Computational Neuroscience: Causal and Non-causal." *British Journal for the Philosophy of Science* 69(3): 849–880.
Chrisman, Matthew. 2012. "Epistemic Expressivism." *Philosophy Compass* 7: 118–126.
Churchland, Paul M. 2012. *Plato's Camera: How the Physical Brain Captures a Landscape of Abstract Universals.* Cambridge, MA: MIT Press.

Clark, Bob. 2017. *Wittgenstein, Mathematics and World*. Cham: Palgrave Macmillan.
Clarke-Doane, Justin. 2020. *Morality and Mathematics*. Oxford: Oxford University Press.
Coltheart, Max. 2005. "Modeling Reading: The Dual-Route Approach." In *The Science of Reading: A Handbook*, edited by Margaret J. Snowling and Charles Hulme, 6–23. Malden: Blackwell.
Coltheart, Max, Kathleen Rastle, Conrad Perry, Robyn Langdon, and Johannes Ziegler. 2001. "DRC: A Dual Route Cascaded Model of Visual Word Recognition and Reading Aloud." *Psychological Review* 108(1): 204–256.
Colyvan, Mark. 1998. "Can the Eleatic Principle Be Justified?" *Canadian Journal of Philosophy* 28: 313–335.
Colyvan, Mark. 2001. *The Indispensability of Mathematics*. Oxford: Oxford University Press.
Colyvan, Mark. 2011. "Fictionalism in Philosophy of Mathematics." In *Routledge Encyclopedia of Philosophy*, edited by Edward J. Craig. New York: Routledge. Online edition, http://www.rep.routledge.com/article/Y093.
Contessa, Gabriele. 2013. *Models and Maps: An Essay on Epistemic Representation*. Unpublished manuscript, Carleton University, Ottawa, ON.
Contessa, Gabriele. 2016. "It Ain't Easy: Fictionalism, Deflationism, and Easy Arguments in Ontology." *Mind* 125(499): 763–773.
Correia, Fabrice, and Benjamin Schnieder, eds. 2012. *Metaphysical Grounding: Understanding the Structure of Reality*. Cambridge: Cambridge University Press.
Craver, Carl F. 2001. "Role Functions, Mechanisms, and Hierarchy." *Philosophy of Science* 68: 31–55.
Craver, Carl F. 2006. "When Mechanistic Models Explain." *Synthese* 153: 355–376.
Craver, Carl F. 2007. *Explaining the Brain: Mechanisms and the Mosaic Unity of Neuroscience*. Oxford: Clarendon Press.
Craver, Carl F. 2014. "The Ontic Account of Scientific Explanation." In *Explanation in the Special Sciences: The Case of Biology and History*, edited by Marie I. Kaiser, Oliver R. Scholz, Daniel Plenge, and Andreas Hüttemann, 27–54. New York: Springer.
Craver, Carl F. 2016. "The Explanatory Power of Network Models." *Philosophy of Science* 83(5): 698–709.
Craver, Carl F., and W. Bechtel. 2007. "Top-Down Causation without Top-Down Causes." *Biology and Philosophy* 22: 547–563.
Craver, Carl F. and Lindley Darden. 2013. *In Search of Mechanisms: Discoveries Across the Life Sciences*. Chicago: University of Chicago Press.
Craver, Carl F., Stuart Glennan, and Mark Povich. 2021. "Constitutive Relevance and Mutual Manipulability Revisited." *Synthese* 199(3–4): 8807–8828.
Craver, Carl F., and David M. Kaplan. 2020. "Are More Details Better? On the Norms of Completeness for Mechanistic Explanations." *British Journal for the Philosophy of Science* 71: 287–319.
Craver, Carl F., and Mark Povich. 2017. "The Directionality of Distinctively Mathematical Explanations." *Studies in History and Philosophy of Science Part A* 63: 31–38.
Creath, Richard. 1980. "Benacerraf and Mathematical Truth." *Philosophical Studies* 37(4): 335–340.
da Costa, Newton C. A., and Steven French. 2003. *Science and Partial Truth: A Unitary Approach to Models and Scientific Reasoning*. Oxford: Oxford University Press.
Daly, Chris, and Simon Langford. 2009. "Mathematical Explanation and Indispensability Arguments." *Philosophical Quarterly* 59(237): 641–658.
Davidson, Donald. 2001. "Truth and Meaning." In *Inquiries into Truth and Interpretation*, edited by Donald Davidson, 17–36. Oxford: Clarendon Press.
Davies, E. Brian. 2005. "A Defence of Mathematical Pluralism." *Philosophia Mathematica* 13(3): 252–276.
Dijksterhuis, Eduard Jan. 1986. *The Mechanization of the World Picture: Pythagoras to Newton*. Princeton, NJ: Princeton University Press.
Donaldson, Thomas. 2020. "Analyticity." In *The Routledge Handbook of Metaphysical Grounding*, edited by Michael J. Raven, 288–299. New York: Routledge.

Donaldson, Thomas, and Jennifer Wang. 2022. "Modal Normativism and De Re Modality." *Argumenta* 7(2): 293–307.

Dorst, Chris. 2019. "Towards a Best Predictive System Account of Laws of Nature." *British Journal for Philosophy of Science* 70: 877–900.

Dorst, Chris. 2022. "Why Do the Laws Support Counterfactuals?" *Erkenntnis* 87(2): 545–566.

Downes, Stephen M. 2009. "Models, Pictures, and Unified Accounts of Representation: Lessons from Aesthetics for Philosophy of Science." *Perspectives on Science* 17(4): 417–428.

Dreier, James. 2004. "Meta-ethics and the Problem of Creeping Minimalism." *Philosophical Perspectives* 18(1): 23–44.

Dummett, Michael. 1973. *Frege: Philosophy of Language*. London: Duckworth.

Dummett, Michael. 1978. *Truth and Other Enigmas*. London: Duckworth.

Dyke, Heather. 2007. *Metaphysics and the Representational Fallacy*. New York: Routledge.

Ebert, Philip A., and Marcus Rossberg, eds. 2016. *Abstractionism: Essays in Philosophy of Mathematics*. Oxford: Oxford University Press.

Einheuser, Iris. 2006. "Counterconventional Conditionals." *Philosophical Studies* 127(3): 459–482.

Einheuser, Iris. 2011. "Toward a Conceptualist Solution of the Grounding Problem." *Noûs* 45: 300–314.

Eklund, Matti. 2013. "Carnap's Metaontology." *Noûs* 47(2): 229–249.

Eklund, Matti. 2016. "Carnap's Legacy for the Contemporary Metaontological Debate." In *Ontology after Carnap*, edited by Stephan Blatti and Sandra Lapointe, 165–189. Oxford: Oxford University Press.

Elgin, Catherine Z. 2009. "Exemplification, Idealization, and Scientific Understanding." In *Fictions in Science: Philosophical Essays on Modeling and Idealization*, edited by M. Suarez, 77–90. London: Routledge.

Ellis, Brian. 1966. *Basic Concepts of Measurement*. Cambridge: Cambridge University Press.

Ellis, Brian. 2001. *Scientific Essentialism*. Cambridge: Cambridge University Press.

Evans, Gareth. 1979. "Reference and Contingency." *The Monist* 62(2): 161–189.

Fang, Wei. 2017. "Holistic Modeling: An Objection to Weisberg's Weighted Feature-Matching Account." *Synthese* 194(5): 1743–1764. doi:10.1007/s11229-016-1018-z

Fang, Wei. 2019. "An Inferential Account of Model Explanation." *Philosophia* 47(1): 99–116.

Field, Hartry. 1980. *Science without Numbers*. Princeton, NJ: Princeton University Press.

Field, Hartry. 1989. *Realism, Mathematics, and Modality*. Oxford: Basil Blackwell.

Field, Hartry. 2022. "Conventionalism about Mathematics and Logic." *Noûs* 57(4): 815–831.

Fiocco, M. Oreste. 2007. "Conceivability, Imagination and Modal Knowledge." *Philosophy and Phenomenological Research* 74(2): 364–380.

Fisher, Ronald A. 1930. *The Genetical Theory of Natural Selection*. Oxford: Clarendon Press.

Fitch, Gregory W. 2004. *Saul Kripke*. Chesham: Acumen.

Florio, Salvatore, and Øystein Linnebo. 2021. *The Many and the One: A Philosophical Study of Plural Logic*. Oxford: Oxford University Press.

Floyd, Juliet, and Hilary Putnam. 2000. "A Note on Wittgenstein's 'Notorious Paragraph' about the Gödel Theorem." *Journal of Philosophy* 97(11): 624–632.

Fodor, Jerry A., and Ernest Lepore. 2001. "Brandom's Burdens: Compositionality and Inferentialism." *Philosophy and Phenomenological Research* 63: 465–481.

Franklin, James. 2014. *An Aristotelian Realist Philosophy of Mathematics: Mathematics as the Science of Quantity and Structure*. London: Palgrave Macmillan.

Frege, Gottlob. 1980. *Philosophical and Mathematical Correspondence*. Oxford: Basil Blackwell.

Friederich, Simon. 2010. "Structuralism and Meta-mathematics." *Erkenntnis* 73: 67–81.

Friederich, Simon. 2011. "Motivating Wittgenstein's Perspective on Mathematical Sentences as Norms." *Philosophia Mathematica* 19(1): 1–19.

Friedman, Michael. 1999. *Reconsidering Logical Positivism*. Cambridge: Cambridge University Press.

Friedman, Michael. 2001. *Dynamics of Reason*. Stanford, CA: CSLI.

Frigg, Roman, and James Nguyen. 2020. *Modelling Nature: An Opinionated Introduction to Scientific Representation*. Cham: Springer.
Gibbard, Allan. 1975. "Contingent Identity." *Journal of Philosophical Logic* 4: 187–221.
Gibbard, Allan. 2009. *Thinking How to Live*. Cambridge, MA: Harvard University Press.
Giere, Ronald N. 1999. *Science without Laws*. Chicago: University of Chicago Press.
Glennan, Stuart. 2002. "Rethinking Mechanistic Explanation." *Philosophy of Science* 69: 342–353.
Glock, Hans-Johann. 1996. "Necessity and Normativity." In *The Cambridge Companion to Wittgenstein*, edited by Hans Sluga and David G. Stern, 198–225. Cambridge: Cambridge University Press.
Goldenfeld, Nigel, and Leo P. Kadanoff. 1999. "Simple Lessons from Complexity." *Science* 284: 87–89.
Goodman, Nelson. 1947. "The Problem of Counterfactual Conditionals." *Journal of Philosophy* 44: 113–128.
Goodman, Nelson. 1976. *Languages of Art: An Approach to a Theory of Symbols*. Indianapolis, IN: Hackett.
Green, Sara, Maria Şerban, Raphael Scholl, Nicholaos Jones, Ingo Brigandt, and William Bechtel. 2018. "Network Analyses in Systems Biology: New Strategies for Dealing with Biological Complexity." *Synthese* 195(4): 1751–1777.
Grice, Herbert P., and Peter Frederick Strawson. 1956. "In Defense of a Dogma." *Philosophical Review* 65(2): 141–158.
Griffith, Aaron M. 2014. "Truthmaking and Grounding." *Inquiry* 57: 196–215.
Gross, Steven. 2015. "Does the Expressive Role of 'True' Preclude Deflationary Davidsonian Semantics?" In *Meaning without Representation: Essays on Truth, Expression, Normativity, and Naturalism*, edited by Steven Gross, Nicholas Tebben, and Michael Williams, 47–63. Oxford: Oxford University Press.
Hale, Bob, and Crispin Wright. 2001. *The Reason's Proper Study: Essays towards a Neo-Fregean Philosophy of Mathematics*. Oxford: Oxford University Press.
Hamilton, William D. 1967. "Extraordinary Sex Ratios." *Science* 156: 477–488.
Haugeland, John. 1998. "Truth and Rule-Following." In Haugeland, *Having Thought: Essays in the Metaphysics of Mind*, 305–361. Cambridge, MA: Harvard University Press.
Hausman, D. 1998. *Causal Asymmetries*. New York: Cambridge University Press.
Hawthorne, John, and Andrew Cortens. 1995. "Towards Ontological Nihilism." *Philosophical Studies* 79(2): 143–165.
Hegarty, Mary. 2011. "The Cognitive Science of Visual-Spatial Displays: Implications for Design." *Topics in Cognitive Science* 3(3): 446–474.
Hegarty, Mary, Micheal Stieff, and Boonie L. Dixon. 2013. "Cognitive Change in Mental Models with Experience in the Domain of Organic Chemistry. *Journal of Cognitive Psychology* 25(2): 220–228.
Heil, John. 2003. *From an Ontological Point of View*. Oxford: Oxford University Press.
Heil, John. 2012. *The Universe as We Find It*. Oxford: Oxford University Press.
Hellman, Geoffrey. 1989. *Mathematics without Numbers: Towards a Modal-Structural Interpretation*. Oxford: Oxford University Press.
Hellman, Geoffrey, and Stuart Shapiro. 2018. *Mathematical Structuralism*. Cambridge: Cambridge University Press.
Hempel, Carl. 1965. *Aspects of Scientific Explanation and Other Essays in the Philosophy of Science*. New York: Free Press.
Henderson, Jared. 2017. "Deflating the Determination Argument." *Thought: A Journal of Philosophy* 6(3): 167–177.
Hendrix, Jimi. 1967. "If 6 Was 9." On *Axis: Bold as Love*. Track Records.
Hilbert, David. 1923. "Die logischen Grundlagen der Mathematik." *Mathematische Annalen* 88: 151–165. English translation in *From Kant to Hilbert: A Source Book in the Foundations of Mathematics*, vol. 2, edited and translated by William Ewald, 1134–1148. Oxford: Clarendon Press, 1996.

Hirsch, Eli. 2011. *Quantifier Variance and Realism: Essays in Metaontology*. Oxford: Oxford University Press.
Hofweber, Thomas. 2005. "Number Determiners, Numbers, and Arithmetic." *Philosophical Review* 114(2): 179–225.
Hofweber, Thomas. 2016. *Ontology and the Ambitions of Metaphysics*. Oxford: Oxford University Press.
Holmes, Travis L. 2021. "Distinctively Mathematical Explanation and the Problem of Directionality: A Quasi-erotetic Solution." *Studies in History and Philosophy of Science Part A* 87: 13–21.
Horisk, Claire. 2008. "Truth, Meaning, and Circularity." *Philosophical Studies* 137: 269–300.
Horwich, Paul. 1998a. *Meaning*. Oxford: Clarendon.
Horwich, Paul. 1998b. *Truth*. 2nd edition. Oxford: Blackwell.
Huang, Kerson. 1987. *Statistical Mechanics*. New York: Wiley and Sons.
Hughes, Christopher. 2004. *Kripke: Names, Necessity, and Identity*. Oxford: Clarendon Press.
Hughes, R. I. G. 1997. "Models and Representation." *Philosophy of Science* 64(4): S325–S336.
Huneman, Philippe. 2010. "Topological Explanations and Robustness in Biological Sciences." *Synthese* 177: 213–245.
Illari, Phyllis. 2013. "Mechanistic Explanation: Integrating the Ontic and Epistemic." *Erkenntnis* 78: 237–255.
Jackson, Frank. 1998. *From Metaphysics to Ethics: A Defence of Conceptual Analysis*. Oxford: Oxford University Press.
Jackson, Frank, and Philip Pettit. 1990. "Program Explanation: A General Perspective." *Analysis* 50(2): 107–117.
Kandel, Eric R., James H. Schwartz, Thomas M. Jessell, Steven A. Siegelbaum, and A. J. Hudspeth, (eds.) 2013. *Principles of Neural Science*. 5th edn. New York: McGraw-Hill.
Kant, Immanuel. (1781/1787) 1998. *Critique of Pure Reason* (*The Cambridge Edition of the Works of Immanuel Kant*), edited by Paul Guyer and Allen W. Wood. New York: Cambridge University Press.
Kaplan, David M. 2011. "Explanation and Description in Computational Neuroscience." *Synthese* 183: 339–373.
Kessler, Glenn. 1980. "Frege, Mill, and the Foundations of Arithmetic." *Journal of Philosophy* 77(2): 65–79.
Khalifa, Kareem, Jared Millson, and Mark Risjord. 2022. "Scientific Representation: An Inferentialist-Expressivist Manifesto." *Philosophical Topics* 50(1): 263–291.
Kim, Jaegwon. 2011. *Philosophy of Mind*. 3rd edition. Boulder: Westview Press.
Kitcher, Philip. 1984. *The Nature of Mathematical Knowledge*. Oxford: Oxford University Press on Demand.
Kitcher, Philip. 1989. "Explanatory Unification and the Causal Structure of the World." In *Minnesota Studies in the Philosophy of Science*, vol. 13: *Scientific Explanation*, edited by Philip Kitcher and Wesley C. Salmon, 410–505. Minneapolis: University of Minnesota Press.
Knuuttila, Tarja. 2011. "Modelling and Representing: An Artefactual Approach to Model-Based Representation." *Studies In History and Philosophy of Science Part A* 42(2): 262–271.
Kocurek, Alexander W. 2021. "Counterpossibles." *Philosophy Compass* 16(11): e12787.
Kocurek, Alexander W., and Ethan Jerzak. 2021. "Counterlogicals as Counterconventionals." *Journal of Philosophical Logic* 50(4): 673–704.
Kocurek, Alexander W., Ethan Jerzak, and Rachel Etta Rudolph. 2020. "Against Conventional Wisdom." *Philosophers' Imprint* 20(22): 1–27.
Kölbel, Max. 2002. *Truth Without Objectivity*. London and New York: Routledge.
Kostić, Daniel. 2020. "General Theory of Topological Explanations and Explanatory Asymmetry." *Philosophical Transactions of the Royal Society B* 375(1796): 20190321.
Kostić, Daniel, and Kareem Khalifa. 2021. "The Directionality of Topological Explanations." *Synthese* 199(5–6): 14143–14165.
Kripke, Saul. 1971. "Identity and Necessity." In *Identity and Individuation*, edited by Milton K. Munitz, 135–164. New York: New York University Press.

Kripke, Saul. 1980. *Naming and Necessity*. Cambridge, MA: Harvard University Press.

Künne, Wolfgang. 2003. *Conceptions of Truth*. Oxford: Clarendon Press.

Künne, Wolfgang. 2005. "The Modest Account of Truth Reconsidered: With a Postscript on Metaphysical Categories." *Dialogue: Canadian Philosophical Review/Revue canadienne de philosophie* 44(3): 563–596.

Kuorikoski, Jaakko. 2021. "There Are No Mathematical Explanations." *Philosophy of Science* 88(2): 189–212.

Lambros, Charles H. 1976. "Are Numbers Properties of Objects?" *Philosophical Studies* 29(6): 381–389.

Lampert, Timm. 2018. "Wittgenstein and Gödel: An Attempt to Make 'Wittgenstein's Objection' Reasonable." *Philosophia Mathematica* 26(3): 324–345.

Lange, Marc. 2007. "Laws and Meta-laws of Nature: Conservation Laws and Symmetries." *Studies in History and Philosophy of Modern Physics* 38: 457–481.

Lange, Marc. 2009. *Laws and Lawmakers*. Oxford: Oxford University Press.

Lange, Marc. 2011. "Conservation Laws in Scientific Explanations: Constraints or Coincidences?" *Philosophy of Science* 78: 333–352.

Lange, Marc. 2013a. "Really Statistical Explanations and Genetic Drift." *Philosophy of Science* 80: 169–188.

Lange, Marc. 2013b. "What Makes a Scientific Explanation Distinctively Mathematical?" *British Journal for Philosophy of Science* 64: 485–511.

Lange, Marc. 2015. "On 'Minimal Model Explanations': A Reply to Batterman and Rice." *Philosophy of Science* 82(2): 292–305.

Lange, Marc. 2016. *Because without Cause: Non-Causal Explanations in Science and Mathematics*. Oxford: Oxford University Press.

Lange, Marc. 2018. "A Reply to Craver and Povich on the Directionality of Distinctively Mathematical Explanations." *Studies in History and Philosophy of Science Part A* 67: 85–88.

Lange, Marc. 2021. "What Could Mathematics Be for It to Function in Distinctively Mathematical Scientific Explanations?" *Studies in History and Philosophy of Science* 87: 44–53.

Lange, Marc. 2022. "In Defense of Really Statistical Explanations." *Synthese* 200(5): 1–15.

Larson, Richard K., and Gabriel Segal. 1995. *Knowledge of Meaning*. Cambridge, MA: MIT Press.

Lavine, Shaughan. 2006. "Something about Everything: Universal Quantification in the Universal Sense of Universal Quantification." In *Absolute Generality*, edited by Agustín Rayo and Gabriel Uzquiano, 98–148. Oxford: Oxford University Press.

Leng, Mary. 2005. "Mathematical Explanation." In *Mathematical Reasoning, Heuristics, and the Development of Mathematics*, edited by Carlo Cellucci and Donald Gillies, 167–189. London: King's College Publications.

Lepore, Ernest, and Kirk Ludwig. 2005. *Donald Davidson: Meaning, Truth, Language, and Reality*. Oxford: Clarendon Press.

Lepore, Ernest, and Kirk Ludwig. 2007. *Donald Davidson's Truth-Theoretic Semantics*. Oxford: Oxford University Press.

Lewis, David. 1973. *Counterfactuals*. Oxford: Blackwell.

Lewis, David. 1983. "New Work for a Theory of Universals." *Australasian Journal of Philosophy* 61: 343–377.

Lewis, David. 1986. "Causal Explanation." In *Philosophical Papers*, vol. 2, edited by David Lewis, 214–240. New York: Oxford University Press.

Linnebo, Øystein. 2018. *Thin Objects: An Abstractionist Account*. Oxford: Oxford University Press.

Linnebo, Øystein. 2023a. "Précis." In "Thin Objects." Special issue of *Theoria* 89(3): 247–255.

Linnebo, Øystein. 2023b "Replies." In "Thin Objects." Special issue of *Theoria* 89(3): 393–406.

Linsky, Bernard, and Edward N. Zalta. 1995. "Naturalized Platonism Versus Platonized Naturalism." *Journal of Philosophy* 92(10): 525–555.

Locke, Theodore. 2020. "Metaphysical Explanations for Modal Normativists." *Metaphysics* 3(1): 33–54.

Locke, Theodore. 2021. "Counterpossibles for Modal Normativists." *Synthese* 198: 1235–1257.
Lowe, Edward Jonathan 1989. *Kinds of Being: A Study of Individuation, Identity and the Logic of Sortal Terms.* Oxford: Blackwell.
Lowe, E. J. 2007. "Sortals and the Individuation of Objects." *Mind and Language* 22(5): 514–533.
Löwenstein David. 2012. "Davidsonian Semantics and Anaphoric Deflationism." *Dialectica* 66(1): 23–44.
Luce, R. Duncan, David H. Krantz, Amos Tversky, and Patrick Suppes. 1990. *Foundations of Measurement.* Vol. 3: *Representation, Axiomatization, and Invariance.* Mineola, NY: Dover.
Ludwig, Kirk. n.d. "De Re Necessities." Indiana University. https://socrates.sitehost.iu.edu/papers/De%20Re%20Necessities.doc.
Lyon, Aidan. 2012. "Mathematical Explanations of Empirical Facts, and Mathematical Realism." *Australasian Journal of Philosophy* 90(3): 559–578.
Lyon, Aidan, and Mark Colyvan. 2008. "The Explanatory Power of Phase Spaces." *Philosophia Mathematica* 16(2): 227–243.
MacFarlane, John. 2000. "What Does It Mean to Say That Logic Is Formal?" PhD diss., University of Pittsburgh. https://johnmacfarlane.net/dissertation.pdf.
Machamer, Peter K., Lindley Darden, and Carl F. Craver. 2000. "Thinking about Mechanisms." *Philosophy of Science* 67: 1–25.
Maddy, Penelope. 1990. *Realism in Mathematics.* Oxford: Oxford University Press.
Mancosu, Paolo. 2008. "Mathematical Explanation: Why It Matters." In *The Philosophy of Mathematical Practice*, edited by Paolo Mancosu, 134–150. Oxford: Oxford University Press.
Matthiessen, Dana. 2022. "Empirical Techniques and the Accuracy of Scientific Representations." *Studies in History and Philosophy of Science Part A* 94: 143–157.
McComb, William David. 2004. *Renormalization Methods: A Guide for Beginners.* Oxford: Oxford University Press.
McGee, Vann. 2000. "Everything." In *Between Logic and Intuition: Essays in Honor of Charles Parsons*, edited by G. Sher and R. Tieszen, 54–78. Cambridge: Cambridge University Press.
McGinn, Colin. 1982. "Rigid Designation and Semantic Value." *Philosophical Quarterly* 32(127): 97–115.
Melia, Joseph. 2000. "Weaseling Away the Indispensability Argument." *Mind* 109(435): 455–480.
Merricks, Trenton. 2001. *Objects and Persons.* Oxford: Clarendon.
Michell, Joel. 1994. "Numbers as Quantitative Relations and the Traditional Theory of Measurement." *British Journal for the Philosophy of Science* 45(2): 389–406.
Michell, Joel. 2021. "Representational Measurement Theory: Is Its Number Up?" *Theory & Psychology* 31(1): 3–23.
Moore, Adrian W. 1998. "More on 'The Philosophical Significance of Godel's Theorem.'" *Grazer Philosophische Studien* 55: 103–126.
Mühlhölzer, Felix. 2012. "Wittgenstein and Metamathematics." *Deutsches Jahrbuch Philosophie* 3: 103–128.
Nguyen, James, and Roman Frigg. 2021. "Mathematics Is Not the Only Language in the Book of Nature." *Synthese* 198: 5941–5962.
Nolan, Daniel. 1997. "Impossible Worlds: A Modest Approach." *Notre Dame Journal of Formal Logic* 38(4): 535–572.
Noonan, Harold. 2014. *Routledge Philosophy Guidebook to Kripke and Naming and Necessity.* Oxon: Routledge.
Nyseth, Fredrik. 2021. "Linguistic Conventionalism and the Truth-Contrast Thesis." *Philosophical Quarterly* 71(2): 264–285.
Nyseth, Fredrik. 2023. "Review of *Shadows of Syntax: Revitalizing Logical and Mathematical Conventionalism*, by Jared Warren." *Mind* 132(527): 880–890.
Oliver, Alex. 1994. "Frege and Dummett Are Two." *Philosophical Quarterly* 44(174): 74–82.
Padilla, Antonio. 2022. *Fantastic Numbers and Where to Find Them: A Cosmic Quest from Zero to Infinity.* New York: Farrar, Straus and Giroux.

Paicu, Marius, and Arghir Zarnescu. 2012. "Energy Dissipation and Regularity for a Coupled Navier-Stokes and Q-Tensor System." *Archive for Rational Mechanics and Analysis* 203: 45–67.

Parker, Wendy S. 2015. "Getting (Even More) Serious about Similarity." *Biology & Philosophy* 30(2): 267–276.

Parsons, Charles. 2008. *Mathematical Thought and Its Objects.* Cambridge: Cambridge University Press.

Peacocke, Christopher. 1992. *A Study of Concepts.* Cambridge, MA: MIT Press.

Pérez Carballo, Alejandro (2014). "Structuring Logical Space." *Philosophy and Phenomenological Research* 92 (2): 460–491.

Pearl, Judea. 2000. *Causality: Models, Reasoning, and Inference.* Cambridge: Cambridge University Press.

Peregrin, Jaroslav. 2014. *Inferentialism: Why Rules Matter.* London: Palgrave Macmillan.

Peregrin, Jaroslav. 2018. "Is Inferentialism Circular?" *Analysis* 78(3): 450–454.

Peregrin, Jaroslav. 2022. "Inferentialism Naturalized." *Philosophical Topics* 50(1): 33–54.

Pexton, Mark. 2014. "How Dimensional Analysis Can Explain." *Synthese* 191(10): 2333–2351.

Pincock, Christopher. 2004. "A New Perspective on the Problem of Applying Mathematics." *Philosophia Mathematica* 12(2): 135–161.

Pincock, Christopher. 2012. *Mathematics and Scientific Representation.* Oxford: Oxford University Press.

Pincock, Christopher. 2015. "Abstract Explanations in Science." *British Journal for the Philosophy of Science* 66: 857–882.

Pincock, Christopher. 2023. *Mathematics and Explanation.* Cambridge: Cambridge University Press.

Plebani, Matteo. 2018. "Fictionalism versus Deflationism: A New Look." *Philosophical Studies* 175: 301–316.

Poincaré, Henri. (1905) 1952. *Science and Hypothesis.* New York: Dover.

Povich, Mark. 2015. "Mechanisms and Model-Based Functional Magnetic Resonance Imaging." *Philosophy of Science* 82(5): 1035–1046.

Povich, Mark. 2018. "Minimal Models and the Generalized Ontic Conception of Scientific Explanation." *British Journal for the Philosophy of Science* 69(1): 117–137. https://doi.org/10.1093/bjps/axw019.

Povich, Mark. 2019. "Model-Based Cognitive Neuroscience: Multifield Mechanistic Integration in Practice." *Theory & Psychology* 29(5): 640–656.

Povich, Mark. 2020. "Modality and Constitution in Distinctively Mathematical Explanations." *European Journal for Philosophy of Science* 10(3): 1–10. https://doi.org/10.1007/s13194-020-00292-y.

Povich, Mark. 2021a. "Information and Explanation: An Inconsistent Triad and Solution." *European Journal for Philosophy of Science* 11(2): 43. https://doi.org/10.1007/s13194-021-00368-3.

Povich, Mark. 2021b. "The Narrow Ontic Counterfactual Account of Distinctively Mathematical Explanation." *British Journal for the Philosophy of Science* 72(2): 511–543. https://doi.org/10.1093/bjps/axz008.

Povich, M. 2023a. "A Conventionalist Account of Distinctively Mathematical Explanation." *Philosophical Problems in Science (Zagadnienia Filozoficzne W Nauce)* 74: 171–223. https://doi.org/10.59203/zfn.74.648.

Povich, Mark. 2023b. "A Scheme Foiled: A Critique of Baron's Account of Extra-mathematical Explanation." *Mind* 132(526): 479–492. https://doi.org/10.1093/mind/fzac019.

Povich, Mark. Forthcoming-a. "Mechanistic Explanation in Psychology." In *The Sage Handbook of Theoretical Psychology*, edited by Hank Stam and Huib Looren de Jong. London: Sage.

Povich, Mark. Forthcoming-b. "(A Little) Quantified Modal Logic for Normativists." *Analysis.*

Povich, Mark. n.d.-a. "Linnebo on Analyticity and Thin Existence."

Povich, Mark. n.d.-b. "The Symbolic Approach to the Omega Rule."

Povich, Mark, and Dan Burnston. n.d. "An Inferentialist Account of Scientific Representation."

Povich, Mark, and Carl F. Craver. 2018. "Review of Marc Lange, *Because without Cause: Non-Causal Explanations in Science and Mathematics*." *Philosophical Review* 127(3): 422–426. doi:https://doi.org/10.1215/00318108-6718870

Poznic, Michael. 2018. "Thin versus Thick Accounts of Scientific Representation." *Synthese* 195(8): 3433–3451.

Price, Huw. 2011. *Naturalism without Mirrors*. Oxford: Oxford University Press.

Price, Huw, Simon Blackburn, Robert Brandom, Paul Horwich, and Michael Williams. 2013. *Expressivism, Pragmatism and Representationalism*. Cambridge: Cambridge University Press.

Priest, Graham. 2013. "Mathematical Pluralism." *Logic Journal of the IGPL* 21(1): 4–13.

Priest, Graham. 2019. "A Note on Mathematical Pluralism and Logical Pluralism." *Synthese* 198(Suppl 20): 4937–4946.

Priestley, E. B., Peter J. Wojtowicz, and Ping Sheng. 1975. *Introduction to Liquid Crystals*. New York: Plenum Press.

Putnam, Hilary. 1979. "What is Mathematical Truth?" In Putnam, *Mathematics Matter and Method: Philosophical Papers, Volume 1*, 2nd edn, 60–78. Cambridge: Cambridge University Press.

Putnam, Hilary. 1981. *Reason, Truth and History*. Cambridge: Cambridge University Press.

Putnam, Hilary. 1987. "Truth and Convention: On Davidson's Refutation of Conceptual Relativism." *Dialectica* 41: 69–77.

Quine, W. V. O. 1948. "On What There Is." *Review of Metaphysics* 2(5): 21–38.

Quine, W. V. O. 1951. "Two Dogmas of Empiricism." *Philosophical Review* 60: 20–43.

Quine W. V. O. 1953. "Reference and Modality." In Quine, *From a Logical Point of View*, 139–159. Cambridge, MA: Harvard University Press.

Quine, W. V. O. 1958. "Speaking of Objects." *Proceedings and Addresses of the American Philosophical Association* 31: 5–22.

Quine, W. V. O. 1976. "Carnap and Logical Truth." In Quine, *The Ways of Paradox and Other Essays*, revised edition, 107–132. Cambridge, MA: Harvard University Press.

Rabinowicz, Wlodek. 2010. "Analyticity and Possible-World Semantics." *Erkenntnis* 72: 295–314.

Railton, Peter. 1978. "A Deductive-Nomological Model of Probabilistic Explanation." *Philosophy of Science* 45: 206–226.

Railton, Peter. 1981. "Probability, Explanation, and Information." *Synthese* 48: 233–256.

Rayo, Agustín. 2009. "Toward a Trivialist Account of Mathematics." In *New Waves in Philosophy of Mathematics*, edited by Otávio Bueno and Øystein Linnebo, 239–260. London: Palgrave Macmillan.

Rayo, Agustín. 2013. *The Construction of Logical Space*. Oxford: Oxford University Press.

Reichenbach, Hans. 1965. *The Theory of Relativity and a Priori Knowledge*. Berkeley: University of California Press.

Resnik, Michael D. 1997. *Mathematics as a Science of Patterns*. Oxford: Oxford University Press.

Reutlinger, Alexander. 2014. "Why Is There Universal Macrobehavior? Renormalization Group Explanation as Noncausal Explanation." *Philosophy of Science* 81: 1157–1170.

Reutlinger, Alexander. 2016. "Is There a Monist Theory of Causal and Noncausal Explanations? The Counterfactual Theory of Scientific Explanation." *Philosophy of Science* 83(5): 733–745.

Reutlinger, Alexander. 2017. "Does the Counterfactual Theory of Explanation Apply to Non-causal Explanations in Metaphysics?" *European Journal for Philosophy of Science* 7(2): 239–256.

Rice, Collin. 2012. "Optimality Explanations: A Plea for an Alternative Approach." *Biology and Philosophy* 27: 685–703.

Rice, Collin. 2015. "Moving beyond Causes: Optimality Models and Scientific Explanation." *Noûs* 49: 589–615.

Rice, Collin. 2019. "Models Don't Decompose That Way: A Holistic View of Idealized Models." *British Journal for the Philosophy of Science* 70(1): 179–208.

Roberts, John T. 2008. *The Law Governed Universe*. Oxford: Oxford University Press.
Robinson, Abraham. 1951. *On the Metamathematics of Algebra*. Amsterdam: North-Holland.
Rodriguez-Pereyra, Gonzalo. 2002. *Resemblance Nominalism: A Solution to the Problem of Universals*. Oxford: Clarendon Press.
Roski, Stefan. 2021. "In Defence of Explanatory Realism." *Synthese* 199: 14121–14141.
Ruben, David-Hillel. 1990. *Explaining Explanation*. London: Routledge.
Rubinov, Mikail, and Ed Bullmore. 2013. "Schizophrenia and Abnormal Brain Network Hubs." *Dialogues in Clinical Neuroscience* 15(3): 339–349.
Russell, Gillian. 2008. *Truth in Virtue of Meaning: A Defence of the Analytic/Synthetic Distinction*. Oxford: Oxford University Press.
Ruyant, Quentin. 2022. "True Griceanism: Filling the Gaps in Callender and Cohen's Account of Scientific Representation." *Philosophy of Science* 88(3): 533–553. doi:10.1086/712882
Saatsi, Juha. 2011. "The Enhanced Indispensability Argument: Representational versus Explanatory Role of Mathematics in Science." *British Journal for the Philosophy of Science* 62(1): 143–154.
Saatsi, Juha. 2012. "Mathematics and Program Explanations." *Australasian Journal of Philosophy* 90: 579–584.
Saatsi, Juha. 2016. "On the 'Indispensable Explanatory Role' of Mathematics." *Mind* 50: 1045–1070.
Saatsi, Juha, and Mark Pexton. 2013. "Reassessing Woodward's Account of Explanation: Regularities, Counterfactuals, and Noncausal Explanations." *Philosophy of Science* 80: 613–624.
Salmon, Nathan. 1996. "Trans-world Identification and Stipulation." *Philosophical Studies: An International Journal for Philosophy in the Analytic Tradition* 84(2–3): 203–223.
Salmon, Wesley. 1977. "A Third Dogma of Empiricism." In *Basic Problems in Methodology and Linguistics*, edited by Robert E. Butts and Jaako Hintikka, 149–166. Dordrecht: Reidel.
Salmon, Wesley. 1984. *Scientific Explanation and the Causal Structure of the World*. Princeton, NJ: Princeton University Press.
Salmon, Wesley. 1989. "Four Decades of Scientific Explanation." In *Scientific Explanation*, edited by Wesley Salmon and Philip Kitcher, 3–219. Minneapolis: University of Minnesota Press.
Samaroo, Ryan. 2022. "Newtonian Mechanics." In *The Routledge Companion to Philosophy of Physics*, edited by Eleanor Knox and Alastair Wilson, 8–20. London: Routledge.
Sayward, Charles. 2001. "On Some Much Maligned Remarks of Wittgenstein on Gödel." *Philosophical Investigations* 24(3): 262–270.
Schaffer, Jonathan. 2010. "The Least Discerning and Most Promiscuous Truthmaker." *Philosophical Quarterly* 60(239): 307–324.
Scharp, Kevin, and Robert B. Brandom, eds. 2007. *In the Space of Reasons: Selected Essays of Wilfrid Sellars*. Cambridge, MA: Harvard University Press.
Schiffer, Stephen. 2003. *The Things We Mean*. Oxford: Clarendon Press.
Schlick, Moritz. 1974. *General Theory of Knowledge*. New York: Springer Verlag.
Schroeder, Severin. 2020. *Wittgenstein on Mathematics*. London: Routledge.
Sellars, Wilfrid. (1963) 1991. *Science, Perception and Reality*. Atascadero, CA: Ridgeview.
Shanker, Stuart. 1987. *Wittgenstein and the Turning Point in the Philosophy of Mathematics*. Albany, NY: SUNY Press.
Shapiro, Stewart. 1997. *Philosophy of Mathematics: Structure and Ontology*. Oxford: Oxford University Press.
Shapiro, Stewart. 2000. *Thinking about Mathematics: The Philosophy of Mathematics*. Oxford: Oxford University Press.
Sheredos, Benjamin. 2017. "Communicating with Scientific Graphics: A Descriptive Inquiry into Non-ideal Normativity." *Studies in History and Philosophy of Science Part C: Studies in History and Philosophy of Biological and Biomedical Sciences* 63: 32–44.
Sidelle, Alan. 1989. *Necessity, Essence and Individuation: A Defense of Conventionalism*. Ithaca, NY: Cornell University Press.

Sidelle, Alan. 1992. "Rigidity, Ontology, and Semantic Structure." *Journal of Philosophy* 89(8): 410–430.

Sidelle, Alan. 1995. "A Semantic Account of Rigidity." *Philosophical Studies* 80(1): 69–105.

Sidelle, Alan. 2002. "On the Metaphysical Contingency of Laws of Nature." In *Conceivability and Possibility*, edited by John Hawthorne and Tamar Szabó Gendler, 309–336. Oxford: Oxford University Press.

Sidelle, Alan. 2009. "Conventionalism and the Contingency of Conventions." *Noûs* 43(2): 224–241.

Sidelle, Alan. 2016. "Frameworks and Deflation in 'Empiricism, Semantics and Ontology' and Recent Metametaphysics." In *Ontology after Carnap*, edited by Stephan Blatti and Sandra Lapointe, 59–80. Oxford: Oxford University Press.

Sider, Theodore. 2003. "Reductive Theories of Modality." In *The Oxford Handbook of Metaphysics*, edited by Michael J. Loux and Dean W. Zimmerman, 180–208. Oxford: Oxford University Press.

Sider, Theodore. 2011. *Writing the Book of the World*. Oxford: Oxford University Press.

Simpson, Matthew. 2020. "Creeping Minimalism and Subject Matter." *Canadian Journal of Philosophy* 50(6): 750–766.

Skow, Bradford. 2014. "Are There Non-causal Explanations (of Particular Events)?" *British Journal for the Philosophy of Science* 65: 445–467.

Skow, Bradford. 2016. *Reasons Why*. Oxford: Oxford University Press.

Soames, Scott. 2003. *Philosophical Analysis in the Twentieth Century*. Vol. 2: *The Age of Meaning*. Princeton, NJ: Princeton University Press.

Sober, Elliott. 1983. "Equilibrium Explanation." *Philosophical Studies* 43: 201–210.

Stalnaker, R. 1978. "Assertion." In *Syntax and Semantics: Pragmatics*, vol. 9, edited by P. Cole, 315–332. New York: Academic Press.

Stalnaker, Robert C. 2001. "On Considering a Possible World as Actual." *Aristotelian Society Supplementary* 75: 141–156.

Stalnaker, Robert C. 2003. "Reference and Necessity." In, *Ways a World Might Be: Metaphysical and Anti-metaphysical Essays*, edited by Robert C. Stalnaker, 165–187. Oxford: Clarendon Press.

Steinberger, Florian. 2017. "Frege and Carnap on the Normativity of Logic." *Synthese* 194(1): 143–162.

Steiner, Mark. 1978. "Mathematics, Explanation, and Scientific Knowledge." *Noûs* 12(1): 17–28.

Steiner, Mark. 1996. "Wittgenstein: 'Mathematics, Regularities, Rules.'" In *Benacerraf and His Critics*, edited by A. Morton and S. P. Stich, 190–212. Oxford: Blackwell.

Steiner, Mark 1998. *The Applicability of Mathematics as a Philosophical Problem*. Cambridge, MA: Harvard University Press.

Steiner, Mark. 2009. "Empirical Regularities in Wittgenstein's Philosophy of Mathematics." *Philosophia Mathematica* 17(1): 1–34.

Stiefel, Klaus M., and G. Brad Ermentrout. 2016. "Neurons as Oscillators." *Journal of Neurophysiology* 116(6): 2950–2960. doi:10.1152/jn.00525.2015

Stieff, Michael, Mary Hegarty, and Ghislain Deslongchamps. 2011. "Identifying Representational Competence with Multi-representational Displays." *Cognition and Instruction* 29(1): 123–145.

Strevens, Michael. 2008. *Depth: An Account of Scientific Explanation*. Cambridge, MA: Harvard University Press.

Strevens, Michael. 2013. "No Understanding without Explanation." *Studies in History and Philosophy of Science Part A* 44(3): 510–515.

Studd, James P. 2019. *Everything, More or Less: A Defence of Generality Relativism*. Oxford: Oxford University Press.

Suárez, Mauricio. 2004. "An Inferential Conception of Scientific Representation." *Philosophy of Science* 71(5): 767–779.

Suárez, Mauricio. 2015. "Deflationary Representation, Inference, and Practice." *Studies In History and Philosophy of Science Part A* 49: 36–47.

Teller, Paul. 1989. *A Modern Formal Logic Primer: Sentence Logic*. Vol. 1. New York: Prentice Hall. https://tellerprimer.ucdavis.edu/.

Thalos, Mariam. 2002. "Explanation Is a Genus: An Essay on the Varieties of Scientific Explanation." *Synthese* 130: 317–354.

Thomasson, Amie. 2007a. "Modal Normativism and the Methods of Metaphysics." *Philosophical Topics* 35: 135–160.

Thomasson, Amie. 2007b. *Ordinary Objects*. New York: Oxford University Press.

Thomasson, Amie. 2013. "Fictionalism versus Deflationism." *Mind* 122(488): 1023–1051.

Thomasson, Amie. 2015. *Ontology Made Easy*. Oxford: Oxford University Press.

Thomasson, Amie. 2017a. "Metaphysics and Conceptual Negotiation." *Philosophical Issues* 27: 364–382.

Thomasson, Amie. 2017b. "Why We Should Still Take It Easy." *Mind* 126(503): 769–779.

Thomasson, Amie. 2019b. "What Can Global Pragmatists Say about Ordinary Objects?" In *The Nature of Ordinary Objects*, edited by Javier Cumpa and Bill Brewer, 235–259. Cambridge: Cambridge University Press.

Thomasson, Amie. 2020a. *Norms and Necessity*. New York: Oxford University Press.

Thomasson, Amie. 2020b. "Truthmakers and Easy Ontology." In *Oxford Studies in Metaphysics*, edited by Karen Bennett and Dean W. Zimmerman, 3–34. Oxford: Oxford University Press.

Thomasson, Amie. 2021. "How Can We Come to Know Metaphysical Modal Truths?" *Synthese* 198(S8): S2077–S2106.

Thomasson, Amie. 2023. "How It All Hangs Together." In *Thomasson on Ontology*, edited by Miguel Garcia-Godinez, 9–38. Cham: Palgrave Macmillan.

Thomasson, Amie. 2024. "How Should We Think about Linguistic Function?" *Inquiry* 67(3): 840–871.

Tononi, Giulio, and Christof Koch. 2015. "Consciousness: Here, There and Everywhere?" *Philosophical Transactions of the Royal Society B: Biological Sciences* 370(1668): 20140167.

Topey, Brett. 2019. "Linguistic Convention and Worldly Fact: Prospects for a Naturalist Theory of the A Priori." *Philosophical Studies* 176: 1725–1752.

Van Fraassen, Bas. 2008. *Scientific Representation: Paradoxes of Perspective*. Oxford: Oxford University Press.

Van Inwagen, Peter. 1995. *Material Beings*. Ithaca, NY: Cornell University Press.

Waismann, Friedrich. (1930) 1986. "The Nature of Mathematics: Wittgenstein's Standpoint." In *Ludwig Wittgenstein: Critical Assessments*, vol. 3, edited by Stuart Shanker, 60–67. London: Croom Helm.

Wang, Qifeng, Tung-Ping Su, Yuan Zhou, Kun-Hsien Chou, I-Yun Chen, Tianzi Jiang, and Ching-Po Lin. 2012. "Anatomical Insights into Disrupted Small-World Networks in Schizophrenia." *Neuroimage* 59(2): 1085–1093.

Ward, Barry. 2003. "Sometimes the World Is Not Enough: The Pursuit of Explanatory Laws in a Humean World." *Pacific Philosophical Quarterly* 84(2): 175–197.

Warren, Jared. 2015a. "Conventionalism, Consistency, and Consistency Sentences." *Synthese* 192(5): 1351–1371

Warren, Jared. 2015b. "The Possibility of Truth by Convention." *Philosophical Quarterly* 65(258): 84–93.

Warren, Jared. 2020. *Shadows of Syntax: Revitalizing Logical and Mathematical Conventionalism*. New York: Oxford University Press.

Warren, Jared. 2021. "Infinite Reasoning." *Philosophy and Phenomenological Research* 103: 385–407.

Warren, Jared. 2022a. *The A Priori without Magic*. Cambridge: Cambridge University Press.

Warren, Jared. 2022b. "Inferentialism, Conventionalism, and A Posteriori Necessity." *Journal of Philosophy* 119(10): 517–541.

Watts, Duncan J. 2000. *Small Worlds: The Dynamics of Networks between Order and Randomness*. Princeton, NJ: Princeton University Press.

Watts Duncan J., and Steven H. Strogatz. 1998. "Collective Dynamics of 'Small-World' Networks." *Nature* 393(6684): 440–442.

Weisberg, Michael. 2013. *Simulation and Similarity: Using Models to Understand the World.* Oxford: Oxford University Press.

West, Geoffrey, James H. Brown, and Brain Enquist. 1999. "The Fourth Dimension of Life: Fractal Geometry and Allometric Scaling of Organisms." *Science* 284: 1677–1679.

Wigner, Eugene P. 1960. "The Unreasonable Effectiveness of Mathematics in the Natural Sciences." *Communications in Pure and Applied Mathematics* 13: 1–14.

Williams, Michael. 1999. "Meaning and Deflationary Truth." *Journal of Philosophy* 96: 545–564.

Williams, Michael. 2007. "Meaning, Truth and Normativity." In *Truth and Speech Acts: Studies in the Philosophy of Language*, edited by Geo Siegwart and Dirk Griemann, 377–395. London: Routledge.

Wittgenstein, Ludwig. (1956) 1978. *Remarks on the Foundations of Mathematics.* Revised edition. Edited by G. H. von Wright, R. Rhees, and G. E. M. Anscombe. Translated by G. E. M. Anscombe. Oxford: Basil Blackwell.

Wittgenstein, Ludwig. 1974. *Philosophical Grammar.* Edited by R. Rhees. Translated by A. Kenny. Oxford: Blackwell.

Wittgenstein, Ludwig. 1976. *Wittgenstein's Lectures on the Foundations of Mathematics.* Edited by Cora Diamond. Ithaca, NY: Cornell University Press.

Wittgenstein, Ludwig. 2013. *Tractatus Logico-philosophicus.* London: Routledge.

Wolff, J. E. 2020. *The Metaphysics of Quantities.* Oxford: Oxford University Press.

Woodward, James. 2003. *Making Things Happen: A Theory of Causal Explanation.* Oxford: Oxford University Press.

Woodward, James. 2013. "Mechanistic Explanation: Its Scope and Limits." *Proceedings of the Aristotelian Society Supplementary* 87: 39–65.

Woodward, James, and Christopher Hitchcock. 2003. "Explanatory Generalizations, Part I: A Counterfactual Account." *Noûs* 37(1): 1–24.

Wright, Cory. 2012. "Mechanistic Explanation without the Ontic Conception." *European Journal of Philosophy of Science* 2: 375–394.

Wright, Cory, and Dingmar van Eck. 2018. "Ontic Explanation Is either Ontic or Explanatory, but Not Both." *Ergo: An Open Access Journal of Philosophy* 5: 997–1029.

Wright, Crispin. 1985. "In Defence of the Conventional Wisdom." In *Exercises in Analysis*, edited by Ian Hacking, 171–197. Cambridge: Cambridge University Press.

Yablo, Stephen. 2001. "Go Figure: A Path through Fictionalism." *Midwest Studies in Philosophy* 25(1): 72–102.

Yablo, Stephen. 2005. "The Myth of the Seven." In *Fictionalism in Metaphysics*, edited by Mark Eli Kalderon, 88–115. Oxford: Oxford University Press.

Index

For the benefit of digital users, indexed terms that span two pages (e.g., 52–53) may, on occasion, appear on only one of those pages.

Figures are indicated by *f* following the page number